Program Authors

Peter Afflerbach
Camille Blachowicz
Candy Dawson Boyd
Elena Izquierdo
Connie Juel
Edward Kame'enui
Donald Leu
Jeanne R. Paratore
P. David Pearson
Sam Sebesta
Deborah Simmons
Alfred Tatum
Sharon Vaughn
Susan Watts Taffe
Karen Kring Wixson

Glenview, Illinois • Boston, Massachusetts
Chandler, Arizona • Upper Saddle River, New Jersey

We dedicate Reading Street to
Peter Jovanovich.

His wisdom, courage,
and passion for education
are an inspiration to us all.

ISBN-13: 978-0-328-46987-1
ISBN-10: 0-328-46987-4
2 3 4 5 6 7 8 9 10 V064 14 13 12 11 10
CC1

Any Path, Any Pace

Reading Street

Calle de la Lectura

PEARSON

Who said so?

The Leading Researchers,

Program Authors

Peter Afflerbach, Ph.D.
Professor
Department of Curriculum and Instruction
University of Maryland at College Park

Camille L. Z. Blachowicz, Ph.D.
Professor of Education
National-Louis University

Candy Dawson Boyd, Ph.D.
Professor
School of Education
Saint Mary's College of California

Elena Izquierdo, Ph.D.
Associate Professor
University of Texas at El Paso

Connie Juel, Ph.D.
Professor of Education
School of Education
Stanford University

Edward J. Kame'enui, Ph.D.
Dean-Knight Professor of Education and Director
Institute for the Development of Educational Achievement and the Center on Teaching and Learning
College of Education
University of Oregon

Donald J. Leu, Ph.D.
John and Maria Neag Endowed Chair in Literacy and Technology
Director, The New Literacies Research Lab
University of Connecticut

Jeanne R. Paratore, Ed.D.
Associate Professor of Education
Department of Literacy and Language Development
Boston University

P. David Pearson, Ph.D.
Professor and Dean
Graduate School of Education
University of California, Berkeley

Sam L. Sebesta, Ed.D.
Professor Emeritus
College of Education
University of Washington, Seattle

Deborah Simmons, Ph.D
Professor
College of Education and Human Development
Texas A&M University

Alfred W. Tatum, Ph.D.
Associate Professor and Director of the UIC Reading Clinic
University of Illinois at Chicago

Sharon Vaughn, Ph.D.
H. E. Hartfelder/Southland Corporation Regents Professor
Director, Meadows Center for Preventing Educational Risk
University of Texas

Susan Watts Taffe, Ph.D.
Associate Professor in Literacy
Division of Teacher Education
University of Cincinnati

Karen Kring Wixson, Ph.D.
Professor of Education
University of Michigan

Consulting Authors

Jeff Anderson, M.Ed.
Author and Consultant
San Antonio, Texas

Jim Cummins, Ph.D.
Professor
Department of Curriculum, Teaching and Learning
University of Toronto

Lily Wong Fillmore, Ph.D.
Professor Emerita
Graduate School of Education
University of California, Berkeley

Georgia Earnest García, Ph.D.
Professor
Language and Literacy Division
Department of Curriculum and Instruction
University of Illinois at Urbana-Champaign

George A. González, Ph.D.
Professor (Retired)
School of Education
University of Texas-Pan American, Edinburg

Valerie Ooka Pang, Ph.D.
Professor
School of Teacher Education
San Diego State University

Sally M. Reis, Ph.D.
Board of Trustees Distinguished Professor
Department of Educational Psychology
University of Connecticut

Jon Scieszka, M.F.A.
Children's Book Author
Founder of GUYS READ
Named First National Ambassador for Young People's Literature 2008

Grant Wiggins, Ed.D.
Educational Consultant
Authentic Education
Concept Development

Lee Wright, M.Ed.
Pearland, Texas

Practitioners, and Authors.

Consultant

Sharroky Hollie, Ph.D.
Assistant Professor
California State University
Dominguez Hills, CA

Teacher Reviewers

Dr. Bettyann Brugger
Educational Support Coordinator—Reading Office
Milwaukee Public Schools
Milwaukee, WI

Kathleen Burke
K–12 Reading Coordinator
Peoria Public Schools, Peoria, IL

Darci Burns, M.S.Ed.
University of Oregon

Bridget Cantrell
District Intervention Specialist
Blackburn Elementary School
Independence, MO

Tahira DuPree Chase, M.A., M.S.Ed.
Administrator of Elementary English Language Arts
Mount Vernon City School District
Mount Vernon, NY

Michele Conner
Director, Elementary Education
Aiken County School District
Aiken, SC

Georgia Coulombe
K–6 Regional Trainer/Literacy Specialist
Regional Center for Training and Learning (RCTL), Reno, NV

Kelly Dalmas
Third Grade Teacher
Avery's Creek Elementary, Arden, NC

Seely Dillard
First Grade Teacher
Laurel Hill Primary School
Mt. Pleasant, SC

Jodi Dodds-Kinner
Director of Elementary Reading
Chicago Public Schools, Chicago, IL

Dr. Ann Wild Evenson
District Instructional Coach
Osseo Area Schools, Maple Grove, MN

Stephanie Fascitelli
Principal
Apache Elementary, Albuquerque Public Schools, Albuquerque, NM

Alice Franklin
Elementary Coordinator, Language Arts & Reading
Spokane Public Schools, Spokane, WA

Laureen Fromberg
Assistant Principal
PS100 Queens, NY

Kimberly Gibson
First Grade Teacher
Edgar B. Davis Community School
Brockton, MA

Kristen Gray
Lead Teacher
A.T. Allen Elementary School
Concord, NC

Mary Ellen Hazen
State Pre-K Teacher
Rockford Public Schools #205
Rockford, IL

Patrick M. Johnson
Elementary Instructional Director
Seattle Public Schools, Seattle, WA

Theresa Jaramillo Jones
Principal
Highland Elementary School
Las Cruces, NM

Sophie Kowzun
Program Supervisor, Reading/Language Arts, PreK–5
Montgomery County Public Schools
Rockville, MD

David W. Matthews
Sixth Grade Teacher
Easton Area Middle School
Easton, PA

Ana Nuncio
Editor and Independent Publisher
Salem, MA

Joseph Peila
Principal
Chappell Elementary School
Chicago, IL

Ivana Reimer
Literacy Coordinator
PS100 Queens, NY

Sally Riley
Curriculum Coordinator
Rochester Public Schools
Rochester, NH

Dyan M. Smiley
Independent Educational Consultant

Michael J. Swiatowiec
Lead Literacy Teacher
Graham Elementary School
Chicago, IL

Dr. Helen Taylor
Director of English Education
Portsmouth City Public Schools
Portsmouth, VA

Carol Thompson
Teaching and Learning Coach
Independence School District
Independence, MO

Erinn Zeitlin
Kindergarten Teacher
Carderock Springs Elementary School
Bethesda, MD

Any Path, Any Pace

Let's Go Exploring

Key
SI Strategic Intervention
OL On Level
A Advanced
ELL ELL

In this Teacher's Edition Unit 4, Volume 1

In the First Stop on Reading Street

GO Digital!

See It!

- Big Question Video
- Concept Talk Video
- Envision It! Animations
- Sing with Me Animations

Hear It!

- Sing with Me Animations
- eReaders
- Grammar Jammer
- Leveled Reader Database

Do It!

- Story Sort
- Letter Tile Drag and Drop

All Together Now

Key
SI Strategic Intervention
OL On-Level
A Advanced
ELL ELL

Look at Us!

Key
- SI Strategic Intervention
- OL On-Level
- A Advanced
- ELL ELL

Changes All Around Us

Key
- SI Strategic Intervention
- OL On-Level
- A Advanced
- ELL ELL

Let's Go Exploring

Key
SI Strategic Intervention
OL On-Level
A Advanced
ELL ELL

Volume 1

Volume 2

Going Places

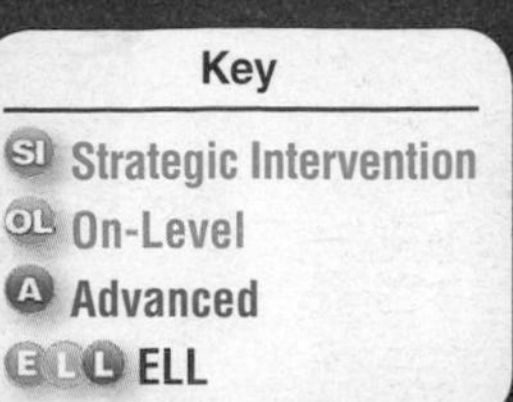

Putting It Together

Key
SI Strategic Intervention
OL On-Level
A Advanced
ELL ELL

Skills Overview

Key
T Tested
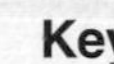 Target Skill

	WEEK 1	WEEK 2
	 **Rooster's Off to See the World** Animal Fantasy pp. 59–69	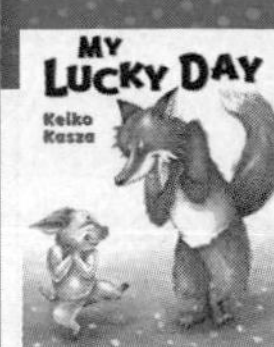 **My Lucky Day** Animal Fantasy pp. 156–171
Get Ready to Read		
Question of the Week	What can we learn from our adventures?	What is a lucky adventure?
Amazing Words	*world, lonely, trip, horizon, journey, homesick*	*piglet, fox, lucky, filthy, cook, scrubber*
Phonemic Awareness	T /h/	T /l/
Phonics	T /h/ Spelled *Hh* Review /o/ Spelled *Oo*	T /l/ Spelled *Ll* Review /h/ Spelled *Hh*
High-Frequency Words	T *are, that, do*	T *are, that, do*
Read and Comprehend		
Comprehension	T **Skill** Sequence Review Compare and Contrast	T **Skill** Cause and Effect Review Plot
Language Arts		
Writing	Directions	Poem
Conventions	Naming Parts	Action Parts
Vocabulary	Sequence Words	Words for Textures
Speaking/Listening	Give Directions	Compare and Contrast

The Big Question

Where will our adventures take us?

WEEK 3	WEEK 4	WEEK 5	WEEK 6
One Little Mouse Animal Fantasy pp. 258–271	**Goldilocks and the Three Bears** Classic Fairy Tale pp. 358–373	**If You Could Go to Antarctica** Nonfiction pp. 459–469	**Abuela** Fantasy pp. 555–570
What adventures can animals have?	How can an adventure cause trouble?	What would it be like to have an Antarctic adventure?	What kind of adventures can you have in the city?
woodland, nest, vale, hollow, comfortable, shadows	*bears, porridge, cottage, big, middle-sized, small*	*Antarctica, continent, icebergs, penguins, seals, whales*	*abuela, adventure, flock, city, airport, harbor*
T Consonant Blends	T /g/	T /e/	T /e/
T Consonant Blends Review /l/ Spelled *Ll*	T /g/ Spelled *Gg* Review Consonant Blends	T /e/ Spelled *Ee* Review /g/ Spelled *Gg*	T /e/ Spelled *Ee* Review /g/ Spelled *Gg*
T *one, two, three, four, five*	T *one, two, three, four, five*	T *here, go, from*	T *here, go, from*
T **Skill** Sequence Review Draw Conclusions	T **Skill** Character Review Setting	T **Skill** Classify and Categorize Review Main Idea	T **Skill** Setting Review Realism and Fantasy
Description	List	Informal Letter	Writing Process: List
Complete Sentences	Telling Sentences	Capital Letters and Periods	Pronouns *I* and *me*
Words for Shapes	Compound Words	Direction Words	Time Words
Listen for Sequence	Discuss Authors and Illustrators	Listen for Story Elements: Character	Listen to Poems

Monitor Progress

Make Data-Driven Decisions

Data Management
- Assess
- Diagnose
- Prescribe
- Disaggregate

Classroom Management
- Monitor Progress
- Group
- Differentiate Instruction
- Inform Parents

Don't Wait Until Friday

SUCCESS PREDICTOR	WEEK 1	WEEK 2	WEEK 3	WEEK 4
Phonemic Awareness — **Phonemic Awareness**	T /h/	T /l/	T Consonant Blends	T /g/
Sound-Spelling — **Phonics**	T /h/ Spelled *Hh*	T /l/ Spelled *Ll*	T Consonant Blends	T /g/ Spelled *Gg*
Word Reading — **High-Frequency Words**	T are T that T do	T are T that T do	T one T two T three T four T five	T one T two T three T four T five
Oral Vocabulary/ Concept Development (assessed informally)	world lonely trip horizon journey homesick	piglet fox lucky filthy cook scrubber	woodland nest vale hollow comfortable shadows	bears porridge cottage big middle-sized small
Retelling — **Comprehension**	T **Skill** Sequence **Strategies** Preview and Predict; Retell	T **Skill** Cause and Effect **Strategies** Preview and Predict; Retell	T **Skill** Sequence **Strategies** Preview and Predict; Retell	T **Skill** Character **Strategies** Preview and Predict; Retell

Key

T Tested

 Target Skill

WEEK 5	WEEK 6
T /o/	T /e/
T /e/ Spelled *Ee*	T /e/ Spelled *Ee*
T here T go T from	T here T go T from
Antarctica continent icebergs penguins seals whales	abuela adventure flock city airport harbor
T **Skill** Classify and Categorize **Strategies** Preview and Predict; Retell	T **Skill** Setting **Strategies** Preview and Predict; Retell

GO Digital!

See It!

- Big Question Video
- Concept Talk Video
- Envision It! Animations
- Sing with Me Animations

Hear It!

- Sing with Me Animations
- eReaders
- Grammar Jammer
- Leveled Reader Database

Do It!

- Story Sort
- Letter Tile Drag and Drop

Assessment and Grouping

for Data-Driven Instruction

4-Step Plan for Assessment

1 Diagnose and Differentiate
2 Monitor Progress
3 Assess and Regroup
4 Summative Assessment

STEP 1 Diagnose and Differentiate

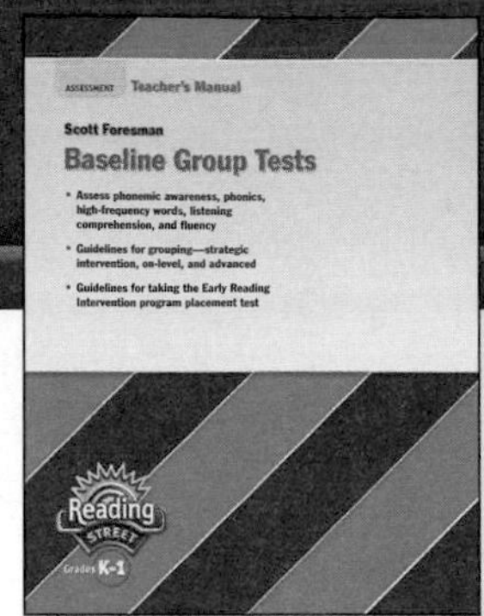

Baseline Group Tests

Diagnose

To make initial grouping decisions, use the Baseline Group Test, the Texas Primary Reading Inventory (TPRI), or another initial placement test. Depending on students' ability levels, you may have more than one of each group.

Differentiate

If... student performance is  SI **then...** use the regular instruction and the daily **Strategic Intervention** small group lessons.

If... student performance is  OL **then...** use the regular instruction and the daily **On-Level** small group lessons.

If... student performance is  A **then...** use the regular instruction and the daily **Advanced** learners small group lessons.

Small Group Time

SI Strategic Intervention

- Daily small group lessons provide more intensive instruction, more scaffolding, more practice, and more opportunities to respond.
- Reteach lessons in the *First Stop* provide more instruction of target skills.
- Leveled readers, decodable readers, and other weekly texts build background and practice target skills and vocabulary.

OL On-Level

- Explicit instructional routines teach core skills and strategies.
- Daily On-Level lessons provide more practice and more opportunities to respond.
- Independent activities provide practice for core skills.
- Student Readers and Get Set, Roll! Readers provide additional reading and practice for core skills and vocabulary.

A Advanced

- Daily Advanced lessons provide instruction for accelerated learning.
- Independent Leveled Readers provide additional reading tied to lesson concepts and skills.

Additional Differentiated Learning Options

Reading Street Response to Intervention Kit

- Focused intervention lessons on the five critical areas of reading: phonemic awareness, phonics, vocabulary, comprehension, and fluency

My Sidewalks on Reading Street

- Early Reading Intervention

STEP 2 Monitor Progress

Use these tools during lesson teaching to **monitor student progress.**

- **Skill and Strategy** instruction during reading
- **Don't Wait Until Friday** boxes to check letter and sound fluency, word reading, retelling, and oral vocabulary
- **Weekly Assessment** on Day 5 to check phonics, high-frequency words, and comprehension
- **Reader's and Writer's Notebook** pages at point of use

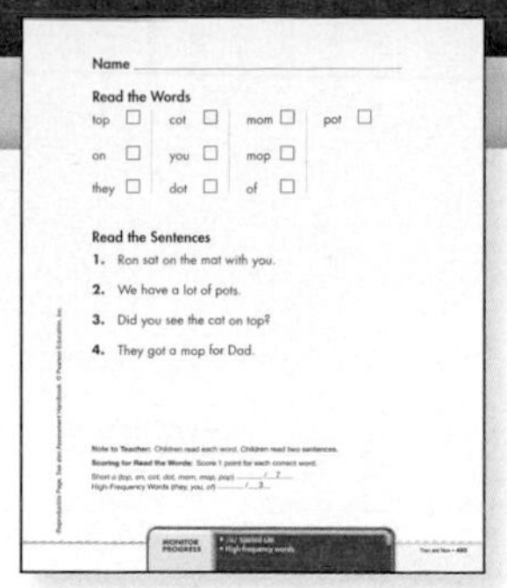

Name

Read the Words

top, cat, mom, pot, on, you, mop, they, dot, of

Read the Sentences

1. Ron sat on the mat with you.
2. We have a lot of pots.
3. Did you see the cat on top?
4. They got a mop for Dad.

Weekly Phonics and High-Frequency Words Assessment

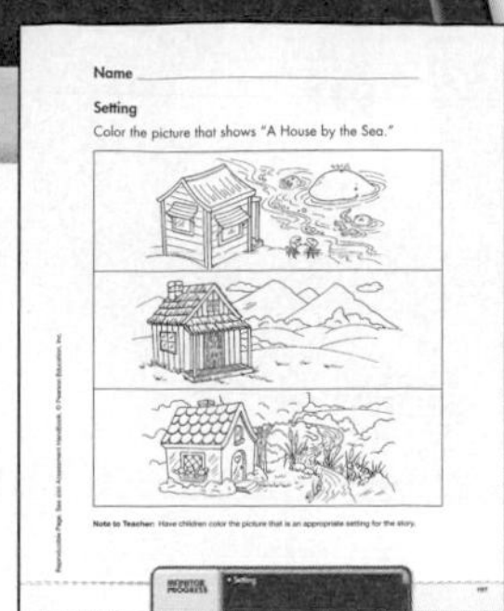

Name

Setting

Color the picture that shows "A House by the Sea."

Weekly Comprehension Assessment

STEP 3 Assess and Regroup

Use these tools during lesson teaching to **assess and regroup.**

- **Weekly Assessments** Record results of weekly assessments for phonics and high-frequency words to track student progress.
- **Unit Benchmark Assessment** Administer this assessment to check progress of unit skills.
- **Regroup** We recommend the first regrouping to be at the end of Unit 2. Use weekly assessment information and Unit Benchmark Assessment performance to inform regrouping decisions. Then regroup at the end of each subsequent unit.

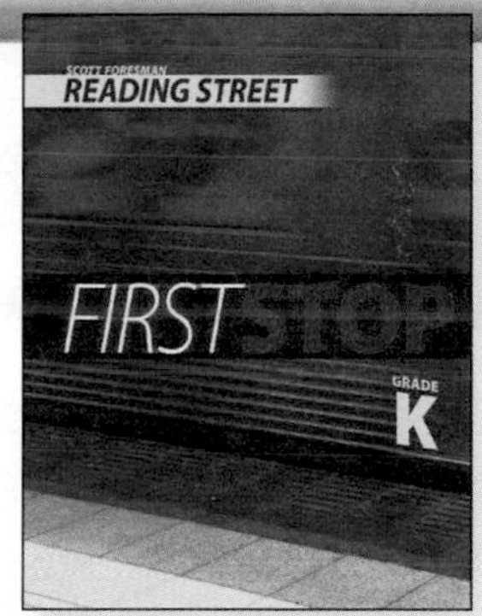

Unit 1 Reading Chart in First Stop

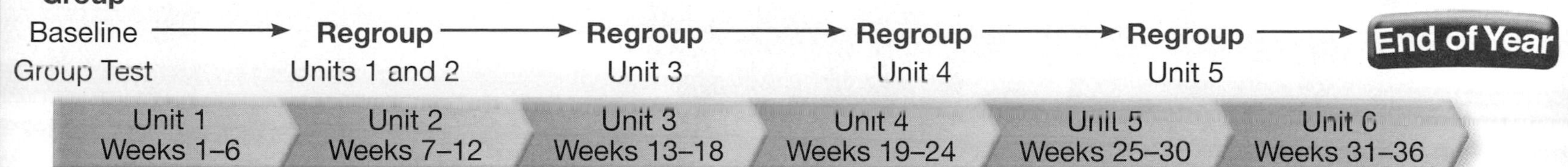

Outside assessments, such as DRA, TPRI, and DIBELS, may recommend regrouping at other times during the year.

STEP 4 Summative Assessment

Use these tools after lesson teaching to **assess students**.

- **Unit Benchmark Assessments** Use to measure a student's mastery of each unit's skills.
- **End-of-Year Benchmark Assessment** Use to measure a student's mastery of program skills covered in all six units.

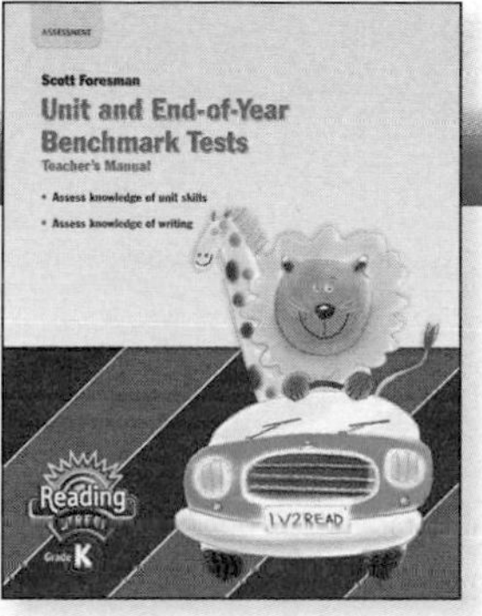

Unit and End-of-Year Benchmark Assessments

Concept Launch

Understanding By Design

Grant Wiggins, Ed. D.
Reading Street Author

"A big idea is a concept, theme, or issue that gives meaning and connection to discrete facts and skills. . . . In an education for understanding, a vital challenge is to highlight the big ideas, show how they prioritize the learning, and help students understand their value for making sense of all the 'stuff' of content."

Let's Go Exploring

Where will our adventures take us?

Reading Street Online

www.ReadingStreet.com

- Big Question Video
- Envision It! Animations
- Story Sort

Small Group Time

Flexible Pacing Plans

Small Group Time

Sometimes you have holidays, programs, assemblies, or other interruptions to the school week. This plan can help you make Small Group Time decisions if you have less time during the week.

Key

- SI Strategic Intervention
- OL On Level
- A Advanced
- ELL ELL

5 Day Plan

DAY 1	• Phonemic Awareness • Phonics • Reading Practice
DAY 2	• Phonemic Awareness • Phonics • Reading Practice
DAY 3	• Phonemic Awareness/ Phonics • Leveled Reader
DAY 4	• Phonemic Awareness • Reading Practice
DAY 5	• Phonics • Reading Practice

4 Day Plan

DAY 1	• Phonemic Awareness • Phonics • Reading Practice
DAY 2	• Phonemic Awareness • Phonics • Reading Practice
DAY 3	• Phonemic Awareness/ Phonics • Leveled Reader
DAY 4	• Phonemic Awareness • Reading Practice

3 Day Plan

DAY 1	• Phonemic Awareness • Phonics • Reading Practice
DAY 2	• Phonemic Awareness/ Phonics • Leveled Reader
DAY 3	• Phonemic Awareness • Reading Practice

ELL

5 Day Plan

DAY 1	• Frontload Concept • Phonemic Awareness/ Phonics • Comprehension
DAY 2	• Comprehension • Vocabulary
DAY 3	• Phonemic Awareness/ Phonics • Conventions
DAY 4	• Phonemic Awareness/ Phonics • Concepts and Oral Language
DAY 5	• Language Workshop • Writing

4 Day Plan

DAY 1	• Frontload Concept • Phonemic Awareness/ Phonics • Comprehension
DAY 2	• Comprehension • Vocabulary
DAY 3	• Phonemic Awareness/ Phonics • Conventions
DAY 4	• Language Workshop • Writing

3 Day Plan

DAY 1	• Frontload Concept • Phonemic Awareness/ Phonics • Comprehension
DAY 2	• Phonemic Awareness/ Phonics • Conventions
DAY 3	• Language Workshop • Writing

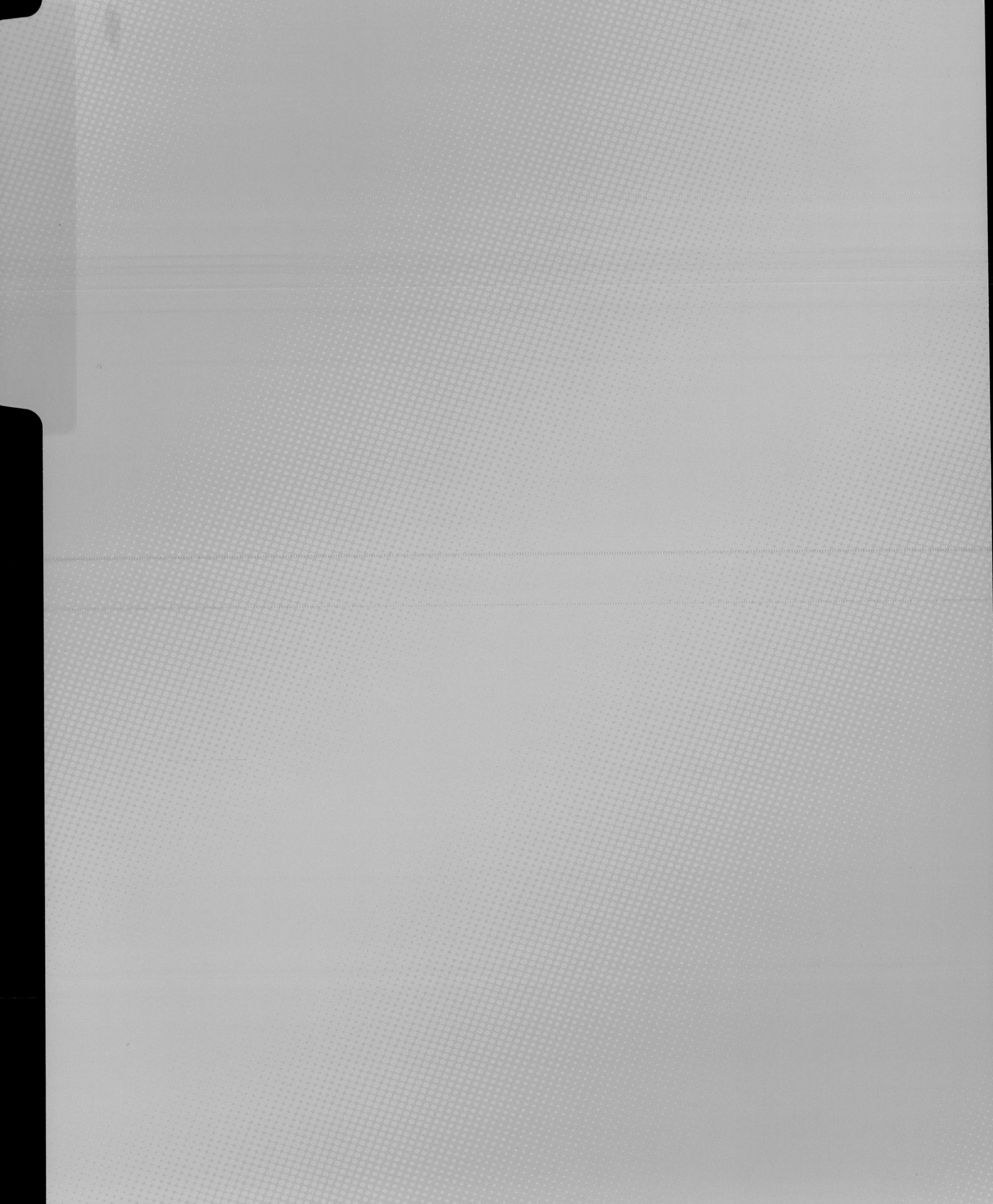

Grade K • Unit 4 • Week 1
Rooster's Off to See the World
16–101

Common Core Standards
Weekly Planning Guide

Selection: Rooster's Off to See the World
Genre: Animal Fantasy

Alignment of the Common Core Standards with This Week's Skills and Strategies

This Week's Common Core Standards for English Language Arts	Instructional Summary
Reading Standards for Literature	
Literature 2. With prompting and support, retell familiar stories, including key details. **Literature 3.** With prompting and support, identify characters, settings, and major events in a story. **Literature 5.** Recognize common types of texts (e.g., storybooks, poems).	The Listening Comprehension selection focuses on how the events of a story happen in a certain order called a **sequence.** The lesson instruction on **predict** and **set a purpose** helps children look at the selection to predict what the selection might be about. Then they learn to set a purpose to help them understand what they read.
Foundational Skills Standards	
Foundational Skills 2.d. Isolate and pronounce the initial, medial vowel, and final sounds (phonemes) in three-phoneme (consonant-vowel-consonant, or CVC) words.* (This does not include CVCs ending with /l/, /r/, or /x/.) **Foundational Skills 2.e.** Add or substitute individual sounds (phonemes) in simple, one-syllable words to make new words. **Foundational Skills 3.a.** Demonstrate basic knowledge of one-to-one letter-sound correspondences by producing the primary or many of the most frequent sounds for each consonant.	The lesson emphasizes **word analysis** skills to decode words. The lesson provides instruction for decoding words using initial, medial, and final phonemes. The lesson also provides **phonics** instruction for listening for initial /h/ and presents sound-symbol association with the consonant /h/ and the letters *Hh.*
Writing Standards	
Writing 2. Use a combination of drawing, dictating, and writing to compose informative/explanatory texts in which they name what they are writing about and supply some information about the topic.	Writing activities include creating **sentences** that tell why everyone is special. Group activities for writing include a **response** to the literature, **directions,** and **sentences** about something they saw as they traveled somewhere. The wrap-up activities ask children to write about the thing that was their favorite in this week's lesson.
Speaking and Listening Standards	
Speaking/Listening 1. Participate in collaborative conversations with diverse partners about *kindergarten topics and texts* with peers and adults in small and larger groups. **Speaking/Listening 4.** Describe familiar people, places, things, and events and, with prompting and support, provide additional detail.	In the **listening** and **speaking** activities, children share their ideas and then learn to tell how to do or make something by giving oral directions. Children restate the directions and focus on the order of the directions.
Language Standards	
Language 1.f. Produce and expand complete sentences in shared language activities. **Language 2.d.** Spell simple words phonetically, drawing on knowledge of sound-letter relationships. **Language 5.c.** Identify real-life connections between words and their use (e.g., note places at school that are *colorful*).	The Conventions section concentrates on the **naming part** or subject of a sentence. Children learn that the subject of a sentence tells who or what the sentence is about and names the person, place, animal, or thing.

Additional Support for a Common Core Standard This Week

Use the following instruction to supplement the teaching of one of this week's Common Core Standards.

Common Core Standard: Literature 2.
Display page 26 of *My Skills Buddy.* Have children retell the events of the story in order.
- Ask children to tell about each picture by identifying what they see in the picture.
- Then close the book and have children retell the events without the aid of the pictures.
- Repeat this procedure with other selections in the unit.

ISBN-13: 978-0-328-64357-8 ISBN-10: 0-328-64357-2

Grade K • Unit 4 • Week 1

Rooster's Off to See the World

Unit 4

Where will our adventures take us?

You Are Here: Week 1

Rooster's Off to See the World

Question of the Week

What can we learn from our adventures?

As children answer this unit's Big Question and this week's Question of the Week, they will address:

Reading 2. Determine central ideas or themes of a text and analyze their development; summarize the key supporting details and ideas. **(Also Reading 3.)**

Concept Talk Guide children as they discuss questions such as:

- What things does the child see?

As children answer this week's Concept Talk question, they will address:

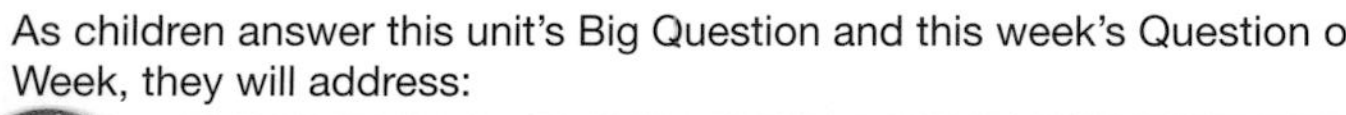

Speaking/Listening 1. Prepare for and participate effectively in a range of conversations and collaborations with diverse partners, building on others' ideas and expressing their own clearly and persuasively.

Writing Have children turn to p. 250 of *Reader's and Writer's Notebook*. Explain that the pictures show how the boy gets from his house to the mailbox around the corner. Tell children that they will give the boy directions. Have them write words to tell the boy how to get to the mailbox.

As children write this week, they will address:

Writing 2. Write informative/explanatory texts to examine and convey complex ideas and information clearly and accurately through the effective selection, organization, and analysis of content.

Listening and Speaking On page 29, children learn to give directions. By doing so, they address:

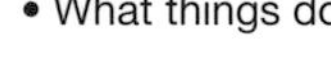

Speaking/Listening 4. Present information, findings, and supporting evidence such that listeners can follow the line of reasoning and the organization, development, and style are appropriate to task, purpose, and audience.

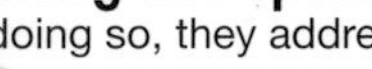

Week 2

My Lucky Day

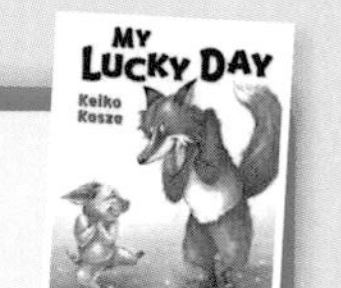

Question of the Week

What is a lucky adventure?

Concept Talk Guide children as they discuss questions such as:

- Why is the boy lucky? Does he know he is lucky at first? How can you tell?

Writing Have children write a class poem on the board. Use the selected topic and one of the suggested rhyming words. Have children copy the class poem on p. 262 of *Reader's and Writer's Notebook*. Then have them draw a picture about the poem.

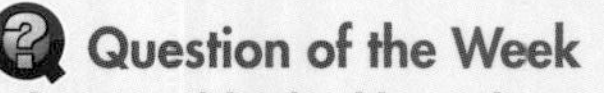

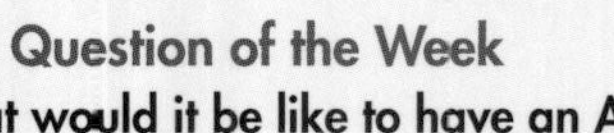

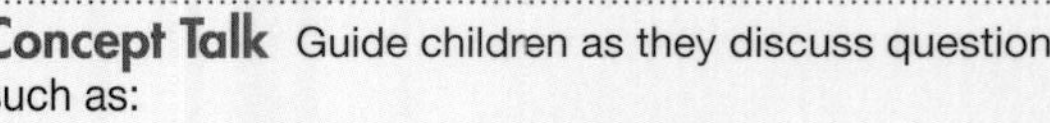

Common Core Standards and Concept Development

- Introduce and explore this unit's weekly concepts through rich, structured conversations
- Develop complex content knowledge and vocabulary
- Expand on a single concept with engaging literature and nonfiction
- Build better readers in all content areas

Align instruction to **Common Core Anchor Standards**

Week 3

One Little Mouse

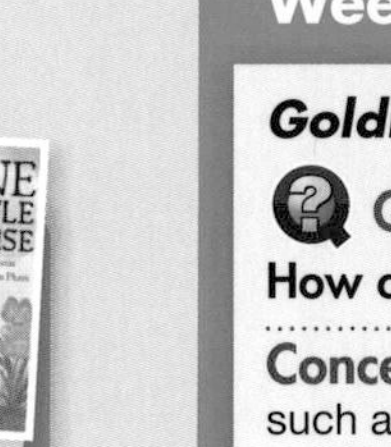

Question of the Week

What adventures can animals have?

Concept Talk Guide children as they discuss questions such as:

- What would a small animal's adventure be like?

Writing Have children turn to p. 274 of *Reader's and Writer's Notebook*. Have them draw a picture of the mouse in the selection. Then have children write or dictate a sentence on the line that tells about the mouse.

Week 4

Goldilocks and the Three Bears

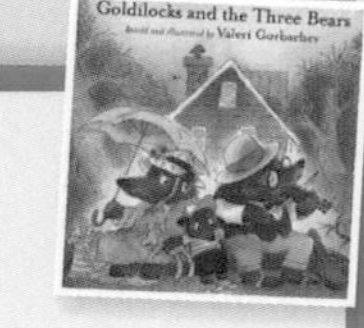

Question of the Week

How can an adventure cause trouble?

Concept Talk Guide children as they discuss questions such as:

- Are these real or make-believe bears? What do real bears do? What do make-believe bears do?

Writing Have children turn to p. 286 of *Reader's and Writer's Notebook*. Have them write or dictate a list of things found in *Goldilocks and the Three Bears*.

Week 5

If You Could Go to Antarctica

Question of the Week

What would it be like to have an Antarctic adventure?

Concept Talk Guide children as they discuss questions such as:

- What would you ask the explorer?
- Would you like to be an explorer?

Writing Have children turn to p. 298 of *Reader's and Writer's Notebook*. Have them write or dictate a letter to someone by finishing the sentence that tells what they like to read about. Then have them write their name at the end of the letter.

Week 6

Abuela

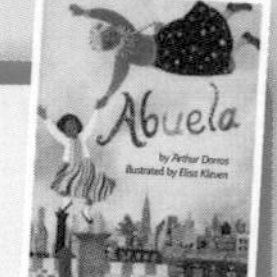

Question of the Week

What kind of adventures can you have in the city?

Concept Talk Guide children as they discuss questions such as:

- How do the children feel about their grandmothers? What do they like best about spending time with their grandmothers?

Writing Reread and discuss your list of things to do in the community, underlining key words in your draft. Have children write or dictate the group draft or copy the underlined key words on p. 314 in *Reader's and Writer's Notebook*. Then have them draw pictures to go with their list.

This Week's ELL Overview

Grade K • Unit 4 • Week 1
Rooster's Off to See the World
7–102
and DI•12–DI•17

ELL Handbook

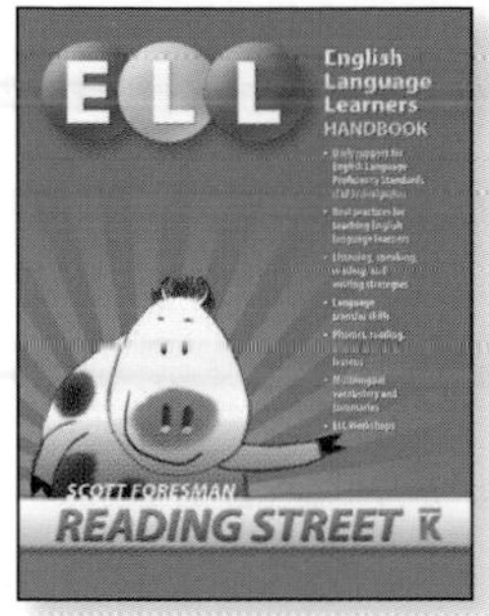

- Maximize Literacy and Cognitive Engagement
- Research Into Practice
- Full Weekly Support for Every Selection

Rooster's Off to See the World
- Routines to Support Instruction

- Transfer Activities
- Professional Development

Daily Leveled ELL Notes

ELL notes appear throughout this week's instruction and ELL Support is on the DI pages of your Teacher's Edition. The following is a sample of an ELL note from this week.

English Language Learners

Beginning Build Background Use the pictures on Talk with Me Chart 19A to help children understand words such as *lonely* and *homesick.* Talk with children about times when they have felt lonely or homesick.

Intermediate Frontload Decodable Story 19 As children learn the letter-sound relationships, it will become easier to introduce them to spelling. Understanding how letter-sounds blend together is the basis for understanding spelling patterns. Help them practice blending words from Decodable Story 19, such as *hat, hop,* and *hit.*

Advanced Frontload Decodable Reader Walk children through *Hob Can Hit.* Have them identify Dan, Hob, Pam, and Sam in the story. Use the pictures to help children identify baseball items, such as *bat, baseball, fan, mitt,* and *hat.*

Advanced High Support Conventions Play a naming parts game with children. Sit in a circle and pass a box of crayons around as you say with children, "Who took a crayon from the crayon box?" When you finish the question, the child holding the box should take a crayon. Use that child's name to say, "José took a crayon from the crayon box." José: "Who, me?" Group: "Yes, you!" José: "Not me!" Point out that *José* is the naming part of the sentence. Then start over by passing the box again.

ELL by Strand

The ELL lessons on this week's Support for English Language Learners pages are organized by strand. They offer additional scaffolding for the core curriculum. Leveled support notes on these pages address the different proficiency levels in your class. See pages DI•12–DI•17.

The Three Pillars of ELL Instruction

ELL Strands	Activate Prior Knowledge	Access Content	Extend Language
Vocabulary p. DI•14	Frontload Vocabulary	Provide Scaffolding	Practice
Reading Comprehension p. DI•14	Provide Scaffolding	Set the Scene	Frontload Vocabulary
Phonics, Spelling, and Word Analysis pp. DI•12, DI•15–DI•16	Frontload Words with /h/	Isolate Initial /h/	Review /o/
Listening Comprehension p. DI•13	Prepare for the Read Aloud	First Listening	Second Listening
Conventions and Writing pp. DI•15, DI•17	Provide Scaffolding/ Introduce and Model	Practice	Leveled Practice Activities/ Leveled Writing Activities
Concept Development p. DI•12	Read the Concept Literacy Reader	Read the Concept Literacy Reader	Develop Oral Language

This Week's Practice Stations Overview

Grade K • Unit 4 • Week 1
Rooster's Off to See the World
7–102

Six Weekly Practice Stations with Leveled Activities can be found at the beginning of each week of instruction. For this week's Practice Stations, see pp. 14–15.

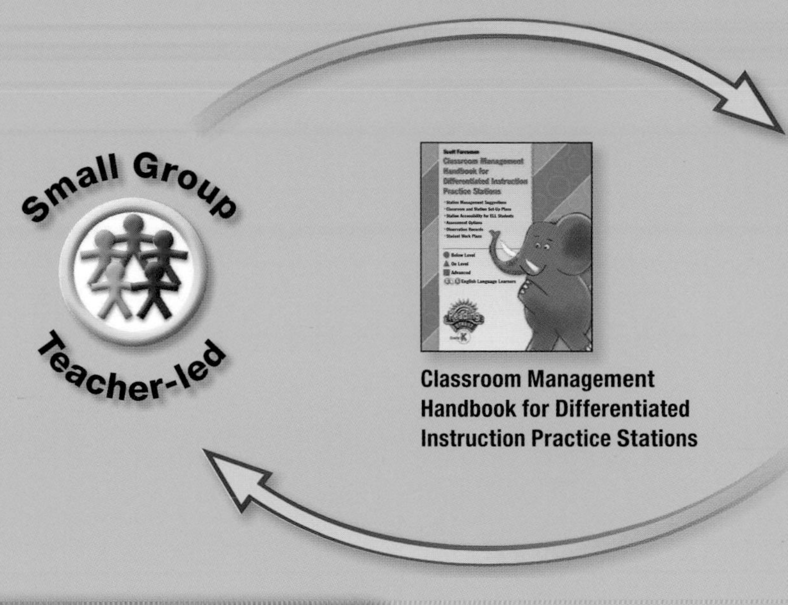

Practice Stations

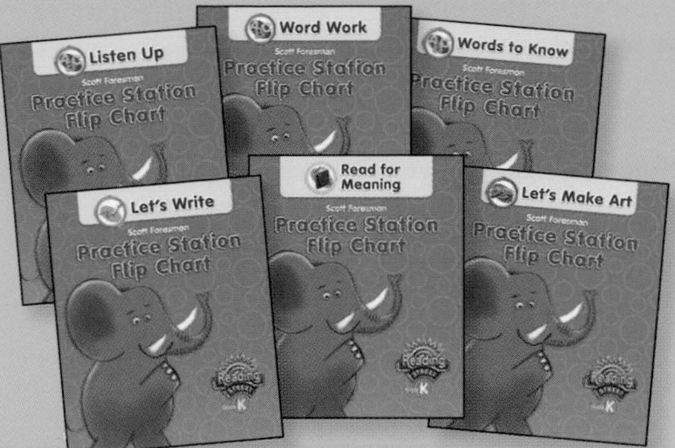

Daily Leveled Center Activities

Below
Advanced
On-Level

Practice Stations Flip Charts

	 Listen Up	 Word Work	 Words to Know	 Let's Write	 Read for Meaning	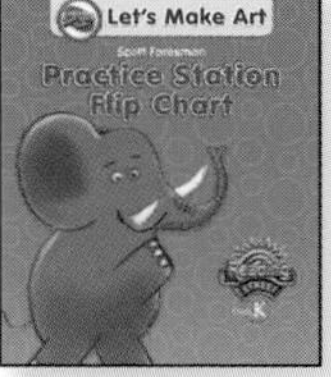 Let's Make Art
Objectives	• Identify words with /o/.	• Identify words with /o/ spelled *Oo.*	• Identify and use words for textures.	• Write a personal narrative.	• Identify the main idea.	• Make faces from clay to show different feelings.
Materials	• *Listen Up* Flip Chart Activity 19 • Picture Cards: *doll, fox, jet, olive, ox, van*	• *Word Work* Flip Chart Activity 19 • Alphabet Card: *Oo* • Picture Cards: *box, cat, mop, octopus, otter, top, web* • Letter Tiles	• *Words to Know* Flip Chart Activity 19 • Teacher-made Word Cards: *hard, soft, smooth, rough* • objects: rock, cotton ball, glossy art paper, sandpaper • paper, pencils	• *Let's Write* Flip Chart Activity 19 • crayons, paper, pencil	• *Read for Meaning* Flip Chart Activity 19 • Trade Book *The Lion and the Mouse* • pencil, crayons, paper	• *Let's Make Art* Flip Chart Activity 19 • Little Book *Rooster's Off to See the World* • art clay

This Week on Reading Street!

Question of the Week

What can we learn from our adventures?

Daily Plan

Whole Group

- /h/ spelled *Hh*
- Sequence
- Vocabulary

Don't Wait Until Friday

MONITOR PROGRESS | **Success Predictor**

Day 1	Day 2	Day 3	Day 4	Day 5
Check Phonemic Awareness	Check Sound Spelling/ Retelling	Check Word Reading	Check Phonemic Awareness	Check Oral Vocabulary

Small Group

Teacher-Led

- Reading Support
- Skill Support
- Fluency Practice

Practice Stations

Independent Activities

Customize Literacy More support for a Balanced Literacy approach, see pp. CL•1–CL•31.

Whole Group

- Writing
- Conventions: Naming Parts
- Listening and Speaking

Assessment

- Day 5 Assessment for Phonics
- Day 5 Assessment for Comprehension

This Week's Reading Selections

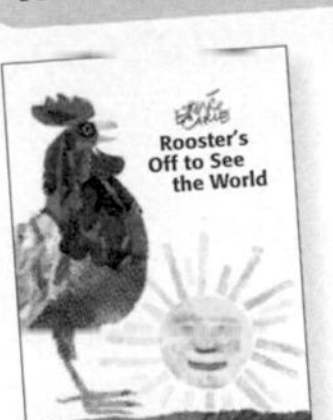

Big Book
Genre: **Animal Fantasy**

Decodable Reader 19

Leveled Readers

Get Set Roll! Reader 19

Resources on Reading Street!

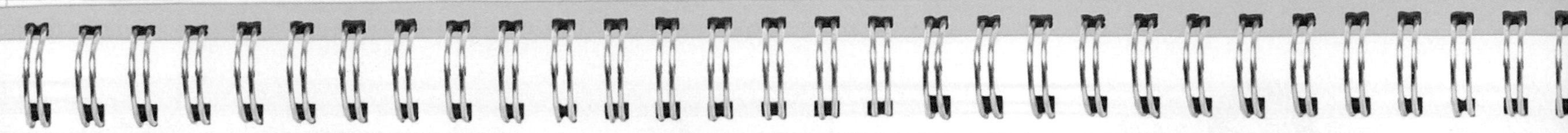

	Build Concepts	Phonemic Awareness and Phonics	Vocabulary
Whole Group	 Talk With Me/ Sing With Me	 Student Edition pp. 12–13 Student Edition p. 16	 Student Edition p. 17 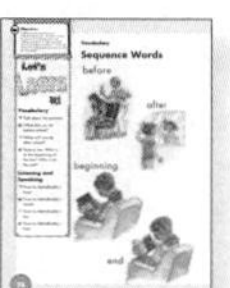 Student Edition p. 28
Go Digital	• Concept Talk Video • Sing with Me Animations	• eReaders	
Small Group and Independent Practice	 Practice Station Flip Chart  Leveled Readers	 Practice Station Flip Chart  Decodable Reader 19  Leveled Readers  Get Set, Roll! Reader 19	 Practice Station Flip Chart 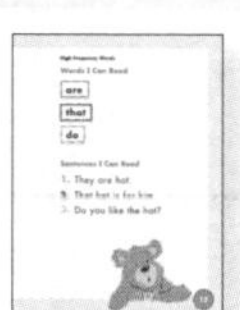 Student Edition p. 17
Go Digital	• eReaders	• eReaders • Letter Tile Drag and Drop	
Customize Literacy	• Leveled Readers	• Decodable Reader	• High-Frequency Word Cards
Go Digital	• Concept Talk Video • Big Question Video • eReaders	• eReaders	• Sing with Me Animations

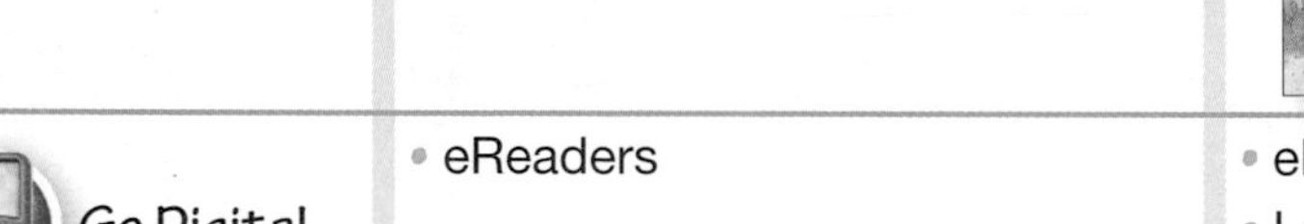

Question of the Week

What can we learn from our adventures?

Comprehension	Fluency	Conventions and Writing
 Student Edition pp. 14–15  Big Book	 Decodable Reader 19  Kdg. Student Reader K.4.1  Get Set, Roll! Reader 19	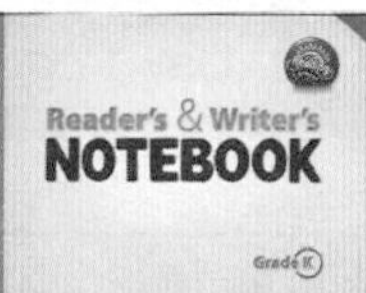 Reader's and Writer's Notebook
• Envision It! Animations	• eReaders	• Grammar Jammer
 Practice Station Flip Chart  Leveled Readers 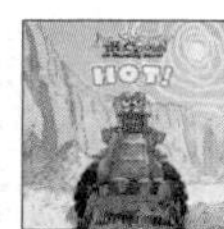 Get Set, Roll! Reader 19	 Practice Station Flip Chart  Leveled Readers	 Practice Station Flip Chart 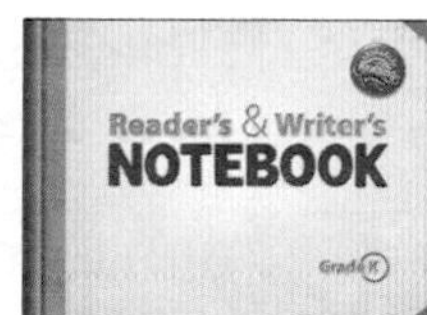 Reader's and Writer's Notebook
• Envision It! Animations • eReaders	• eReaders	• Grammar Jammer
• Leveled Readers	• Leveled Readers	• *Reader's and Writer's Notebook*
• Envision It! Animations • eReaders	• eReaders	• Grammar Jammer

My 5-Day Planner for Reading Street!

Don't Wait Until Friday MONITOR PROGRESS

	Day 1	Day 2
Don't Wait Until Friday MONITOR PROGRESS	Check Phonemic Awareness **Day 1** Day 1 pages 16–31	Check Sound-Spelling Check Retelling **Day 2** pages 32–49
Get Ready to Read	**Concept Talk,** 16 **Oral Vocabulary,** 17 *world, lonely, trip, horizon, journey, homesick* **Phonemic Awareness,** 18–19 ◎ Initial /h/ **Phonics,** 20–21 ◎ /h/ Spelled *Hh* **Handwriting,** 22 Letters *H* and *h* **High-Frequency Words,** 23 Introduce *are, that, do* **READ Decodable Story 19,** 24–25	**Concept Talk,** 32 **Oral Vocabulary,** 33 *world, lonely* **Phonemic Awareness,** 34–35 ◎ Initial /h/ **Phonics,** 36–37 ◎ /h/ Spelled *Hh* **Handwriting,** 38 Words with *Hh* **High-Frequency Words,** 39 *are, that, do* **READ Decodable Reader 19,** 40–41
Read and Comprehend	**Listening Comprehension,** 26–27 ◎ Sequence	**Listening Comprehension,** 42 ◎ Sequence **READ Big Book—First Read,** 42 Rooster's Off to See the World **Retell,** 43 **Think, Talk, and Write,** 44
Language Arts	**Conventions,** 28 Naming Parts **Writing,** 29 Wonderful, Marvelous Me! **Daily Handwriting,** 29 Letters *H* and *h* **Listening and Speaking,** 30 Give Directions **Wrap Up Your Day,** 30 **Extend Your Day!,** 31	**Conventions,** 45 Naming Parts **Writing,** 46 Respond to Literature **Daily Handwriting,** 46 Letters *H* and *h* **Vocabulary,** 47 Sequence Words **Wrap Up Your Day,** 48 **Extend Your Day!,** 49

You Are Here! Unit 4 Week 1

Question of the Week

What can we learn from our adventures?

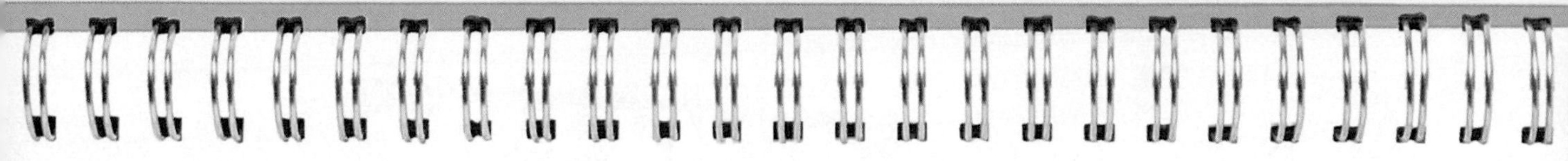

Check Word Reading **Day 3** pages 50–75	Check Phonemic Awareness **Day 4** pages 76–87	Check Oral Vocabulary **Day 5** pages 88–101
Concept Talk, 50 **Oral Vocabulary,** 51 *trip, horizon* **Phonemic Awareness,** 52–53 ◉ Initial /h/ **Phonics,** 54–55 ◉ /h/ Spelled *Hh* **READ Kindergarten Student Reader K.4.1,** 56–57	**Concept Talk,** 76 **Oral Vocabulary,** 77 *journey, homesick* Review **Phonemic Awareness,** 78 /o/ Review **Phonics,** 79 /o/ Spelled *Oo* **Spelling,** 80 ◉ /h/ Spelled *Hh* **READ Get Set, Roll! Reader 19,** 81	**Concept Wrap Up,** 88 **Oral Vocabulary,** 89 *world, lonely, trip, horizon, journey, homesick* Review **Phonemic Awareness,** 90 ◉ /h/ Review **Phonics,** 91 ◉ /h/ Spelled *Hh* **Assessment,** 92–93 Monitor Progress
Comprehension, 58 ◉ Sequence **READ Big Book—Second Read,** 58–69 Rooster's Off to See the World	**Comprehension,** 82 ◉ Sequence Review Compare and Contrast **READ Big Book—Third Read,** 83 Rooster's Off to See the World	**Let's Practice It!,** 94–95 Lullaby **Assessment,** 96–97 Monitor Progress
Conventions, 70 Sentences **Writing,** 71 Genre: Directions **Daily Handwriting,** 71 Letters *H* and *h* **Listening and Speaking,** 72–73 Give Directions **Wrap Up Your Day,** 74 **Extend Your Day!,** 75	**Conventions,** 84 Naming Parts **Writing,** 85 Extend the Concept **Daily Handwriting,** 85 Letters *H* and *h* **Vocabulary,** 86 Sequence Words **Wrap Up Your Day,** 86 **Extend Your Day!,** 87	Review **Conventions,** 98 Naming Parts **Writing,** 99 This Week We… **Daily Handwriting,** 99 Letters *H* and *h* **Wrap Up Your Week!,** 100 What can we learn from our adventures? **Extend Your Day!,** 101

Week 1

Grouping Options for Differentiated Instruction
Turn the page for the small group time lesson plan.

Planning Small Group Time on Reading Street!

SMALL GROUP TIME RESOURCES

DAY 1 Look for this Small Group Time box each day to help meet the individual needs of all your children. Differentiated instruction lessons appear on the DI pages at the end of each week.

Teacher-Led

SI Strategic Intervention	OL On-Level	A Advanced
Teacher-Led • Phonemic Awareness and Phonics **Reread** Decodable Story	**Teacher-Led** • Phonemic Awareness and Phonics **Reread** Decodable Story	**Teacher-Led** • Phonemic Awareness and Phonics **Reread** Decodable Story for Fluency

ELL Place English language learners in the groups that correspond to their reading abilities in English.

Practice Stations	Independent Activities
• Listen Up • Word Work	• Read Independently • *Reader's and Writer's Notebook* • Concept Talk Video

ELL

ELL Poster 19

Day 1	
SI Strategic Intervention	**Phonemic Awareness and Phonics,** DI•1 **Reread** Decodable Story 19, DI•1
OL On-Level	**Phonemic Awareness and Phonics,** DI•6 **Reread** Decodable Story 19, DI•6
A Advanced	**Phonemic Awareness and Phonics,** DI•9 **Reread** Decodable Story 18 for Fluency, DI•9
 **English Language Learners**	DI•12–DI•13 Frontload Concept Phonemic Awareness and Phonics Comprehension Skill

You Are Here! Unit 4 Week 1

Reading Street Response to Intervention Kit

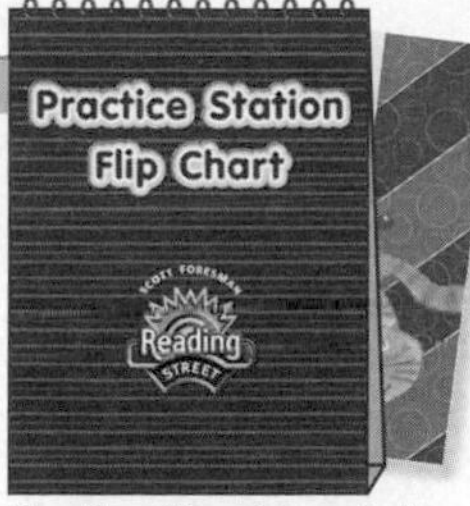

Reading Street Leveled Practice Stations Kit

Question of the Week

What can we learn from our adventures?

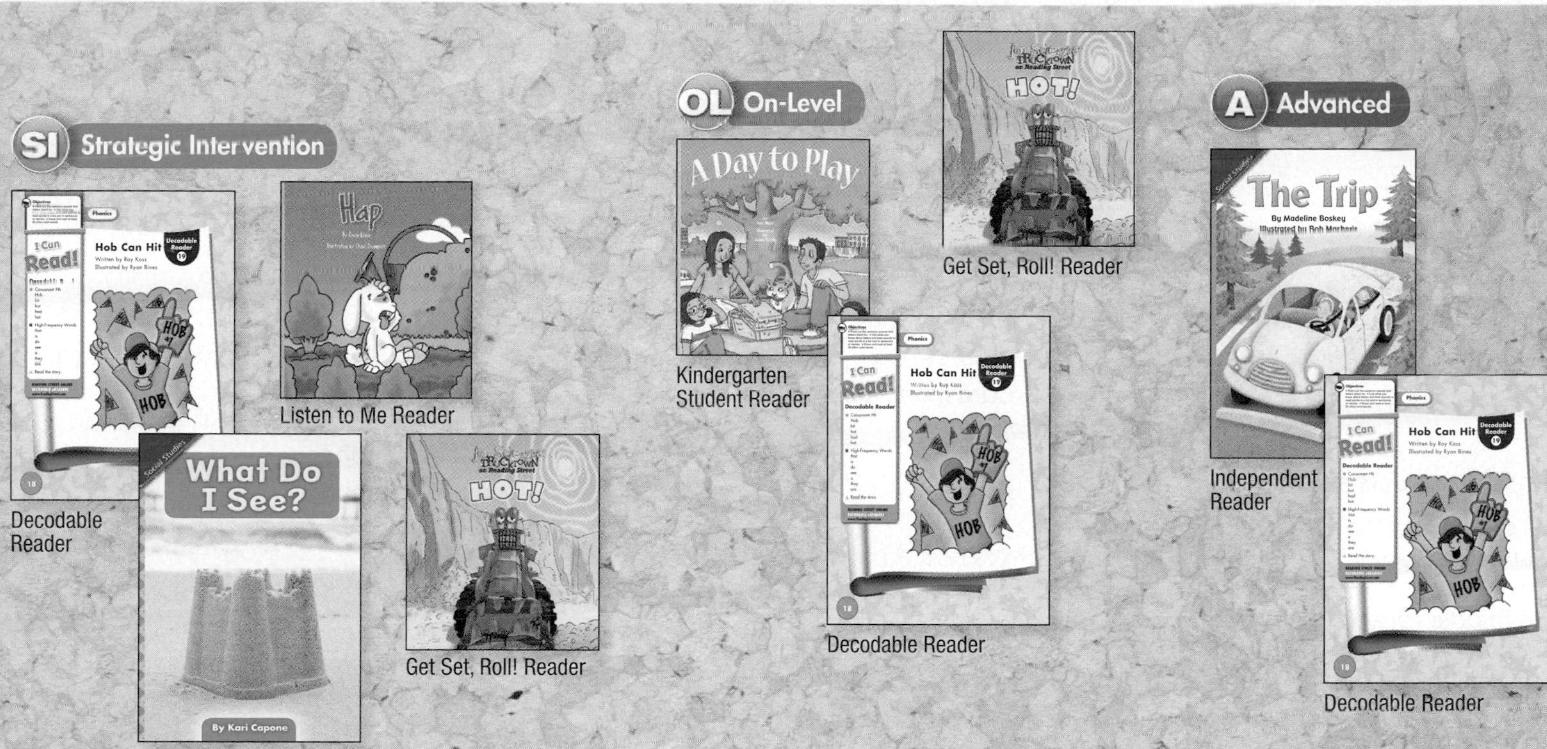

Small Group Weekly Plan

Day 2	Day 3	Day 4	Day 5
Phonemic Awareness and Phonics, DI•2 **Reread** Decodable Reader 19, DI•2	**Phonemic Awareness and Phonics,** DI•3 **Read** Concept Literacy Reader K.4.1, DI•3	**Phonemic Awareness and Phonics,** DI•4 **Read** Get Set, Roll! Reader 19, DI•4	**Phonics Review,** DI•5 **Read** Listen to Me Reader K.4.1, DI•5
Phonemic Awareness and Phonics, DI•6 **Reread** Decodable Reader 19, DI•6	**Phonemic Awareness and Phonics,** DI•7 **Read** Kindergarten Student Reader K.4.1, DI•7	Review Phonics and High-Frequency Words **Read** Get Set, Roll! Reader 19, DI•8	**Phonics Review,** DI•8 **Reread** Leveled Books, DI•8
Phonics and Spelling, DI•9 **Reread** Decodable Reader 19 for Fluency, DI•9	**Read** Independent Reader K.4.1 or Kindergarten Student Reader K.4.1, DI•10	**Read** Get Set, Roll! Reader 19 or **Reread** Kindergarten Student Reader K.4.1, DI•11	**Fluency and Comprehension,** DI•11 **Reread** Independent Reader for Fluency, DI•11
DI•14 Comprehension Skill Frontload Vocabulary	DI•15 Review Phonemic Awareness and Phonics Scaffold Conventions	DI•16 Review Phonemic Awareness and Phonics Revisit Concept and Oral Language	DI•17 Language Workshop Writing

Practice Stations for Everyone on Reading Street!

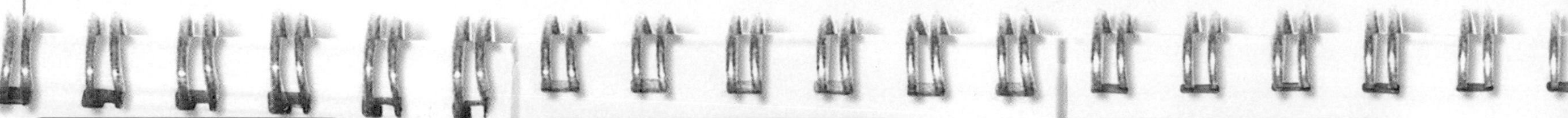

Listen Up!
Words with /o/

Objectives
- Identify words with /o/.

Materials
- *Listen Up!* Flip Chart Activity 19
- Picture Cards: *doll, fox, jet, olive, ox, van*

Differentiated Activities

● Find the Picture Card for *ox*. Say the sound you hear at the beginning. Find the Picture Card for *doll*. Say the sound you hear in the middle. Draw a picture of something whose name has the sound you hear at the beginning of *ox* and in the middle of *doll*.

▲ Find the Picture Card for *ox*. Say the sound you hear at the beginning. Find the Picture Card for *doll*. Say the sound you hear in the middle. Find other Picture Cards whose names begin like *ox* or have the middle sound you hear in *doll*.

■ Find the Picture Card for *ox*. Say the sound you hear at the beginning. Find the Picture Card for *doll*. Say the sound you hear in the middle. Look around the room. Find other objects whose names have the sound you hear at the beginning of *ox* and in the middle of *doll*.

Word Work
/o/ Spelled *Oo*

Objectives
- Identify words with /o/ spelled *Oo*.

Materials
- *Word Work* Flip Chart Activity 19
- Alphabet Cards: *Oo*
- Picture Cards: *box, cat, mop, octopus, otter, top, web*
- Letter Tiles

Differentiated Activities

● Find the Alphabet Card for *Oo*. Say *otter*. Find a Picture Card that begins with *Oo* like *otter* or has *Oo* in the middle like *box*.

▲ Find the Alphabet Card for *Oo*. Say *otter*. Find a Picture Card that begins with *Oo* like *otter* or has *Oo* in the middle like *box*. Look around the room. Find other objects whose names begin with *Oo* or have *Oo* in the middle like *otter* and *box*.

■ Find the Alphabet Card for *Oo*. Say *otter*. Find all the Picture Cards that begin with *Oo* like *otter* or have *Oo* in the middle like *box*. Look around the room. Find other objects whose names begin with *Oo* or have *Oo* in the middle like *otter* and *box*. Use Letter Tiles to spell words with *Oo*.

Technology
- Letter Tile Drag and Drop

Words To Know
Words for textures

Objectives
- Identify and use words for textures.

Materials
- *Words to Know* Flip Chart Activity 19
- Teacher-made word cards: *hard, soft, smooth, rough*
- objects: rock, cotton ball, glossy art paper, sandpaper
- paper, pencils

Differentiated Activities

● Find objects that are *hard, soft, smooth, rough*. Tell a partner how each feels.

▲ Find objects that are *hard, soft, smooth,* and *rough*. Match each object with a word card.

■ Match the Word Cards with the objects that are *hard, soft, smooth,* and *rough*. Write a sentence to tell about something that is *hard* and something that is *soft*. Write a sentence to tell about something that is *rough* and something that is *smooth*.

You Are Here! Unit 4 Week 1

Use this week's materials from the Reading Street Leveled Practice Stations Kit to organize this week's stations.

Key

● Below-Level Activities
▲ On-Level Activities
■ Advanced Activities

Practice Station Flip Chart

Week 1

Let's Write!

Personal narrative

Objectives

• Write a personal narrative.

Materials

• *Let's Write!* Flip Chart Activity 19
• crayons, paper, pencil

Differentiated Activities

● Draw a picture that shows something you do with a friend. Write a sentence that tells about your picture.

▲ Draw a picture to shows something you do with a friend. Write three sentences to tell about your picture.

■ Draw a picture that shows something you do with a friend. Write three sentences to tell about your picture. With a partner, tell each other how to make your sentences better.

Read For Meaning

Main idea

Objectives

• Identify the main idea.

Materials

• *Read for Meaning* Flip Chart Activity 19
• Trade Book *The Lion and the Mouse*
• pencil, crayons, paper

Differentiated Activities

● Look at the book. Think about the big idea. Tell a partner what the book is mostly about.

▲ Look at the book. Point to pictures and words that tell what the book is mostly about. Draw a picture that tells about the big idea.

■ Look at the book. Draw a picture and write a sentence that tells what the book is mostly about.

Let's Make Art!

Objectives

• Make animals from clay.

Materials

• *Let's Make Art!* Flip Chart Activity 19
• Little Book *Rooster's Off to See the World*
• art clay

Differentiated Activities

● Look at the pictures in the Little Book. Use clay to make one of the animals that set off to see the world.

▲ Look at the pictures in the Little Book. Choose an animal. Use clay to make that animal. Tell a partner why that animal joins Rooster.

■ Look at the pictures in the Little Book. Use clay to make one or two animals that joined Rooster. Use your animals to tell the story to a partner.

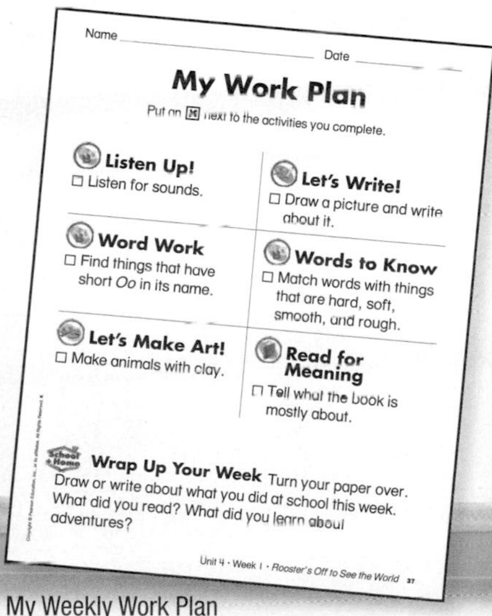

Name ________ Date ________

My Work Plan

Put on ☒ next to the activities you complete.

Listen Up!
☐ Listen for sounds.

Let's Write!
☐ Draw a picture and write about it.

Word Work
☐ Find things that have short *Oo* in its name.

Words to Know
☐ Match words with things that are hard, soft, smooth, and rough.

Let's Make Art!
☐ Make animals with clay.

Read for Meaning
☐ Tell what the book is mostly about.

Wrap Up Your Week Turn your paper over. Draw or write about what you did at school this week. What did you read? What did you learn about adventures?

Unit 4 • Week 1 • Rooster's Off to See the World 37

My Weekly Work Plan

Objectives

- Share information and ideas about the concept.

Today at a Glance

Oral Vocabulary
world, lonely, trip, horizon, journey, homesick

Phonemic Awareness
◎ Initial /h/

Phonics
◎ /h/ Spelled *Hh*

Handwriting
H and *h*

High-Frequency Words
are, that, do

Comprehension
◎ Sequence

Conventions
Naming Parts

Writing
Wonderful, Marvelous Me!

Listening and Speaking
Give Directions

TRUCKTOWN on Reading Street

Start your engines! Display p. 23 of *Truckery Rhymes.*

- Read aloud "Hey Diddle Diddle" and track the print.
- Reread the rhyme and have children chime in as they wish.
- Ask children to identify the rhyming words. (*diddle, middle; moon, tune*)

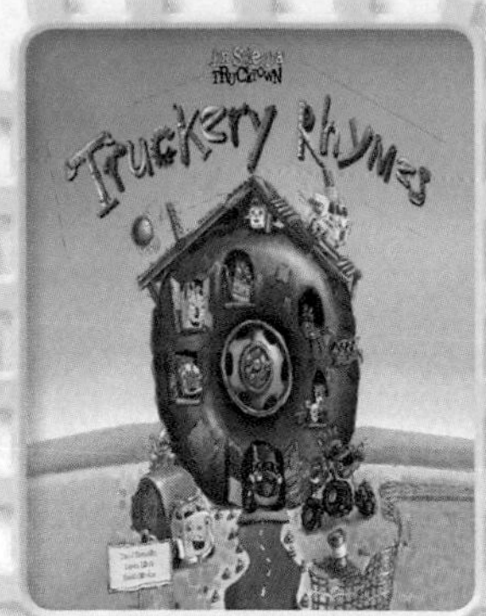

Truckery Rhymes

Concept Talk

Question of the Week

What can we learn from our adventures?

Introduce the concept To build concepts and to focus their attention, tell children that they will have an opportunity to talk, sing, read, and write about **learning from adventures.** Track each word as you read the question of the week.

Play the CD that features a song about an adventure. What things does the child see?

Background Building Audio

ROUTINE Activate Prior Knowledge — Team Talk

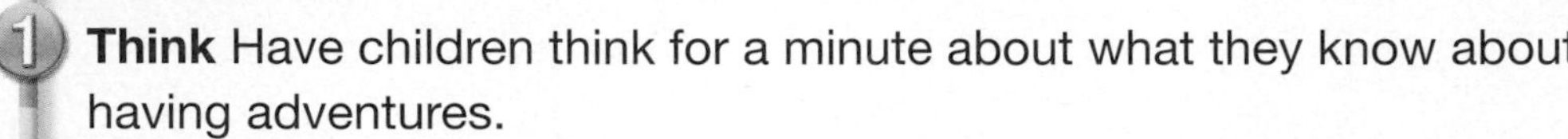

1. **Think** Have children think for a minute about what they know about having adventures.
2. **Pair** Have pairs of children discuss the question of the week. Remind them to take turns speaking. Have children use complete sentences in their discussions about having adventures.
3. **Share** Call on a few children to share their ideas with the group. Guide discussion and encourage elaboration with prompts such as: What does it mean to go on an adventure?

Routines Flip Chart

Anchored Talk

Develop oral language

Display Talk with Me Chart 19A. What do you see in the pictures? Look at the picture of the family at the airport. Where do you think they are going? What kind of adventure do you think they will have? What do you think they will learn on their adventure?

We are going to learn six Amazing Words this week. Listen as I say each word: *world, lonely, trip, horizon, journey, homesick.* Have children say each word as you point to the picture.

Display Sing with Me Chart 19B. Tell children they are going to sing a song about taking a special trip. Read the title. Have children describe the illustration. Sing the song several times to the tune of "Head and Shoulders, Knees and Toes." Listen for the Amazing Words: *world, lonely, trip, horizon, journey, homesick.* Have children march around the classroom and sing the song with you.

Sing with Me Audio

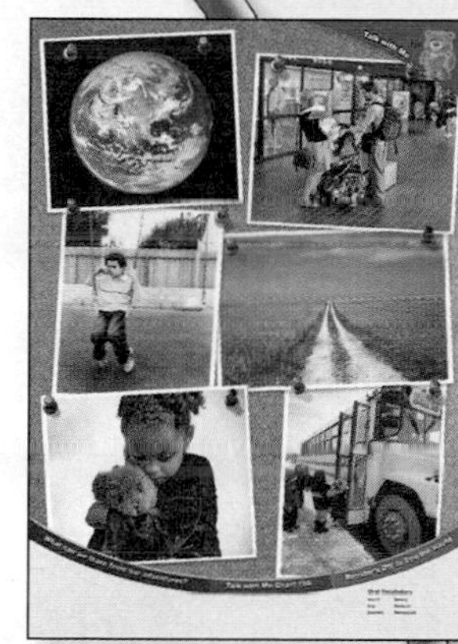
Talk with Me/Sing with Me Chart 19A

Talk with Me/Sing with Me Chart 19B

ELL Preteach Concepts Use the Day 1 instruction on ELL Poster 19 to assess and build background knowledge, develop concepts, and build oral vocabulary.

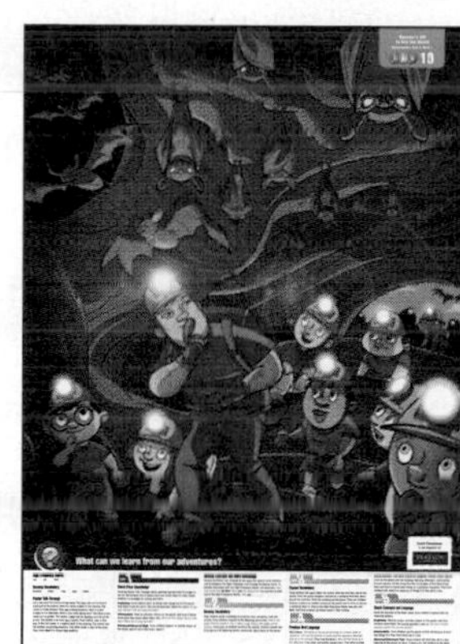
ELL Poster 19

Amazing Words

world	lonely
trip	horizon
journey	homesick

Differentiated Instruction

SI Strategic Intervention

Build Background Discuss what taking a trip means. Ask children how they prepare to go away to visit someone, even if it is only a short trip. Discuss things they need to take with them and how taking a trip makes them feel.

English Language Learners

Build Background Use the pictures on Talk with Me Chart 19A to help children understand words such as *lonely* and *homesick*. Talk with children about times when they have felt lonely or homesick.

ELL Support Additional ELL support and modified instruction is provided in the *ELL Handbook* and in the ELL Support lessons on pp. DI•12–17.

DAY 1 Get Ready to Read

Objectives

- ◎ Learn initial /h/.
- Identify words with initial /h/.
- Discriminate words with final /h/.
- Identify initial sounds.

Check Phonemic Awareness
SUCCESS PREDICTOR

My Skills Buddy, pp. 12–13

Phonemic Awareness

◎ Initial /h/

Introduce Today we will learn a new sound. Listen carefully as I say the sound: /h/ /h/ /h/. Say it with me: /h/ /h/ /h/. Display the *hat* Picture Card. *Hat* begins with /h/ /h/ /h/, *hat*. What sound does *hat* begin with? Use Picture Cards for *house, hen,* and *hammer* to continue the routine.

Picture Card

Model Have children look at the picture on pages 12–13 of *My Skills Buddy*. Tell them that they will be listening for a new sound—/h/. I see some hooks in the picture. What sound do you hear at the beginning of *hooks?* I hear /h/ at the beginning of *hooks*. The first sound in *hooks* is /h/. What other things do you see that begin with that sound?

Guide practice As children name example words from the picture, guide them in stating that /h/ is the beginning sound. Discuss some of the bulleted items on p. 12 of *My Skills Buddy*. Save the other bulleted items for Day 2.

Corrective feedback **If...** children have difficulty naming words with /h/,
then... say *hooks* again, stretching the beginning sound—/h/ /h/ /h/, *hooks*.

Use this week's materials from the Reading Street Leveled Practice Stations Kit to organize this week's stations.

Key

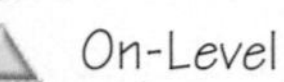

Below-Level Activities

On-Level Activities

Advanced Activities

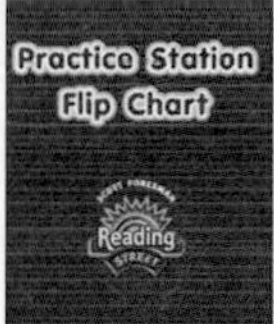

Practice Station Flip Chart

Week 1

Let's Write!

Personal narrative

Objectives

- Write a personal narrative.

Materials

- *Let's Write!* Flip Chart Activity 19
- crayons, paper, pencil

Differentiated Activities

● Draw a picture that shows something you do with a friend. Write a sentence that tells about your picture.

▲ Draw a picture to shows something you do with a friend. Write three sentences to tell about your picture.

■ Draw a picture that shows something you do with a friend. Write three sentences to tell about your picture. With a partner, tell each other how to make your sentences better.

Read For Meaning

Main idea

Objectives

- Identify the main idea.

Materials

- *Read for Meaning* Flip Chart Activity 19
- Trade Book *The Lion and the Mouse*
- pencil, crayons, paper

Differentiated Activities

● Look at the book. Think about the big idea. Tell a partner what the book is mostly about.

▲ Look at the book. Point to pictures and words that tell what the book is mostly about. Draw a picture that tells about the big idea.

■ Look at the book. Draw a picture and write a sentence that tells what the book is mostly about.

Let's Make Art!

Objectives

- Make animals from clay.

Materials

- *Let's Make Art!* Flip Chart Activity 19
- Little Book *Rooster's Off to See the World*
- art clay

Differentiated Activities

● Look at the pictures in the Little Book. Use clay to make one of the animals that set off to see the world.

▲ Look at the pictures in the Little Book. Choose an animal. Use clay to make that animal. Tell a partner why that animal joins Rooster.

■ Look at the pictures in the Little Book. Use clay to make one or two animals that joined Rooster. Use your animals to tell the story to a partner.

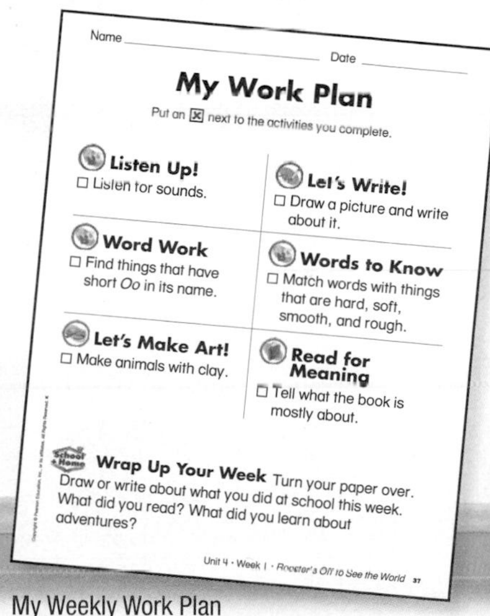
Name _______ Date _______

My Work Plan

Put an ☒ next to the activities you complete.

Listen Up!
☐ Listen for sounds.

Let's Write!
☐ Draw a picture and write about it.

Word Work
☐ Find things that have short *Oo* in its name.

Words to Know
☐ Match words with things that are hard, soft, smooth, and rough.

Let's Make Art!
☐ Make animals with clay.

Read for Meaning
☐ Tell what the book is mostly about.

Wrap Up Your Week Turn your paper over. Draw or write about what you did at school this week. What did you read? What did you learn about adventures?

Unit 4 • Week 1 • Rooster's Off to See the World

My Weekly Work Plan

Objectives

- Share information and ideas about the concept.

Today at a Glance

Oral Vocabulary
world, lonely, trip, horizon, journey, homesick

Phonemic Awareness
◎ Initial /h/

Phonics
◎ /h/ Spelled *Hh*

Handwriting
H and *h*

High-Frequency Words
are, that, do

Comprehension
◎ Sequence

Conventions
Naming Parts

Writing
Wonderful, Marvelous Me!

Listening and Speaking
Give Directions

TRUCKTOWN on Reading Street

Start your engines! Display p. 23 of *Truckery Rhymes.*

- Read aloud "Hey Diddle Diddle" and track the print.
- Reread the rhyme and have children chime in as they wish.
- Ask children to identify the rhyming words. (*diddle, middle; moon, tune*)

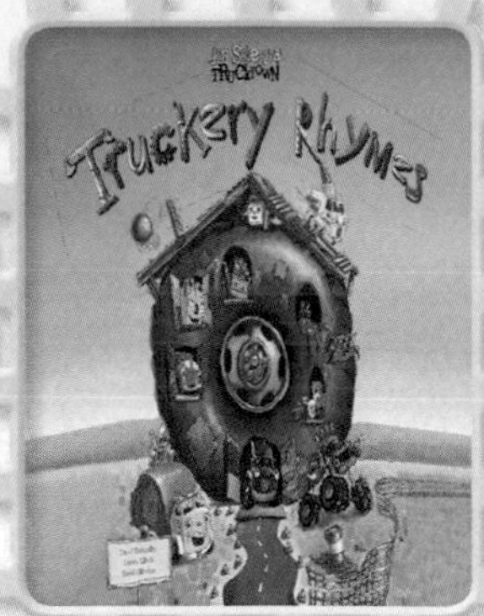

Truckery Rhymes

Concept Talk

Question of the Week

What can we learn from our adventures?

Introduce the concept To build concepts and to focus their attention, tell children that they will have an opportunity to talk, sing, read, and write about **learning from adventures.** Track each word as you read the question of the week.

Play the CD that features a song about an adventure. What things does the child see?

Background Building Audio

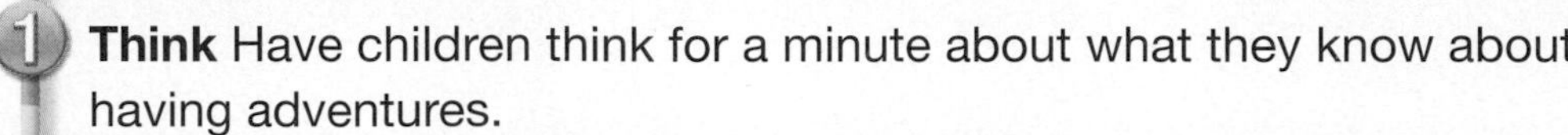

ROUTINE **Activate Prior Knowledge** Team Talk

1. **Think** Have children think for a minute about what they know about having adventures.
2. **Pair** Have pairs of children discuss the question of the week. Remind them to take turns speaking. Have children use complete sentences in their discussions about having adventures.
3. **Share** Call on a few children to share their ideas with the group. Guide discussion and encourage elaboration with prompts such as: What does it mean to go on an adventure?

Routines Flip Chart

Discriminate sounds

I am going to read a list of words. Clap your hands when you hear a word that begins with /h/. Listen carefully. I will do the first one: *hill* (clap), *boy, head* (clap). Continue with these sets of words: him, hen, more; moon, hop, hose.

Display the *hat* Picture Card. This is a *hat*. *Hat* begins with /h/ /h/ /h/, *hat*. What sound does *hat* begin with? Display the *mop* Picture Card. This is a *mop*. The first sound in *mop* is /m/. Do *hat* and *mop* both begin with /h/? No, *hat* and *mop* do not both begin with /h/. Which word begins with /h/, *hat* or *mop?* Continue with the following pairs of Picture Cards: *hen, bat; house, doll; kangaroo, hippopotamus*.

Corrective feedback

If... children cannot discriminate initial /h/,
then... have them enunciate /h/ as they say *hen*.

When you say /h/, you can feel the air explode as you breathe out. Say /h/ and feel how the air explodes. Have children say *hen* and feel the air movement. Then repeat the activity with *hang, hand, happy,* and *hope*.

Identify initial sounds

I am going to say a word. I want you to tell me what sound you hear at the beginning of the word. Let's do the first one together. Listen: *fan*. What is the beginning sound in *fan?* I hear /f/. *Fan* begins with /f/. Continue the routine with these words: *dig, ran, net, bed, cob, pop, sad, ten, map*.

Don't Wait Until Friday

MONITOR PROGRESS — Check Phonemic Awareness — Words with Initial /h/

Say *ham* and *kite*. Have children identify the word that begins with /h/. Continue with *hot, slide; tent, hip; hut, soap*.

If... children cannot discriminate initial /h/,
then... use the small-group Strategic Intervention lesson, p. DI•1, to reteach /h/.

Day 1	Day 2	Day 3	Day 4	Day 5
Check Phonemic Awareness	Check Sound-Spelling/ Retelling	Check Word Reading	Check Phonemic Awareness	Check Oral Vocabulary

Success Predictor

Differentiated Instruction

 Strategic Intervention

Support Phonemic Awareness Have children hold their hands in front of their faces and say the word *ha* three times. Tell them that they should be able to feel their breath on their hands as they say /h/. Have them say the words *happy, hot,* and *hand*.

Teacher Tip

After children have distinguished /h/ from other initial sounds, have them identify /h/ words on their own to share with the class.

ELL

English Language Learners

Language Transfer Children may pronounce /h/ with a harsher sound that resembles the sound of the letter *j* in Spanish. Show how /h/ is pronounced by puffing air from the throat and provide extra practice with /h/ words such as *high, honey, hatch, hear,* and *hop*.

ELL Support For additional support for language transfer, see Linguistic Contrastive Analysis in the *ELL Handbook.*

Objectives

- Recognize uppercase *H* and lowercase *h*.
- ◎ Associate the sound /h/ with the spelling *h*.
- Blend and read words with /h/.

Skills Trace

◎ /h/ Spelled *Hh*

Introduce U4W1D1
Practice U4W1D2; U4W1D3
Reteach/Review U4W1D5; U4W2D4
Assess/Test Benchmark Assessment U4

KEY:
U=Unit W=Week D=Day

Phonics—Teach/Model

◎ /h/ Spelled *Hh*

Introduce Display the *Hh* Alphabet Card and point to the *helicopter. Helicopter* begins with /h/. Say the word with me: *helicopter*. Write *helicopter* on the board and point to the *h*. *Helicopter* begins with /h/ spelled *h*. Now point to the letters *Hh* on the card. The sound for this letter is /h/. The names of these letters are uppercase *H* and lowercase *h*. What is the sound for this letter? What are the names of these letters?

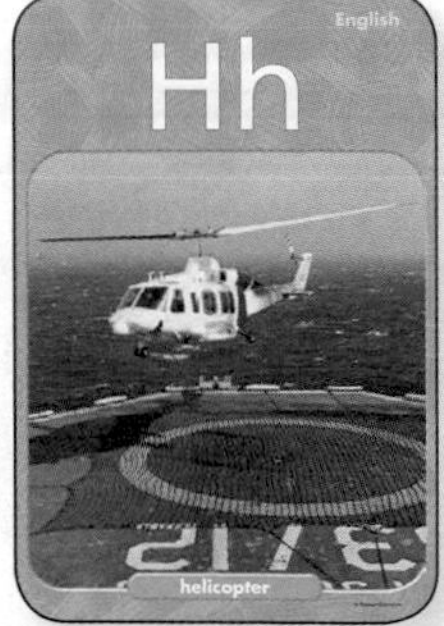

Alphabet Card

Model Write *We're Hiking Home* on the board. Point to the first *H*. When I see this letter, I think of the sound /h/. This word is *Hiking*—/h/, *Hiking*. Point to *Home*. This word also beings with *H*. I know that when I see an *H,* the sound will be /h/. This word is /h/, *Home*. The song we will sing is "We're Hiking Home."

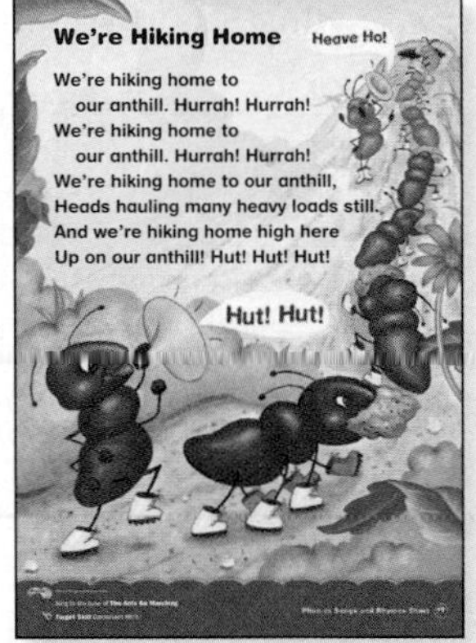

Phonics Songs and Rhymes Chart 19

Guide practice Display Phonics Songs and Rhymes Chart 19. Teach children the song "We're Hiking Home" sung to the tune "The Ants Go Marching." Play the CD and sing the song several times. I hear many words that begin with /h/. When you hear a word that begins with /h/, hop on one foot. As you sing the song, point to words that begin with *h*.

Phonics Songs and Rhymes Audio

On their own Have children hunt for uppercase *H* and lowercase *h* on the classroom alphabet chart or in other places around the classroom.

Blend Words

Review

To review sound-spellings, use Alphabet Cards *Aa, Cc, Ii, Nn, Oo, Tt* and the *ant, cap, igloo, nose, octopus,* and *tent* Picture Cards. Then use this routine for sound-by-sound blending to have children blend new words.

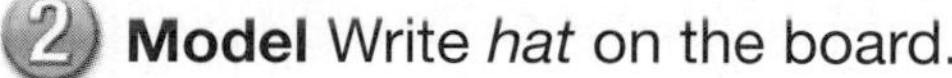

ROUTINE Sound-by-Sound Blending

1. **Connect** Write the letter *h*. What is the sound for this letter? The sound is /h/. Say it with me: /h/ /h/ /h/. When you see this letter in a word, what sound will you say?
2. **Model** Write *hat* on the board.
   - Touch under the letter *h*. What is the sound for this letter? Say it with me: /h/ /h/ /h/. Repeat the routine for *a* and *t*.
   - Let's blend the sounds together. Listen as I blend the sounds: /h/ /a/ /t/. Say it with me: /h/ /a/ /t/. Now say it without me.
   - Listen as I use *hat* in a sentence: *I wear a hat on my head*. Say the sentence with me. Then have children use *hat* in their own sentences.

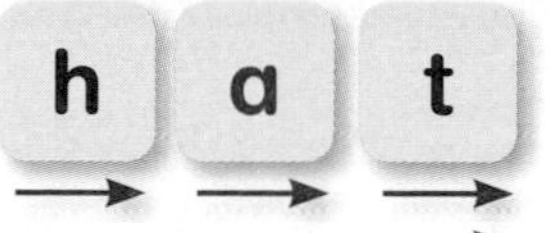

3. **Guide Practice** Continue the routine established in step 2 with the words below:

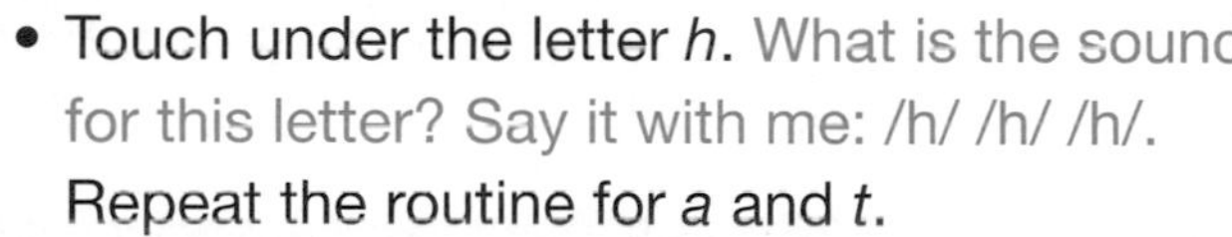

on it can hop hit

Children should successfully read these words before reading Decodable Story 19 on p. 243–244 of *Reader's and Writer's Notebook.*

Corrective Feedback If children have trouble reading a word, model blending the sounds to read the word. Then have children say it with you.

Routines Flip Chart

Differentiated Instruction

 Advanced

Hunting for *Hh* Have children write *Hh* on self-stick notes. Give children five minutes to hunt around the classroom for things that begin with /h/ spelled *Hh* and attach a self-stick note to it. Remind them to include their own heads, hands, and hearts.

Teacher Tip

Help children remember that /h/ is spelled *Hh* by having them brainstorm words that begin with /h/ for you to write on the board. Point out that the beginning /h/ in each word corresponds to the letter *H* or *h* at the beginning of the word.

English Language Learners

Support Phonics Children may spell /h/ as *j*. Model the correct sound-spelling by saying and writing a short sentence with both /h/ and /j/, such as *I can jump high*. Have children repeat the sentence, and call their attention to /h/ spelled *Hh*.

DAY 1 Get Ready to Read

Objectives

- Write *H* and *h*.
- Learn high-frequency words.

Handwriting

Introduce Write *Hh* on the board. Words that begin with /h/ are written with an uppercase *H* or a lowercase *h*. Which letter is uppercase *H*? Which letter is lowercase *h*?

Model uppercase *H* Write *Henry* on the board. Point to the uppercase *H*. This is the uppercase *H*. We use uppercase letters to begin sentences and for the first letter in a person's name. Watch as I trace the uppercase *H* with my finger. Follow the stroke instructions pictured below.

Guide practice Have children write the uppercase *H* in the air. Use your finger to make an uppercase *H* in the air. Now write it on the palm of your hand.

Model lowercase *h* Write *happy* on the board and point to the lowercase *h*. This is lowercase *h*. Watch as I trace a lowercase *h* with my finger. Write another lowercase *h* on the board following the stroke instructions. Again, have children write *h* in the air and on their hands.

Guide practice Have children use their Write-On Boards to write a row each of uppercase *H* and lowercase *h*.

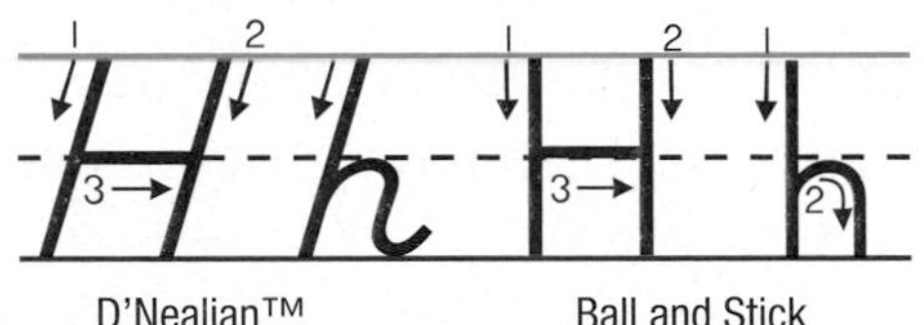
D'Nealian™ Ball and Stick

More practice Use *Reader's and Writer's Notebook,* pp. 241, 242, for additional practice with initial *h*.

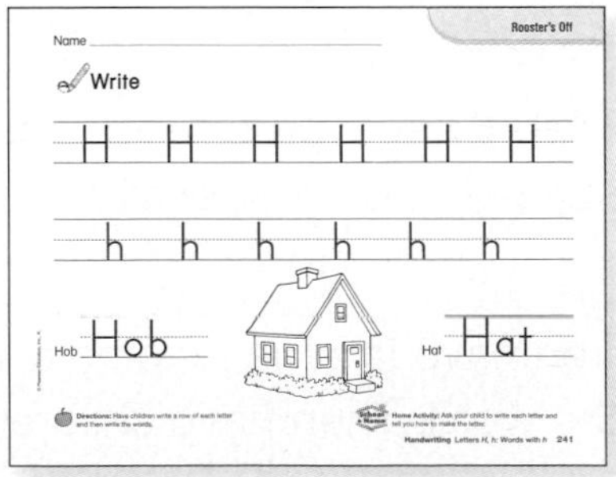

Reader's and Writer's Notebook, p. 241

Reader's and Writer's Notebook, p. 242

High-Frequency Words

Introduce

Use the routine below to teach high-frequency words *are, that,* and *do*.

ROUTINE **Nondecodable Words**

1. **Say and Spell** Some words we have to learn by remembering the letters rather than saying the sounds. We will say and spell the words to help learn them. Write *do* on the board. This is the word *do*. It has two letters. The letters in *do* are *d* and *o*. Have children say and spell the word with you.
2. **Demonstrate Meaning** I can use the word *do* in lots of sentences. Here is one sentence: *I do my homework*. Now you use the word in a sentence.

Repeat the routine with the words *are* and *that*.

Add *do, are,* and *that* to the Word Wall.

Routines Flip Chart

Differentiated Instruction

Advanced

High-Frequency Words Write the words *are, that,* and *do* on the board. Say the words aloud. Have several children write the words on their Write-On Boards and use them in sentences.

Academic Vocabulary

Write the following words on the board:

sequence	**naming part**
retell	**directions**
lullaby	**rhythm**

Point to the list. This week we are going to learn these important words. They are tools for learning. As we work this week, you will hear them many times. Read the words. Preteach the Academic Vocabulary at point-of-use by providing a child-friendly description, explanation, or example that clarifies the meaning of each term. Then ask children to restate the meaning of the Academic Vocabulary in their own words.

Objectives

- Read high-frequency words.
- Decode and read words in context and isolation.

Decodable Story 19
/h/ Spelled *Hh* and High-Frequency Words

Review Review the following high-frequency words by having children read each word as you point to it on the Word Wall.

I	have	a	the	is	little	that
my	me	do	you	with	like	

Read Decodable Story 19

Display Decodable Story 19. Today we will read a story about a girl and her hat. Point to the title of the story. The title of this story is *I Have!* What sound do you hear at the beginning of *have?* We will read lots of words that begin with /h/ in this story. Have children read Decodable Story 19 on pp. 243–244 in *Reader's and Writer's Notebook*.

Reader's and Writer's Notebook, pp. 243–244

Use the routine for reading decodable books to read Decodable Story 19.

ROUTINE Reading Decodable Books

1. **Read Silently** Have children whisper read the story page by page as you listen in.
2. **Model Fluent Reading** Have children finger point as you read a page. Then have children reread the page without you.
3. **Read Chorally** Have children finger point as they chorally read the page. Continue reading page by page, repeating steps 1 and 2.
4. **Read Individually** Have children take turns reading aloud a page.
5. **Reread and Monitor Progress** As you listen to individual children reread, monitor progress and provide support.
6. **Reread with a Partner** Have children reread the story page by page with a partner.

Routines Flip Chart

Differentiated Instruction

SI Strategic Intervention

Support Reading Pair less able children with more able children so that they can get a clear understanding of what fluent reading sounds like.

Small Group Time

DAY 1 Break into small groups after reading the Decodable Story and before the comprehension lesson.

Teacher-Led

SI Strategic Intervention	OL On-Level	A Advanced
Teacher-Led Page DI•1 • Phonemic Awareness and Phonics • **Reread** Decodable Story 19	**Teacher-Led** Page DI•6 • Phonemic Awareness and Phonics • **Reread** Decodable Story 19	**Teacher-Led** Page DI•9 • Phonemic Awareness and Phonics • **Reread** Decodable Story 19 for Fluency

Place English language learners in the groups that correspond to their reading abilities in English.

Practice Stations
- Visit the Listen Up! Station
- Visit the Word Work Station

Independent Activities
- Read independently
- Concept Talk Video
- *Reader's and Writer's Notebook*

English Language Learners

Frontload Decodable Story 19 As children learn the letter-sound relationships, it will become easier to introduce them to spelling. Understanding how letter-sounds blend together is the basis for understanding spelling patterns. Help them practice blending words from Decodable Story 19, such as *hat, hop,* and *hit.*

Objectives

◎ Identify sequence.

Skills Trace

◎ **Sequence**

Introduce U1W3D1; U2W5D1; U4W1D1; U4W3D1

Practice U1W3D2; U1W3D3; U1W3D4; U2W5D2; U2W5D3; U2W5D4; U4W1D2; U4W1D3; U4W1D4; U4W3D2; U4W3D3; U4W3D4

Reteach/Review U1W3D5; U1W5D4; U2W2D4; U2W5D5; U2W6D4; U4W1D5; U4W3D5; U5W2D4

Assess/Test Benchmark Assessment U4

KEY:

U=Unit W=Week D=Day

My Skills Buddy, pp. 14–15

Listening Comprehension

◎ Sequence

Introduce

Envision It!

In a story, events happen in a certain order. Something happens first, next, and last. The order in which these things happen is called the **sequence.** Good readers pay attention to the order of events in a story so they can better understand the story. What do good readers do?

Have children turn to pp. 14–15 in *My Skills Buddy* and look at the three pictures. These pictures tell a story in sequence. They tell what happens first, next, and last. Help me tell this story. Guide children as they describe the order of the story.

- What happens first? (A mother bird sits on her eggs.)
- What happens next? (The mother bird feeds the baby birds.)
- What happens last? (The baby birds fly away.)

Model

Today I will read a story about a kitten that takes a walk. Read **"Kate Kitten Takes a Walk"** and model how to identify sequence.

When I read, I pay attention to the order in which things happen. I notice what happens first, next, and last. In "Kate Kitten Takes a Walk," Kate skips her daily nap to take a walk while the weather is nice. She tries to find someone to walk with her. First, she asks a robin. Next, she asks a squirrel. Last, she asks a puppy, and he walks with her.

Guide practice After reading, ask children questions about the sequence in which events happened.

- Who does Kate ask to walk with her first? (a robin) What is the robin's answer? (He can't because he has to find worms for his babies.)
- Who does Kate ask to walk with her next? (a squirrel) What is the squirrel's answer? (He can't because he has to bury nuts for winter.)
- Who does Kate ask to walk with her last? (a puppy) What is the puppy's answer? (He thinks it sounds like fun.)

More practice Display the Big Book *The Little School Bus.* Page through the story. Help children recall the sequence in which the animals are picked up for school. Who gets on the school bus first? next? then? last?

Connect to everyday life During the day, we do things in order. Think about what you do when you get to school. What are three things you do when you get to school? Tell us what you do first, next, and last.

Differentiated Instruction

Strategic Intervention

Support Sequence As you review the story, write numbered sentences on the board to help children keep track of the order of events.

Academic Vocabulary

sequence the order in which story events happen

English Language Learners

Oral Comprehension To prepare English learners for the Read Aloud, use the modified Read Aloud in the ELL Support lesson p. DI•13.

Kate Kitten Takes a Walk

After lunch, Kate usually took a nap. But today she didn't. The sun was shining, and a breeze tickled her whiskers. Instead, she took a walk. First, she met a robin hopping in the grass.

"Will you walk with me?" Kate asked.

"I can't," he said. "I have to find worms for my babies."

Kate went on. Next, she saw a squirrel racing down a tree. Kate asked him too. But he said he had to bury nuts for winter. Kate walked on. Finally, she noticed a puppy digging a hole.

"Will you walk with me?" she asked.

He wagged his tail. "That sounds like fun!" he said. They had a lovely time in the sun.

DAY 1 Language Arts 20–25 mins.

Objectives

- Identify and use naming parts of sentences.
- Write or dictate a sentence about how you are special.

Conventions
Naming Parts

Model Remind children that a sentence tells a complete thought. The naming part of the sentence tells who or what the sentence is about. Show the *cat* Picture Card. Then write this sentence on the board: *The cat ran fast.* Let's read this sentence together: *The cat ran fast.* What ran fast? (the cat) This sentence is about the cat. The cat is the naming part of the sentence. What is the naming part of the sentence? (the cat)

Guide practice Use the following Picture Cards to make simple sentences: *astronaut, box, dog, flag, truck, zebra, man.* Write the sentences on the board and read them aloud to children. Have them place the correct Picture Card under each sentence to show who or what the sentence is about.

Team Talk Pair children and have them use images from the Picture Cards in the guide practice activity to make up their own complete sentences.

Daily Fix-It Use the Daily Fix-It for more conventions practice.

Writing
Wonderful, Marvelous Me!
I Am Special Because...

Introduce Talk with children about how everyone is special. Everyone in this room is special. What makes us special? Lots of wonderful, marvelous things make each of special. We are special because of who we are on the inside, what we can do, and even how we look. Someone may be special because he is a good artist. Someone else may be special because she can say the ABCs without stopping. Someone else may be special because she has dark hair or freckles. Encourage children to share their thoughts and ideas about things that make them special.

Model Today we are going to write about something that makes us special. I'm going to close my eyes and think about things I can do. One thing that makes me special is that I can sing. Sing a short, familiar tune. Another thing that is special about me is that I wear glasses. Draw a picture of yourself with glasses and write the word *glasses.* I am also special because I am a good listener and a good speaker.

Guide practice Encourage children to help you think of other things that make you special. Write words and draw pictures on the board to show their ideas.

Independent writing Now you are going to write a sentence about something special about you. Close your eyes and think about the wonderful, marvelous things that make you special. Have children write or dictate their ideas and illustrate them.

Daily Handwriting

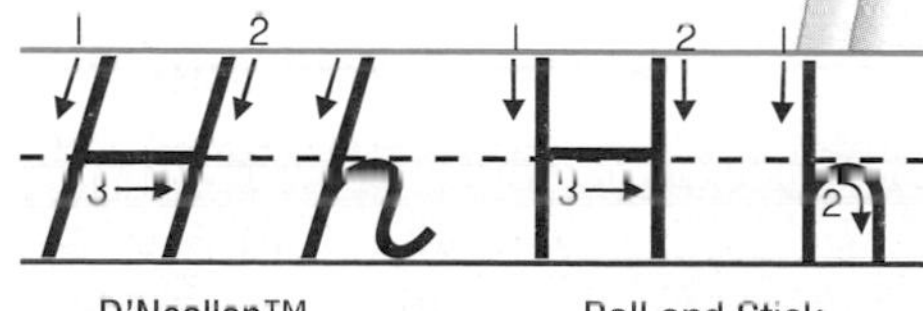

Write *Hank* and *had* on the board. Review correct letter formation of uppercase *H* and lowercase *h*.

Have children write *Hank* and *had* on their Write-On Boards. Remind them to use proper left-to-right and top-to-bottom progression and proper spacing between letters when writing *H* and *h*.

Write Guy
Jeff Anderson

Show Off—in a Good Way

Post children's successful sentences. Celebrate them as writers. Select a sentence of the week, and write it large! Display it as a poster inside or outside the classroom door. Students learn from each others' successes.

Academic Vocabulary

naming part the part of a sentence that tells who or what the sentence is about

Daily Fix-It

dan hit the ball
Dan hit the ball.

This week's practice sentences appear on Teacher Resources DVD-ROM.

Writing Routine

Day 1 Wonderful, Marvelous Me!
Day 2 Respond to Literature
Day 3 Genre Writing
Day 4 Extend the Concept
Day 5 This Week We...

DAY 1 Language Arts

Objectives
- Introduce giving directions.
- Follow directions.
- Give directions.
- Share information by speaking loudly and clearly.

Listening and Speaking
Give Directions

Teach When I tell you how to do something, I am giving you directions. Directions are the steps you need to do or make something. The steps should be done in order. When I give you directions, I try to speak loudly and clearly. I give the directions in the order that you will need to do them. Have children recall a time when they have followed your directions.

Model I am going to give directions on how to wash your hands. I want you to follow my directions as you pretend to wash your hands. Have children pretend to wash their hands as you give directions.

Guide practice Have children give simple directions for something they do every day, such as making their bed. Refer children to the Rules for Listening and Speaking on pp. 1–2 of the *Reader's and Writer's Notebook.* Remind them to speak loudly and clearly when giving directions.

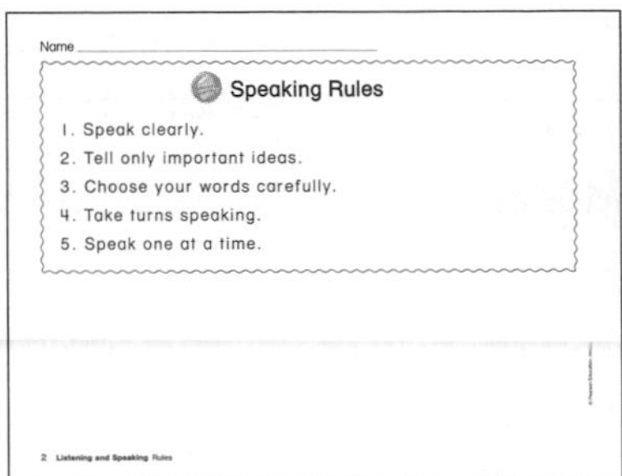
Name
Speaking Rules
1. Speak clearly.
2. Tell only important ideas.
3. Choose your words carefully.
4. Take turns speaking.
5. Speak one at a time.

Reader's and Writer's Notebook, p. 2

Wrap Up Your Day

- ✔ **Concept Talk** Today we talked about learning from our adventures. What are some things we can learn from adventures we may take some day?
- ✔ **Oral Language** Today we learned some Amazing Words as we talked about having adventures. Let's say the Amazing Words again: *world, lonely, trip, horizon, journey, homesick.*
- ✔ **Homework Idea** Send home the Family Times Newsletter, Let's Practice It! TR DVD•37–38.

Social Studies

What an Adventure!

Materials: child-friendly magazines, scissors, construction paper, glue, pencils

A New Place Have children look through magazines to find pictures of people having outdoor adventures, such as those in cars or at parks, campsites, or zoos. Discuss the pictures, asking children what kind of adventure they think the people are having. Have them cut out and glue the pictures into a collage to show the various adventures people are having.

Write a Label Allow children to talk about their collages. Then have them tell one word they would use to describe their picture. Have children write or dictate their word on the paper.

Conventions

Naming Parts

Materials: drawing paper, crayons

Draw Pictures of Naming Parts Divide a sheet of drawing paper into four sections for each child. Have children draw pictures for four nouns—a person, an animal, a place, and a thing—each of which could be the naming part of a sentence. Then have them write or dictate a sentence about each picture that uses the noun as the naming part.

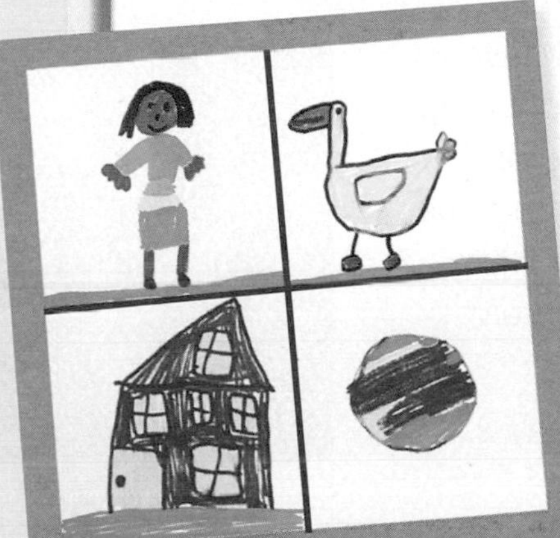

Comprehension

Sequence

Materials: 3 sentence strips

Put a Story in Order Write one story event from *Farfallina and Marcel* on each sentence strip.

Farfallina and Marcel meet for the first time.

Farfallina and Marcel grow up.

Farfallina and Marcel meet again after they have grown up.

Have three children show the sentences out of order. Read each sentence. Have the class rearrange the children with their sentences to put them in the correct story order and then reread all three sentences.

20–25 mins.

Objectives

- Discuss the concepts to develop oral language.
- Build oral vocabulary.

Today at a Glance

Oral Vocabulary
world, lonely

Phonemic Awareness
◉ Initial /h/

Phonics
◉ /h/ Spelled *Hh*

Handwriting
Words with *Hh*

Comprehension
◉ Sequence

Conventions
Naming Parts

Writing
Respond to Literature

Vocabulary
Sequence Words

TRUCKTOWN on Reading Street

Start your engines! Display page 23 of *Truckery Rhymes*. Point to "Hey Diddle Diddle." Who can tell us what kind of truck this rhyme is about? Yes, it's about an ice cream truck. Let's read the rhyme together. Have children point to the rhyming words as the class reads the rhyme again. Give additional children the opportunity to say the rhyme aloud and track the print.

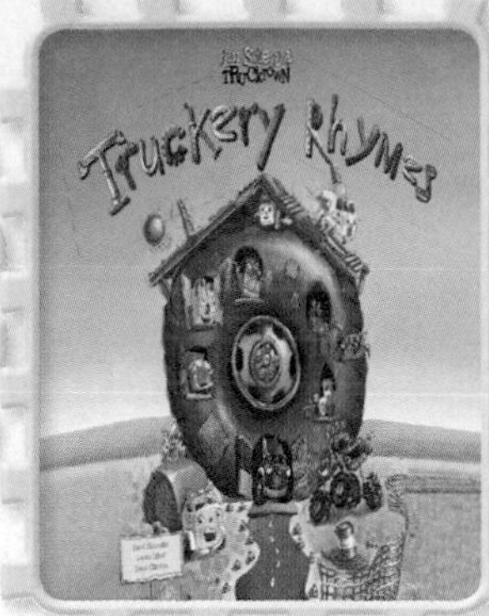

Truckery Rhymes

Concept Talk

Question of the Week

What can we learn from our adventures?

Build concepts Write the question of the week on the board and track the print as you read it aloud. Have children speak loudly and clearly as they answer the question in complete sentences. To reinforce the concept and focus children's attention, display Talk with Me/Sing with Me Chart 19B. Tell children they are going to sing about taking a special trip.

Sing with Me Audio

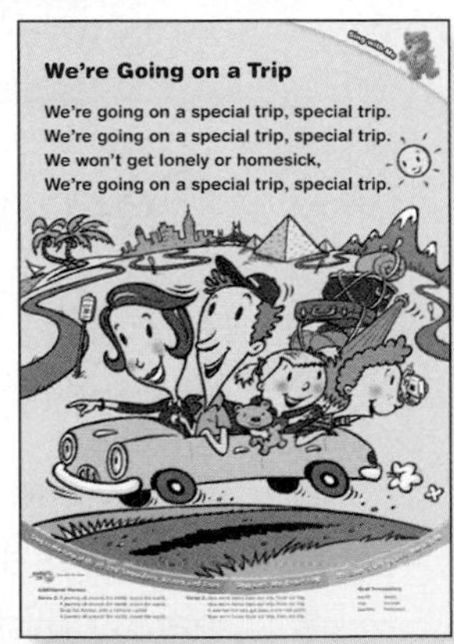

Talk with Me/Sing with Me Chart 19B

Listen for Amazing Words The Amazing Words *world* and *lonely* are in the song "We're Going on a Trip." Read the title and have children describe the sights in the illustration. Sing the song several times to the tune of "Head and Shoulders, Knees and Toes" until children become familiar with the words and can sing along. Have children stand when they hear *world* and *lonely*.

ELL Reinforce Vocabulary Use the Day 2 instruction on ELL Poster 19 to reinforce the meanings of high-frequency words.

ELL Poster 19

Oral Vocabulary
Amazing Words

Amazing Words Oral Vocabulary Routine

Teach Amazing Words

1. **Introduce the Word** In the story *Rooster's Off to See the World,* we will read about a rooster who decides to travel and see the world. Our planet, Earth, is also called the *world*. What's our new Amazing Word for Earth? Say it with me: *world.*

2. **Demonstrate** Provide examples to show meaning. *I would like to travel around the whole world.*

Repeat steps 1 and 2.

Introduce the Word After the rooster in the story starts to walk, he feels lonely. To be *lonely* is to feel alone. What's our new Amazing Word for feeling alone? Say it with me: *lonely.*

Demonstrate *When my friend went away, I was lonely.*

3. **Apply** Tell children to use *world* and *lonely* in complete sentences. Have pairs of children tell where in the world they would like to go and what it feels like to be lonely.

Routines Flip Chart

Use Amazing Words

To reinforce the concept and the Amazing Words, have children supply the appropriate Amazing Word for each sentence.

The boy was _____ as he sat by himself. (lonely)

We all live in this _____. (world)

Amazing Words

world	lonely
trip	horizon
journey	homesick

Differentiated Instruction

Strategic Intervention

Build Concepts Display and discuss a world map or a globe. Tell children that *world* and *Earth* both mean the planet we live on. Have children find different places on the map or globe, including where they live.

English Language Learners

Access Content Have children share words in their home languages that are used for *world* and *lonely.* For example, the Spanish words *mundo* and *solitario* are used for *world* and *lonely.*

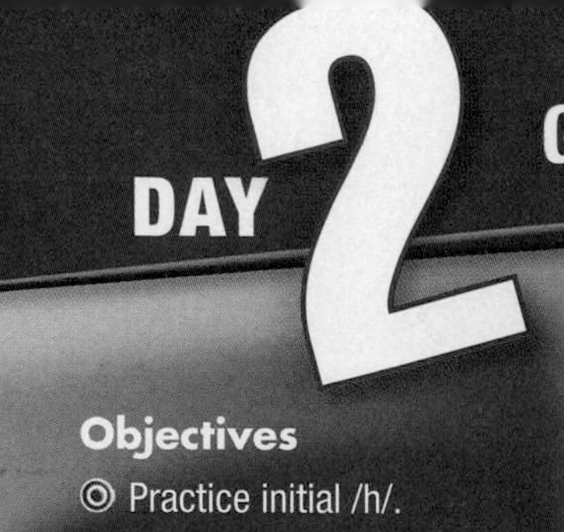

Get Ready to Read

Objectives
- ◎ Practice initial /h/.
- Substitute initial and final sounds.

Phonemic Awareness
Initial /h/

Picture Card

Teach

Display the *hose* Picture Card. This is a *hose*. *Hose* begins with /h/. What is this picture? What sound does it begin with?

Model

Display the *hen* Picture Card. This is a *hen.* Listen carefully to the sounds: /h/ *-en*. I hear /h/ at the beginning of *hen*. What is the beginning sound you hear in *hen?* Say it with me: /h/ /h/ /h/, *hen.*

Continue with the *house* and *hat* Picture Cards.

Picture Card

Guide practice

Have children look at the picture on *My Skills Buddy,* pp. 12–13. When we looked at this page, we saw *hooks* and other things that begin with /h/. Can you name other things in the room that begin with /h/?

Corrective feedback

If... children cannot discriminate initial /h/,
then... have them enunciate /h/ as they segment initial /h/ words.

Listen as I segment a word: /h/ /i/ /p/. What sound do you hear at the beginning? I hear /h/ at the beginning of *hip*. Continue with the following words: *had, hop, hit.*

My Skills Buddy, pp. 12–13

On their own Display Phonics Songs and Rhymes Chart 19, "We're Hiking Home." Remind children of the tune "The Ants Go Marching." Sing the song several times. Have children join in. Tell children to raise their hands when they hear /h/ words.

We're Hiking Home

Heave Ho!

We're hiking home to
our anthill. Hurrah! Hurrah!
We're hiking home to
our anthill. Hurrah! Hurrah!
We're hiking home to our anthill,
Heads hauling many heavy loads still.
And we're hiking home high here
Up on our anthill! Hut! Hut! Hut!

Hut! Hut!

Phonics Songs and Rhymes Chart 19

Review **Sound Substitution** Tell children they are going to make new words by changing either the beginning sound or the ending sound. Listen as I say a word: *hip,* /h/ *-ip.* I will change the beginning sound to say a new word: /s/ *-ip, sip.* I can change the ending sound of words too. Listen to the word *hot: ho-* /t/. I will change the ending /t/ in *hot* to /p/. The new word is *ho-* /p/, *hop.* I changed *hot* to *hop*. Say the words with me: *ho-* /t/, *ho-* /p/. Continue the routine with the following pairs of words: *dog, hog; hat, ham; beat, heat*.

Differentiated Instruction

 Strategic Intervention

Support Phonemic Awareness Take children on a Hiking Hunt around the classroom. Have them look for things whose name begins with /h/. When they spot an item, they should stop, raise their hands, and say the item's name.

Teacher Tip

Phonemic awareness activities can be used throughout the day as transition activities. Name a set of words and have children identify which word begins with /h/.

English Language Learners

Support Phonemic Awareness Point to images in the picture on pp. 12–13 of *My Skills Buddy* as you say the corresponding words. To clarify understanding, have children point to the images as you say the words.

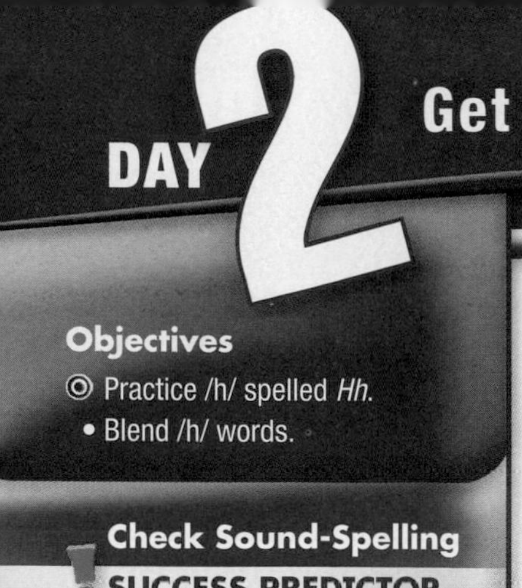

Get Ready to Read

Phonics—Teach/Model

/h/ Spelled *Hh*

Review ***/h/Hh*** Point to the *helicopter* on the *Hh* Alphabet Card. What is this? What sound does *helicopter* begin with? *Helicopter* begins with /h/. Write *helicopter* on the board and point to the letter *h*. The letter for /h/ is *h*.

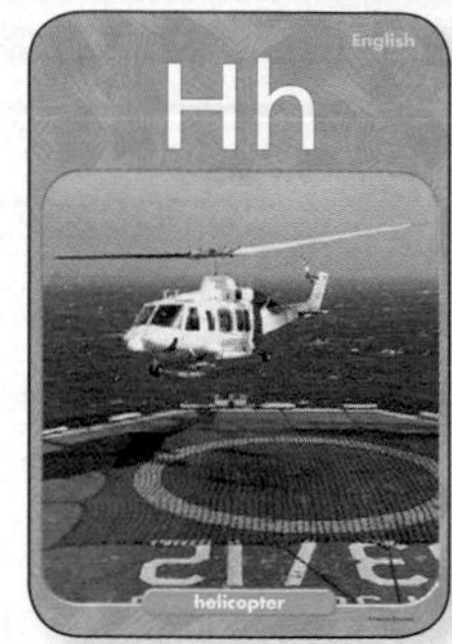

Alphabet Card

Model Display the *hat* Picture Card. What is this? Say the sounds in *hat* with me: /h/ /a/ /t/, *hat*. Where do you hear /h/ in *hat?* (at the beginning)

Write *hat* on the board. Point to each letter as you say the sounds: /h/ /a/ /t/, *hat.* Continue the routine with the following words: *hop, hip*.

Picture Card

Guide practice

Envision It!

Have children open *My Skills Buddy* to p. 16. Demonstrate using the blending arrows on *My Skills Buddy* p. 16 as you model blending the first word. Put your finger on the red arrow below the *h*. Say the sound that *h* stands for: /h/. Continue with letters *o* and *t.* Now I run my fingers along the blue arrow as I blend the letter quickly to read *hot.* Note that the letter *o* in *hot* changed to *a* to make the word *hat.* Repeat with the word *hat.* Have children work with a partner to blend the rest of the words on the page.

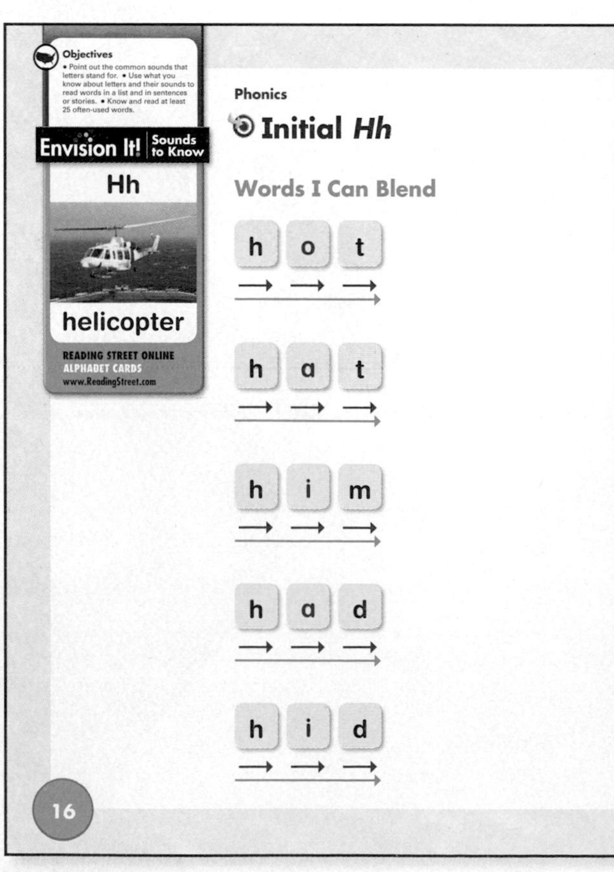

My Skills Buddy, p. 16

Blend Use the following routine to blend *h* words.

ROUTINE **Sound-by-Sound Blending**

1. **Connect** Write the letter *h*. What is the sound for this letter? The sound is /h/. Say it with me: /h/ /h/ /h/. When you see this letter in a word, what sound will you say?
2. **Model** Write the word *hot* on the board.
   - Touch under the *h*. What is the sound for this letter? Say it with me: /h/ /h/ /h/. Repeat the routine for *o* and *t*.
   - Let's blend the sounds together. Listen as I blend the sounds: /h/ /o/ /t/. Say it with me: /h/ /o/ /t/. Now say it without me.
   - Listen as I use *hot* in a sentence: *The stove is hot.* Say it with me. Have children use *hot* in a sentence.
3. **Guide Practice** Continue the routine in step 2 with these words:

man Dan Hob hit fan had hat pop

Have children successfully read all of the words before reading Decodable Reader 19 on pp. 18–25 of *My Skills Buddy.*

Corrective Feedback If children have difficulty blending words, model blending the sounds to read the word. Then have children say it with you.

Routines Flip Chart

MONITOR PROGRESS **Check Sound-Spelling /h/ Spelled *Hh***

Have children write *Hh* on a card. I will say some sentences. If a word in the sentence begins with /h/, hold up your card. Say: *The hippo and hen have lunch; Harry and Holly play with the hose; Harold and Helen fix the house with hammers.*

If... children cannot discriminate /h/,

then... use the small-group Strategic Intervention lesson, p. DI•2, to reteach /h/.

Continue to monitor children's progress using other instructional opportunities during the week so that children can be successful with the Day 5 Assessment.

Day 1	Day 2	Day 3	Day 4	Day 5
Check Phonemic Awareness	Check Sound-Spelling/ Retelling	Check Word Reading	Check Phonemic Awareness	Check Oral Vocabulary

Success Predictor

Differentiated Instruction

Advanced

Blending Sounds Have available cards with all the sound-spellings children have learned. Call out a word such as *hot*. Have children repeat the word and choose the correct letter cards to spell out the word for the class.

English Language Learners

Support Phonics The letter *h* is silent in Spanish, French, and Portuguese, so children with some literacy in those languages may need to practice associating /h/ with the letter *h.*

DAY 2 Get Ready to Read

Objectives

- Write *H* and *h*.
- Read high-frequency words.

Handwriting
Write Words with *Hh*

Review Write *Henry* on the board. This is the name *Henry*. I use an uppercase *H* for the first letter in *Henry's* name. Watch me make an uppercase *H*. Write another uppercase *H* on the board using the instructional strokes indicated in the model.

Write *him* on the board. This word is *him*. I use a lowercase *h* at the beginning of *him*. Watch me make a lowercase *h*. Write another *h* on the board using the proper instructional strokes.

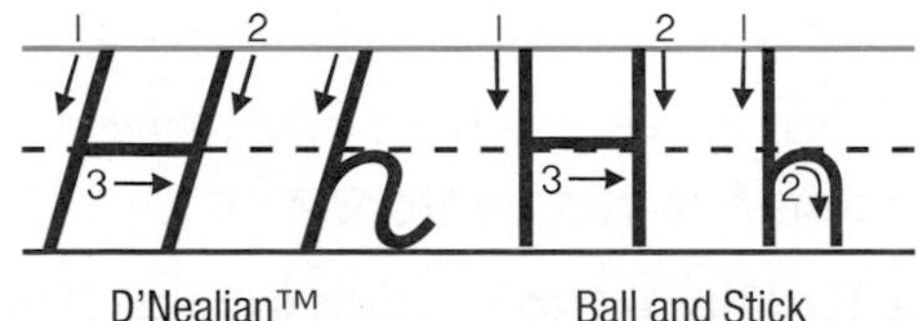

Guide practice Have children use their Write-On Boards to make a row of uppercase *H* and a row of lowercase *h*. Circulate around the room, assisting children as necessary. Have children then write the following words: *ham, hid, hop.*

High-Frequency Words

Model reading

Have children turn to p. 17 of *My Skills Buddy.* Read the high-frequency words *are, that,* and *do* together. Then have children point to each word and read it themselves. Read the sentences on the *My Skills Buddy* page together to read the new high-frequency words in context.

Team Talk Pair children and have them take turns reading each of the sentences aloud.

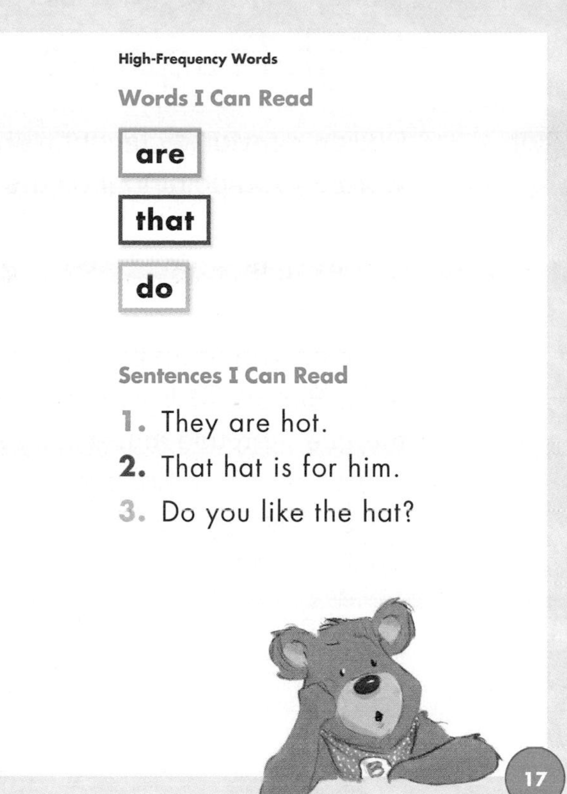
High-Frequency Words

Words I Can Read

are

that

do

Sentences I Can Read

1. They are hot.
2. That hat is for him.
3. Do you like the hat?

17

My Skills Buddy, p. 17

On their own

Use *Reader's and Writer's Notebook,* p. 245, for additional practice with this week's high-frequency words.

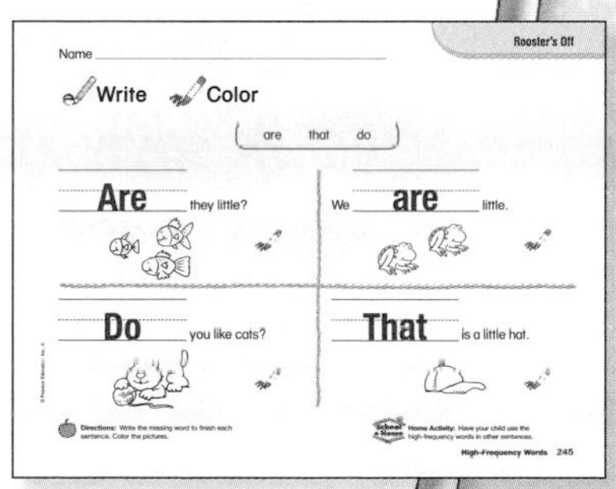

Reader's and Writer's Notebook, p. 245

Differentiated Instruction

SI Strategic Intervention

High-Frequency Words Write this week's high-frequency words on cards for children to tape to the tops of their desks. As they read stories this week, remind them to look at this week's high-frequency words and practice saying them. They can also keep track on the card of how many times they read the words this week by making a mark on the card for each use.

DAY 2 Get Ready to Read

Objectives

- Read high-frequency words.
- Decode and read words in context and isolation.

Decodable Reader 19
/h/ Spelled *Hh* and High-Frequency Words

Review Review previously taught high-frequency words. Have children read each word as you point to it on the Word Wall.

that	is	do	see	a	they	are

Have children turn to Decodable Reader 19, *Hob Can Hit,* on p. 18 of *My Skills Buddy*. Today we will read a story about a baseball player. Point to the title. The title of the story is *Hob Can Hit*. What is the title? Point to the names of the author and illustrator. The author's name is Roy Kass. What does an author do? This book is illustrated by Ryan Bines. What does an illustrator do? We will read lots of words beginning with *h* in the book.

Use the routine for reading decodable books to read Decodable Reader 19.

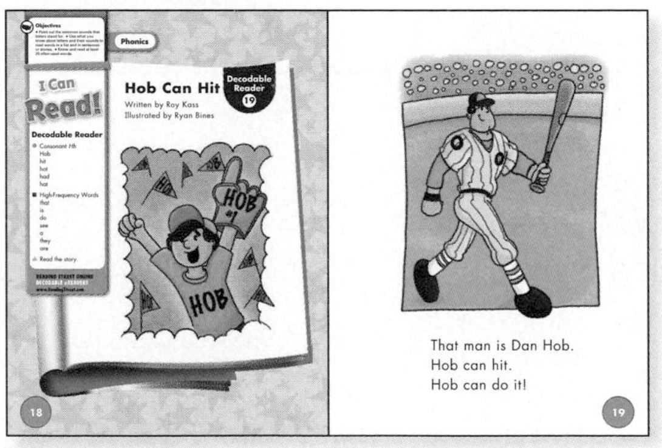

My Skills Buddy, pp. 18–25

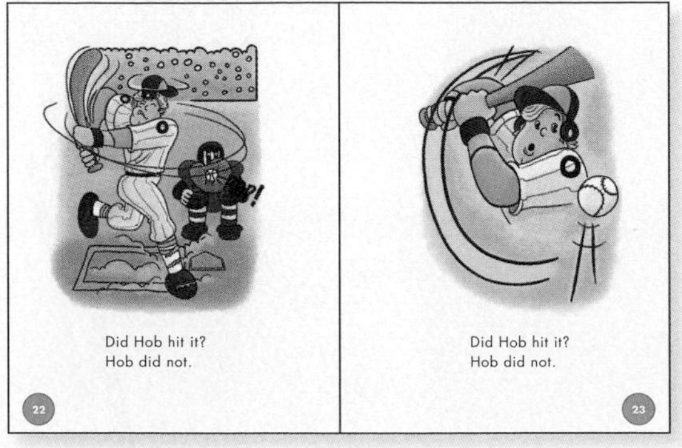

ROUTINE Reading Decodable Books

1. **Read Silently** Have children whisper read the book page by page as you listen in.
2. **Model Fluent Reading** Have children finger point as you read a page. Then have children reread the book without you.
3. **Read Chorally** Have children finger point as they chorally read the page. Continue reading page by page, repeating steps 1 and 2.
4. **Read Individually** Have children take turns reading aloud a page.
5. **Reread and Monitor Progress** As you listen to individual children reread, monitor progress and provide support.
6. **Reread with a Partner** Have children reread the book page by page with a partner.

Routines Flip Chart

Differentiated Instruction

 Strategic Intervention

Practice Blending Words
Before reading Decodable Reader 19, write *Pam, Sam, hot,* and *hat* on the board. Have children practice blending these words so they can be more successful when reading the book.

Small Group Time

DAY 2 Break into small groups after reading the Decodable Reader and before the comprehension lesson.

Teacher-Led

SI Strategic Intervention	OL On-Level	A Advanced
Teacher-Led Page DI•2 • Phonemic Awareness and Phonics • **Reread** Decodable Reader 19	**Teacher-Led** Page DI•6 • Phonemic Awareness and Phonics • **Reread** Decodable Reader 19	**Teacher-Led** Page DI•9 • Phonics and Spelling • **Reread** Decodable Reader 19 for Fluency

 Place English language learners in the groups that correspond to their reading abilities in English.

Practice Stations
- Visit the Word Work Station
- Visit the Words to Know Station

Independent Activities
- Read independently
- Background Building Audio
- *Reader's and Writer's Notebook*

English Language Learners

Frontload Decodable Reader
Walk children through *Hob Can Hit.* Have them identify Dan, Hob, Pam, and Sam in the story. Use the pictures to help children identify baseball items, such as *bat, baseball, fan, mitt,* and *hat.*

Objectives

- ◎ Practice sequence.
- Preview and predict.
- Retell a story.

Check Retelling
SUCCESS PREDICTOR

Listening Comprehension
◎ Sequence

Review

Envision It!

Have children turn to p. 14 of *My Skills Buddy.* Remind children that events in the story happen in a certain order, or sequence. Good readers pay attention to the sequence, or order in which things occur, because it helps them understand what is happening in the story.

My Skills Buddy, pp. 14–15

First Read—Big Book
Rooster's Off to See the World

Concepts of print Display the cover of *Rooster's Off to See the World.* Explain that the printed words tell us the title of the story and who wrote it.

Preview and predict

What do you see on the cover? I see the sun and a rooster looking happy. The title of the book is *Rooster's Off to See the World.* What do you think this book will be about? Let's read to find out.

Use illustrations Take children on a picture walk through the book. Have them tell about what they see in each picture.

Introduce genre An animal fantasy is a story about animal characters that talk and act like people. We will read about animals who decide to take an adventure.

Set purpose Say the question of the week: *What can we learn from our adventures?* Listen as I read to see what happens to the rooster on his adventure.

Model Read *Rooster's Off to See the World* with expression for enjoyment.

Read for enjoyment

Reread using Develop Vocabulary notes

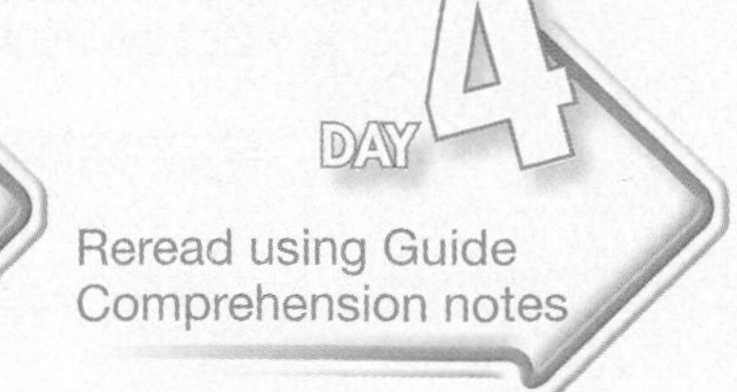

Reread using Guide Comprehension notes

Retell

Check retelling

Envision It!

Have children turn to p. 26 of *My Skills Buddy.* Walk through the retelling boxes as children retell *Rooster's Off to See the World.* Let's retell what happens in the first box. The rooster decides that he wants to travel, so he starts walking. How does he feel? Let's retell what happens in the next box. Continue with the rest of the boxes. After children retell the story as a group, have them draw a picture to retell a favorite part of the story. Have them write or dictate a word or sentence to go with the picture.

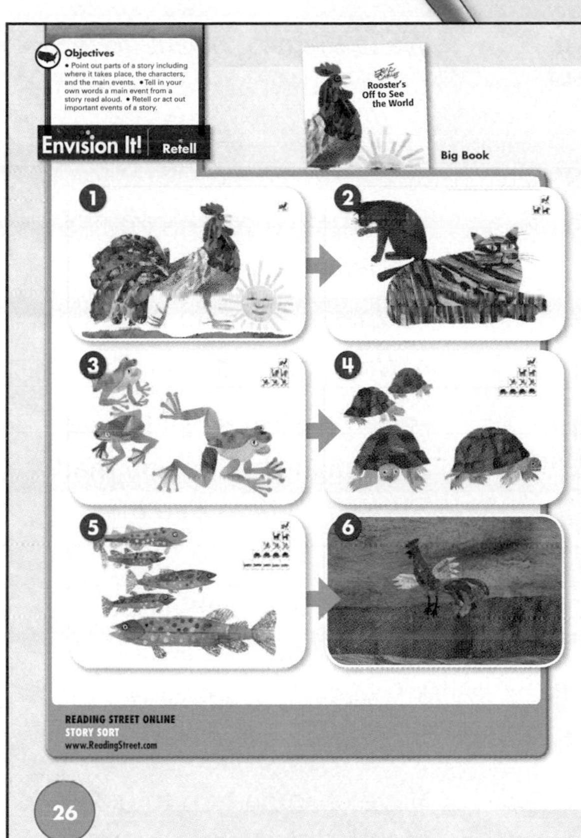

My Skills Buddy, p. 26

Top-Score Response A top-score response describes events in sequence with details.

MONITOR PROGRESS **Check Retelling**

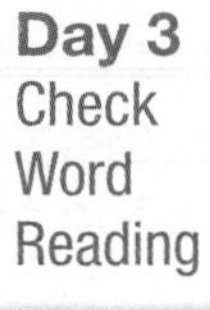
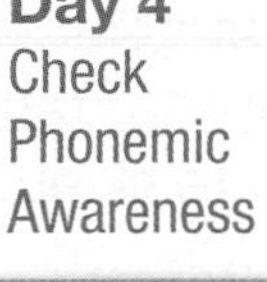
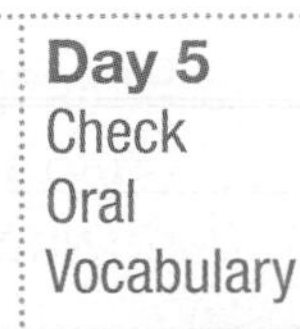

If... children have difficulty retelling the story,

then... go through the story one page at a time, and ask children to tell what happens in their own words.

Day 1	Day 2	Day 3	Day 4	Day 5
Check Phonemic Awareness	Check Sound-Spelling/ Retelling	Check Word Reading	Check Phonemic Awareness	Check Oral Vocabulary

Success Predictor

Differentiated Instruction

SI Strategic Intervention

Using Illustrations As children page through the selection, have them note the smaller pictures on each page as they go along. Explain that these pictures will help them keep track of the number of animals that are on the adventure during that part of the story.

Academic Vocabulary

retell telling a story in one's own words

Retelling Plan

- [x] **This week assess Advanced students.**
- [ ] **Week 2** Assess On-Level students.
- [ ] **Week 3** Assess Strategic Intervention students.
- [ ] **Week 4** Assess Advanced students.
- [ ] **Week 5** Assess On-Level students.
- [ ] **Week 6** Assess Strategic Intervention students.

DAY 2 Read and Comprehend

Objectives

- ◎ Practice sequence.
- Confirm predictions.
- Practice naming parts.

Think, Talk, and Write

Discuss concept

We're learning about adventures and what we can learn from them. Think about an adventure you have had.

- Where did you go on this adventure?
- What did you do there?
- What things did you learn?

Confirm predictions

Have children recall their predictions before you read *Rooster's Off to See the World.*

- What did you think the story would be about?
- Was your prediction correct?

Have children turn to p. 27 of *My Skills Buddy.* Read the questions and directives and have children respond.

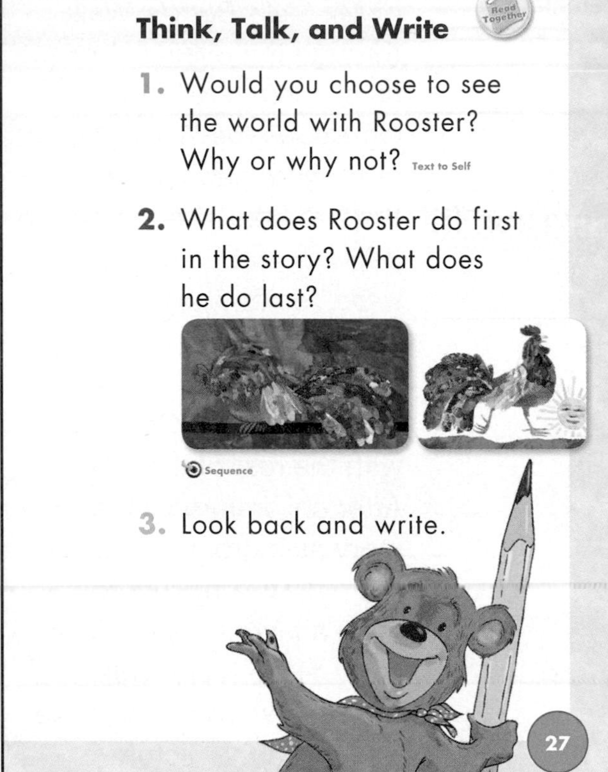

My Skills Buddy, p. 27

Text to self

1. Would you choose to see the world with Rooster? Why or why not? If you did, where would you like to go? Would you be afraid to keep going when it got dark?

◎ Sequence

2. Let's look at pp. 2 and 3. What does Rooster do first in the story? (He decides to set off and see the world by himself.) Let's look at the last two pages of the story. What does he do last? (He decides to go back home and sit on his very own perch.)

Look back and write

3. Let's look back at our story and write about it. We remember that the rooster and all his animal friends decide to go off and see the world. After walking along for a while, it begins to get dark because the sun is going down. Listen for what happens to their adventure. Read pp. 12–13 of *Rooster's Off to See the World.* Let's write about why the adventure stops. Discuss with children why the animals do not want to keep going on the adventure and record children's responses on chart paper. (Possible responses: They have nothing to eat. They have nowhere to sleep. It is too cold. They are afraid.)

Conventions
Naming Parts

Review Remind children that each sentence contains a naming part. The naming part tells who or what the sentence is about.

Guide practice Show the *hen* Picture Card. Listen to this sentence: *The rooster wants an adventure.* Who or what is this sentence about? (the rooster) *The rooster* is the naming part of the sentence.

Say the following sentences and have children identify the naming part in each sentence:

The rooster met three frogs. (The rooster)

Five fish came along too. (Five fish)

The sun went down. (The sun)

On their own Use *Reader's and Writer's Notebook,* p. 246, for more practice with naming parts.

Daily Fix-It Use the Daily Fix-It exercise for more conventions practice.

INTERACT with TEXT

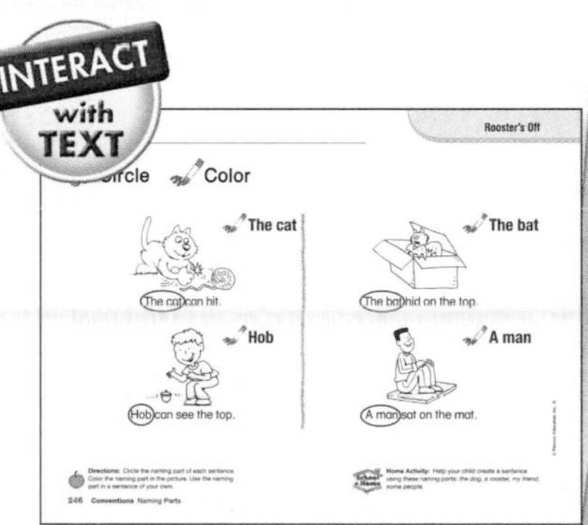

Rooster's Off

Circle Color

The cat | The bat

The cat can hit. | The bat hid on the top.

Hob | A man

Hob can see the top. | A man sat on the mat.

246 Conventions Naming Parts

Reader's and Writer's Notebook, p. 246

Differentiated Instruction

A Advanced

Support Conventions Call out an action verb phrase such as *danced happily.* Have children think of a naming part to make a complete sentence, such as *The girls danced happily.*

Daily Fix-It

will Heidi hear the horn

W̲ill Heidi hear the horn?̲

This week's practice sentences appear on Teacher Resources DVD-ROM.

ELL

English Language Learners

Support Conventions Play a naming parts game with children. Sit in a circle and pass a box of crayons around as you say with children, "Who took a crayon from the crayon box?" When you finish the question, the child holding the box should take a crayon. Use that child's name to say, "José took a crayon from the crayon box." José: "Who, me?" Group: "Yes, you!" José: "Not me!" Point out that *José* is the naming part of the sentence. Then start over by passing the box again.

DAY 2 Language Arts

15–20 mins.

Objectives

- Write sentences about *Rooster's Off to See the World.*
- Identify and use sequence words.
- Write *H* and *h.*

Writing

Respond to Literature

Discuss Display Big Book *Rooster's Off to See the World.* Discuss with children who the rooster meets along his way.

Model In the story, the rooster meets many different animals as he sets off to see the world. When the rooster talks to these animals, they decide to join him on his adventure. I am going to write:

The rooster meets two cats.

Guide practice Invite children to help you write more sentences about who the rooster meets on his adventure to see the world.

The rooster meets three frogs.
The rooster meets four turtles.

Independent writing Have children write or dictate a sentence about the rooster and the animals he meets along the way. Some children may wish to use this sentence frame:

The rooster meets _____.

Then have children illustrate their sentences.

Daily Handwriting

Write *Hap* and *hot* on the board. Review correct letter formation of uppercase *H* and lowercase *h.*

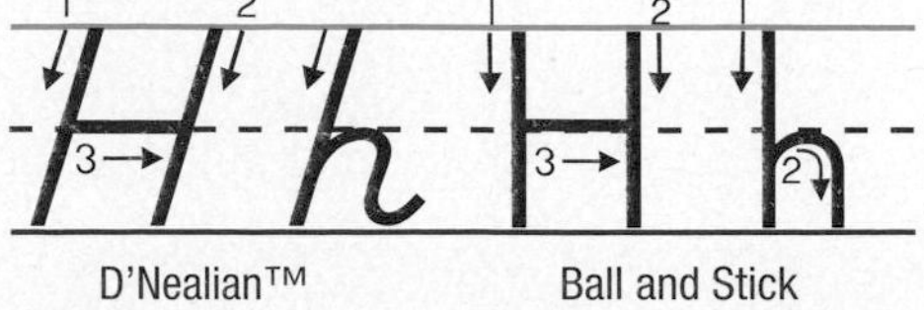

Have children write *Hap* and *hot* on their Write-On Boards. Remind children to use proper left-to-right and top-to-bottom progression when writing *H* and *h.*

Vocabulary
Sequence Words

Model Have children turn to p. 28 of *My Skills Buddy.* Direct them to the picture of the girl preparing to get her hair cut. What is the girl with long hair doing? Then direct them to the picture of the girl with shorter hair. The girl got her hair cut. Now her hair is short. *Before* the haircut, the girl's hair was long. *After* the haircut, her hair is short. *Before* and *after* are sequence words. They tell the order in which things happen. Repeat the process for the words *beginning* and *end.* Use the first three Vocabulary bullets on p. 28 to guide the discussion.

My Skills Buddy, p. 28

Guide practice Write the words *before, after, beginning,* and *end* on the board. Point to each word as you read it.

before **after** **beginning** **end**

These words tell the order in which things happen. Display Big Book *Rooster's Off to See the World.* This book has a beginning and an end. Open to the first page of the story. This is the *beginning* of the story. Open to the last page. This is the *end* of the story. *Beginning* and *end* are sequence words. They tell the order in which things happen. Let's talk about *before* and *after.* Who can show me something they did *before* they came to school this morning? Who can show me something they did *after* they got to the classroom? *Before, after, beginning,* and *end* are all words that tell the order in which things happen.

On their own Have children do a series of actions to show *before* and *after* and *beginning* and *end.* For example, they can show what their shoes look like before and after they are tied, or how they feel before and after they eat breakfast. They can point out what month starts the beginning of the year and what month ends it, or what day starts their school week and what day ends it.

Differentiated Instruction

SI Strategic Intervention

Sequence Words Reinforce the use of sequence words with children. Ask them to tell what happens *before* reading and *after* reading. Ask them to tell how the school day *begins* and how it *ends.* Do this throughout the day to help them understand sequence.

English Language Learners

Access Content Help children visualize the sequence words by having them stand in a line. Point to and name the child at the *beginning* and *end* of the line. Stand in the middle of the line and identify the child who is *before* and *after* you in line.

Objectives

- Review skills learned and practiced today.

Wrap Up Your Day

✔ **Concept Talk** Today we talked about things we can learn from taking an adventure. We heard a story about a rooster who sets out to see the world and what he finds there. What happens when the rooster sets out on his adventure?

✔ **Phonemic Awareness** Today we talked about words that begin with /h/. Listen to the following rhyme. Raise you hand high when you hear words that begin with /h/.

Happy Hap jumped up high.
Happy Hap reached the sky.
Happy Hap hopped and hopped.
But Happy Hap could not stop!

✔ **Vocabulary Skill** Today we talked about the sequence words *before, after, beginning,* and *end.* Who can show me the *beginning* of the alphabet? Who can show me the *end* of the alphabet? What letter comes *before Hh?* What letter comes *after Hh?*

Preview DAY 3

Tomorrow we will read more about the rooster who went off to see the world.

✔ **Homework Idea** Have children find pictures of things whose names begin with /h/ to share with the class.

Social Studies

My Own Adventure

Materials: local, state, or U.S. map; paper; drawing tools; pencils

From Here to There Display a map and discuss with children where they live. Have them trace a route on the map to get from where they live to another place of your choosing. Discuss what they may see on their way there as well as what they might do. Keep track of the places children will visit during their travels by writing a list on the board.

Draw an Adventure Have children choose one of the places you wrote about on the board. Have them draw a picture of themselves there and write or dictate a sentence about the visit. Display children's drawings around the classroom.

Phonics

Initial Sounds

Materials: large bag; objects whose names begin with *h, b, a, s,* or *t*

Guess What Is in the Bag Put several objects whose names begin with *h, b, a, s,* or *t* into the bag. Give clues about each object. It begins with /h/ and you wear it on your head. What is it? (hat) When children correctly identify the object, take it out of the bag. Continue with other objects.

- It begins with /b/, and it is round. (ball)
- It begins with /a/, and you eat it. (apple)
- It begins with /s/; you wash with it. (soap)

Conventions

Sequence

Materials: paper, drawing tools, pencils

How It Happens Give each child a sheet of drawing paper divided into four sections, labeled *1, 2, 3,* and *4.* Then discuss the order in which they do something, such as brushing their teeth, getting a drink of water, or making their beds. Have children choose one activity for which they can give pictorial directions. Have them draw a picture in each box to show the steps for doing their activity.

Objectives

- Share information and ideas about the concept.
- Build oral vocabulary.

Today at a Glance

Oral Vocabulary
trip, horizon

Phonemic Awareness
◉ Initial /h/

Phonics
◉ /h/ Spelled *Hh*

Comprehension
◉ Sequence

Conventions
Sentences

Writing
Directions

Listening and Speaking
Give Directions

TRUCKTOWN on Reading Street

Start your engines! Display p. 23 of *Truckery Rhymes.* Recite the original rhyme "Hey Diddle Diddle" and then have children repeat it with you:

Hey diddle, diddle, the cat and the fiddle,
The cow jumped over the moon.
The little dog laughed to see such
sport,
And the dish ran away with
the spoon.

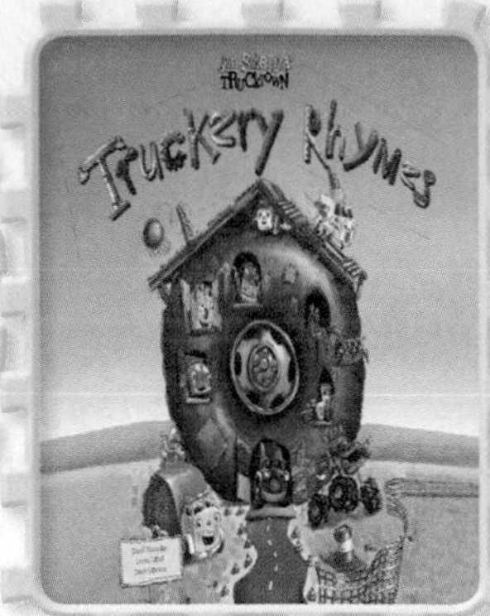

Truckery Rhymes

Concept Talk

Question of the Week
What can we learn from our adventures?

Write the question of the week on the board. Read the question as you track the print. Talk with children about things you can learn from an adventure. Have children speak loudly and clearly and respond in complete sentences.

Listen for Amazing Words

Let's Sing Display Sing with Me Chart 19B. Remind children that yesterday they sang about a special trip and listened for the words *world* and *lonely*. Today we are going to listen for the Amazing Words *trip* and *horizon*. Sing the song several times to the tune of "Head and Shoulders, Knees and Toes." Have children sing with you.

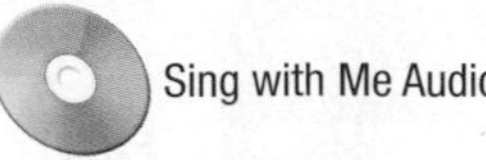
Sing with Me Audio

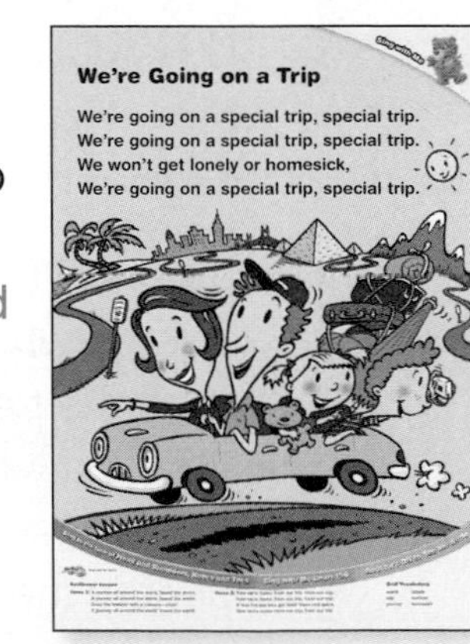

Talk with Me/Sing with Me Chart 19B

Oral Vocabulary
Amazing Words

Amazing Words Oral Vocabulary Routine

Teach Amazing Words

1. **Introduce the Word** In *Rooster's Off to See the World,* Rooster decides to take a *trip* to see the world. To take a *trip* is to leave home and go someplace else. What's our new Amazing Word for leaving home and going someplace else? Say it with me: *trip.*
2. **Demonstrate** Provide examples to show meaning. *I will take a trip to the store with my mom.*

Repeat steps 1 and 2.

Introduce the Word I could see far off toward the *horizon.* The *horizon* is the place where the sky and the land seem to meet. What's our new Amazing Word for the place where the sky and land seem to meet? Say it with me: *horizon.*

Demonstrate *At the horizon, it is hard to tell sky from water.*

3. **Apply** Tell children to use *trip* and *horizon* in complete sentences. Have them illustrate the words.

Routines Flip Chart

Use Amazing Words

To reinforce the concept and the Amazing Words, have children supply the appropriate Amazing Word for each sentence.

The sky seems to touch the land at the _____. (horizon)

We took a little _____ to my favorite store. (trip)

ELL Expand Vocabulary
Use the Day 3 instruction on ELL Poster 19 to help children expand vocabulary.

ELL Poster 19

Amazing Words

world	lonely
trip	horizon
journey	homesick

Differentiated Instruction

SI Strategic Intervention

Amazing Words Display the picture on pp. 12–13 of *Rooster's Off to See the World.* Discuss how the moon seems so close to the land. That place where the land seems to meet the sky is called the *horizon.*

DAY 3 Get Ready to Read

Objectives
- ◎ Isolate initial /h/.
- Discriminate sounds.
- Substitute phonemes.

Phonemic Awareness
◎ Initial /h/

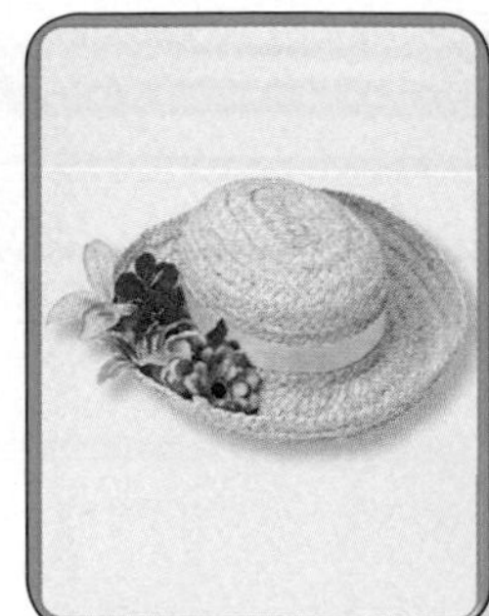
Picture Card

Review **Initial /h/** Display the *hat* Picture Card. Listen as I say this word: *hat*. What is the first sound in *hat?* Say it with me: /h/, *hat.* Today we will listen for /h/ words.

Discriminate sounds I am going to say two words. Tell me which word begins with /h/. Listen carefully: *hand, foot.* Which word begins with /h/? *Hand* begins with /h/. Continue with the following pairs of words: *horse, donkey; low, high; seek, hide; happy, sad; house, mouse.*

On their own Display Picture Cards for *ant, bus, crab, hen, hippopotamus, kangaroo, house,* and *hammer.* Have children choose one of the cards, name the picture, and tell if it begins with /h/.

Substitute phonemes

Listen to the word I am going to say: *hit.* Say it with me: /h/ /i/ /t/, *hit.* I can make a new word by changing the last sound. Listen: /h/ /i/ /d/. Say it with me: /h/ /i/ /d/. What is the new word? The new word is *hid.* Let's try again. Now I will change the middle sound. Listen: /h/ /a/ /d/. What is the new word? The new word is *had.* Now I will change the first sound. Listen: /m/ /a/ /d/. What is the new word? The new word is *mad*. I started with *hit*. I changed /t/ to /d/ and made *hid.* Then I changed /i/ to /a/ and made *had*. Finally I changed /h/ to /m/ and made *mad.*

Continue the routine with the following set of words: *tap, tip, hip, him, hum.*

Corrective feedback

If... children cannot substitute phonemes,
then... repeat the words, emphasizing the changed phoneme.

Segment

Listen to the sounds in the word *ham:* /h/ /a/ /m/. Say them with me: /h/ /a/ /m/. How many sounds do you hear? There are three sounds in *ham.* Let's try some more words. Continue the routine with *had, hop,* and *hit.*

Differentiated Instruction

Strategic Intervention

Substitute Phonemes When substituting phonemes, emphasize the sound that is changing. Have children repeat the new sound, noting the difference between the old word and the new one. Make sure that children understand that when they change the sound, the new word must be a real word.

Get Ready to Read

Objectives

- ◎ Practice /h/ spelled *Hh.*
- Substitute phonemes.
- Read /h/ words.
- Read high-frequency words.

Check Word Reading
SUCCESS PREDICTOR

Phonics—Teach/Model
◎ /h/ Spelled *Hh*

Alphabet Card

Review ***/h/Hh*** Display the *Hh* Alphabet Card and point to the *helicopter.* What sound do you hear at the beginning of *helicopter?* What letter spells that sound? Point to the letters *Hh*. What is the sound for these letters? What is the name of these letters?

Review **Letter Names and Sounds** Use Alphabet Cards to review the following letter names and sounds: *Aa, Bb, Cc, Dd, Ff, Ii, Mm, Nn, Oo, Pp, Rr, Ss, Tt.*

Blend sounds Write *him* on the board. Point to each letter as you say the sound: /h/ /i/ /m/. When I blend these sounds together, I make the word *him*. Say the sounds with me: /h/ /i/ /m/, *him*. Repeat the blending with *top, dad, fit, pot, can, bat, fin,* and *had.*

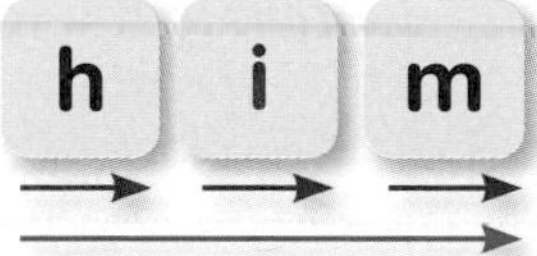

More practice Use *Reader's and Writer's Notebook,* p. 247, for additional practice with /h/.

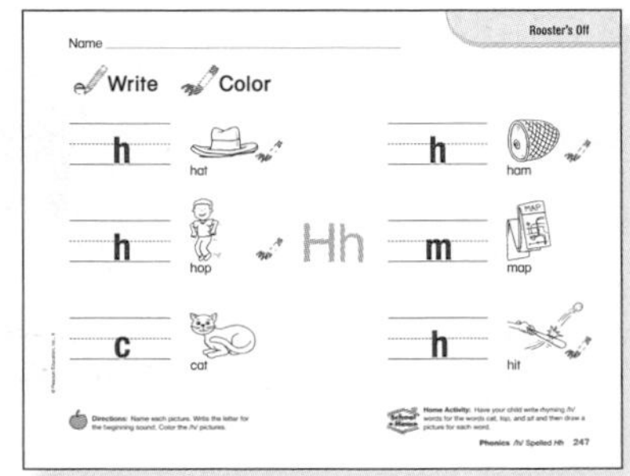

Reader's and Writer's Notebook, p. 247

Review **Sound-Spelling** Display the *Nn* Alphabet Card. What sound do you hear at the beginning of *nest?* What letter spells that sound? Yes, the letter *n* spells /n/. Review the following sounds and letters with Alphabet Cards: *Aa, Hh, Ii, Oo, Pp, Tt*.

Review **High-Frequency Words** Write *are* on the board. This is the word *are*. What is this word? Repeat the routine with *that, do, they, you,* and *of.*

Alphabet Card

Don't Wait Until Friday

MONITOR PROGRESS Check Word Reading High-Frequency Words

Write *are, that, do, they, you,* and *of* on the board. Have children take turns reading the words.

Practice reading these words from the Kindergarten Student Reader K.4.1, *A Day to Play.*

Nan	**and**	**Nat**	**can**	**hit**	**top**	**bin**	**it**
tin	**hot**	**fan**	**nap**	**man**	**at**	**sip**	**not**

If... children cannot read the high-frequency words,
then... write the words on cards for them to practice at home.

If... children cannot blend sounds to read the words,
then... provide practice blending the words in chunks, /n/ *-an.*

If... children can successfully blend sounds to read the words,
then... have them read Kindergarten Student Reader K.4.1, *A Day to Play.*

Day 1	Day 2	Day 3	Day 4	Day 5
Check Phonemic Awareness	Check Sound-Spelling/ Retelling	Check Word Reading	Check Phonemic Awareness	Check Oral Vocabulary

Success Predictor

Differentiated Instruction

A Advanced

Support Sound-Spelling Use the letters children have learned to make a spelling list of simple decodable words. Conduct a spelling bee with children to see how many words they can spell.

Objectives

- Read /h/ words.
- Read high-frequency words.

Kindergarten Student Reader K.4.1

/h/ Spelled *Hh* and High-Frequency Words

Review

High-Frequency Words Review the previously taught high-frequency words. Have children read each word as you point to it on the Word Wall.

do	you	see	the	of
a	are	they	look	that

Teach rebus words

Write *stand* on the board. This is the word *stand*. Say the letters with me: *s, t, a, n, d, stand.* Look for this word in our book today. The word will have a picture above it to help you read it.

Read Kindergarten Student Reader K.4.1

Display Kindergarten Student Reader K.4.1. Today we are going to read a new book. Point to the title. The title of this book is *A Day to Play*. The author's name is Ann Rossi. Jaime Smith illustrated this book.

Use the reading decodable books routine to read the Kindergarten Student Reader.

ROUTINE Reading Decodable Books

1. **Read Silently** Have children whisper read the book page by page as you listen in.
2. **Model Fluent Reading** Have children finger point as you read a page. Then have children reread the page without you.
3. **Read Chorally** Have children finger point as they chorally read the page. Continue reading page by page, repeating steps 1 and 2.
4. **Read Individually** Have children take turns reading aloud a page.
5. **Reread and Monitor Progress** As you listen to individual children reread, monitor progress and provide support.
6. **Reread with a Partner** Have children reread the book page by page with a partner.

Routines Flip Chart

Do you see Nan and Nat?

2

Nat can hit the top of the bin.
Do you see Nat hit it?

3

Nan can hit the top of a tin can.
Nan can hit it.

4

Kindergarten Student Reader K.4.1

Nat and Nan are hot, hot, hot!
They can fan, fan, fan.

5

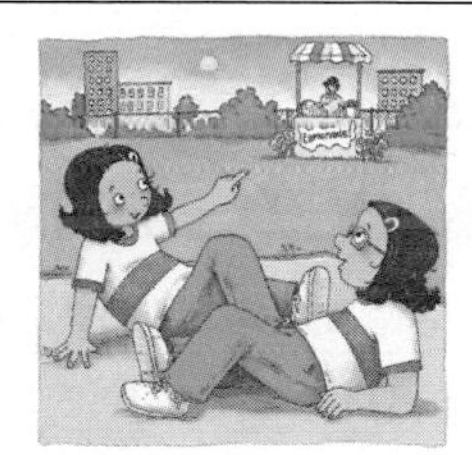

Nat and Nan can nap, nap, nap.
They can see a man.

6

Nat and Nan are at the stand.
They can sip, sip, sip.

7

Look at that.
Nat and Nan are not hot.

8

Differentiated Instruction

SI Strategic Intervention

Support Reading Pair less able readers with more able ones so that they may get an understanding of what more fluent reading sounds like from their peers.

Small Group Time

DAY 3 **Break into small groups to read the Kindergarten Student Reader before the comprehension lesson.**

Teacher-Led

SI Strategic Intervention	OL On-Level	A Advanced
Teacher-Led Page DI•3 • Phonemic Awareness and Phonics • **Read** Concept Literacy Reader K.4.1 or Kindergarten Student Reader K.4.1	**Teacher-Led** Page DI•7 • Phonemic Awareness and Phonics • **Read** Kindergarten Student Reader K.4.1	**Teacher-Led** Page DI•10 • **Read** Independent Reader K.4.1 or Kindergarten Student Reader K.4.1

Place English language learners in the groups that correspond to their reading abilities in English.

Practice Stations
- Visit the Words to Know Station
- Visit the Let's Write! Station

Independent Activities
- Read independently
- Audio Text of Big Book
- *Reader's and Writer's Notebook*

English Language Learners

Access Content Have children point out the naming parts of the sentences, such as *Nan, Nat, bin,* and *man.* Then have them identify each of these people or things in the illustrations.

DAY 3 Read and Comprehend 20–25 mins.

Objectives

- Recall and retell a story.
- ◎ Practice sequence.
- Develop and use vocabulary.
- Develop and use comprehension skills.

Comprehension

Retell the story Have children turn to p. 26 of *My Skills Buddy* and use the retelling boxes to retell the story *Rooster's Off to See the World*.

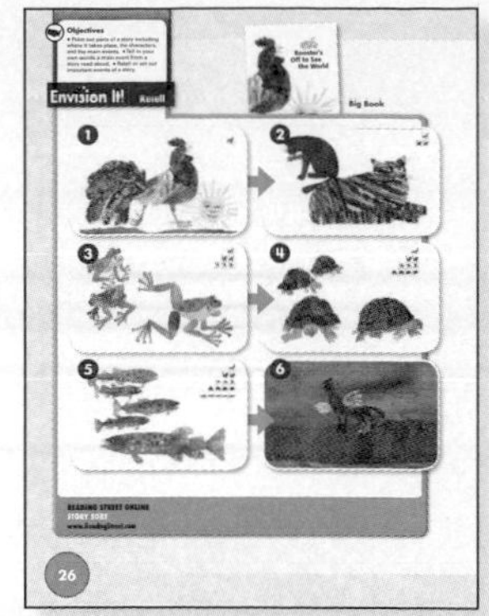

My Skills Buddy, p. 26

Direct children to the first retell box. Here the rooster decides to set off on an adventure. Tell me how the rooster feels after he starts walking.

Continue reviewing the retelling boxes and having children tell the story.

Review **Sequence** Display illustrations of *Rooster's Off to See the World*. Let's recall what happened to the rooster on his trip to see the world.

- What animals does the rooster meet when he first starts his trip? (two cats) What do the cats decide to do? (They join the rooster on his trip.)
- After the cats and the frogs join the rooster, what animals decide to go on the trip next? (four turtles)
- What does the rooster do last? (He decides to go back to his perch.)

More practice Use *Reader's and Writer's Notebook,* p. 248, for additional practice with sequence.

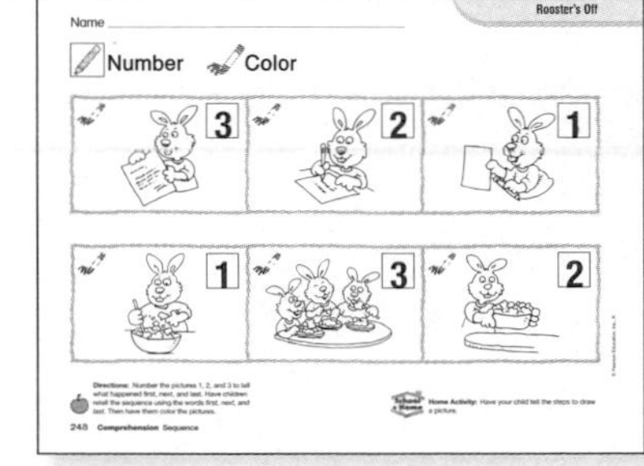

Reader's and Writer's Notebook, p. 248

Second Read—Big Book
Rooster's Off to See the World

Reread *Rooster's Off to See the World*. Follow the Day 3 arrow beginning on p. 59, and use the Develop Vocabulary notes to prompt conversations about the story.

Have children use the Amazing Words *world, lonely, trip, horizon, journey,* and *homesick* to talk about the story.

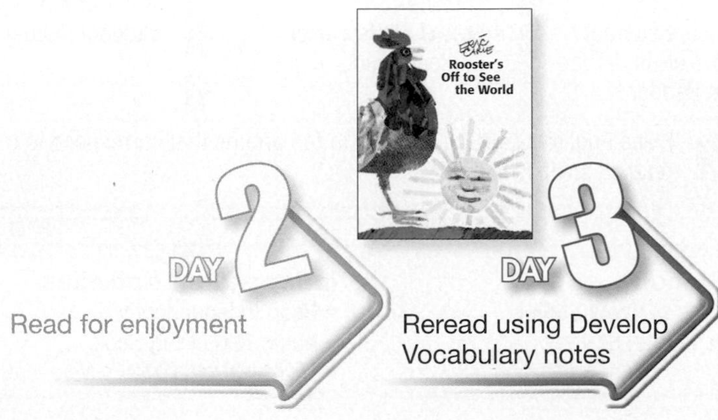

DAY 3

Develop Vocabulary

***Wh-* question**

What does the rooster decide to do one morning? (travel to see the world)

- When you travel, you set out to go somewhere new. What new places have you traveled to?

Big Book, pp. 2–3

DAY 4

Guide Comprehension

Distancing

How does the rooster feel early in his journey? (lonely)

- The rooster feels lonely. When have you felt lonely? What did you do to feel better?

Develop Vocabulary, continued

DAY 3

Open-ended

What do the cats decide to do? (go on the trip with the rooster)

- A trip can be short or long. What would be a short trip? a long trip?

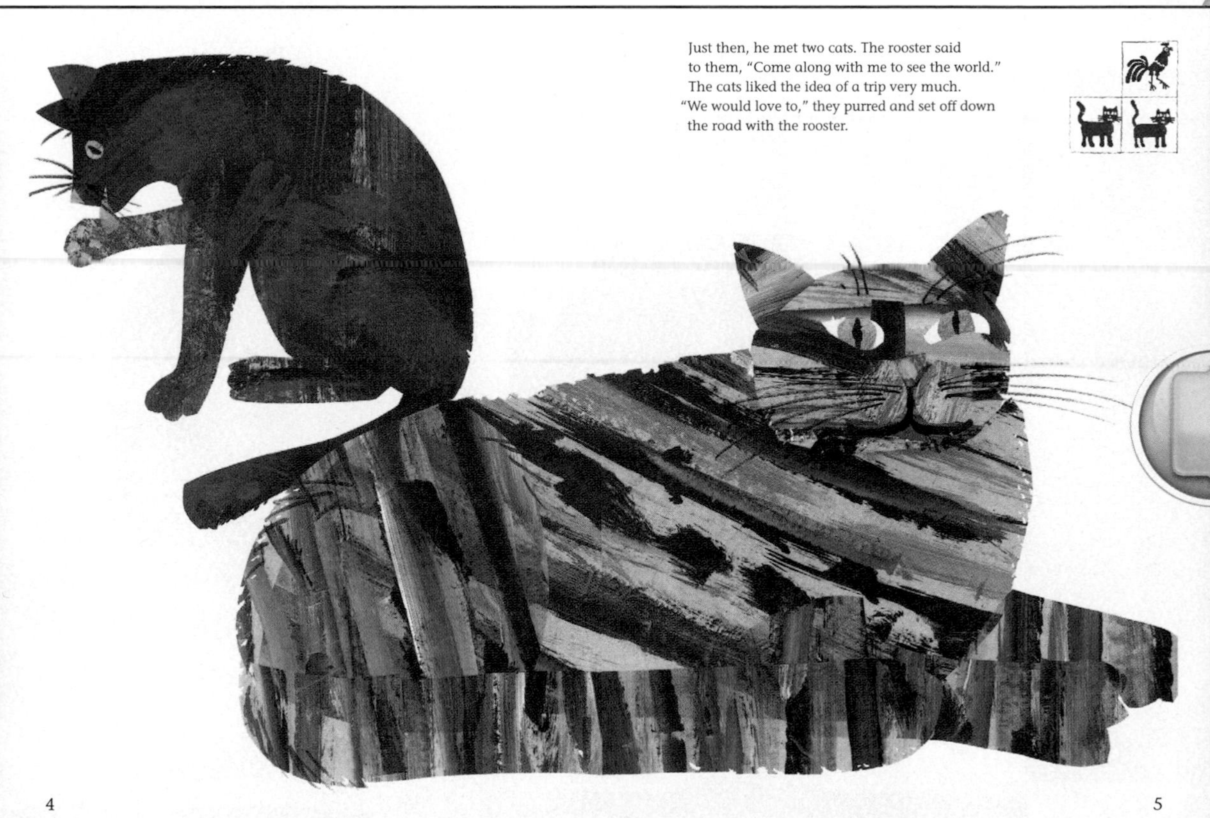
Just then, he met two cats. The rooster said to them, "Come along with me to see the world." The cats liked the idea of a trip very much. "We would love to," they purred and set off down the road with the rooster.

4 5

Big Book, pp. 4–5

Guide Comprehension, continued

DAY 4

Inferential

Why do you think the rooster invites the cats to go with him? (He wants company on his long trip. He likes the cats.)

***Wh-* question**

What new animals does the rooster meet now? (three frogs)

- The rooster is eager for more company, so he invites the frogs along. What does it mean to be "eager for more company"?

Expand Vocabulary eager

Expand Vocabulary company

Big Book, pp. 6–7

***Wh-* question**

The frogs say they are not busy now. What kinds of things do you think would keep a frog busy? (finding food, croaking or singing, swimming in a pond)

Develop Vocabulary, continued

DAY 3

***Wh*- question**

What are the turtles doing when the rooster sees them? (crawling slowly down the road)

- Turtles walk so slowly that it looks like they are crawling. Can you crawl like the turtles in the story?

Develop Vocabulary crawling

After a while, the rooster, the cats, and the frogs saw four turtles crawling slowly down the road.

"Hey," said the rooster, "how would you like to see the world?"

"It might be fun," snapped one of the turtles and they joined the others.

8 9

Big Book, pp. 8–9

Guide Comprehension, continued

DAY 4

Open-ended

What do you think the animal friends will find as they see the world?
(They may find things to eat or other animals to make friends with.)

Distancing

Where are the fish? (in a brook)

- The rooster is "delighted" to have the fish come along on the adventure. When have you been delighted, or very happy, about something?

Expand Vocabulary delighted

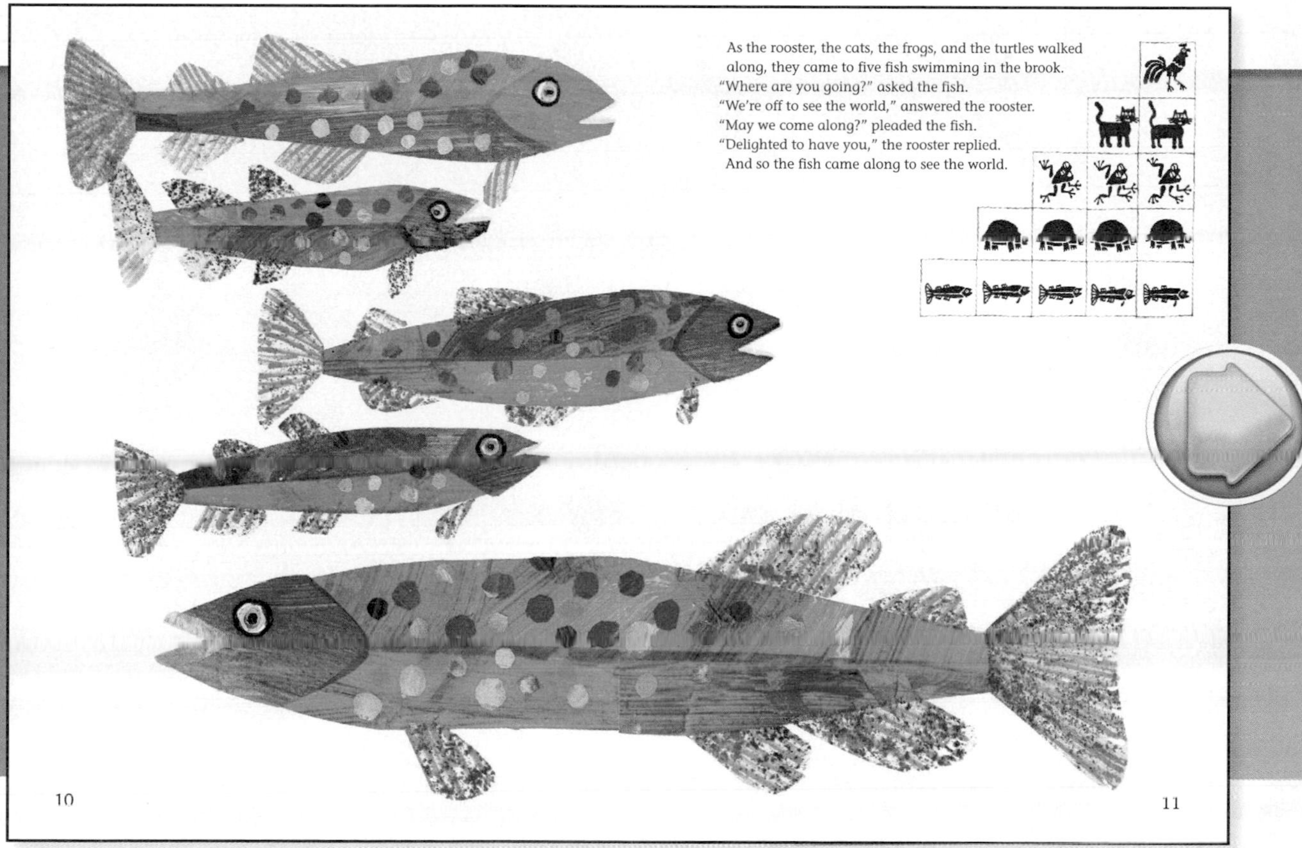
As the rooster, the cats, the frogs, and the turtles walked along, they came to five fish swimming in the brook.
"Where are you going?" asked the fish.
"We're off to see the world," answered the rooster.
"May we come along?" pleaded the fish.
"Delighted to have you," the rooster replied.
And so the fish came along to see the world.

10 11

Big Book, pp. 10–11

Sequence

What has happened so far in the story? Use sequence words. (First, the rooster decides to travel and see the world. Next, he invites two cats to join him. Then he invites three frogs and four turtles. Finally, he invites five fish.)

Develop Vocabulary, continued

DAY 3

***Wh-* question**
What does the rooster forget to think about? (food and shelter)

- He forgets to think about food and shelter, or what the animals will eat and where they will sleep. How do you think the rooster feels now?

Expand Vocabulary shelter

The sun went down. It began to get dark. The moon came up over the horizon. "Where's our dinner?" asked the cats. "Where are we supposed to sleep?" asked the frogs. "We're cold," complained the turtles.

12

Just then, some fireflies flew overhead. "We're afraid," cried the fish. Now, the rooster really had not made any plans for the trip around the world. He had not remembered to think about food and shelter, so he didn't know how to answer his friends.

13

Big Book, pp. 12–13

Guide Comprehension, continued

Inferential
Why are the fish afraid? (The fireflies' lights scared them. They are not used to the dark.)

- Do you think the other animals might be afraid too? Why or why not?

Open-ended

What does it mean to be "headed for home"? (to go back home)

- After a few minutes of silence, the fish decide to go back home. What do you think they were doing during those few minutes of silence?

Develop Vocabulary silence

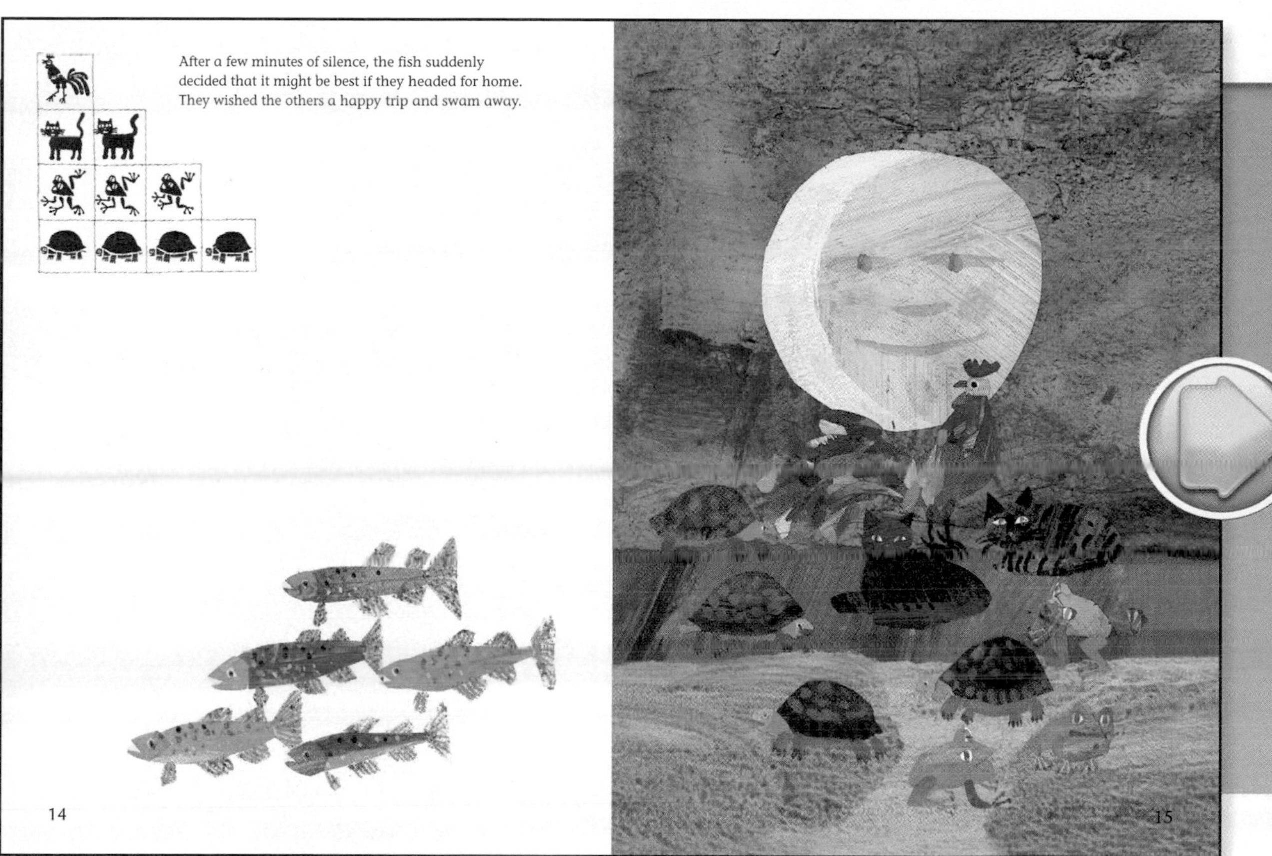

Big Book, pp. 14–15

Monitor and Fix Up

What do the small pictures in the corner show? (the animals that are on the adventure during this part of the story)

- When I don't understand a story, I can look at the pictures. If you forget which animals are with the rooster, how can you use these pictures to help you?

DAY 3

Develop Vocabulary, continued

Wh- question
How many animals are left on the trip? (six)

- *Good-bye* is something you say when you leave. What are some other ways to say good-bye?

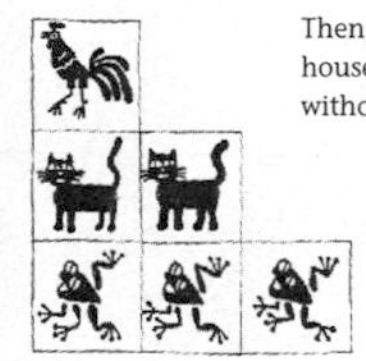

Then, the turtles began to think about their warm house. They turned and crawled back down the road without so much as a good-bye.

16

17

Big Book, pp. 16–17

Guide Comprehension, continued

Distancing
Why do you think the turtles don't say good-bye? (They are in a hurry to get back home. They are rude.)

- If you go to someone's house, it is polite to say *good-bye* and *thank you* before you leave. Why is it important to be polite?

***Wh-* question**

Which animals disappear now? (three frogs)

- The frogs are polite when they leave the rooster and the cats. What does it mean to be polite?

Develop Vocabulary disappeared

Expand Vocabulary polite

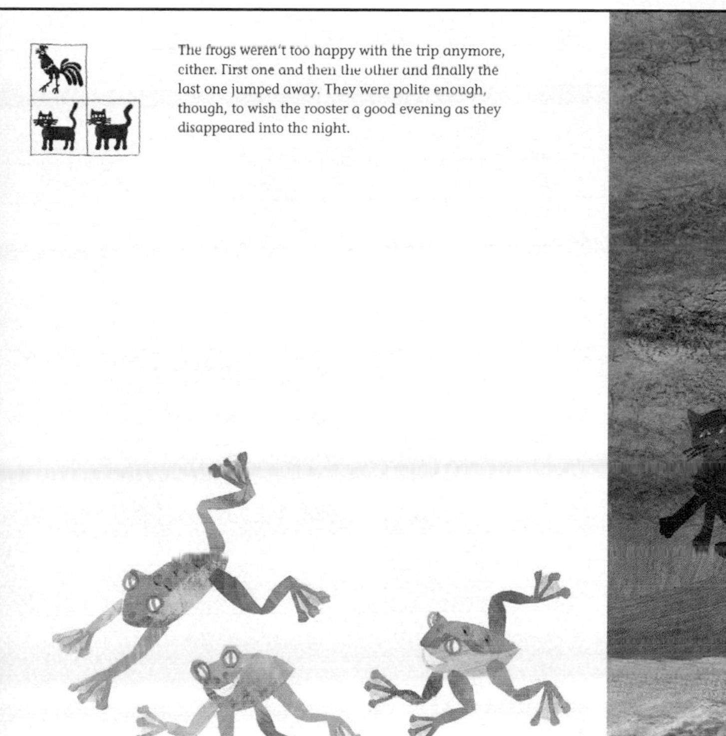

The frogs weren't too happy with the trip anymore, either. First one and then the other and finally the last one jumped away. They were polite enough, though, to wish the rooster a good evening as they disappeared into the night.

18

19

Big Book, pp. 18–19

***Wh-* question**

Why do the frogs leave? (They aren't happy with the trip anymore.)

- Where do you think the frogs will go now?

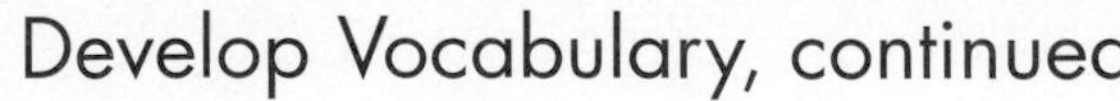

Develop Vocabulary, continued

DAY 3

Wh- question

How does the rooster feel now that he is alone? (homesick)

- To be homesick is to miss home when you are away. When have you ever felt homesick?

The cats then remembered an unfinished meal they had left behind. They kindly wished the rooster a happy journey and they, too, headed for home.

Now the rooster was all alone – and he hadn't seen anything of the world. He thought for a minute and then said to the moon, "To tell you the truth, I am not only hungry and cold, but I'm homesick as well."
The moon did not answer. It, too, disappeared.

20

21

Big Book, pp. 20–21

Guide Comprehension, continued

DAY 4

Sequence

In what order did the animals leave the rooster? Use sequence words. (First, the fish left. Then the turtles left. Next, the frogs left. Finally, the cats left.)

Distancing

Where does the rooster sit after a good meal? (his own perch)

- The rooster doesn't travel all the way around the world, but he does dream about it. What are some good dreams you have had?

Conventions p. 70

Big Book, pp. 22–23

Draw Conclusions

Why do you think the rooster "knew what he had to do"? (It was dark and he had nowhere to eat and sleep. The rooster decided home was the best place to be.)

- The rooster decides to go home. Do you think the rooster makes the right choice?

Conventions p. 84

DAY 3 Language Arts 20–25 mins.

Objectives

- Review sentences.
- Write or dictate directions.

Conventions

Sentences

Review Remind children of what they learned about sentences. A sentence tells a complete thought. It starts with a capital, or uppercase, letter and ends with a punctuation mark. All sentences have a naming part that tells who or what the sentence is about.

Guide practice Hold up AlphaBuddy holding a ball. AlphaBuddy is going to help us write a sentence. Write the following sentence on the board:

alphaBuddy plays with a ball

Where does the capital letter go? (at the beginning of the sentence) Have a child capitalize *AlphaBuddy.* Where does the punctuation mark go? (at the end) Have a child make a period at the end of the sentence. What is the naming part of this sentence? (AlphaBuddy) What does AlphaBuddy do in the sentence? (plays with a ball)

Write these sentences on the board:

mac runs to school
the bunny likes Pam
she walks home

Read each sentence aloud. Have children capitalize the first word, add a period, and underline the naming part of each sentence. How do you know these are complete sentences?

Team Talk Pair children and have them use the *dog, hippopotamus, rabbit,* and *zebra* Picture Cards and other pictures of animals to make oral sentences using the animal as the naming part.

On their own Use *Reader's and Writer's Notebook,* p. 249, for more practice with sentences.

Daily Fix-It Use the Daily Fix-It exercise for more conventions practice.

INTERACT with TEXT

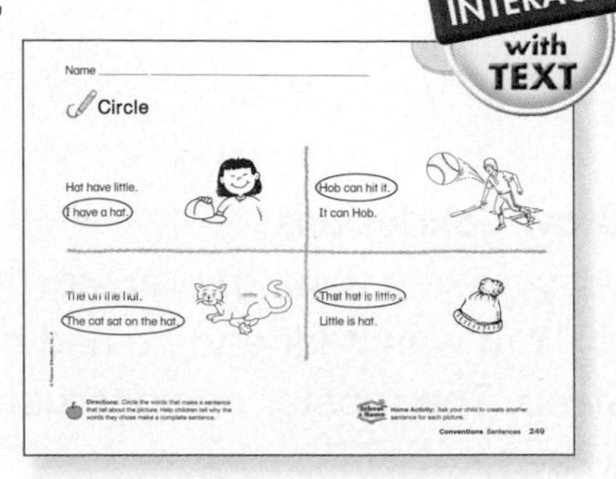

Reader's and Writer's Notebook, p. 249

Writing
Directions

Teach Tell children that directions are steps that tell how to do or make something. Display a child-friendly board game. Every game has directions for how to play it. The people who make the game write the directions on the box or on a sheet of paper in the game box. If you didn't know how to play the game, the directions would tell you.

Model When people go somewhere they have never been before, they get directions on how to get there so that they don't get lost. I will write directions to get from the classroom to the library. I can use pictures and words to give directions. Write simple directions on the board. As you write, say aloud what you are writing. Use pictures as well as words in your written directions.

Guide practice We can write directions to get from the classroom to the doors we use when we go outside. Let's write them together. Take children's suggestions for how to get from the classroom to the doors that lead them outside. Use pictures and simple words, such as *walk, turn,* and *go out,* in your directions.

Independent writing Have children turn to p. 250 of *Reader's and Writer's Notebook.* These pictures show how this boy gets from his house to the mailbox around the corner. Give him directions to the mailbox. Have children write words to tell the boy how to get to the mailbox.

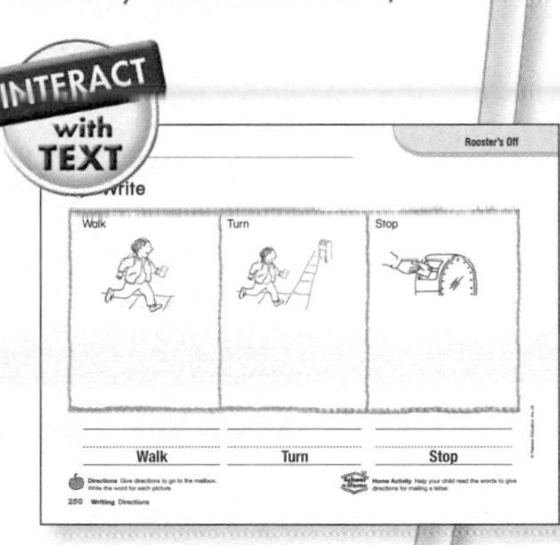

Reader's and Writer's Notebook, p. 250

Daily Handwriting

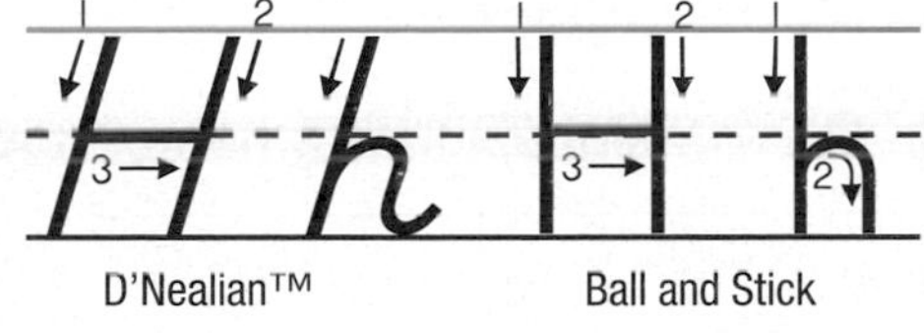

Write *Hob* and *him* on the board. Review correct letter formation of uppercase *H* and lowercase *h.*

Have children write *Hob* and *him* on the Write-On Boards. Remind children to use proper left-to-right and top-to-bottom progression and proper spacing between letters when writing *H* and *h.*

Differentiated Instruction

Strategic Intervention

Support Directions Bring in empty food containers with pictures showing preparation instructions. Review the pictorial directions with children. Tell them that every day, people use directions to do things. Have them list different directions they give and follow.

Academic Vocabulary

directions steps that tell how to do or make something

Daily Fix-It

nan and Nat hit it

Nan and Nat hit it.

This week's practice sentences appear on Teacher Resources DVD ROM.

Objectives

- Practice giving directions.

Listening and Speaking
Give Directions

Review Remind children that directions are steps that tell you how to do or make something. When you speak, remember to speak loudly and clearly. Give your directions in the order that they need to be done.

Model Today, AlphaBuddy will give directions. Listen carefully so that you can follow his directions. When you listen to directions, face the speaker so you better understand what he or she is saying. Have AlphaBuddy give the following directions:

- Stand up.
- Put your hand on your head.
- Sit down with your hands on your knees.

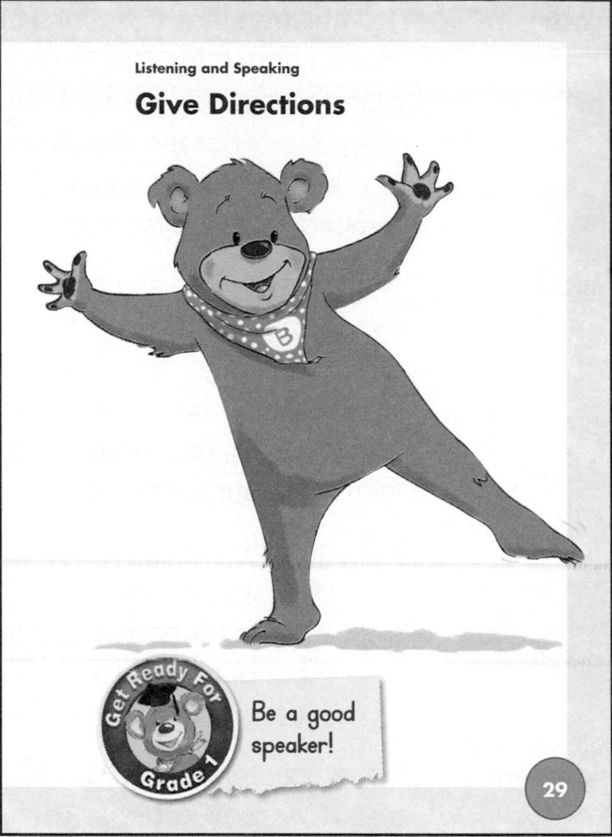

My Skills Buddy, p. 29

When AlphaBuddy was telling you what to do, he was giving you directions.

Guide practice Have children turn to p. 29 of *My Skills Buddy*. I see a picture of AlphaBuddy. Listen as I give some directions for you to follow. Use the Listening and Speaking bullets on p. 28 to have children point in turn to AlphaBuddy's nose, mouth, ear, and foot.

Independent practice Have children take turns using AlphaBuddy to give directions to their classmates. They should give simple directions and begin each with *AlphaBuddy says* ________. Refer children to their Rules for Listening and Speaking from pp. 1–2 of the *Reader's and Writer's Notebook.* Remind children to speak loudly and clearly when giving their directions.

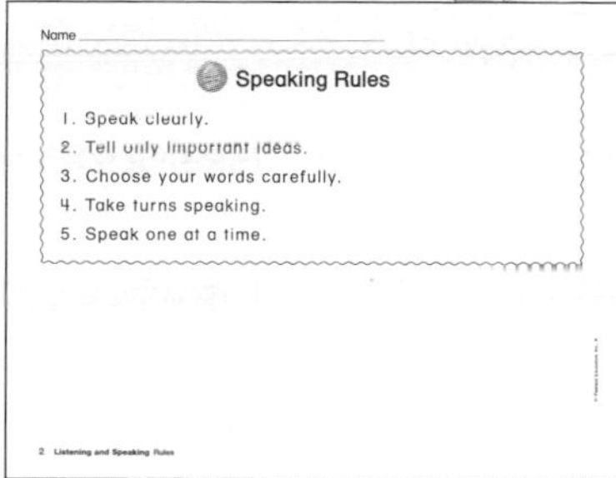
Name

Speaking Rules

1. Speak clearly.
2. Tell only important ideas.
3. Choose your words carefully.
4. Take turns speaking.
5. Speak one at a time.

Reader's and Writer's Notebook, pp. 1–2

Be a Good Speaker

1. Speak clearly.
2. Tell only important ideas.
3. Choose your words carefully.
4. Take turns speaking.
5. Speak one at a time.

Differentiated Instruction

Advanced

Giving Directions Discuss with children different ways directions can be given without words, such as through symbols on signs or using gestures and pointing. Then have children give directions to a partner, without using words, on how to get from one place in the class to another.

English Language Learners

Professional Development

Access Content Experts say that Total Physical Response (TPR) helps children learn English by following directions with movements. Give children practice following AlphaBuddy's directions. Make up other directions for children to follow.

Objectives

- Review skills learned and practiced today.

Wrap Up Your Day

✔ **Respond to Literature** Today we read about Nan and Nat. What did they do? They played ball, took a nap, drank lemonade, and played at the park.

✔ **Conventions** Have children tell you the naming part in the following sentence: *The child put on the red shirt.*

✔ **Homework Idea** Have children bring to school an object or a picture of an object that begins with /h/.

Social Studies
Playground Map

Materials: large sheet of paper, pencils, crayons or markers

Where I Play Take children on a walk through the school playground. Have them note where important features are, such as swings, the slide, or a large tree. When you return to the classroom, discuss what you saw on your playground walk.

Make a Map On a large sheet of paper, draw an outline of the playground. Have each child draw a feature they noted during the playground walk. Discuss with children what directions they would need to follow to get from place to place on your map.

Comprehension
Sequence

Materials: Kindergarten Student Reader K.4.1; props such as a ball, cups, and sitting mats

Act Out the Sequence Reread Kindergarten Student Reader K.4.1, *A Day to Play.* Have children tell you what happens first, next, and last in the story. Then have groups of three children act out the story sequence.

Phonics
Writing /h/ words

Materials: paper, pencils

Hands Down Have children trace their hands on a sheet of paper. Have them write the letters *Hh* at the top of the paper. Then have them write as many words as they can that begin with /h/ inside their handprints. They can use their decodable readers or other books they can read independently to find words.

Objectives
- Discuss the concept to develop oral language.
- Build oral vocabulary.

Today at a Glance

Oral Vocabulary
journey, homesick

Phonemic Awareness
Initial and Medial /o/

Phonics
/o/ Spelled *Oo*
Spell Words

Comprehension
◉ Sequence

Conventions
Naming Parts

Writing
Extend the Concept

Vocabulary
Sequence Words

TRUCKTOWN on Reading Street

Start your engines!

- Display "Hey Diddle Diddle" and lead the group in saying the rhyme a few times.
- Next, have the group clap the rhythm as they recite the rhyme.
- When the rhythm is smooth, have them march around the room as they say the rhyme.

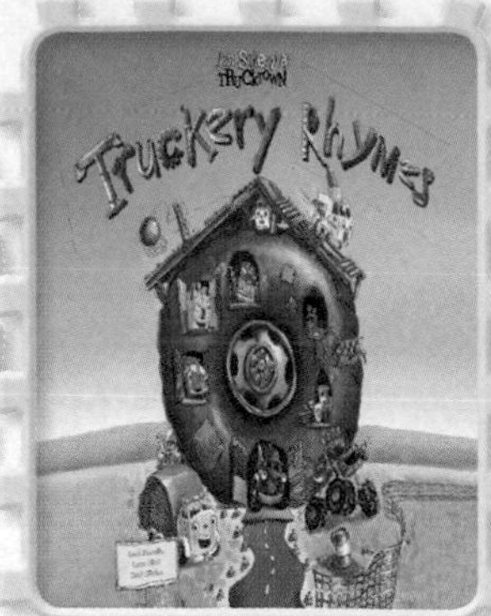

Truckery Rhymes

Concept Talk

Question of the Week
What can we learn from our adventures?

Build concepts Write and read the question of the week as you track the print. Tell children to respond in complete sentences. Display Sing with Me Chart 19B.

Listen for Amazing Words We are going to sing this song again. Listen for the Amazing Words *journey* and *homesick*. Sing the song several times with children to the tune of "Head and Shoulders, Knees and Toes." Have them clap when they hear *journey* and *homesick*.

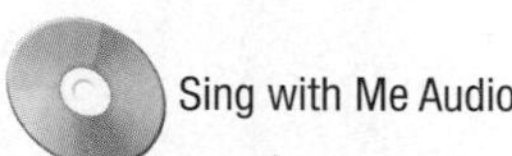
Sing with Me Audio

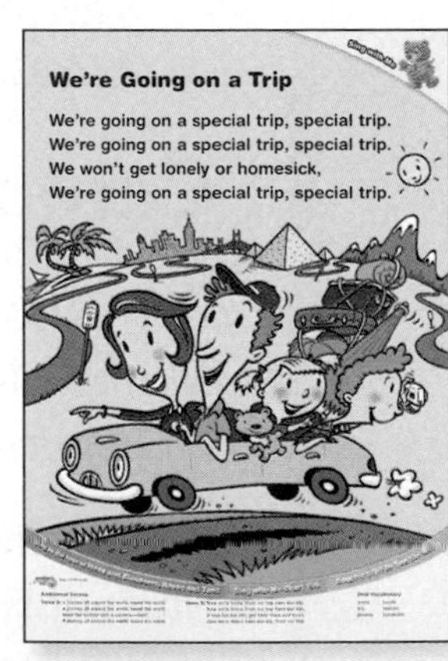

Talk with Me/Sing with Me Chart 19B

ELL Produce Oral Language Use the Day 4 instruction on ELL Poster 19 to extend and enrich language.

ELL Poster 19

Oral Vocabulary
Amazing Words

Amazing Words Oral Vocabulary Routine

Teach Amazing Words

1 **Introduce the Word** The rooster decides to take a *journey* to see the world. To take a *journey* is to travel somewhere. What's our Amazing Word for traveling somewhere? Say it with me: *journey*.

2 **Demonstrate** *I took a journey to see the seashore.* Where can a *journey* take you?

Repeat steps 1 and 2.

Introduce The rooster gets *homesick* for his perch. To be *homesick* is to miss being at home. What's our Amazing Word for missing home? Say it with me: *homesick*.

Demonstrate *When I am away for long, I get homesick.* Have you ever gotten *homesick?*

3 **Apply** Tell children to use *journey* and *homesick* in complete sentences. Have them illustrate the words.

Routines Flip Chart

Use Amazing Words

To reinforce the concept and the Amazing Words, have children supply the appropriate Amazing Word for each sentence.

The turtles decided not to complete the _______. (journey)

The frogs were _______ for their pond. (homesick)

Amazing Words

world	lonely
trip	horizon
journey	homesick

Differentiated Instruction

Advanced

Amazing Words As you discuss the Amazing Words for the day, have children compare the words *journey* and *trip*. Have them tell how the words are similar and different by asking questions such as *Would you journey to the store or take a trip to the store?*

Objectives

- Review /o/.
- Review /o/ spelled *Oo*.

Check Phonemic Awareness
SUCCESS PREDICTOR

Phonemic Awareness

Review /o/

Review

Display the *olive* Picture Card. This is an *olive*. *Olive* begins with /o/. What sound does *olive* begin with? Continue the routine with the *octopus* and *otter* Picture Cards.

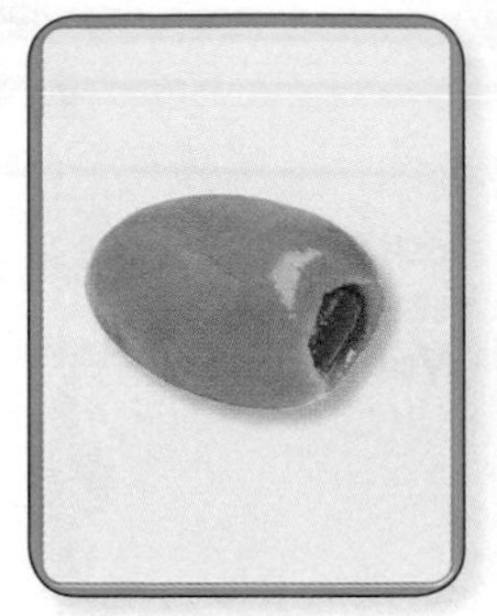

Picture Card

Display the *box* Picture Card. This is a *box*. *Box* has /o/ in the middle. What sound do you hear in the middle of *box?* Continue the routine with the *mop, rock,* and *top* Picture Cards.

Picture Card

Corrective feedback

If... children cannot discriminate /o/,
then... have them say /o/ several times, /o/, /o/, /o/.

When you say /o/, you drop your mouth open and say the sound at the back of your throat. Have children practice saying /o/.

Phonics
/o/ Spelled *Oo*

Review

Display the *Oo* Alphabet Card. This is an *otter*. *Otter* begins with /o/. What letter spells the sound /o/? Yes, the letter *o*.

Write the word *hop* on the board. Help me blend this word. Listen as I say each sound: /h/ /o/ /p/. Now let's blend the sounds together to read the word: /h/ /o/ /p/, *hop*. What is the word? (*hop*) Let's try some more. Continue blending with *hot, top, Tom,* and *Don*.

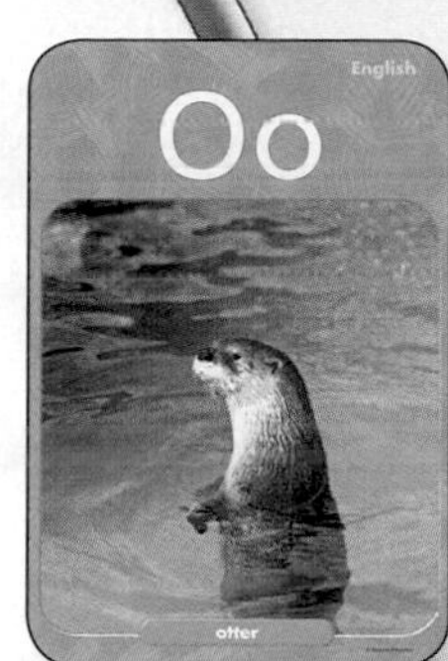

Alphabet Card

Don't Wait Until Friday

MONITOR PROGRESS — Check Phonemic Awareness

Phoneme Segmentation I am going to say a word. Tell me all the sounds you hear in the word. Use the following words:

Hob	**can**	**hit**	**man**	**Dan**	**it**	**fan**	**Pam**
Sam	**did**	**not**	**hot**	**had**	**hat**	**pop**	

If... children cannot segment the sounds,
then... use the small-group Strategic Intervention lesson, p. DI•4, to reteach segmentation skills.

Continue to monitor children's progress using other instructional opportunities during the week so that they can be successful with the Day 5 Assessment. See the Skills Trace on p. 26.

Day 1	Day 2	Day 3	Day 4	Day 5
Check Phonemic Awareness	Check Sound-Spelling/ Retelling	Check Word Reading	Check Phonemic Awareness	Check Oral Vocabulary

Success Predictor

Differentiated Instruction

SI Strategic Intervention

Support Phonemic Awareness Review /o/ with children. Tell them to listen for action words with /o/. When they hear it, they are to do the action. Say the following words: *hop, drop, jump, plop, stand, sit, mop, stop*.

Phonemic Awareness Success Predictor

Get Ready to Read

Objectives
- Spell words.
- Blend and segment words.
- Read decodable text.
- Read high-frequency words.

Spelling
/h/ Spelled *Hh*

ROUTINE **Spell Words**

Spell words

1. **Review Sound-Spellings** Display the *Hh* Alphabet Card. This is a *helicopter*. *Helicopter* begins with /h/. What letter spells this sound? (*h*) Continue the routine with the following Alphabet Cards: *Aa, Bb, Dd, Ii, Mm, Oo, Pp, Tt*.

2. **Model** Today we are going to spell some words. Listen to the three sounds in *him*: /h/ /i/ /m/.

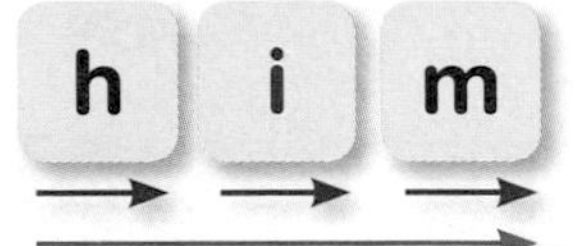

- What is the first sound in *him?* (/h/) What is the letter for /h/? (*h*) Write *h* on the board.
- What is the middle sound in *him?* (/i/) What is the letter for /i/? (*i*) Write *i* on the board.
- What is the last sound in *him?* (/m/) What is the letter for /m/? (*m*) Write *m* on the board.
- Point to *him*. Help me blend the sound of each letter together to read this word: /h/ /i/ /m/. The word is *him*. Repeat the modeling with the word *hid*.

3. **Guide Practice** Now let's spell some words together. Listen to this word: /h/ /i/ /p/. What is the first sound in *hip?* (/h/) What is the letter for /h/? (*h*) Write *h* on the board. Now you write *h* on your paper. What is the middle sound in *hip?* (/i/) What is the letter for /i/? (*i*) Write *i* on the board. Now you write *i* on your paper. What is the last sound in *hip?* (/p/) What is the letter for /p/? (*p*) Write *p* on the board. Now you write *p* on your paper. Now we can blend the sound of each letter together to read the word: /h/ /i/ /p/. What is the word? (*hip*) Continue the spell and blend practice with the following words: *hat, ham, hop*.

4. **On Your Own** This time I am going to say a word and I want you to write it on your paper. Remember, first, say the word slowly in your head and then write the letter for each sound. Listen carefully. Write the word hit. Give children time to write the word. How do you spell the word *hit?* Listen to the sounds: /h/ /i/ /t/. The first sound is /h/. What is the letter for /h/? Did you write *h* on your paper? What is the letter for /i/? Did you write *i* on your paper? What is the letter for /t/? Did you write *t* on your paper? Name the letters in *hit*. *Hit* is spelled *h, i, t*. Continue the activity with the following words: *hot, top, bad, had*.

Routines Flip Chart

eReaders 

Get Set, Roll! Reader 19
Practice /h/ Spelled *Hh*

Review Review the high-frequency words *see, are, you, look, do, is, the, I, a, like,* and *that*. Have children find each word on the Word Wall.

Teach rebus words Write the word *button* on the board. This is *button*. Name the letters with me: *b, u, t, t, o, n*. Repeat the routine with the word *Pete*. Look for the words *button* and *Pete* in the story today. A picture above each word will help you read it.

Read Get Set, Roll! Reader 19 Today we will read about Payloader Pete. Point to the title of the book. What is the title of this book? (*Hot!*) We will read lots of words with /h/ in this book.

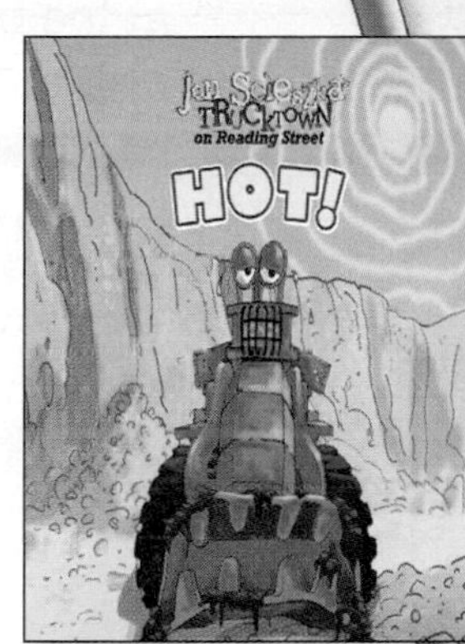

Get Set, Roll! Reader 19

Small Group Time

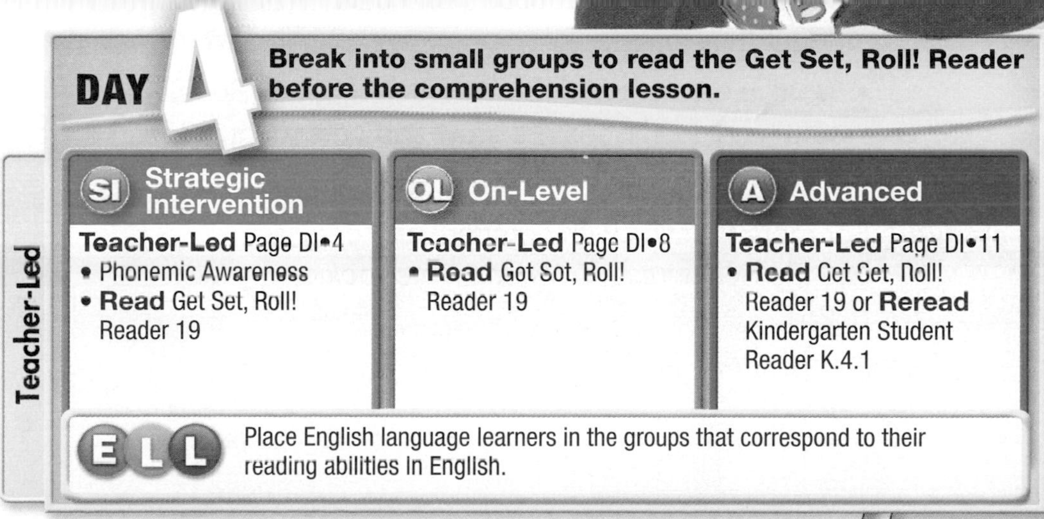

DAY 4 Break into small groups to read the Get Set, Roll! Reader before the comprehension lesson.

Teacher-Led

SI Strategic Intervention	OL On-Level	A Advanced
Teacher-Led Page DI•4 • Phonemic Awareness • **Read** Get Set, Roll! Reader 19	**Teacher-Led** Page DI•8 • **Read** Get Set, Roll! Reader 19	**Teacher-Led** Page DI•11 • **Read** Get Set, Roll! Reader 19 or **Reread** Kindergarten Student Reader K.4.1

ELL Place English language learners in the groups that correspond to their reading abilities in English.

Practice Stations
- Visit the Let's Write! Station
- Visit the Read for Meaning Station

Independent Activities
- Read independently
- Audio Text of the Big Book
- *Reader's and Writer's Notebook*

Differentiated Instruction

SI Strategic Intervention

Concept Development Review with children the different kinds of trucks they have learned about so far and what these trucks do.

English Language Learners

Frontload Reader Take a picture walk with children to preview the reader before starting the routine.

DAY 4 Read and Comprehend

20–25 mins.

Objectives

- ◎ Practice sequence.
- Review and practice compare and contrast.

Comprehension

◎ Sequence

Practice sequence Have children turn to the Sequence picture on p. 14 of *My Skills Buddy.* As you look at the pictures, remind children that all stories follow a sequence of events.

My Skills Buddy, pp. 14–15

Envision It! Team Talk Pair children and have them recall the sequence of events in a story they have read in class.

Compare and Contrast

Review When we compare and contrast, we look at how things are alike and different, or the same and not the same. Good readers pay attention to how things are alike and different because it helps them understand the story.

Display pp. 2–5 of Big Book *Rooster's Off to See the World.* Let's look at these pictures to tell how roosters and cats are alike and how they are different.

- What is alike about roosters and cats? (They are both animals. They are about the same size.)
- What is different about roosters and cats? (Roosters have two legs and cats have four. Roosters crow and cats meow. Roosters have feathers and cats have fur.)

More practice For more practice with compare and contrast, use the *Reader's and Writer's Notebook,* p. 251.

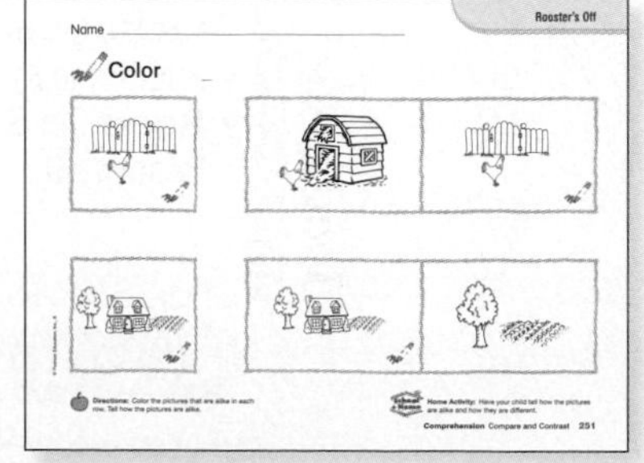

Reader's and Writer's Notebook, p. 251

Third Read—Big Book
Rooster's Off to See the World

Guide comprehension

Display *Rooster's Off to See the World*. The rooster decides one day to see the world. Let's compare and contrast the start and end of the rooster's adventure.

- Display pp. 2–3. What is the setting, or the time and place, at the start of the journey? (daytime, on the road near the rooster's perch)
- How does the rooster feel when he starts his journey? (lonely)
- Display pp. 22–23. What is the setting, or the time and place, at the end of the journey? (nighttime, on the rooster's perch)
- How does the rooster feel when he ends his journey? (happy)
- What is the same? (The rooster is near his home.)
- What is different? (the time of day; how the rooster is feeling)

Reread *Rooster's Off to See the World.* Return to p. 59. Follow the Day 4 arrow and use the Guide Comprehension notes to give children the opportunity to gain a more complete understanding of the story.

Read for enjoyment

Reread using Develop Vocabulary notes

DAY 4
Reread using Guide Comprehension notes

Differentiated Instruction

Strategic Intervention

Support Comprehension Review with children the story *Rooster's Off to See the World.* Have them recall what they remember about the story before they hear it again.

DAY 4 Language Arts

20–25 mins.

Objectives
- Identify naming parts.
- Practice naming parts.
- Use a picture dictionary.

Conventions
Naming Parts

Review Remind children that the naming part of a sentence tells who or what that sentence is about. Listen to this sentence: *The dog drank water.* Who or what is this sentence about? Who drank water? Yes, the dog drank water, so *the dog* is the naming part of the sentence. Repeat using these words instead of *dog* in the sentence: *bear, cat, deer, bunny*.

Guide practice Have children turn to p. 132 of *My Skills Buddy.* This is a picture dictionary. It can help you find out what a word means or how to spell it. This page shows words for things that go. Let's use one of these words as the naming part of a sentence. Have children dictate a sentence using a word from the picture dictionary as the naming part. (The boat floats.) Write their sentences on the board. What is the naming part of this sentence? *The boat* is the naming part, because the boat is the thing that is floating. Repeat with other words from the picture dictionary.

On their own Use *Reader's and Writer's Notebook,* p. 252 for more practice with naming parts.

Daily Fix-It Use the Daily-Fix It exercise for more conventions practice.

INTERACT with TEXT

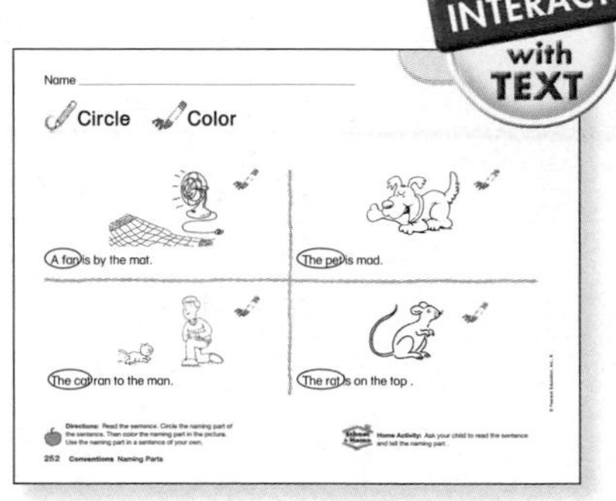

Reader's and Writer's Notebook, p. 252

Writing
Extend the Concept: Text to Self

Discuss learning from adventures

We read a story about a rooster who wanted to go out and see the world. He wanted to have an adventure. We too can have an adventure when we walk out our doors to go anywhere, even to and from school or the store!

Guide practice

Ask children to recall anything they saw or learned or noticed on their way to school that morning or any other morning. Suggest things, such as a bird flying, flowers blooming, or a new car on the street, to stimulate their minds. Discuss how sometimes we can learn from even small things.

Use children's contributions to the discussion to write sentences.

On my way to school, I saw...	**birds making a nest.**
	a very big flower.
	a mother and her baby.

Independent writing

Have children write or dictate a sentence about what they saw on a different outing, such as to the store or to a friend or relative's house, or they may copy one of the sentences from the board. Invite volunteers to read their sentences to the class. Have children to illustrate their sentences.

Daily Handwriting

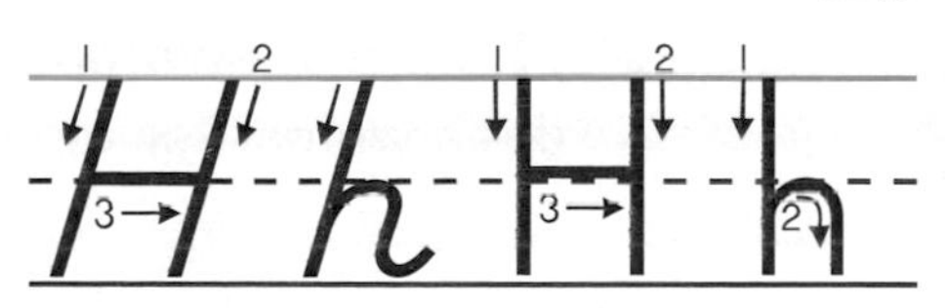

Write uppercase *H* and lowercase *h* on the board. Review correct letter formation with children.

Have children write a row each of uppercase *H* and lowercase *h* on their Write-On Boards. Remind them to use proper left-to-right and top-to-bottom progression when writing *H* and *h.*

Differentiated Instruction

 Strategic Intervention

Support Writing Pair more capable children with less capable ones to help them as they write their sentences telling what they see on their way to school.

Daily Fix-It

the little brown bunnies ran

The little brown bunnies ran.

This week's practice sentences appear on Teacher Resources DVD-ROM.

English Language Learners

Support Writing As children write or dictate, supply English words if needed to express their ideas.

Objectives

- Practice using sequence words in sentences.

Vocabulary
Sequence Words

Teach

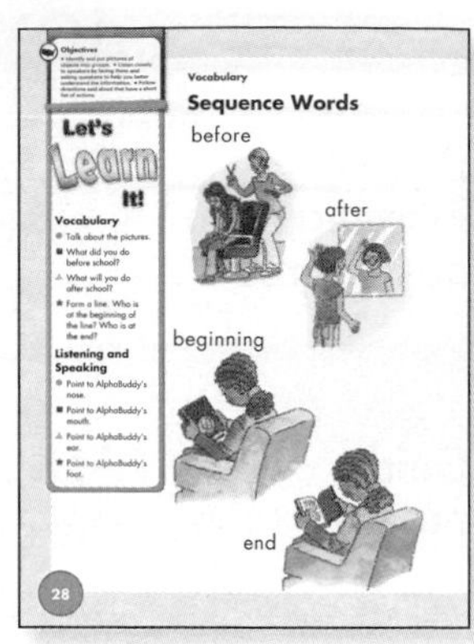

My Skills Buddy, p. 28

Write the words *before, after, beginning*, and *end* on the board. Point to each word as you read it. These are sequence words. They tell the order in which things happen. Have children turn to p. 28 of *My Skills Buddy*. Point to the picture of the girl looking at the cover of a book. Is this person reading from the beginning or the end of the book? Then point to the picture of the girl reading the last page of the book. Is this person reading at the beginning or the end of the book? Have children point to the before and after pictures of the girl getting her hair cut. Use the last Vocabulary bullet on p. 28 to discuss the sequence of children in line.

Team Talk Pair children and have them list things that show *beginning* and *end* or *before* and *after.*

Wrap Up Your Day

✔ **Concept Talk** Today we read again about a rooster taking a trip and learning from his adventure. What do you think the rooster learned?

✔ **Phonemic Awareness** Today we reviewed /o/ words. I am going to say three words. Tell me which words have /o/: *mop, tan, hot.*

✔ **Conventions** We know that naming parts tell who or what a sentence is about. What is the naming part of the sentence *Three frogs hopped away*?

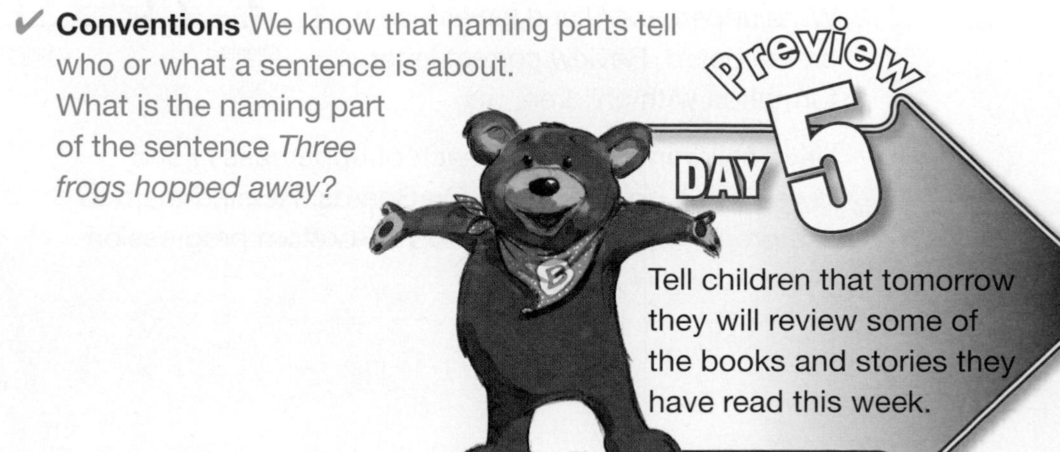

Tell children that tomorrow they will review some of the books and stories they have read this week.

Social Studies
The Whole Wide World

Materials: map or globe, magazines, construction paper, glue, pencils

Where to Roam On a map or globe, point to the United States, your state, and the community in which the school is located. Discuss with children several different geographical regions in the state or country. Then have them use magazines to find pictures of mountains, rivers, lakes, valleys, cities, farms, and so on. Have children choose a place they might want to visit and explain their reasoning.

Write a Sentence Have children think about the place they have chosen. What would they expect to see there and what would they expect to learn? Have them glue their picture to paper and write a sentence telling what they expect to see in this place. You may want to use the sentence starter: *I see* ________.

Phonics
Short *o* Words

Build Words Write the word *nod* on the board. Read the word. Have a child change the *n* to *c* and then say the new word: *cod.* Continue making new words by changing the initial consonant: *pod, rod.* Then have children change the final consonant *d* to *t* to make new words that end with *-ot: not, cot, pot, rot.*

nod	not
cod	cot
pod	pot
rod	rot

Drama
Dramatize a Song

Act Out "Frère Jacques" Teach children the song "Frère Jacques." Have children decide whether "Frère Jacques" is a song about getting up in the morning or going to sleep at night. Have children sing the song several times or until they are familiar with it. Then have them pretend to sleep like Brother John as they sing. Ask children to draw a picture that shows what they think Brother John looks like when he hears the morning bells.

Are you sleeping,
are you sleeping,
Brother John,
Brother John?
Morning bells are ringing,
morning bells are ringing.
Ding, ding, dong;
Ding, ding, dong.

Objectives

- Review the concepts.
- Build oral vocabulary.

Today at a Glance

Oral Vocabulary
world, lonely, trip, horizon, journey, homesick

Phonemic Awareness
⊙ Initial /h/

Phonics
⊙ /h/ Spelled *Hh*

Comprehension
⊙ Sequence

Conventions
Naming Parts

Writing
This Week We…

Check Oral Vocabulary
SUCCESS PREDICTOR

TRUCKTOWN on Reading Street

Start your engines!

- Display "Hey Diddle Diddle" and lead the group in saying the rhyme a few times.
- Have children walk around the room in a line pretending to be ice cream trucks as they say the rhyme again.

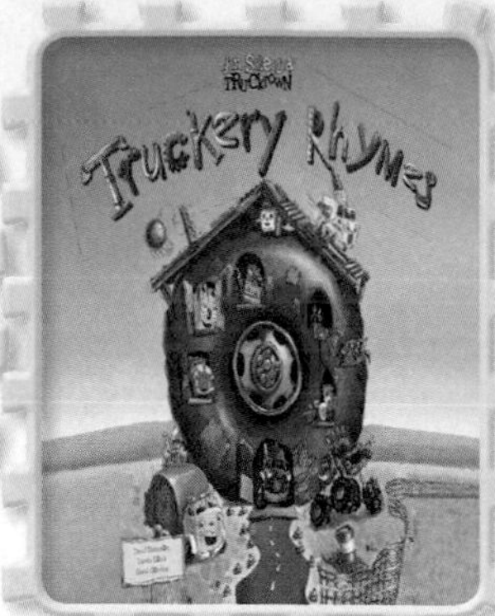
Truckery Rhymes

Concept Wrap Up

Question of the Week

What can we learn from our adventures?

Listen for Amazing Words

Write the question of the week on the board. Track the print as you read it to children. Have them use Amazing Words in their responses (*world, lonely, trip, horizon, journey, homesick*). Remind them to answer the question in complete sentences. Display Sing with Me Chart 19B. Let's sing "We're Going on a Trip." I want you to listen for the Amazing Words we learned this week. Remind children that the words *world, lonely, trip, horizon, journey,* and *homesick* are in the song. Sing the song several times to the tune of "Head and Shoulders, Knees and Toes." Then discuss what the family in the song learned from their trip.

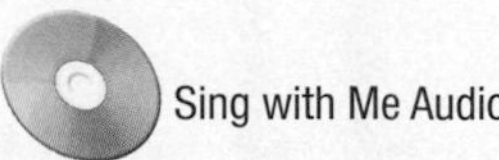
Sing with Me Audio

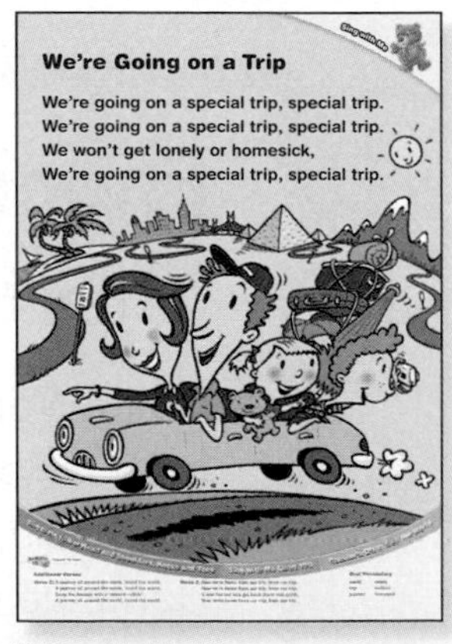

Talk with Me/Sing with Me Chart 19B

ELL Check Concepts and Language Use the Day 5 instruction on ELL Poster 19 to monitor children's understanding of the lesson concept.

ELL Poster 19

Oral Vocabulary
Amazing Words

Review

Let's Talk Display Talk with Me Chart 19A. We learned six new Amazing Words this week. Let's say the Amazing Words as I point to the pictures on the chart. Point to each picture and give children the chance to say the appropriate Amazing Word before offering it.

Have children supply the missing Amazing Word to complete each sentence.

In the summer my family goes on a ________ . (trip)

The ________ is a big place. (world)

Where sky and land meet is called the ________. (horizon)

The ________ home was a long one. (journey)

Being all by yourself can be ________. (lonely)

I get ________ when I am away from home too long. (homesick)

It's Friday

MONITOR PROGRESS Check Oral Vocabulary

Demonstrate Word Knowledge Monitor the Amazing Words by asking the following questions. Have children use the Amazing Words in their answer.

- **What does it mean to miss being at home?** (homesick)
- **What can you call short travel away from home?** (trip)
- **Where do the land and sky seem to meet?** (horizon)
- **What do we call Earth and everything on it?** (world)
- **How might you feel when you are all by yourself?** (lonely)
- **What do you call travel to some place far away?** (journey)

If... children have difficulty using the Amazing Words,
then... reteach the words using the Oral Vocabulary Routine on the Routines Flip Chart.

Day 1	Day 2	Day 3	Day 4	Day 5
Check Phonemic Awareness	Check Sound-Spelling/ Retelling	Check Word Reading	Check Phonemic Awareness	Check Oral Vocabulary

Success Predictor

Amazing Words

world	lonely
trip	horizon
journey	homesick

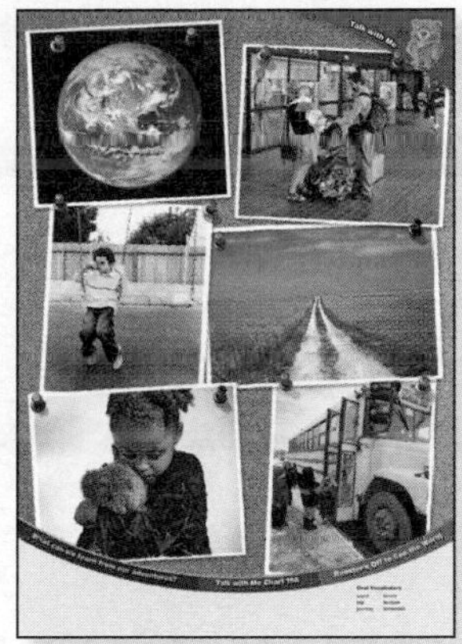
Talk with Me/Sing with Me Chart 19A

Differentiated Instruction

 **Advanced**

Amazing Words Have children choose one Amazing Word to illustrate. Then have them write or dictate a sentence to go with their pictures that uses the Amazing Word.

DAY 5 Wrap Up your Week

10–15 mins.

Objectives

- ◎ Review initial /h/.
- ◎ Review /h/ spelled *Hh*.

Phonemic Awareness Review

◎ Initial /h/

Isolate initial /h/ Display the *hammer* Picture Card. What is the first sound in *hammer?* Say the word with me: *hammer,* /h/ /h/ /h/, *hammer*. Review initial /h/ with the following Picture Cards: *hose, house, hippopotamus*.

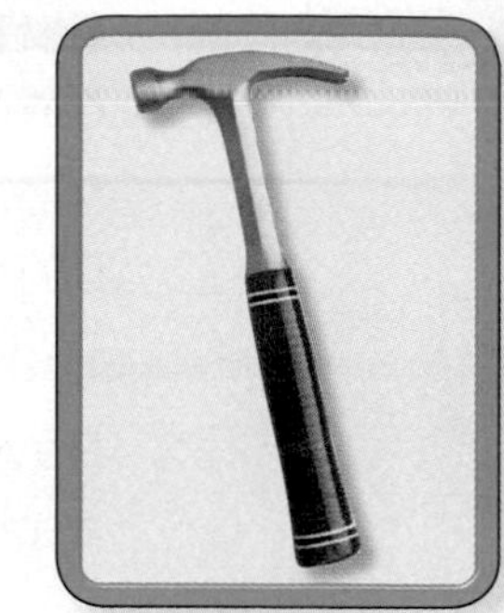
Picture Card

Tell children that you will say some words. Have them raise their hands when you say a word that begins with /h/. Use these words: *tip, hip, pot, hot, hat, cat, mill, hill, hop, mop, hen, pen*.

Substitute sounds I am going to say a word. Listen carefully: /h/ /a/ /t/, *hat*. I can make a new word by changing the first or last sound. I will change the first sound. Listen: /k/ /a/ /t/. What is the new word? The new word is *cat*. Let's try some more. Practice substituting initial and final phonemes with the following pairs of words: *man, pan; bit, fit; pot, pod*.

Phonics Review
/h/ Spelled *Hh*

Teach /h/*Hh* Display the *Hh* Alphabet Card. This is a *helicopter*. What sound do you hear at the beginning of *helicopter*? What letter spells that sound?

Alphabet Card

High-frequency words Write the word *are* on the board. This is the word *are*. Let's say it together. What is this word? Continue the routine with *that* and *do*.

Apply phonics in familiar text **Let's Reread** Have children reread one of the books specific to the target letter sounds. You may wish to review the decodable words and high-frequency words that appear in each book prior to rereading.

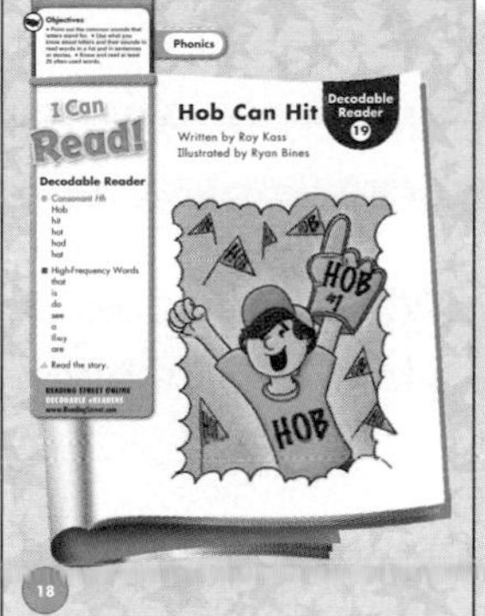
Decodable Reader 19
My Skills Buddy, p. 18

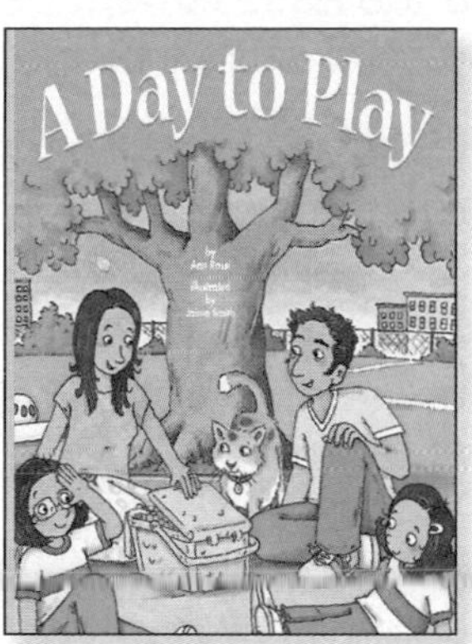

Kindergarten
Student Reader K.4.1

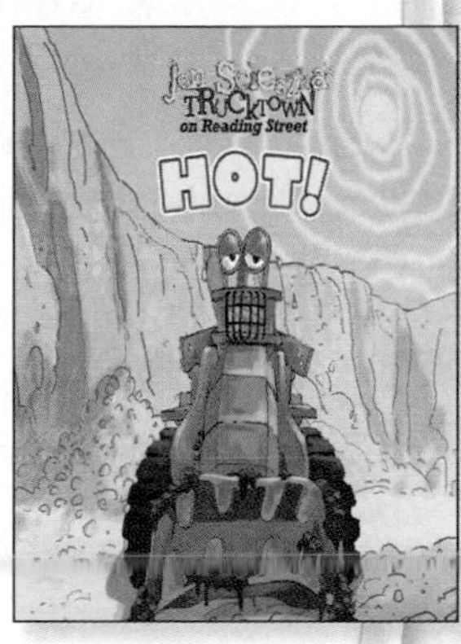

Get Set, Roll!
Reader 19

Differentiated Instruction

A Advanced

Support Phonics Draw an outline of a person on the board. Have children write the letter *h* on labels. Name different body parts. When children hear one that starts with /h/, have them put a label note on that part of the drawing. Use the following body parts: *head, arm, leg, heart, hand, knee, heel, toe, hip*.

Small Group Time

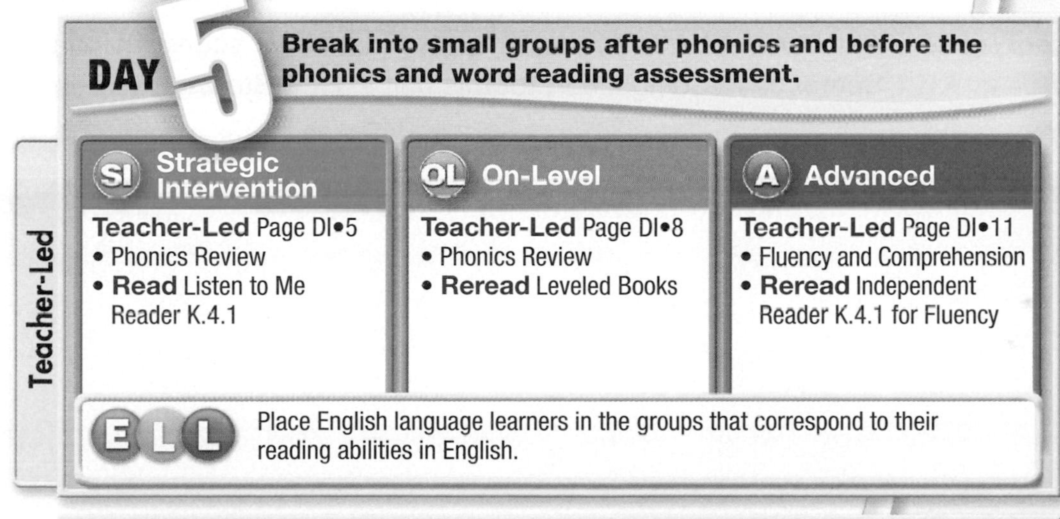

DAY 5 Break into small groups after phonics and before the phonics and word reading assessment.

Teacher-Led

SI Strategic Intervention	OL On-Level	A Advanced
Teacher-Led Page DI•5 • Phonics Review • **Read** Listen to Me Reader K.4.1	**Teacher-Led** Page DI•8 • Phonics Review • **Reread** Leveled Books	**Teacher-Led** Page DI•11 • Fluency and Comprehension • **Reread** Independent Reader K.4.1 for Fluency

ELL Place English language learners in the groups that correspond to their reading abilities in English.

Practice Stations
- Visit the Read for Meaning Station
- Visit the Let's Make Art Station

Independent Activities
- Read independently
- Story Sort
- Concept Talk Video

DAY 5 Wrap Up your Week

Assess

- ◎ Read words with /h/.
- Read high-frequency words.
- Read sentences.

Assessment
Monitor Progress

/h/ Spelled *Hh*

Whole Class Divide a paper into four equal sections for each child. Have children draw something that begins with /h/ in each box. Then have them label the pictures with the word or the letter *h*.

MONITOR PROGRESS — **Check Word and Sentence Reading**

If... children cannot complete the whole-class assessment,
then... use the Reteach lesson in *First Stop.*

If... you are unsure of a child's grasp of this week's skills,
then... use the assessment below to obtain a clearer evaluation of the child's progress.

/h/ Spelled *Hh* and high-frequency words

One-on-One To facilitate individual progress monitoring, assess some children on Day 4 and the rest on Day 5. While individual children are being assessed, the rest of the class can reread this week's books and look for words that begin with /h/.

Word reading

Use the word lists on reproducible p. 93 to assess a child's ability to read words that begin with /h/ and high-frequency words. We're going to read some words. I'll read the first word, and you read the rest. The first word is *hip,* /h/ /i/ /p/. For each child, record any decoding problems.

Sentence reading

Use the sentences on reproducible p. 93 to assess a child's ability to read words in sentences. Have the child read two sentences aloud. Have each child read different sentences. Start over with sentence one if necessary.

Record scores

Monitor children's accuracy by recording their scores using the Word and Sentence Reading Chart for this unit in *First Stop*.

Name ____________________

Read the Words

hip	☐	ham	☐
hot	☐	that	☐
hop	☐	hid	☐
had	☐	hit	☐
are	☐	do	☐
hat	☐	him	☐

Read the Sentences

1. Hap can see that dot.
2. Are you hot?
3. That man is Hal.
4. We are with him.
5. Do not hit the cab.

Note to Teacher: Children read each word. Children read two sentences.

Scoring for Read the Words: Score 1 point for each correct word.

/h/*Hh* (*hip, hot, hop, had, hat, ham, hid, hit, him*) ______ / 9

High-Frequency Words (*are, that, do*) ______ / 3

MONITOR PROGRESS
- /h/*Hh*
- High-frequency words

Objectives

- Recognize a lullaby.
- Identify rhythm in a lullaby.

My Skills Buddy, pp. 30–31

Let's Practice It!
Lullaby

Teach

Tell children that today they will hear a lullaby. A lullaby is a kind of poem or soft song that is used to put children to sleep. Review the features of a lullaby with children.

- A lullaby is a soft song or poem.
- A lullaby has rhythm. Rhythm is a strong beat found in songs and poems.
- A lullaby repeats a line or phrase.
- Babies or children are often mentioned as characters in a lullaby.

Have children turn to pp. 30–31 of *My Skills Buddy*. I am going to read you a lullaby called "The Evening Is Coming." Look at the picture as I read. Read the text of "The Evening Is Coming." As you read, direct children to look at the appropriate part of the picture.

Guide practice

Discuss the features of a lullaby with children and the bulleted text on *My Skills Buddy,* p. 30.

- A lullaby is a soft song or poem. Does this lullaby sound like a song or poem? (Yes, it rhymes like a poem and has rhythm like a poem. It has soft words like a song.)
- A lullaby has rhythm. Rhythm is a strong beat found in songs and poems. Listen to the rhythm in "The Evening Is Coming" as I read and tap your feet to the beat. Reread the lullaby, tapping to the beat. Then read the lullaby again and have children tap with you to the rhythm.
- A lullaby repeats a line or phrase. What line or phrase is repeated in the lullaby? ("It's time little children were going to bed.")
- Aside from the animals, what characters are in this lullaby and in other lullabies?

Differentiated Instruction

Strategic Intervention

Support Genre Discuss poems and rhymes children are familiar with. Have them note how a lullaby is like a poem or rhyme. Have them tell why they think people use lullabies to put children to sleep.

Academic Vocabulary

lullaby a soft song or poem used to put babies to sleep

rhythm a strong beat found in songs and poems.

The Evening Is Coming

The evening is coming.
The sun sinks in to rest.
The birds are all flying
Straight home to their nests.
"Caw, caw," says the crow
As it flies overhead.
It's time little children
Were going to bed.

Here comes the pony.
Its work is all done.
Down through the meadow
It has a good run.
Up go its heels,
And down goes its head.
It's time little children
Were going to bed.

Objectives

◎ Review sequence.

Assess

◉ Identify sequence.

Comprehension Assessment

Monitor Progress

Review ◉ **Sequence** In most stories, things happen in a certain order. Something happens first, next, and last. This order of events in a story is called sequence. Good readers pay attention to the sequence in the story to help them understand what is happening.

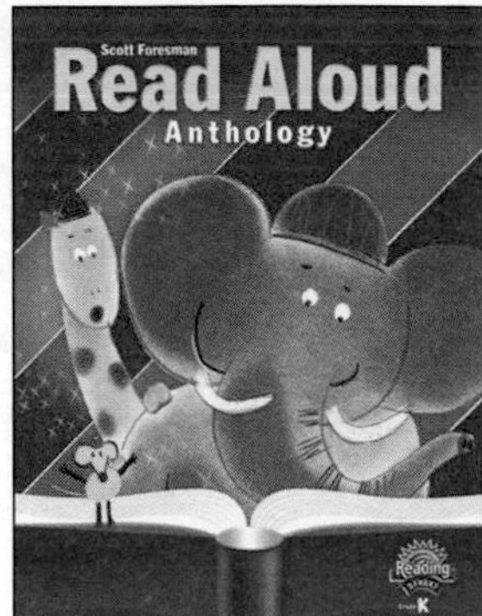

Read Aloud Anthology

Read "A Day Like Every Other Day" Tell children that you are going to read them a story called "A Day Like Every Other Day." Have them listen to the sequence, or order in which things happen in the story. Listen carefully. After I read, I am going to ask you what happens first, next, and last. Read "A Day Like Every Other Day" on p. 44 of the Read Aloud Anthology.

Check sequence After you read the story, have children tell what happens in the story by answering these questions:

- What does the child do first? (wakes up and gets ready for school)
- What does the child do next? (walks to school with Mom and Dad)
- What does the child do then? (takes the bus with Mom to the bookstore)
- What does the child do last? (goes to bed)

Corrective feedback **If...** children cannot identify the sequence of the story,
then... reteach sequence using the Reteach lesson in *First Stop.*

Assess sequence Use the blackline master found on p. 97. Make one copy for each child. Have children cut out the three scenes and glue them onto another sheet of paper in the correct order.

Name ______________________________

Sequence

Put these events from "A Day Like Every Other Day" in order.

Note to Teacher: Have children cut out the scenes and glue them in the correct order onto another sheet of paper.

MONITOR PROGRESS

• Sequence

DAY 5 Wrap Up your Week

10–15 mins.

Objectives

- Review naming parts.
- Dictate or write a list.

Conventions
Naming Parts

Review Remind children of what they learned about naming parts. Naming parts tell who or what a sentence is about.

Model Have AlphaBuddy clap his hands. Who is clapping his hands? AlphaBuddy is clapping his hands. Write this sentence on the board:

AlphaBuddy claps his hands.

AlphaBuddy is the naming part of the sentence. He is who the sentence is about.

Guide practice One at a time, have children stand and do various actions, such as laugh, sing, jump, or hop. Have the class say a complete sentence using the child's name and telling the action. Point out that the child's name is the naming part of the sentence. It tells who or what the sentence is about.

On their own Have children draw a picture of themselves doing an action. Have them write or dictate a sentence about the action and circle the naming part.

Daily Fix-It Use the Daily Fix-It exercise for more conventions practice.

Writing
This Week We...

Review Display *Rooster's Off to See the World,* Sing With Me Chart 19B, Phonics Songs and Rhymes Chart 19, Decodable Reader 19 from *My Skills Buddy,* Kindergarten Student Reader K.4.1, and Get Set, Roll! Reader 19. This week we learned about things we can learn from an adventure. We read new books, and we sang new songs. Which book or song was your favorite? Let's share our ideas with each other.

Team Talk Pair children and have them take turns telling which book or song was their favorite and why.

Model writing a list Today we will write a list of the adventures we took through our songs and stories this week. The rooster and his new friends have an adventure while walking to see the world. I will write *walking to see the world* on the list.

Adventures

1. walking to see the world

Guide practice Continue the list with children. Then read through the list and have children act out the action words.

Adventures

1. walking to see the world	**4. watching a baseball game**
2. driving on a special trip	**5. playing in the park**
3. hiking home to an anthill	**6. driving with Payload Pete**

On their own Have children write or dictate a sentence by adding a naming part to one of the items on the list.

Daily Handwriting

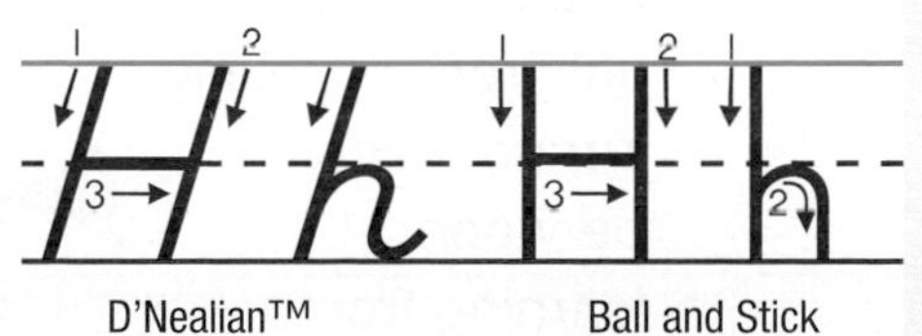

Write uppercase *H* and lowercase *h* on the board. Review correct letter formation with children.

Have children write a row each of uppercase *H* and lowercase *h* on their Write-On Boards. Remind them to use proper left-to-right and top-to-bottom progression.

Differentiated Instruction

SI Strategic Intervention

Support Writing Have children discuss what they read about learning from an adventure this week. Have them share their sentences and pictures with the class.

Daily Fix-It

they are little bears

They are little bears.

This week's practice sentences appear on Teacher Resources DVD-ROM.

English Language Learners

Poster Preview Prepare children for next week by using Week 2 ELL Poster number 20. Read the Poster Talk-Through to introduce the concept and vocabulary. Ask children to identify and describe objects and actions they see.

Objectives

- Review weekly concept.
- Review sequence.

Wrap Up Your Week!

Question of the Week

What can we learn from our adventures?

Amazing Words

You've learned 006 words this week!

You've learned 111 words this year!

Illustrate sequence

This week we talked about things we can learn from an adventure.

- Make a sequence chart like the one below or use Graphic Organizer 21 and fill it with children's responses about *Rooster's Off to See the World*.
- Have children draw three events from the story.
- Help children arrange their pictures to show the order of story events.

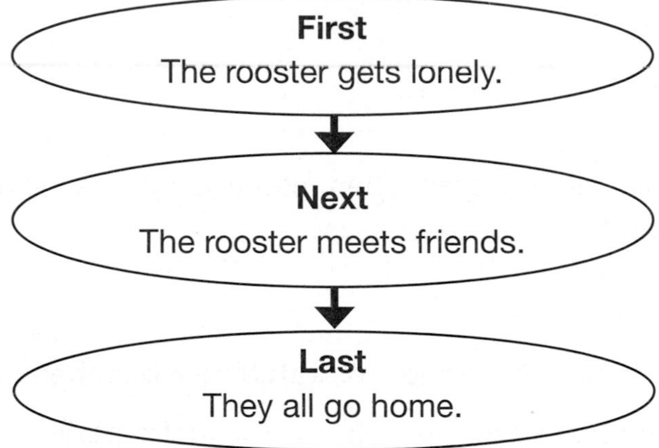

Next Week's Question

What is a lucky adventure?

Discuss next week's question. Guide children in making connections between learning from adventures and having a lucky adventure.

Science
Adventure Underwater

Materials: books or magazines with underwater scenes, paper, pencils, crayons or markers

Thinking About Adventures Remind children that in *Rooster's Off to See the World,* most of the characters that joined Rooster on his adventures spend all or some of their time in water. Have them speculate what it would be like to take an adventure underwater and what things they might learn or discover. Have them view pictures of what the world looks like underwater to aid the discussion.

Write Sentences Have children think of one thing they might learn in an underwater adventure. Have them draw a picture of an underwater scene and write or dictate a sentence about it.

Time for Math
Graphing

Materials: Big Book *Rooster's Off to See the World;* Decodable Reader 19, *Hob Can Hit;* Kindergarten Student Reader K.4.1, *A Day to Play;* Get Set, Roll! Reader 19, *Hot!*

Recall and Graph Favorite Stories Display each book. I am going to hold up each book again. I want you to stand up when I hold up your favorite book from this week.

Prepare a graph with the title of each book at the bottom. Count the children standing and record the results for each book.

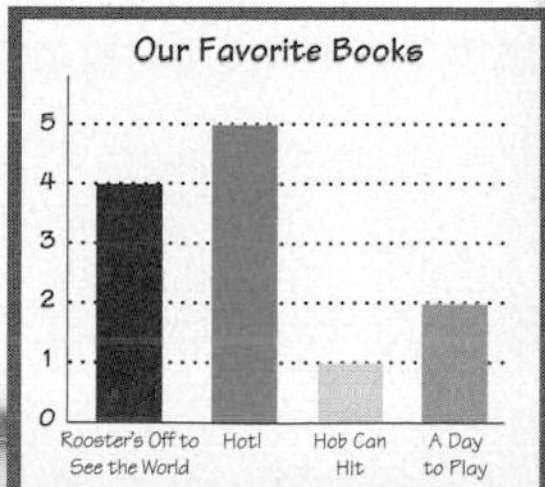

Comprehension
Listen for Sequence

Act Out a Song Have children learn the words and actions for the song "The Hokey Pokey." Have them sing it with you. First, have children use their foot.

What do we do first with our foot? (We put our foot in.)

What do we do next? (We take our foot out.)

What do we do then? (We put our foot back in and shake it all about.)

What do we do last? (We turn ourselves around.)

DAY 5 Assessment Checkpoints for the Week

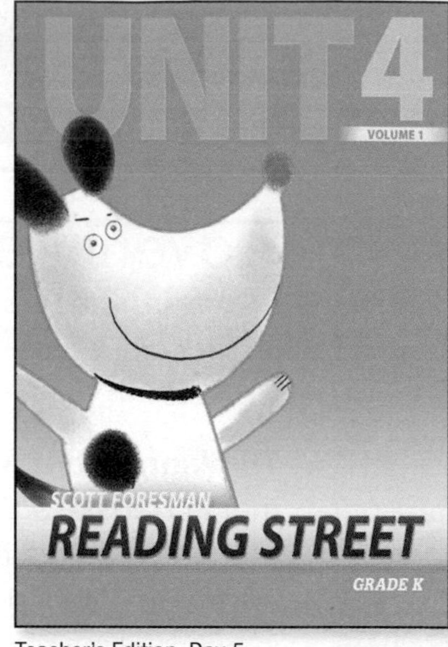

Teacher's Edition, Day 5

Weekly Assessment

Use the whole-class assessment on pages 92–93 and 96–97 in this Teacher's Edition to check:

- ✔ **/h/ Spelled *Hh***
- ✔ **Comprehension Skill** *Sequence*
- ✔ **High-Frequency Words** *are* *that* *do*

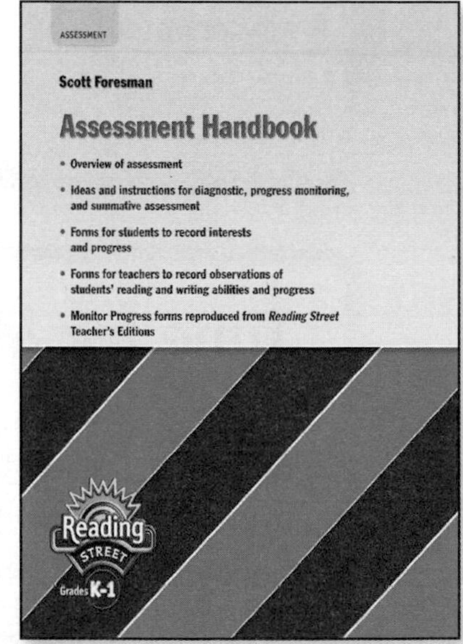

Assessment Handbook

Managing Assessment

Use the Assessment Handbook for:

- ✔ **Observation Checklists**
- ✔ **Record-Keeping Forms**
- ✔ **Portfolio Assessment**

Teacher Notes

Pacing Small Group Instruction

5 Day Plan

DAY 1	• Phonemic Awareness/ Phonics • Decodable Story 19
DAY 2	• Phonemic Awareness/ Phonics • Decodable Reader 19
DAY 3	• Phonemic Awareness/ Phonics • Concept Literacy Reader K.4.1 or Kindergarten Student Reader K.4.1
DAY 4	• Phonemic Awareness/ Phonics • Get Set, Roll! Reader 19
DAY 5	• Phonics Review • Listen to Me Reader K.4.1

3 or 4 Day Plan

DAY 1	• Phonemic Awareness/ Phonics • Decodable Story 19
DAY 2	• Phonemic Awareness/ Phonics • Decodable Reader 19
DAY 3	• Phonemic Awareness/ Phonics • Concept Literacy Reader K.4.1 or Kindergarten Student Reader K.4.1
DAY 4	• Phonemic Awareness/ Phonics • Get Set, Roll! Reader 19

3 Day Plan: Eliminate the shaded box.

SI Strategic Intervention

DAY 1

Phonemic Awareness • Phonics

- **Isolate /h/** Display the *hammer* Picture Card. This is a *hammer*. *Hammer* begins with /h/. Say it with me: /h/ /h/ /h/, *hammer*. Repeat with the *hat, hen,* and *hose* Picture Cards.
- **Connect /h/ to *Hh*** Write *Hh* on the board. This is uppercase *H* and lowercase *h.* /h/ is spelled *Hh.* Say /h/ with me: /h/ /h/ /h/. I am going to say three words. I want you to tell me which word begins with /h/. Listen carefully: *cabin, house, room.* Which word begins with /h/? *House* begins with /h/. *Cabin* and *room* do not begin with /h/. What letter does *house* begin with? Continue the routine with the following sets of words: *half, quarter, dollar; sad, happy, mad; cold, hot, warm*.

Decodable Story 19

- **Review** Review the high-frequency words *I, have, a, the, is, little, that, my, me, do, you, with,* and *like.* Write each word on the board and have children read the word with you.

  If... children have difficulty reading the words,
  then... say a word and have children point to the word. Repeat several times, giving assistance as needed.

- **Read** Have children read the story orally. Then have them reread the story several times individually.

Reader's and Writer's Notebook, pp. 243–244

Objectives
- Isolate the initial sound in spoken one-syllable words.
- Identify the common sounds that letters represent.
- Read at least 25 high-frequency words from a commonly used list.

DAY 2

Phonemic Awareness • Phonics

- **Discriminate /h/** Display Phonics Songs and Rhymes Chart 19. Sing the song "We're Hiking Home" to the tune of "The Ants Go Marching" with children. Tell children to hop when they hear an /h/ word. Then have children identify the *h* words on the chart. After children identify the word, say the word aloud. Ask children to identify the beginning sound of the word and the letter that spells that sound.

Decodable Reader 19

- **Review** Review the high-frequency words by writing *that* on the board. This is the word *that*. What word is this? Continue with the following words: *is, do, see, a they, are.*

  If... children have difficulty reading the words,
  then... say a word and have children point to the word. Repeat several times, giving assistance as needed.

- **Read** Display the cover of *Hob Can Hit* on p. 18 of *My Skills Buddy.* Ask a volunteer to read the first page of the story. Have children identify the child in each picture and what he or she is doing. Continue through the story in this manner.

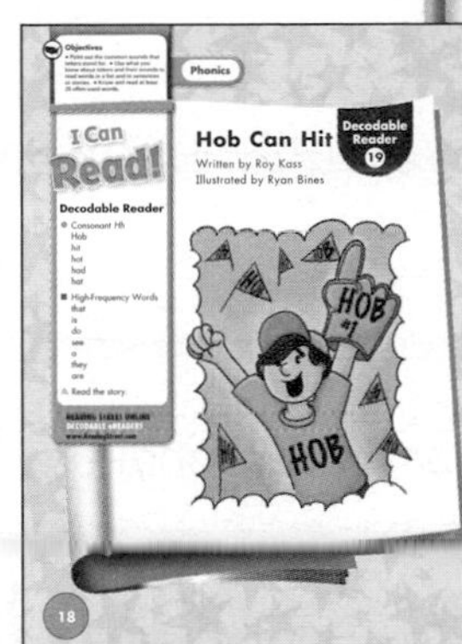

My Skills Buddy

More Reading

Use Leveled Readers or other text at children's instructional level.

Objectives

- Identify the common sounds that letters represent.
- Read at least 25 high-frequency words from a commonly used list.
- Retell a main event from a story read aloud.

Phonemic Awareness • Phonics

- **Isolate /h/** Display the *hat* Picture Card. This is a *hat*. What sound does *hat* begin with? *Hat* begins with /h/. Continue with the *hen* and *hose* Picture Cards.
- **Connect /h/ to *Hh*** Write *Hh* on the board. These are the letters *Hh*. When I see *Hh*, I know I will say /h/. Write the word *hand* on the board and point to your own hand. This is my hand. *Hand* begins with /h/. Say it with me: /h/ /h/ /h/, *hand*. Demonstrate for children how to wave their hands above their heads. When you hear a word that begins with /h/, wave your hands high in the air. Use the following words: *host, most, nose, hose, pose, house, pan, hot.*
- **Blend Sounds** Write *hat* on the board. Have children blend the sound of each letter to read the word. Repeat the routine with the words *hop* and *hit.*
- **Review High-Frequency Words** Write *are* on the board. Have volunteers say the word and use it in a sentence. Continue with the word *that* and *do.*
- To practice phonics and high-frequency words, have children read Kindergarten Student Reader K.4.1. Use the instruction on pp. 56–57.

For a complete lesson plan and additional practice, see the **Leveled Reader Teaching Guide**.

Concept Literacy Reader K.4.1

- **Preview and Predict** Display the cover of the Concept Literacy Reader K.4.1. Point to the title of the book. The title of the book is *What Do I See?* What do you think the book is about? Have children tell about the picture and what they think the book might be about.
- **Set a Purpose** We talked about the title of the book. Let's read the book to count things we can see. Have children read the Concept Literacy Reader.
- **Read** Provide corrective feedback as children read the book orally. During reading, ask them if they are able to confirm any of the predictions they made prior to reading.

If... children have difficulty reading the book individually,
then... read a sentence aloud as children point to each word. Then have the group reread the sentences as they continue pointing to the words.

- **Retell** Have children retell the content as you page through the book. Help them identify what the book is about. Also call attention to the number in the text and the number of things in the picture.

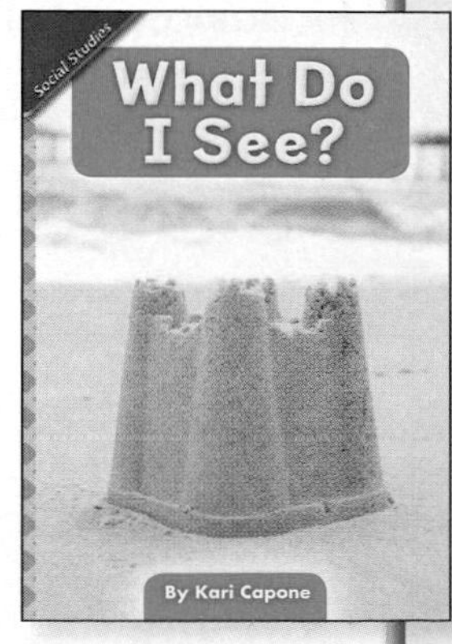

Concept Literacy Reader K.4.1

Objectives

- Identify the common sounds that letters represent.
- Predict what might happen next based on the cover.
- Predict what might happen next based on the title.
- Retell important facts in a text, heard or read.

Phonemic Awareness • Phonics

- **Sing a Song** Write the song on the board. Have children sing the song to the tune of "Mary Had A Little Lamb." Have children sing it with you several times. Then have them hop when they hear an /h/ word. The letter *Hh* makes the /h/ sound. Ask volunteers to find an uppercase *H* and a lowercase *h* in the song and circle the letters.

  Henry Hippo hops to town,
  Hops to town, hops to town.
  Henry Hippo hops to town.
  Hopping with his hard hat on!

- **Segmenting** Say *hit.* I hear three sounds in *hit,* /h/ /i/ /t/. How many sounds do you hear in *had?* What are they? (three, /h/ /a/ /d/) Continue with *hat, hot, hid, hip, hop,* and *kit.*

Get Set, Roll! Reader 19

- **Review** Review the following high-frequency words with children prior to reading the story: *see, are, you, look, do, is, the, I, a, like, that.*

- **Teach Rebus Words** Write the word *button* on the board. This is the word *button.* Who has buttons on their clothes today? Repeat the routine with the word *Pete.* These words are in the story we will read. A picture above the word will help us read it.

- **Read** Display Get Set, Roll! Reader 19, *Hot!* Point to the title of the story. What is the title of the story? *Hot!* is the title of the story. Look at the picture and think about the title. What do you think this story will be about?

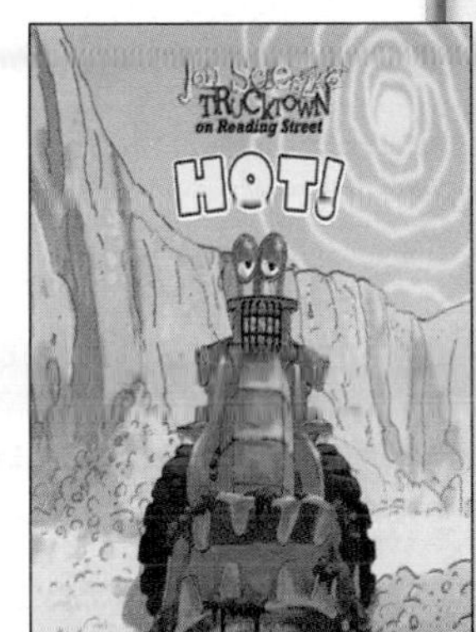

Get Set, Roll! Reader 19

  If... children have difficulty reading the story individually,
  then... read a sentence aloud as children point to each word. Then have the group reread the sentences as they continue pointing to the words.

- **Reread** Use echo reading of Get Set, Roll! Reader 19 to model fluent reading. Use your oral reading to model for children where to pause, when to change pitch, and which words to stress. Then have children reread orally three to four times, or until they can read with few or no mistakes.

Objectives

- Identify the common sounds that letters represent.
- Predict what might happen next based on the title.

More Reading

Use Leveled Readers or other text at children's instructional level.

More Reading

Use Leveled Readers or other text at children's instructional level.

Phonics Review

- **Recognize /h/** Write lowercase *h* on the board. Name the letter. Have children make the letter in the air as you trace the letter. Next, write uppercase *H* on the board. Name the letter as you write it several times. Then give each child three strips of paper to set into the shape of an uppercase *H*.
- **Make an *Hh* Picture** Supply children with construction paper, glue, and a variety of straight objects, such as chenille sticks, uncooked spaghetti, cotton swabs, straws, craft sticks, or twigs. Have children glue the objects onto the construction paper in the shape of an uppercase *H.*

Listen to Me Reader K.4.1

- **Preview and Predict** Display the cover of the book. The title of this story is *Hap.* It is written by Kevin Reese. It is illustrated by Chad Thompson. What kind of animal is Hap? Tell me what Hap looks like.
- **Set a Purpose** Review children's ideas. Point out that after they read, they will know if they predicted correctly. Tell children that you will read the story with them. Follow along with your finger as I read. Then we will take turns reading this page. Repeat this routine through all of the pages. Guide children to decode words.

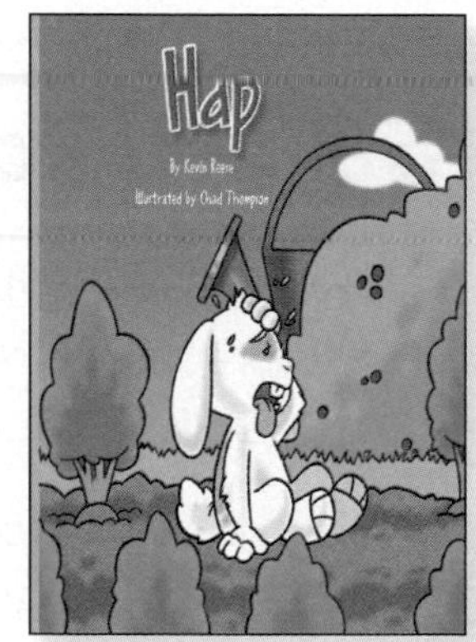

Listen to Me Reader K.4.1

- **Reread for Fluency** Use echo reading of Listen to Me Reader K.4.1 to model reading fluently. Use your oral reading to model for children when to pause, when to change pitch, and which words to stress. Then have children reread orally three to four times, or until they can read with few or no mistakes.

Objectives

- Identify the common sounds that letters represent.
- Predict what might happen next based on the cover.

On-Level

DAY 1

Phonemic Awareness•Phonics

- **Recognize *Hh*** Write the letters *Hh* on the board. What are these letters? When you see these letters, what sound will you say? Ask children to name words that begin with /h/. List the words on the board as children say them. Have children echo read the list of words. Then ask them to take turns circling *h* in the words on the board.

Objectives

- Identify the common sounds that letters represent.

On-Level

DAY 2

Phonemic Awareness•Phonics

- **Listen for /h/** Tell children you will tell them a story and they should listen for /h/. When you say a word that begins with /h/, children should hop and repeat the word. Tell a simple story, emphasizing the initial /h/ words and pausing to give children a chance to hop and repeat the word. *Hope* likes to *hop*. She *hops* all around *her house*. She can *hop high!* She *hops* with *Henry* up the *hill*. She *hops* with *him* down the *hill. Hope hops* and *hops* until she is *hot. Hopping* makes *Hope happy. Hop! Hop! Hop!* Write several sentences from the story on the board. The letter *Hh* stands for the sound /h/. Ask children to circle *H* and *h* in the sentences.
- **High-Frequency Words** Display the following word cards: *that, do, are, of, they, you.* Say the word *that* and select a child to point to the word. Have children say the word and use it in a sentence. Continue with the other words.

Objectives

- Isolate the initial sound in spoken one-syllable words.
- Read at least 25 high-frequency words from a commonly used list.

Pacing Small Group Instruction

20–30 mins.

5 Day Plan

DAY 1	• Phonemic Awareness/ Phonics • Decodable Story 19
DAY 2	• Phonemic Awareness/ Phonics • High-Frequency Words • Decodable Reader 19
DAY 3	• Phonemic Awareness/ Phonics • Kindergarten Student Reader K.4.1
DAY 4	• Get Set, Roll! Reader 19
DAY 5	• Phonics Review • Reread Leveled Books

3 or 4 Day Plan

DAY 1	• Phonemic Awareness/ Phonics • Decodable Story 19
DAY 2	• Phonemic Awareness/ Phonics • High-Frequency Words • Decodable Reader 19
DAY 3	• Phonemic Awareness/ Phonics • Kindergarten Student Reader K.4.1
DAY 4	• Get Set, Roll! Reader 19

3 Day Plan: Eliminate the shaded box.

More Practice

For additional practice with this week's phonics skills, have children reread the Decodable Story (Day 1) and the Decodable Reader (Day 2).

Phonemic Awareness • Phonics

- **Discriminate /h/** Ask six volunteers to draw around the shape of their hands on the board. Collect twelve Picture Cards, including the following *Hh* cards: *hammer, hat, hen, hippopotamus, hose, house*. Mix the cards and display them one at a time. Have a child name the picture. If the name has initial /h/, have the child write a lowercase *h* in one of the handprints.

Kindergarten Student Reader K.4.1

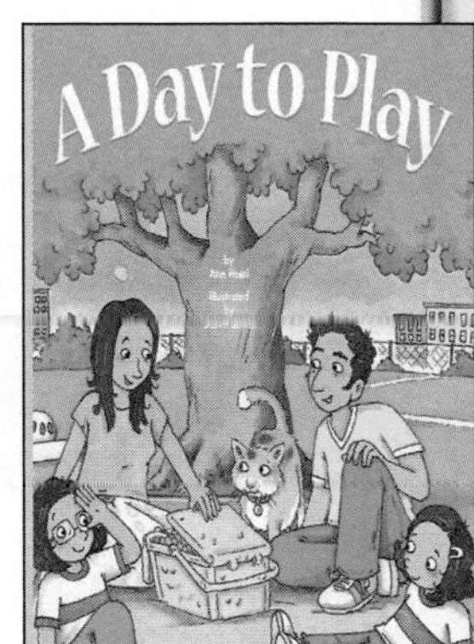

Kindergarten Student Reader K.4.1

- **Preview and Predict** Display the cover of the book. The title of this story is *A Day to Play.* Look at the cover. Where do you think the story takes place? What do you think this story is about? Tell me your ideas.
- **Set a Purpose** Review the list of things children think might happen in the story. Remind children they want to find out what the characters play during the day.
- **Read** Have children follow along as they read the story with you. After reading p. 3, ask children to tell about what Nan and Nat do. Continue with each page. Ask the following questions:
  - What can Nan and Nat do?
  - How do Nan and Nat get hot? What do they do to cool off?
- **Summarize** Have children retell the story to a partner and tell what Nan and Nat do at the end.
- **Text to Self** Help children make personal connections to the story as they tell what they would play.

Objectives

- Identify the common sounds that letters represent.
- Predict what might happen next based on the cover.
- Make connections to own experiences.

On-Level DAY 4

Get Set, Roll! Reader 19

- **Review** Review the words *see, are, you, look, do, is, the, I, a, like,* and *that* by writing each word on the board and saying the word with children. Then give clues to a word and have children tell which word it is.
- **Review Rebus Words** Write *Pete* on the board and read the word with children. This is the name *Pete.* Pete is the name of one of the trucks. What kind of truck is Pete? Continue with the word *button.* Remember, there will be a picture above the words to help us read them.
- **Read** Display Get Set, Roll! Reader 19, *Hot!* Point to the title of the story. What is the title of the story? *Hot!* is the title of the story. Let's read the story together.

Objectives

- Read at least 25 high-frequency words from a commonly used list.

More Reading

Use Leveled Readers or other text at children's instructional level.

On-Level DAY 5

Phonics Review

- **Exercise to the Alphabet** Tell children it is time to try a new exercise routine. Suggest one of the letters *B, H, S,* or *T.* Ask children to think of an activity for that letter, such as *bend, hop, sit,* or *touch your toes.* Once you have chosen an exercise for each letter, call out a letter and help children exercise to the alphabet! When you call out a letter, have children say the word for the letter and then do the exercise.

Objectives

- Identify the common sounds that letters represent.

Pacing Small Group Instruction

20–30 mins.

5 Day Plan

DAY 1	• Phonemic Awareness/ Phonics • Decodable Story 19
DAY 2	• Phonics • Spelling • Decodable Reader 19
DAY 3	• Independent Reader K.4.1 or Kindergarten Student Reader K.4.1
DAY 4	• Get Set, Roll! Reader or Kindergarten Student Reader K.4.1
DAY 5	• Fluency/Comprohoncion • Independent Reader K.4.1

3 or 4 Day Plan

DAY 1	• Phonemic Awareness/ Phonics • Decodable Story 19
DAY 2	• Phonics • Spelling • Decodable Reader 19
DAY 3	• Independent Reader K.4.1 or Kindergarten Student Reader K.4.1
DAY 4	• Get Set, Roll! Reader or Kindergarten Student Reader K.4.1

3 Day Plan: Eliminate the shaded box.

More Practice

For additional practice with this week's phonics skills and to develop fluency, have children reread the Decodable Story (Day 1) and the Decodable Reader (Day 2).

A Advanced — DAY 1

Phonemic Awareness • Phonics

- **Words with *Hh*** Display the following Picture Cards in random order: *bat, cat, hat, hen, pen, ten.* Have children name each picture and identify the two words that begin with *Hh.* Then have them find two sets of rhyming words *(hat, bat, cat* and *hen, pen, ten).* Ask volunteers to write the sets on the board. Show children that only the first letter changes to make these rhyming words.

Objectives

- Distinguish orally presented rhyming pairs of words from non-rhyming pairs.
- Isolate the initial sound in spoken one-syllable words.

A Advanced — DAY 2

Phonics • Spelling

- **Connect /h/ to *Hh*** Display the *Hh* Alphabet Card. What sound does *helicopter* begin with? What letter spells that sound?
- **Spell Sounds** Give each child the following letter tiles: *a, h, i, o, p, t.* Listen to the sounds in the word *hat:* /h/ /a/ /t/, *hat.* What is the letter for /h/? It is *h.* Place your *h* tile in front of you. Continue with the remaining sounds.

Let's blend the sounds to read the word: /h/ /a/ /t/, *hat*. Continue the routine with the words *hit* and *hop*.

Objectives

- Identify the common sounds that letters represent.
- Use letter-sound correspondences to spell consonant-vowel-consonant (CVC) words.

Advanced
DAY 3

For a complete lesson plan and additional practice, see the **Leveled Reader Teaching Guide**.

Independent Reader K.4.1

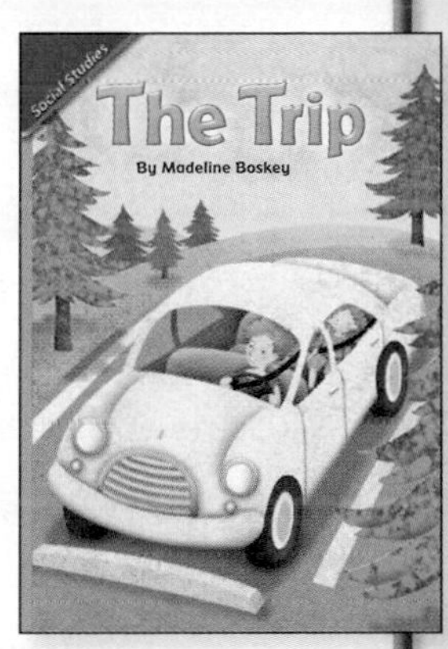

Independent Reader K.4.1

- **Practice High-Frequency Words** Write *do* on the board. Have volunteers say the word and use it in a sentence. Continue with the words *are* and *that.*
- **Activate Prior Knowledge** Remind children that we can explore many things outdoors. Have you ever been hiking? Have you ever been fishing? What things do you like to do outside? What kinds of nature things can you see outdoors? After children discuss exploring nature, have children take turns reading *The Trip* for their group.
- **Sequence** After reading the selection, have children draw a picture that shows where Jen and her mom went first, next, and last.
- **Reread for Fluency** After rereading with children, model reading fluently for them. I am going to read this book aloud. I will read the words with no mistakes. I want you to read it aloud with me. Try to read the words just as I do.
  - 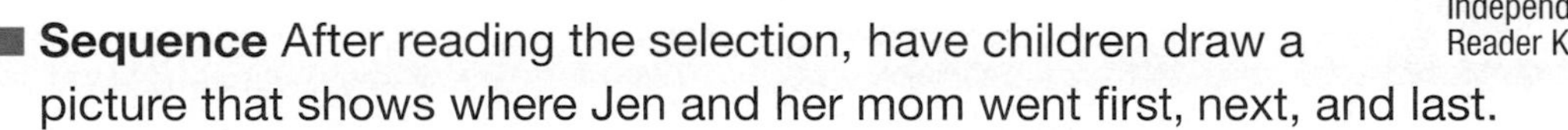Use echo reading of Independent Reader K.4.1 to model reading fluently. Use your oral reading to model for children where to pause, when to change pitch, and which words to stress. Then have children reread orally three to four times, or until they can read with few or no mistakes.
- 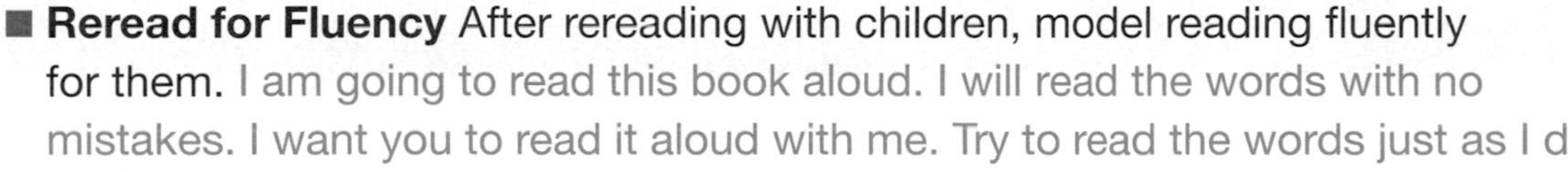For more practice with phonics and high-frequency words and to develop fluency, have children read Kindergarten Student Reader K.4.1. Use the instruction on pp. 56–57.

More Reading

Use Leveled Readers or other text at children's instructional level.

Objectives

- Read at least 25 high-frequency words from a commonly used list.
- Retell a main event from a story read aloud.

More Reading

Use Leveled Readers or other text at children's instructional level.

Kindergarten Student Reader K.4.1

- **Revisit Rebus Words** Write *stand* on the board. This is the word *stand.* The word stand can mean more than one thing, but in this story, it means a place to sell something.
- **Reread** Use Kindergarten Student Reader K.4.1 to practice reading fluently.
- **Text to World** Ask children to think about summer. Nan and Nat get hot because it is summer and the sun is out. Have children draw a picture of what it looks like outside during the summer.
- **Read** Have children read Get Set, Roll! Reader 19, *Hot.* Use the instruction on p. 81.

Kindergarten Student Reader K.4.1

Objectives

- Read at least 25 high-frequency words from a commonly used list.
- Make connections to the larger community.

Fluency•Comprehension

- **Reread for Fluency** Use the Independent Reader K.4.1 to model reading fluently for children. I am going to read this selection aloud. I will read the words with no mistakes. I want you to read it aloud with me. Try to read the words just as I do.
- **Comprehension** After children have finished reading, have them retell what happens in the selection. Then have children write or draw a picture of what happens first and what happens last.

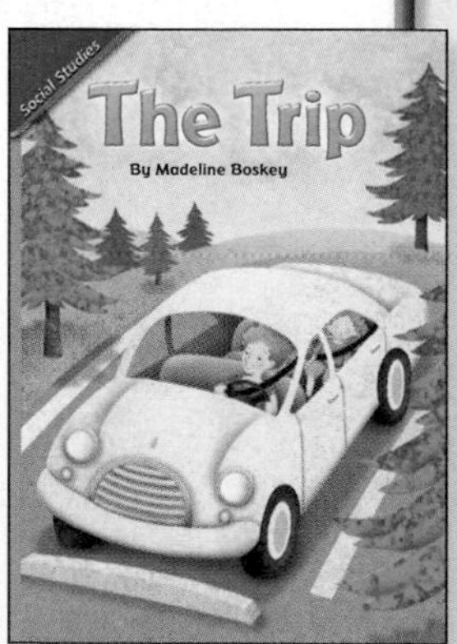

Independent Reader K.4.1

Objectives

- Read at least 25 high-frequency words from a commonly used list.

DAY 1

Concept Development

- **Read the Concept Literacy Reader** To build background and vocabulary, read *What Do I See?* with children. Begin by having children look at the pictures in the book. What things do you see? How many of each are there? Read the book aloud, pausing to discuss each page. Model sentence patterns and vocabulary that describe the objects on the page. This is a pinwheel. It blows in the wind. There is one pinwheel. How many pinwheels are there? On a second reading, invite children to talk about how the number of objects grows on each page.
- **Develop Oral Language** Revisit *What Do I See?,* pointing out that there is a different number of each of the things shown. Then have children sing the following song with you to the tune of "Row, Row, Row Your Boat":

> I can count them off,
> Things seen at the beach.
> There's one pinwheel and two seashells,
> Five clouds are out of reach.

Phonemic Awareness/Phonics

- **Frontload Words with /h/** Have children look at the picture on pp. 12–13 of *My Skills Buddy.* These children are playing in a house. Listen to the word *house.* What sound does *house* begin with? *House* begins with /h/; /h/, *house.* Then use this chant to introduce picture words beginning with /h/. For example: In this picture there is a hat. Who can point to the hat? Have children point to the hat in the picture. *Hat* begins with /h/. /h/ sounds like ha, ha, ha.

  Repeat the exercise with other words in the picture that begin with /h/, including *hanger, helicopter, hamster, hippo, horse, hammer, hand, hair,* and *helmet.*
- **Connect /h/ to *Hh*** Use letter tiles to display the word *ham* or write it on the board. This word is *ham:* /h/ /a/ /m/, *ham.* Say the word with me. Have children write the word *ham* and circle the letter that makes /h/. Write and read aloud the following sentence: *My friend Hannah has a hamster at her house.* Point to the letter *h* in *Hannah* and ask: What letter is this? Yes, this is *h.* Repeat with the *h* in *has, hamster,* and *horse.*

Objectives

• Distinguish sounds of English with increasing ease. • Recognize elements of the English sound system in newly acquired vocabulary. • Learn relationships between sounds and letters of the English language.

Content Objective

- Develop content knowledge related to taking adventures.

Language Objectives

- Understand and use grade-level content area vocabulary.
- Recognize the sounds of English.

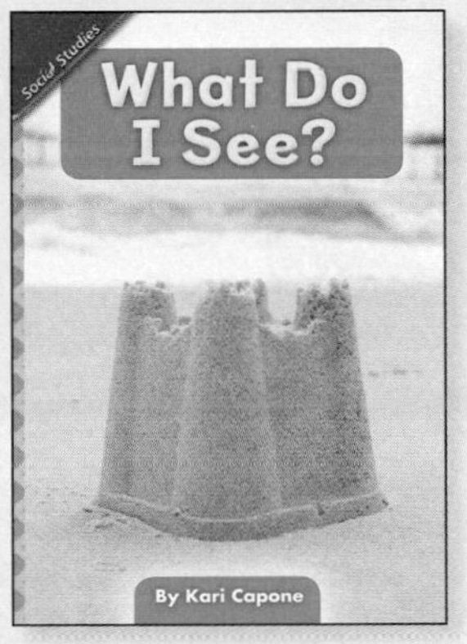

Concept Literacy Reader K.3.1

Daily Planner

DAY 1	• Concept Development • Phonemic Awareness/ Phonics • Listening Comprehension
DAY 2	• Comprehension • Vocabulary
DAY 3	• Phonemic Awareness/ Phonics • Conventions
DAY 4	• Phonemic Awareness/ Phonics • Concepts and Oral Language
DAY 5	• Language Workshop • Writing

Content Objective

- Understand sequence.

Language Objective

- Learn and use academic vocabulary.

My Skills Buddy, pp. 14–15

ELL English Language Learners — DAY 1

Comprehension: Sequence

- **Frontload Vocabulary** Discuss the illustrations on pp. 14–15 in *My Skills Buddy.* Point to the first picture. What do you see? How many eggs are there? Why do you think the momma bird is sitting on the eggs? Point to the middle picture. What do you see here? How many baby birds are there? Where do you think the baby birds came from? Point to the third picture. What do you see here? How can you tell they are leaving? Why do you think they are leaving?
- **Provide Scaffolding** Point to the illustrations on pp. 14–15. Explain what is happening in each illustration. Help children understand that these drawings show events in sequence, or in the order they happen. Point to the first picture. The baby birds are in the eggs. The momma bird is keeping them warm. Point to the middle picture. This happens next. The babies have hatched. They are being fed by their mother. Point to the third picture. This happens last. Now, the babies are old enough to fly away. Support your words with gestures or simple drawings. Tell children that many times sequence is shown from left to right.
- **Prepare for the Read Aloud** The modified Read Aloud below prepares children for listening to the oral reading "Kate Kitten Takes a Walk" on p. 27.

Kate Kitten

Kate is a kitten. She likes to nap after lunch. Today she does not nap. It is very nice outside. She takes a walk.

She meets a bird and a squirrel. They are too busy to walk with Kate. Then she sees a puppy.

"Will you walk with me?" she asks.

The puppy wags his tail. "That sounds like fun!" he says.

Kate and the puppy have a great time on their walk.

- **First Listening: Listen to Understand** Write the title of the Read Aloud on the board. This is about a kitten named Kate. She decides to go for a walk. Listen to find out what she does on her walk. After reading, ask children to recall the animals and the events. Who is too busy to walk with Kate?
- **Second Listening: Listen to Check Understanding** Write the words *bird, squirrel,* and *puppy* on the board. As you listen to the story, think about the animals Kate meets. After reading, ask children to point to the animal that actually walks with Kate. How does the story end?

Objectives

• Understand the main points of spoken language ranging from situations in which topics are familiar to unfamiliar. • Use visual and contextual support to enhance and confirm understanding needed to comprehend increasingly challenging language.

ELL English Language Learners DAY 2

Comprehension

- **Provide Scaffolding** Display *Rooster's Off to See the World*. Lead a detailed picture walk through the story, naming what you see in the illustrations and describing what is happening. Use gestures and facial expressions to convey meaning.
  - **Set the Scene** Use the cover of the Big Book to help children understand that this story takes place on the road leading away from rooster's perch. Describe what the road is like. The road away from rooster's perch has many different animals. There is also a brook that runs along the road. Explain that a brook is like a small river. Have you ever seen a brook? What kind of animals do you think live there?
  - **Frontload Vocabulary** As you lead the picture walk, use the illustrations to introduce unfamiliar words in the text, including words about travel. Look at the picture on page 12. Have you ever taken a trip with a group? Where did you go? Did you like it? Why? Include some of the following words from the story: *travel, lonely* (p. 2); *trip* (p. 5); *wandered* (p. 7); *journey* (p. 20).

Vocabulary: Sequence Words

- **Frontload Vocabulary** Have children turn to p. 28 of *My Skills Buddy.* Talk about what is happening in each picture, using the sequence words *before, after, beginning,* and *end.* For example, point to the before picture. This girl is getting her hair cut. Her hair is long. This is how her hair looks *before* it is cut. Then invite children to talk about the pictures using the sequence words.
- **Provide Scaffolding** Write *before, after, beginning,* and *end* on the board. These words tell us about the order, or sequence. Point to *beginning.* What do you do at the *beginning* of the day? (wake up, eat breakfast, dress) Point to the word *end.* What do you do at the *end* of the day? (brush my teeth, go to bed) Ask more questions with the other sequence words.
- **Practice** Invite four children to the front of the class. Have them stand in a line. Point to the word *beginning* on the board. Who is standing at the beginning of the line? Point to the word *end.* Who is at the end of the line? Ask other sequence questions using the words *before* and *after.*

Objectives

- Use prior experiences to understand meanings in English.
- Speak using learning strategies.
- Learn new basic and academic vocabulary heard during classroom instruction and interactions.

Content Objective

- Develop background knowledge.

Language Objective

- Learn and use sequence words.

Use Learning Strategies

Remind children that if they are having trouble understanding the vocabulary words, they can ask the teacher for help.

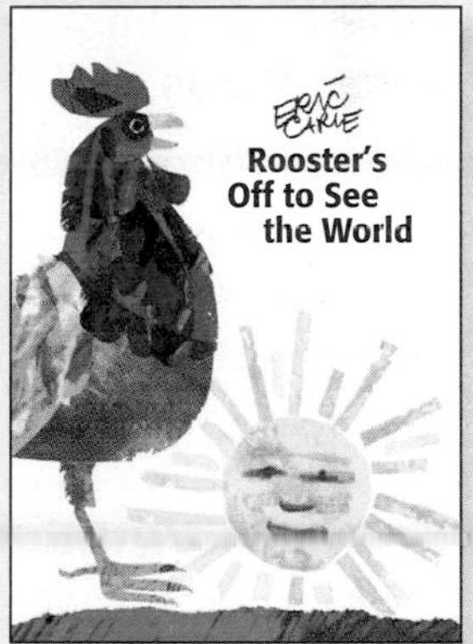

Big Book

Content Objective

- Use learning strategies.

Language Objectives

- Connect /h/ and *Hh.*
- Use naming parts.

Transfer Skills

Pronouncing /h/ Speakers of several languages pronounce /h/ as other sounds, such as /j/ or /kh/. For children who have trouble pronouncing /h/, model making the sound. Show that the mouth, as well as the throat, are open and relaxed. Practice saying /h/ a few times, and then say the words *hot* and *hit.* Have children repeat after you.

Use Learning Strategies

Help children understand that in English, the naming part is usually listed at the beginning of the sentence. In many foreign languages, the naming part is often found in the middle or end of a sentence.

ELL English Language Learners DAY 3

Phonemic Awareness/Phonics

- **Isolate Initial /h/** Say *hot,* and then model segmenting sounds by saying /h/ /o/ /t/. Emphasize the initial sound in the word. Repeat with *had* and *ham.* Help children identify the initial sound in each word.
- **/h/ Spelled *Hh*** Write the words *hat, hip,* and *hop* on the board. As you read them aloud, track the sounds and letters with your fingers. Help children recognize that these words all begin with /h/.

Conventions: Naming Parts

- **Provide Scaffolding** Point to the image on p. 2 of *Rooster's Off to See the World.* A rooster wants to travel. *A rooster* is what the sentence is about. The naming part of the sentence is *a rooster.* It tells what the sentence is about.
- **Practice** What are some other naming parts in this story? Page through the Big Book and have children name different subjects that they see. Make sure they include the article along with the noun, for the complete naming part: *The cats* (p. 5); *the frogs* (p. 7); *The moon* (p. 12); *some fireflies* (p. 13).

Leveled Support

Beginning/Intermediate For each animal naming part, have a child stand up and mimic the sounds or actions of that animal. While the child is acting out the animal, say the naming part aloud, such as *a cat* or *the rooster.* Have children repeat the naming part after you and then make up their own sentences using it. For example, *A cat meows.*

Advanced/Advanced-High Instruct children to make up their own version of the story by replacing some of the naming parts. For example, ask children to change *a rooster* (p. 2) to a different animal. Make sure children change other parts of the story to match the change to the naming parts. For example, if they change the *two cats* (p. 5) to *two dogs,* have them change *purred* to *barked.*

Objectives

- Develop repertoire of learning strategies commensurate with grade-level learning expectations.
- Speak using a variety of grammatical structures with increasing accuracy and ease as more English is acquired.
- Learn relationships between sounds and letters of the English language.

DAY 4

Phonemic Awareness/Phonics

- **Review /o/** To review /o/, ask a question with words that contain initial and medial /o/: Is Bob on the cot? Then remind children that some words have /o/ at the beginning and others have /o/ in the middle. Repeat the question a few words at a time, and have children chorally repeat after you. Listen to these words: *Bob, on, cot.* Which word starts with /o/? Which words have /o/ in the middle?
- **/o/ Spelled *Oo*** Write the letters *Oo.* What letter is this? Yes, this letter is *Oo.* Use word tiles to form these words: *on, or, top, rod, not, pot.* Model reading each word, isolating /o/. Show all the sound-letter correspondences (for example, /t/ /o/ /p/ = *top*).

Concepts and Oral Language

- **Revisit Talk with Me Chart 19A** Display the chart. Have children describe the people or objects in the photos. Use the naming parts such as *the world* and *the boy* when talking about each picture.
- **Develop Oral Language** Introduce language patterns that help describe the pictures on Talk with Me Chart 19A. Use the Amazing Word associated with each picture. This is the *world.* We all live there. What else do we call the world? Then divide the class into small groups. Have groups ask and answer each other's questions about the pictures on the chart. If necessary, help each group develop questions to ask one another. For example, direct students to the second picture on the chart of the *journey:* Where are the people? What do they have with them? Where are they going? Allow groups to discuss their answers.

Beginning/Intermediate Ask questions to help children notice more details about the people and objects in the pictures, such as Does the girl who is homesick look happy or sad? Does the horizon look close or far away?

Advanced/Advanced-High Encourage children to use their own experiences to understand the actions in the pictures. For example, *The boy is lonely. I am lonely when...* or *The class goes on a trip. Our class went on a trip to...*

Objectives

- Ask [for] information ranging from using a very limited bank of high-frequency, high-need, concrete vocabulary, including key words and expressions needed for basic communication in academic and social contexts, to using abstract and content-based vocabulary during extended speaking assignments

Content Objectives

- Develop oral language.
- Use learning strategies.

Language Objectives

- Connect /o/ with *Oo*.
- Learn English language patterns.

Use Learning Strategies

Draw a two-column chart on the board titled *Taking a Trip.* Label one side of the chart *Good* and the other side *Bad.* Help children fill in the chart with good things about taking a trip, such as getting to see new places, and bad things, such as getting homesick.

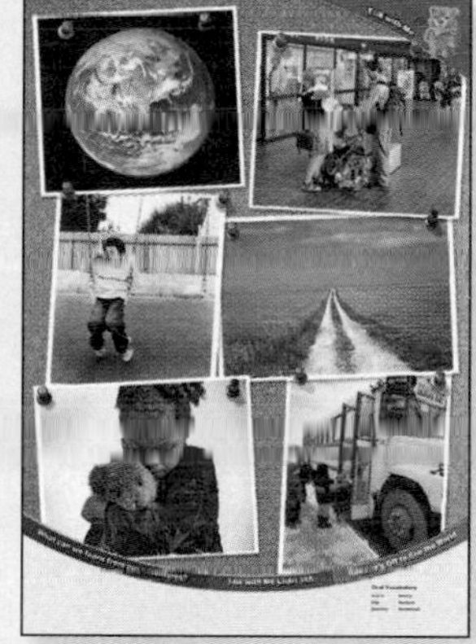

Talk with Me Chart 19A

Content Objectives

- Understand *Rooster's Off to See the World.*
- Practice sequence.

Language Objectives

- Retell a selection through speaking and writing.
- Write using grade-level vocabulary.

Monitor and Self-Correct

Remind children that if they don't know how to say a word, they can ask for help.

Home Language Support

Invite children to share ideas in their home languages before creating their sentences.

ELL English Language Learners — DAY 5

Language Workshop: Retell

- **Introduce and Model** Display pp. 2–3 of *Rooster's Off to See the World.* Look at the rooster in this picture. Do you remember what he wants to do? Ask students questions about the story: How does rooster feel when he's walking all alone? (lonely) What does the rooster do to make the trip more fun? (asks other animals to come along) Explain that by discussing what happens in the story, children are retelling it. It is best to retell a story in sequence, or in the order that it happens.
- **Practice** Organize children into groups to represent the animals in the story. Choose one child to be the rooster. Now we are going to retell the story by acting it out. Tell the "rooster" to walk around the class. In the beginning, the rooster wants to see the world. He soon gets lonely. Then he sees two cats. They join his group. Tell the "cats" to join the rooster and walk around the class. After that, the rooster meets three frogs. . . Continue to retell the story by having all the groups join, and then eventually leave, the rooster.

Writing: Retell

- **Prepare for Writing** We acted out what the animals do in the story. We talked about what the animals do in the story. Now let's write about what the animals do. Have each child fold a piece of paper in half to create two sections.
- **Create Sentences Retelling the Story** Have children copy the sentence starter *On the walk, rooster meets* _____ at the bottom of each section. Have children choose and draw a picture of the animals that rooster meets on the page. Have them complete the sentence frames. When children finish their sentences, have them read their sentences to a partner several times. Have children edit their partner's sentences for spelling and grammar.

Leveled Support

Beginning Provide the sentence frame in each section, and have children dictate or write words to complete the sentences.

Intermediate Guide children in writing words to complete the sentences.

Advanced/Advanced-High Encourage children to write their sentences on their own. You might also have children help less-proficient partners complete their sentences.

Objectives

- Write using content-based grade-level vocabulary.
- Spell familiar English words with increasing accuracy.
- Write using a variety of grade-appropriate sentence lengths in increasingly accurate ways as more English is acquired.

My Lucky Day

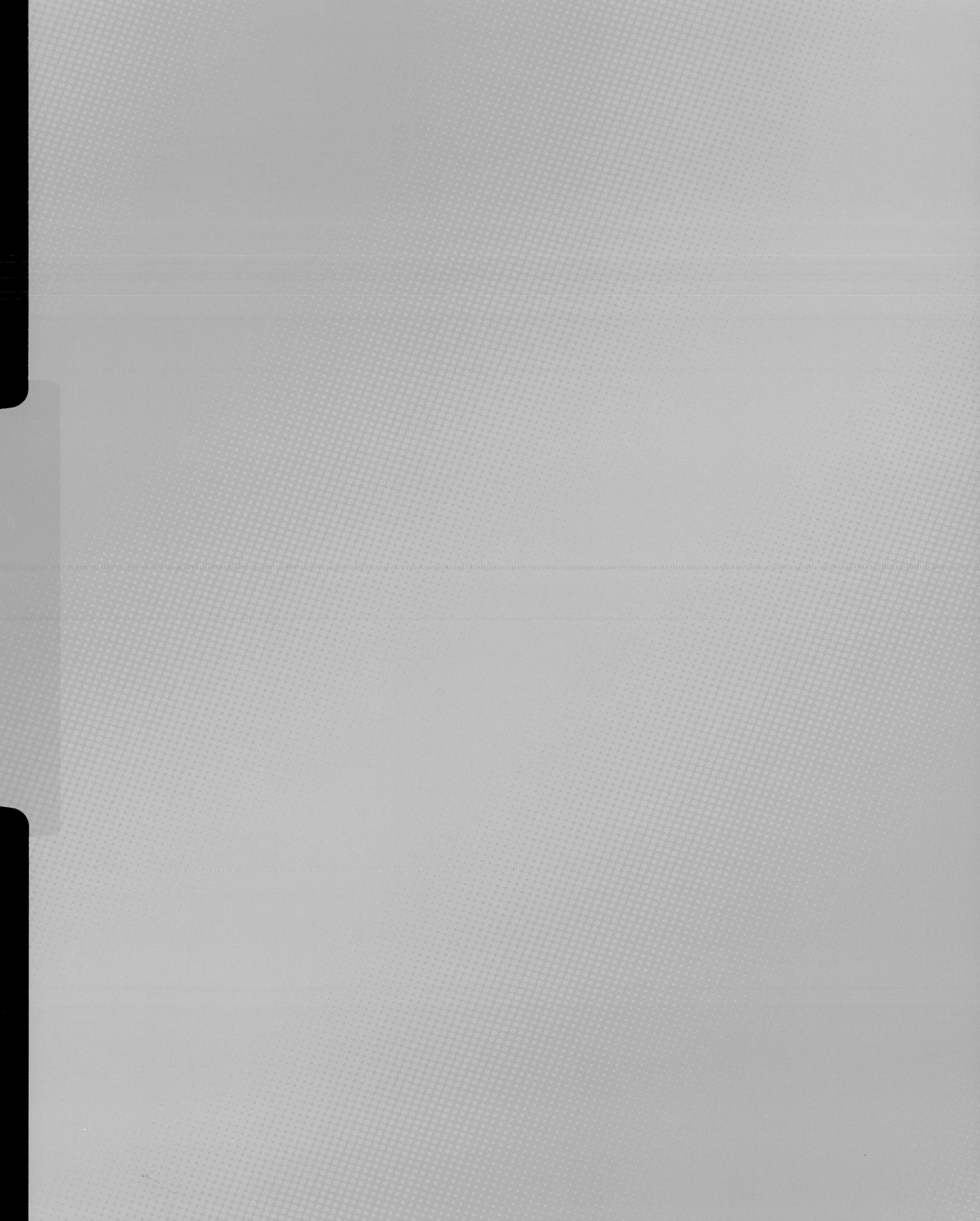

Common Core Standards
Weekly Planning Guide

Grade K • Unit 4 • Week 2
My Lucky Day
112–203

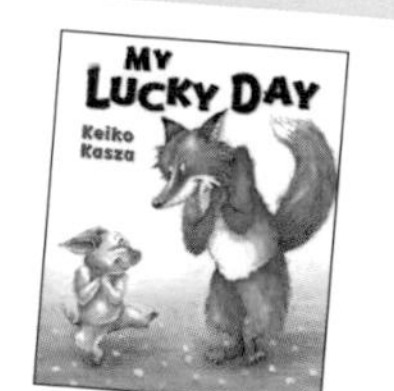

Selection: My Lucky Day
Genre: Animal Fantasy

Alignment of the Common Core Standards with This Week's Skills and Strategies

This Week's Common Core Standards for English Language Arts	Instructional Summary
Reading Standards for Literature	
Literature 1. With prompting and support, ask and answer questions about key details in a text.	The skill of **cause and effect** is taught in this lesson. The lesson explains that a cause is *why* something happens and an effect is *what* happens. The lesson instruction on **predict** and **set a purpose** helps children look at the selection to predict what the selection might be about and to set a purpose to help them understand what they read.
Literature 7. With prompting and support, describe the relationship between illustrations and the story in which they appear (e.g., what moment in a story an illustration depicts).	
Literature 10. Actively engage in group reading activities with purpose and understanding.	
Foundational Skills Standards	
Foundational Skills 1.b. Recognize that spoken words are represented in written language by specific sequences of letters.	Children learn that letters in a specific order make a word and that they can blend the sounds to read the word. The lesson provides **phonics** instruction for listening for /l/ and presents sound-symbol association with the consonant /l/ and the letters *Ll.*
Foundational Skills 2.a. Recognize and produce rhyming words.	
Writing Standards	
Writing 2. Use a combination of drawing, dictating, and writing to compose informative/explanatory texts in which they name what they are writing about and supply some information about the topic.	Writing activities include creating **sentences** about ways we feel. Group activities for writing include a **response** to the literature, a **poem,** and **sentences** about a lucky adventure. The wrap-up activities ask children to write about a favorite adventure they have had.
Writing 8. With guidance and support from adults, recall information from experiences or gather information from provided sources to answer a question.	
Speaking and Listening Standards	
Speaking/Listening 1. Participate in collaborative conversations with diverse partners about *kindergarten topics and texts* with peers and adults in small and larger groups.	Children **compare and contrast** the pig and fox from the selection. The lesson explains that comparing is telling how two things are alike and contrasting is telling how two things are different.
Language Standards	
Language 1.e. Use the most frequently occurring prepositions (e.g., *to, from, in, out, on, off, for, of, by, with*).	*My Skills Buddy,* page 48, introduces **words for textures** *(fuzzy, bumpy, sharp, furry).* Children use the words in sentences. Language skills also concentrate on learning about the **action part** of sentences. Children learn that the action part is the part of a sentence that tells what someone or something is doing.
Language 1.f. Produce and expand complete sentences in shared language activities.	
Language 5.a. Sort common objects into categories (e.g., shapes, foods) to gain a sense of the concepts the categories represent.	

Additional Support for a Common Core Standard This Week

Use the following instruction to supplement the teaching of one of this week's Common Core Standards.

Common Core Standard: Foundational Skills 1.b.
Write the word *cap* on the board. Ask a volunteer to point to the first letter in the word and make the sound the letter stands for. Continue with the other letters.

- Ask children to identify the first letter in the word and show the direction to move to decode the word.
- Have volunteers sound out the word and show how to blend the sounds to make a word.
- Continue with the words *mop, cot, rat, ran, pan, bat, sat,* and *man.*

ISBN-13: 978-0-328-64357-8 ISBN-10: 0-328-64357-2

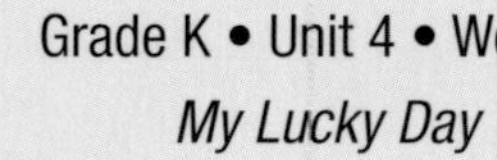

Grade K • Unit 4 • Week 2

My Lucky Day

Unit 4

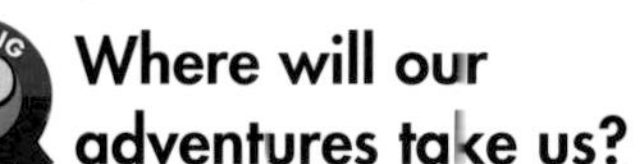

Where will our adventures take us?

Week 1

Rooster's Off to See the World

Question of the Week

What can we learn from our adventures?

Concept Talk Guide children as they discuss questions such as:

- What things does the child see?

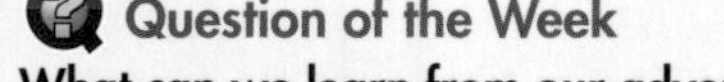

Writing Have children turn to p. 250 of *Reader's and Writer's Notebook*. Explain that the pictures show how the boy gets from his house to the mailbox around the corner. Tell children that they will give the boy directions. Have them write words to tell the boy how to get to the mailbox.

You Are Here: Week 2

My Lucky Day

Question of the Week

What is a lucky adventure?

As children answer this unit's Big Question and this week's Question of the Week, they will address:

Reading 1. Read closely to determine what the text says explicitly and to make logical inferences from it; cite specific textual evidence when writing or speaking to support conclusions drawn from the text.

Concept Talk Guide children as they discuss questions such as:

- Why is the boy lucky? Does he know he is lucky at first? How can you tell?

As children answer this week's Concept Talk questions, they will address:

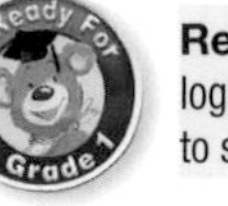

Speaking/Listening 1. Prepare for and participate effectively in a range of conversations and collaborations with diverse partners, building on others' ideas and expressing their own clearly and persuasively.

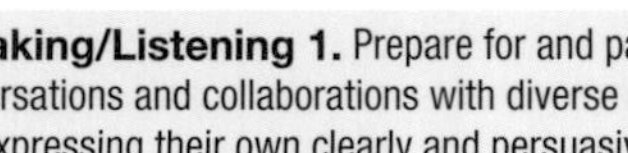

Writing Have children write a class poem on the board. Use the selected topic and one of the suggested rhyming words. Have children copy the class poem on p. 262 of *Reader's and Writer's Notebook*. Then have them draw a picture about the poem.

As children write this week, they will address:

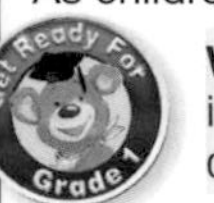

Writing 2. Write informative/explanatory texts to examine and convey complex ideas and information clearly and accurately through the effective selection, organization, and analysis of content.

Listening and Speaking On page 49, children learn how to compare and contrast. By doing so, they address:

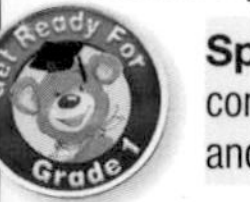

Speaking/Listening 1. Prepare for and participate effectively in a range of conversations and collaborations with diverse partners, building on others' ideas and expressing their own clearly and persuasively.

Common Core Standards and Concept Development

- Introduce and explore this unit's weekly concepts through rich, structured conversations
- Develop complex content knowledge and vocabulary
- Expand on a single concept with engaging literature and nonfiction
- Build better readers in all content areas

Align instruction to **Common Core Anchor Standards**

Week 3

One Little Mouse

Question of the Week

What adventures can animals have?

Concept Talk Guide children as they discuss questions such as:

- What would a small animal's adventure be like?

Writing Have children turn to p. 274 of *Reader's and Writer's Notebook*. Have them draw a picture of the mouse in the selection. Then have children write or dictate a sentence on the line that tells about the mouse.

Week 4

Goldilocks and the Three Bears

Question of the Week

How can an adventure cause trouble?

Concept Talk Guide children as they discuss questions such as:

- Are these real or make-believe bears? What do real bears do? What do make-believe bears do?

Writing Have children turn to p. 286 of *Reader's and Writer's Notebook*. Have them write or dictate a list of things found in *Goldilocks and the Three Bears*.

Week 5

If You Could Go to Antarctica

Question of the Week

What would it be like to have an Antarctic adventure?

Concept Talk Guide children as they discuss questions such as:

- What would you ask the explorer?
- Would you like to be an explorer?

Writing Have children turn to p. 298 of *Reader's and Writer's Notebook*. Have them write or dictate a letter to someone by finishing the sentence that tells what they like to read about. Then have them write their name at the end of the letter.

Week 6

Abuela

Question of the Week

What kind of adventures can you have in the city?

Concept Talk Guide children as they discuss questions such as:

- How do the children feel about their grandmothers? What do they like best about spending time with their grandmothers?

Writing Reread and discuss your list of things to do in the community, underlining key words in your draft. Have children write or dictate the group draft or copy the underlined key words on p. 314 in *Reader's and Writer's Notebook*. Then have them draw pictures to go with their list.

This Week's ELL Overview

Grade K • Unit 4 • Week 2

My Lucky Day

103–204

and DI•29–DI•34

ELL Handbook

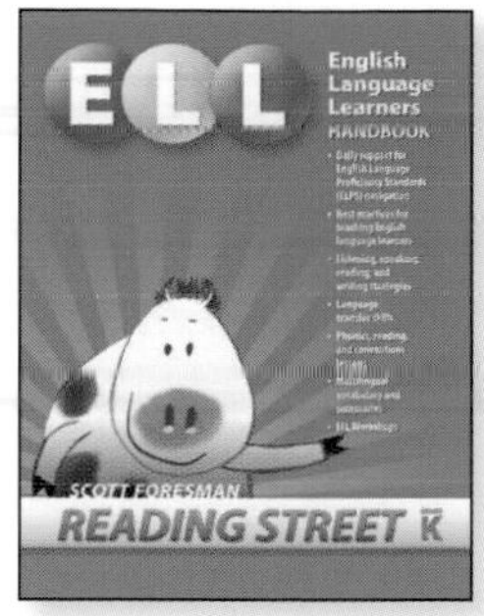

- Maximize Literacy and Cognitive Engagement
- Research Into Practice
- Full Weekly Support for Every Selection

My Lucky Day

- Routines to Support Instruction

- Transfer Activities
- Professional Development

Daily Leveled ELL Notes

ELL notes appear throughout this week's instruction and ELL Support is on the DI pages of your Teacher's Edition. The following is a sample of an ELL note from this week.

English Language Learners

Beginning Listening Comprehension English learners will benefit from additional visual support to understand words from the song. For example, point to the *piglet* and the *fox* in the art to scaffold meaning.

Intermediate Extend Language Explain that when talking about two similar objects, we use *this* to refer to the closer object and *that* to refer to the object that is farther away. Have children practice using the words *this* and *that* to point out objects in the classroom.

Advanced Conventions In English action parts (predicates), verbs are often followed by objects, as in *drank the water.* Korean- and Hindi-speaking children, however, may place the verb at the end of the sentence. Provide opportunities for children to practice building English sentences.

Advanced High Language Transfer Display pictures of a fox and a piglet. Say the animal names aloud and have children repeat. Then have them share the words for *fox* and *piglet* in their native languages. Note any similarities between the English and non-English words.

ELL by Strand

The ELL lessons on this week's Support for English Language Learners pages are organized by strand. They offer additional scaffolding for the core curriculum. Leveled support notes on these pages address the different proficiency levels in your class. See pages DI•29–DI•34.

The Three Pillars of ELL Instruction

ELL Strands	Activate Prior Knowledge	Access Content	Extend Language
Vocabulary p. DI•31	Frontload Vocabulary	Provide Scaffolding	Practice
Reading Comprehension p. DI•31	Provide Scaffolding	Set the Scene	Frontload Vocabulary
Phonics, Spelling, and Word Analysis pp. DI•29, DI•32–DI•33	Frontload Words with /l/	Isolate Initial and Final /l/	Review /h/
Listening Comprehension p. DI•30	Prepare for the Read Aloud	First Listening	Second Listening
Conventions and Writing pp. DI•32, DI•34	Provide Scaffolding/ Introduce and Model	Practice	Leveled Practice Activities/ Leveled Writing Activities
Concept Development p. DI•29	Read the Concept Literacy Reader	Read the Concept Literacy Reader	Develop Oral Language

This Week's Practice Stations Overview

Grade K • Unit 4 • Week 2
My Lucky Day
103–204

Six Weekly Practice Stations with Leveled Activities can be found at the beginning of each week of instruction. For this week's Practice Stations, see pp. 110–111.

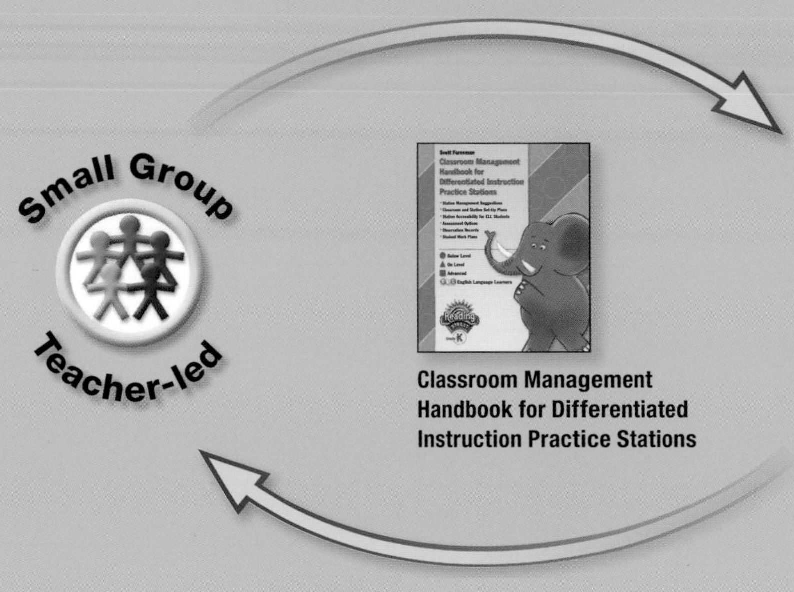

Classroom Management Handbook for Differentiated Instruction Practice Stations

Practice Stations

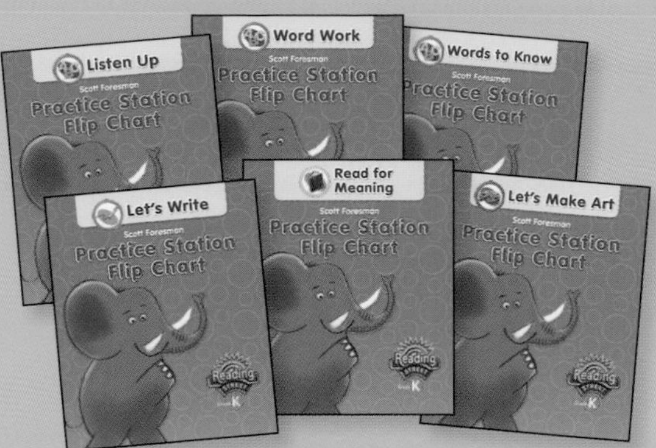

Daily Leveled Center Activities

Below — Advanced

On-Level — 

Practice Stations Flip Charts

	 **Listen Up**	 **Word Work**	 **Words to Know**	 **Let's Write**	 **Read for Meaning**	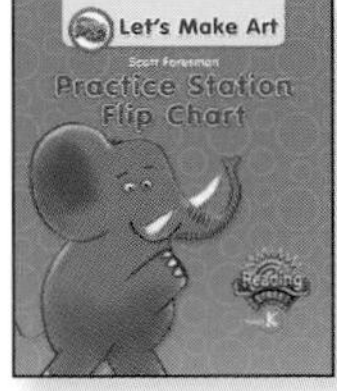 **Let's Make Art**
Objectives	• Identify words with /h/.	• Identify words with /h/ spelled *Hh.*	• Identify and use sequence words.	• Write directions.	• Identify the sequence of events in a story.	• Make a drawing of the story.
Materials	• *Listen Up* Flip Chart Activity 20 • Picture Cards: *hammer, hat, hose, kite, taxi, vest* • paper, crayons	• *Word Work* Flip Chart Activity 20 • Alphabet Card: *Hh* • Picture Cards: *bus, garden, hen, hippopotamus, house, soap* • Letter Tiles	• *Words to Know* Flip Chart Activity 20 • Teacher-made Word Cards: *before, after, beginning, end* • paper, pencils, crayons	• *Let's Write* Flip Chart Activity 20 • Trade Book *My Lucky Day* • crayons, paper, pencil	• *Read for Meaning* Flip Chart Activity 20 • Little Book *Rooster's Off to See the World* • pencil, crayons, paper	• *Let's Make Art* Flip Chart Activity 20 • crayons, paper, pencils

This Week on Reading Street!

Question of the Week

What is a lucky adventure?

Daily Plan

Whole Group
- /l/ spelled *Ll*
- Cause and Effect
- Vocabulary

MONITOR PROGRESS Success Predictor

Day 1	Day 2	Day 3	Day 4	Day 5
Check Phonemic Awareness	Check Sound Spelling/ Retelling	Check Word Reading	Check Phonemic Awareness	Check Oral Vocabulary

Small Group

Teacher-Led
- Reading Support
- Skill Support
- Fluency Practice

Practice Stations

Independent Activities

Customize Literacy More support for a Balanced Literacy approach, see pp. CL•1–CL•31.

Whole Group
- Writing
- Conventions: Action Parts
- Listening and Speaking

Assessment
- Day 5 Assessment for Phonics
- Day 5 Assessment for Comprehension

You Are Here! Unit 4 Week 2

This Week's Reading Selections

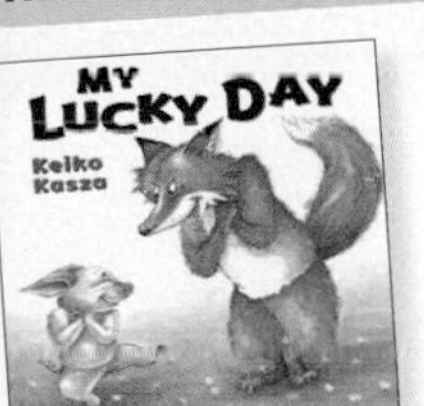

Trade Book
Genre: **Animal Fantasy**

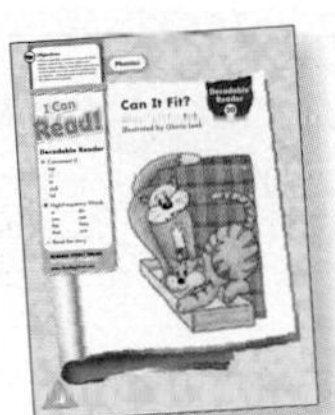
Decodable Reader 20

Leveled Readers

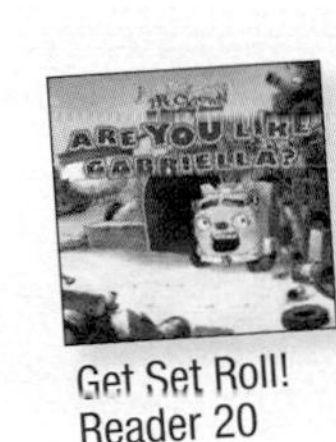
Get Set Roll! Reader 20

Resources on Reading Street!

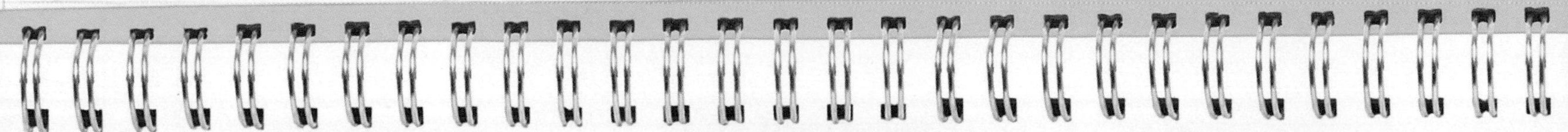

	Build Concepts	Phonemic Awareness and Phonics	Vocabulary
Whole Group	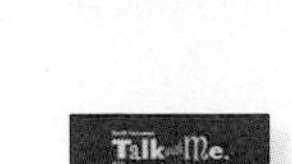 Talk With Me/ Sing With Me	 Student Edition pp. 32–33 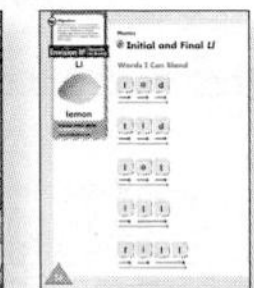 Student Edition p. 36	 Student Edition p. 37 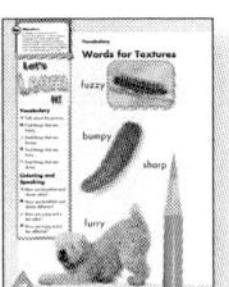 Student Edition p. 48
 Go Digital	 • Concept Talk Video • Sing with Me Animations	• eReaders	
 **Small Group and Independent Practice**	 Practice Station Flip Chart  Leveled Readers	 Practice Station Flip Chart  Decodable Reader 20  Leveled Readers   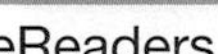 Get Set, Roll! Reader 20	 Practice Station Flip Chart 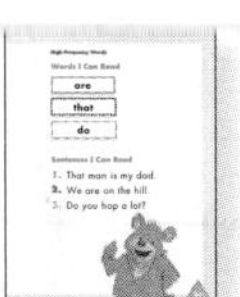 Student Edition p. 37
Go Digital	• eReaders	• eReaders • Letter Tile Drag and Drop	
Customize Literacy	• Leveled Readers	• Decodable Reader	• High-Frequency Word Cards
 Go Digital	• Concept Talk Video • Big Question Video • eReaders	• eReaders	• Sing with Me Animations

Question of the Week

What is a lucky adventure?

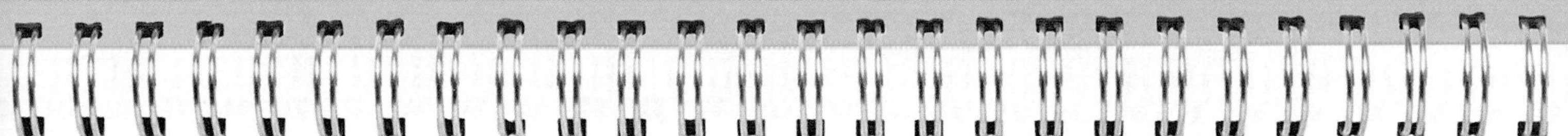

Comprehension	Fluency	Conventions and Writing
 Student Edition pp. 34–35 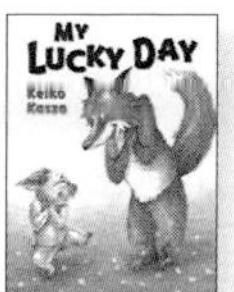 Trade Book	Decodable Reader 20  Kdg. Student Reader K.4.2  Get Set, Roll! Reader 20	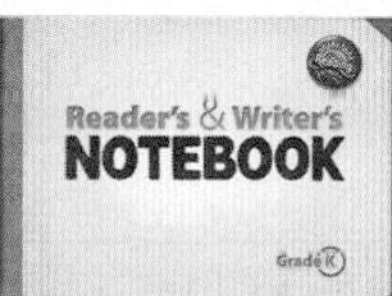 Reader's and Writer's Notebook
• Envision It! Animations	• eReaders	• Grammar Jammer
 Practice Station Flip Chart  Leveled Readers 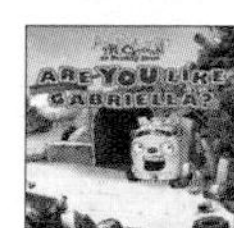 Get Set, Roll! Reader 20	 Practice Station Flip Chart  Leveled Readers	 Practice Station Flip Chart 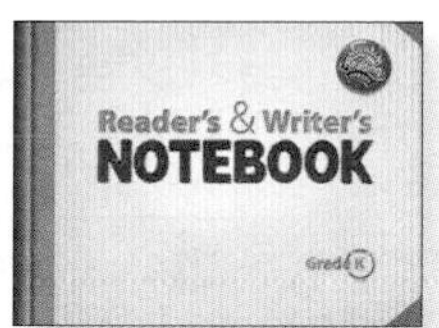 Reader's and Writer's Notebook
• Envision It! Animations • eReaders	• eReaders	• Grammar Jammer
• Leveled Readers	• Leveled Readers	• *Reader's and Writer's Notebook*
• Envision It! Animations • eReaders	• eReaders	• Grammar Jammer

Week 2

My 5-Day Planner for Reading Street!

Don't Wait Until Friday MONITOR PROGRESS	Check Phonemic Awareness **Day 1** pages 112–127	Check Sound-Spelling Check Retelling **Day 2** pages 128–145
Get Ready to Read	**Concept Talk,** 112 **Oral Vocabulary,** 113 *piglet, fox, lucky, filthy, cook, scrubber* **Phonemic Awareness,** 114–115 ◉ Initial /l/ **Phonics,** 116–117 ◉ /l/ Spelled *Ll* **Handwriting,** 118 Letters *L* and *l* **High-Frequency Words,** 119 *are, that, do* **READ Decodable Story** 20, 120–121	**Concept Talk,** 128 **Oral Vocabulary,** 129 *piglet, fox* **Phonemic Awareness,** 130–131 ◉ Final /l/ **Phonics,** 132–133 ◉ /l/ Spelled *Ll* **Handwriting,** 134 Words with *Ll* **High-Frequency Words,** 135 *are, that, do* **READ Decodable Reader 20,** 136–137
Read and Comprehend	**Listening Comprehension,** 122–123 ◉ Cause and Effect	**Listening Comprehension,** 138 ◉ Cause and Effect **READ Trade Book—First Read,** 138 My Lucky Day **Retell,** 139 **Think, Talk, and Write,** 140
Language Arts	**Conventions,** 124 Action Parts **Writing,** 125 Wonderful, Marvelous Me! **Daily Handwriting,** 125 Letters *L* and *l* **Listening and Speaking,** 126 Compare and Contrast **Wrap Up Your Day,** 126 **Extend Your Day!,** 127	**Conventions,** 141 Action Parts **Writing,** 142 Respond to Literature **Daily Handwriting,** 142 Letters *L* and *l* **Vocabulary,** 143 Words for Textures **Wrap Up Your Day,** 144 **Extend Your Day!,** 145

You Are Here! Unit 4 Week 2

Question of the Week

What is a lucky adventure?

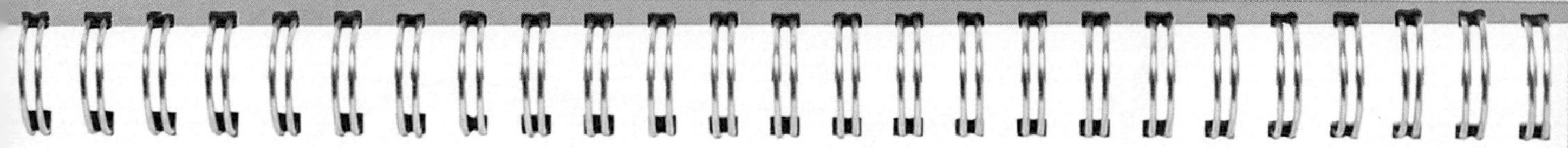

Check Word Reading	Check Phonemic Awareness	Check Oral Vocabulary
Day 3 pages 146–177	**Day 4** pages 178–189	**Day 5** pages 190–203
Concept Talk, 146 **Oral Vocabulary,** 147 *lucky, filthy* **Phonemic Awareness,** 148–149 ◉ Initial and Final /l/ **Phonics,** 150–151 ◉ /l/ Spelled *Ll* **READ Kindergarten Student Reader K.4.2,** 152–153	**Concept Talk,** 178 **Oral Vocabulary,** 179 *cook, scrubber* **Review Phonemic Awareness,** 180 /h/ **Review Phonics,** 181 /h/ Spelled *Hh* **Spelling,** 182 ◉ /l/ Spelled *Ll* **READ Get Set, Roll! Reader 20,** 183	**Concept Wrap Up,** 190 **Oral Vocabulary,** 191 *piglet, fox, lucky, filthy, cook, scrubber* **Review Phonemic Awareness,** 192 ◉ /l/ **Review Phonics,** 193 ◉ /l/ Spelled *Ll* **Assessment,** 194–195 Monitor Progress
Comprehension, 154 ◉ Cause and Effect **READ Trade Book—Second Read,** 155–171 My Lucky Day	**Comprehension,** 184 ◉ Cause and Effect **Review** Plot **READ Trade Book—Third Read,** 185 My Lucky Day	**Let's Practice It!,** 196–197 Fable **Assessment,** 198–199 Monitor Progress
Conventions, 172 Naming Parts **Writing,** 172 Genre: Poem **Daily Handwriting,** 173 Letters *L* and *l* **Listening and Speaking,** 174–175 Compare and Contrast **Wrap Up Your Day,** 176 **Extend Your Day!,** 177	**Conventions,** 186 Action Parts **Writing,** 187 Extend the Concept **Daily Handwriting,** 187 Letters *L* and *l* **Vocabulary,** 188 Words for Textures **Wrap Up Your Day,** 188 **Extend Your Day!,** 189	**Review Conventions,** 200 Action Parts **Writing,** 201 This Week We… **Daily Handwriting,** 201 Letters *L* and *l* **Wrap Up Your Week!,** 202 What is a lucky adventure? **Extend Your Day!,** 203

Week 2

Grouping Options for Differentiated Instruction
Turn the page for the small group time lesson plan.

Planning Small Group Time on Reading Street!

SMALL GROUP TIME RESOURCES

DAY 1 Look for this Small Group Time box each day to help meet the individual needs of all your children. Differentiated instruction lessons appear on the DI pages at the end of each week.

Teacher-Led

SI Strategic Intervention	OL On-Level	A Advanced
Teacher-Led • Phonemic Awareness and Phonics **Reread** Decodable Story	**Teacher-Led** • Phonemic Awareness and Phonics **Reread** Decodable Story	**Teacher-Led** • Phonemic Awareness and Phonics **Reread** Decodable Story for Fluency

ELL Place English language learners in the groups that correspond to their reading abilities in English.

Practice Stations
- Listen Up
- Word Work

Independent Activities
- Read Independently
- *Reader's and Writer's Notebook*
- Concept Talk Video

ELL

ELL Poster 20

	Day 1
 SI Strategic Intervention	**Phonemic Awareness and Phonics,** DI•18 **Reread** Decodable Story 20, DI•18
OL On-Level	**Phonemic Awareness and Phonics,** DI•23 **Reread** Decodable Story 20, DI•23
 A Advanced	**Phonemic Awareness and Phonics,** DI•26 **Reread** Decodable Story 20 for Fluency, DI•26
ELL English Language Learners	DI•29–DI•30 Frontload Concept Phonemic Awareness and Phonics Comprehension Skill

You Are Here! Unit 4 Week 2

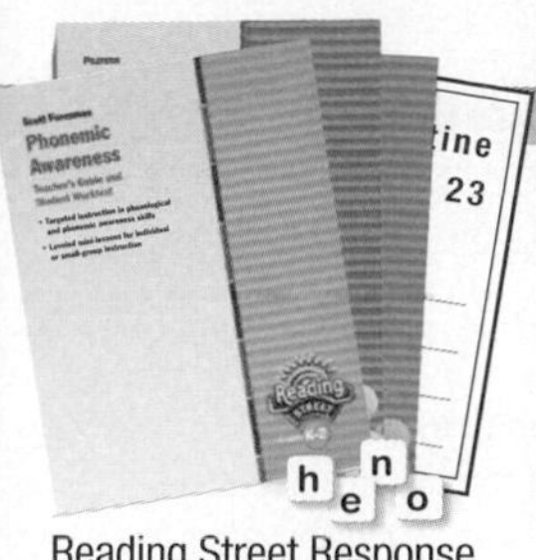
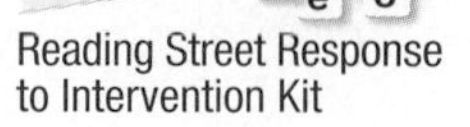

Reading Street Response to Intervention Kit

Reading Street Leveled Practice Stations Kit

Question of the Week
What is a lucky adventure?

Decodable Reader

Listen to Me Reader

Concept Literacy Reader

Get Set, Roll! Reader

Kindergarten Student Reader

Get Set, Roll! Reader

Decodable Reader

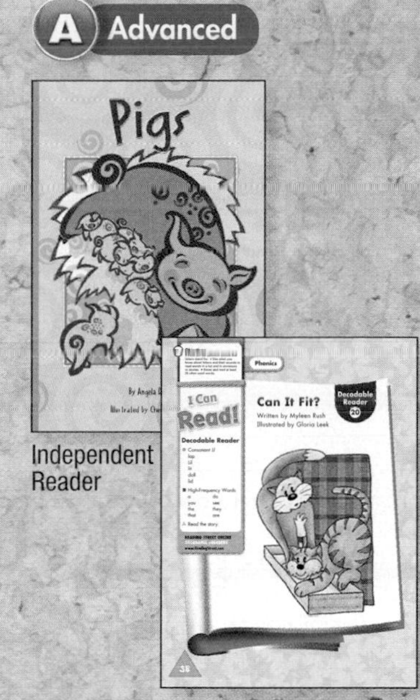

Independent Reader

Decodable Reader

Week 2

Small Group Weekly Plan

Day 2	Day 3	Day 4	Day 5
Phonemic Awareness and Phonics, DI•19 **Reread** Decodable Reader 20, DI•19	**Phonemic Awareness and Phonics,** DI•20 **Read** Concept Literacy Reader K.4.2 or Kindergarten Student Reader K.4.2, DI•20	**Phonemic Awareness and Phonics,** DI•21 **Read** Get Set, Roll! Reader 20, DI•21	**Phonics Review,** DI•22 **Read** Listen to Me Reader K.4.2, DI•22
Phonemic Awareness and Phonics, DI•23 **Reread** Decodable Reader 20, DI•23	**Phonemic Awareness and Phonics,** DI•24 **Read** Kindergarten Student Reader K.4.2, DI•24	Review Phonics and High-Frequency Words **Read** Get Set, Roll! Reader 20, DI•25	**Phonics Review,** DI•25 **Reread** Leveled Books, DI•25
Phonics and Spelling, DI•26 **Reread** Decodable Reader 20 for Fluency, DI•27	**Read** Independent Reader K.4.2 or Kindergarten Student Reader K.4.2, DI•27	**Read** Get Set, Roll! Reader or **Reread** Kindergarten Student Reader K.4.2, DI•28	**Fluency and Comprehension,** DI•28 **Reread** Independent Reader for Fluency, DI•28
DI•31 Comprehension Skill Frontload Vocabulary	DI•32 Review Phonemic Awareness and Phonics Scaffold Conventions	DI•33 Review Phonemic Awareness and Phonics Revisit Concept and Oral Language	DI•34 Language Workshop Writing

Practice Stations for Everyone on Reading Street!

Listen Up!
Words with /h/

Objectives
• Identify words with /h/.

Materials
• *Listen Up!* Flip Chart Activity 20
• Picture Cards: *hammer, hat, hose, kite, taxi, vest*
• paper, crayons

Differentiated Activities
● Find the Picture Card for *hat*. Say the sound you hear at the beginning. Find another Picture Card whose name begins like *hat*.

▲ Find the Picture Card for *hat*. Say the sound you hear at the beginning. Find all the Picture Cards whose names begin like *hat*.

■ Find the Picture Card for *hat*. Find all the Picture Cards whose names begin like *hat*. Look around the room. Find other things whose names begin like *hat*. Draw a picture of something that has the same beginning sound as hat.

Word Work
/h/ Spelled *Hh*

Objectives
• Identify words with /h/ spelled *Hh*.

Materials
• *Word Work* Flip Chart Activity 20
• Alphabet Card: *Hh*
• Picture Cards: *bus, garden, hen, hippopatamus, house, soap*
• Letter Tiles

Differentiated Activities
● Find the Alphabet Card for *Hh*. Find Picture Cards whose names begin with *Hh* like *helicopter*.

▲ Find the Alphabet Card for *Hh*. Find Picture Cards whose names begin with *Hh* like *helicopter*. Look around the room. Find other objects whose names begin with *Hh* like *helicopter*.

■ Find the Alphabet Card for the letter *Hh*. Find Picture Cards whose names begin with *Hh* like *helicopter*. Look around the room. Find other objects whose names begin with *Hh* like *helicopter*. Use the Letter Tiles to spell other words that begin with *Hh*.

Technology
• Letter Tile Drag and Drop

Words To Know
Sequence words

Objectives
• Identify and use sequence words.

Materials
• *Words to Know* Flip Chart Activity 20
• Teacher-made word cards: *before, after, beginning, end*
• paper, pencils, crayons

Differentiated Activities
● Draw a picture of children lined up for school. Write *1* at the beginning of the line. Write *2* at the end of the line. Find the word cards for *beginning* and *end*.

▲ Draw a picture of children lined up for school. Write *1* at the beginning of the line. Write *2* at the end of the line. Draw another picture of you before lunch and after lunch. Match your pictures with the word cards *before, after, beginning, end*.

■ Draw a picture of children lined up for school. Write *1* at the beginning of the line. Write *2* at the end of the line. Draw another picture of you before lunch and after lunch. Write the words *before, after, beginning, end* on your pictures.

You Are Here! Unit 4 Week 2

Use this week's materials from the Reading Street Leveled Practice Stations Kit to organize this week's stations.

Key

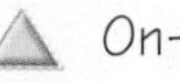

Below-Level Activities

On-Level Activities

Advanced Activities

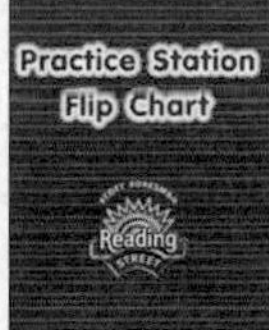

Practice Station Flip Chart

Let's Write!

Directions

Objectives

- Write directions.

Materials

- *Let's Write!* Flip Chart Activity 20
- Trade Book *My Lucky Day*
- crayons, paper, pencil

Differentiated Activities

● Look at the book. Draw a picture that shows the steps fox took to give the piglet a bath. Write numbers to show the order in which the fox did these things.

▲ Look at the book. Draw a picture that shows the steps fox took to give the piglet a bath. Write a word or two to tell what the fox did.

■ Look at the book. Draw a picture that shows the steps fox took to give the piglet a bath. Write a sentence for each step to tell what the fox did.

Read For Meaning

Sequence

Objectives

- Identify the sequence of events in a story.

Materials

- *Read for Meaning* Flip Chart Activity 20
- Little Book *Rooster's Off to See the World*
- pencil, crayons, paper

Differentiated Activities

● Look at the Little Book. What happened? Point to pictures in the story and tell a partner what happened *first*, what happened *next*, and what happened *last*.

▲ Look at the Little Book. Think about what happened. Draw pictures to show what happened *first*, what happened *next*, and what happened *last*. Tell a partner about it.

■ Look at the Little Book. Draw pictures to show what happened *first*, what happened *next*, and what happened *last*. Write a sentence to tell about each picture.

Technology

- Story Sort

Let's Make Art!

Objectives

- Make a drawing of the story.

Materials

- *Let's Make Art!* Flip Chart Activity 20
- crayons, paper, pencils

Differentiated Activities

● Think about *My Lucky Day*. Draw a picture of your favorite part of the story.

▲ Think about *My Lucky Day*. Draw a picture of your favorite part of the story. Write words or a sentence to tell about your picture.

■ Think about *My Lucky Day*. Draw a picture of your favorite part of the story. Then draw who you think the piglet went to visit next. Write a sentence or two to tell about your pictures.

Week 2

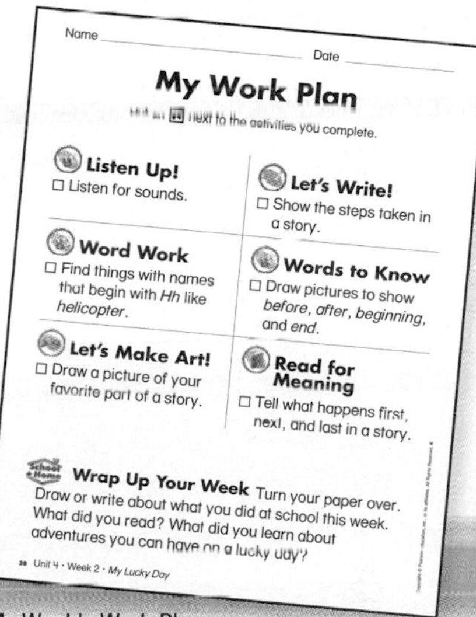

Name Date

My Work Plan

Put an ☒ next to the activities you complete.

Listen Up!
☐ Listen for sounds.

Let's Write!
☐ Show the steps taken in a story.

Word Work
☐ Find things with names that begin with *Hh* like *helicopter*.

Words to Know
☐ Draw pictures to show *before, after, beginning,* and *end*.

Let's Make Art!
☐ Draw a picture of your favorite part of a story.

Read for Meaning
☐ Tell what happens first, next, and last in a story.

Wrap Up Your Week Turn your paper over. Draw or write about what you did at school this week. What did you read? What did you learn about adventures you can have on a lucky day?

Unit 4 • Week 2 • My Lucky Day

My Weekly Work Plan

DAY 1 Get Ready to Read 30–35 mins.

Objectives

- Share information and ideas about the concept.

Today at a Glance

Oral Vocabulary
piglet, fox, lucky, filthy, cook, scrubber

Phonemic Awareness
◉ Initial /l/

Phonics
◉ /l/ Spelled *Ll*

Handwriting
L and *l*

High-Frequency Words
are, that, do

Comprehension
◉ Cause and Effect

Conventions
Action Parts

Writing
Wonderful, Marvelous Me!

Listening and Speaking
Compare and Contrast

TRUCKTOWN on Reading Street

Start your engines! Display p. 5 of *Truckery Rhymes.*

- Read aloud "Jack Be Nimble" and track the print.
- Reread the rhyme and have children chime in as they wish.
- Ask children to identify the rhyming words. (*quick, brick*)

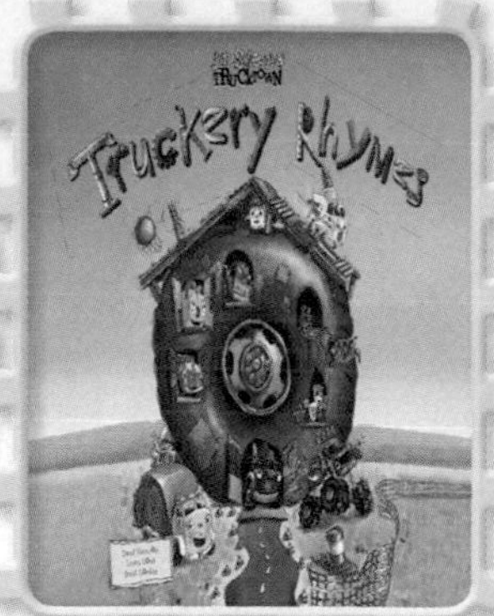

Truckery Rhymes

Concept Talk

Question of the Week
What is a lucky adventure?

Introduce the concept To build concepts and to focus their attention, tell children that they will talk, sing, read, and write about **lucky adventures.** Track each word as you read the question of the week.

Play the CD that features a boy who has a lucky day. Why is the boy lucky? Does he know he is lucky at first? How can you tell?

Background Building Audio

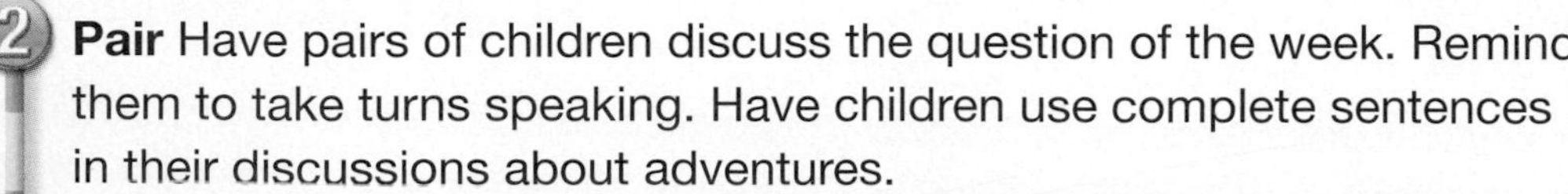

Activate Prior Knowledge Team Talk

1. **Think** Have children think for a minute about what they know about lucky adventures.
2. **Pair** Have pairs of children discuss the question of the week. Remind them to take turns speaking. Have children use complete sentences in their discussions about adventures.
3. **Share** Call on a few children to share their ideas with the group. Guide discussion and encourage elaboration with prompts such as: What makes an adventure lucky?

Routines Flip Chart

Anchored Talk

Develop oral language

Display Talk with Me Chart 20A. Which pictures show adventures? Look at these boys laughing. What is on their faces? Why do you think they are so dirty? What else do you see in these pictures? Prompt children to respond in complete sentences.

We are going to learn six new Amazing Words this week. Listen as I say each word: *piglet, fox, lucky, filthy, cook, scrubber*. Have children say each word as you point to the picture.

Display Sing with Me Chart 20B. Tell children that they are going to sing a song about a piglet. Read the title. Have children describe the pictures. Sing the song several times to the tune of "Baby Bumble Bee." Listen for the Amazing Words *piglet, fox, lucky, filthy, cook,* and *scrubber*. Have children stand up and sing with you.

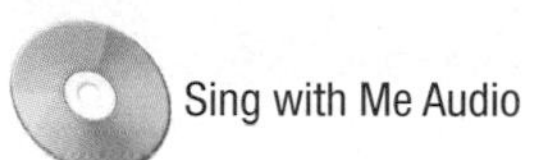
Sing with Me Audio

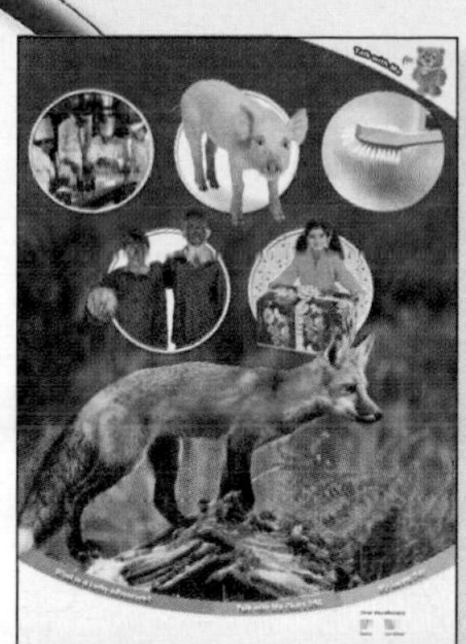
Talk with Me/Sing with Me Chart 20A

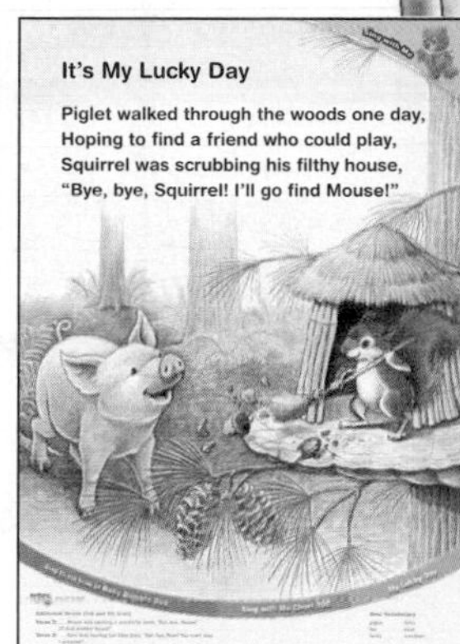

Talk with Me/Sing with Me Chart 20B

ELL Preteach Concepts Use the Day 1 instruction on ELL Poster 20 to assess and build background knowledge, develop concepts, and build vocabulary.

ELL Poster 20

Amazing Words

piglet	fox
lucky	filthy
cook	scrubber

Differentiated Instruction

Strategic Intervention

Build Background To help children understand words in the song such as *cook* and *scrubber*, have children pantomime what they would do if they were cooks and how they might use scrubbers.

English Language Learners

Listening Comprehension English learners will benefit from additional visual support to understand words from the song. For example, point to the *piglet* and the *fox* in the art to scaffold meaning.

ELL Support Additional ELL support and modified instruction is provided in the *ELL Handbook* and in the ELL Support Lessons on pp. DI•29–34.

Objectives

- ◎ Learn initial /l/.
- Identify words with initial /l/.
- Discriminate words with initial /l/.
- Identify initial sounds.

Check Phonemic Awareness
SUCCESS PREDICTOR

My Skills Buddy, pp. 32–33

Phonemic Awareness
◎ Initial /l/

Introduce Today we are going to learn a new sound. Listen carefully: /l/ /l/ /l/. Say it with me: /l/ /l/ /l/. Display the *lake* Picture Card. *Lake* begins with /l/ /l/, *lake*. What sound does *lake* begin with? Continue the routine with the *lamp, leaf,* and *lemon* Picture Cards.

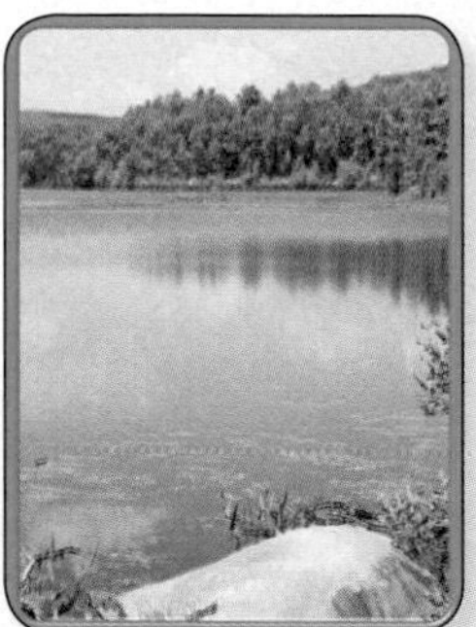
Picture Card

Model Have children look at the picture on pp. 32–33 of *My Skills Buddy*. Tell them that they will be listening for a new sound—/l/. I see a loaf of bread in the picture. What sound do you hear at the beginning of *loaf?* I hear /l/ at the beginning of *loaf*. The first sound in *loaf* is /l/. What other things do you see that begin with that sound?

Guide practice As children name example words from the picture, guide them in stating that /l/ is the beginning sound. Discuss with children some of the bulleted items on p. 32 of *My Skills Buddy*. Save the other bulleted items for discussion on Day 2.

Corrective feedback **If...** children have difficulty naming words with /l/,
then... say *lake* again, stretching out the beginning sound—/l/ /l/ /l/, *lake*.

Discriminate sounds I am going to say two words. Listen carefully to the first sound in each word. One word begins with /l/ and the other word does not: *cap, lap*. Which word begins with /l/? (*lap*).

Now let's play a sound game. I will say two words. If the words begin with same sound, clap your hands. If the words begin with different sounds, stomp your foot. Listen carefully: *leaf, list* (clap), *moon, socks* (stomp), *lemon, line* (clap), *ten, sun* (stomp), *ladder, look* (clap).

Corrective feedback **If...** children cannot discriminate initial /l/,
then... have them enunciate /l/ as they say *leaf*.

When you say the first sound in *leaf,* your tongue is behind your top teeth and your mouth is open. Say /l/ with me: /l/ /l/ /l/. Is your tongue behind your top teeth? Say *leaf* with me: *leaf*. Repeat the activity with the words *log, lap, lit,* and *last*.

Initial sounds Review initial sounds. I am going to read some words. Tell me the first sound in each word. Listen to this word: *lion*. What is the first sound in *lion?* (/l/) Continue with these words: *fog, mat, nap, leg, pick, hike, lamp, duck, rock, tip, ball.*

Don't Wait Until Friday

MONITOR PROGRESS Check Phonemic Awareness Words with Initial /l/

Say *lucky* and *fox*. Have children identify the word that begins with /l/. Continue with *leaf, house; lamp, map; ladybug, cat; lemon, tub.*

If... children cannot discriminate initial /l/,

then... use the small-group Strategic Intervention lesson, p. DI•18, to reteach /l/.

Day 1	Day 2	Day 3	Day 4	Day 5
Check Phonemic Awareness	Check Sound-Spelling/ Retelling	Check Word Reading	Check Phonemic Awareness	Check Oral Vocabulary

Success Predictor

Differentiated Instruction

Advanced

Initial /l/ Say the words *lion, monkey, ant, lizard,* and *tiger*. Have children draw a picture of one of the animals whose name begins with /l/.

ELL

English Language Learners

Support Phonemic Awareness Speakers of Chinese, Japanese, Korean, and Vietnamese may confuse the sounds of /l/ and /r/. Give children additional practice in producing /l/ by itself and at the beginning of words.

Objectives

- Recognize uppercase *L* and lowercase *l*.
- ◎ Associate the sound /l/ with the spelling *l*.
- Blend and read words with /l/.

Skills Trace

◎ /l/ Spelled *Ll*

Introduce U4W2D1

Practice U4W2D2; U4W2D3

Reteach/Review U4W2D5; U4W3D4

Assess/Test Benchmark Assessment U4

KEY:

U=Unit W=Week D=Day

Phonics—Teach/Model

◎ /l/ Spelled *Ll*

Introduce Display the *Ll* Alphabet Card. Point to the *lemon* on the Alphabet Card. *Lemon* begins with /l/. Say the word with me: *lemon*. Write *lemon* on the board and point to the *l*. *Lemon* begins with /l/ spelled *l*. Now point to the letters *Ll* on the card. The sound for this letter is /l/. The names of these letters are uppercase *L* and lowercase *l*. What is the sound for this letter? What are the names of these letters?

Alphabet Card

Model Write "Lucy Leopard Loves Her Lunch" on the board. Point to the first *L*. When I see this letter, I think of the sound /l/. The first word is *Lucy*—/l/, *Lucy*. Point to *Leopard*. The next word begins with *L* too. I know that when I see *L*, the sound will be /l/. The second word is /l/, *Leopard*. Repeat with the words *Loves* and *Lunch*. The song we will sing is "Lucy Leopard Loves Her Lunch."

Guide practice Display Phonics Songs and Rhymes Chart 20. Teach children the song "Lucy Leopard Loves Her Lunch," sung to the tune of "Twinkle, Twinkle, Little Star." Play the CD and sing the song several times. I hear many words that begin with /l/. When you hear a word that begins with /l/, clap your hands. As you sing the song, point to words that begin with *l*.

Phonics Songs and Rhymes Audio

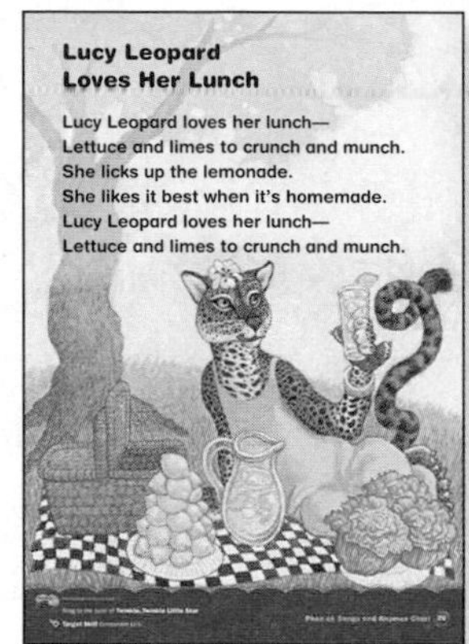

Phonics Songs and Rhymes Chart 20

On their own Have children find uppercase *L* and lowercase *l* on the classroom alphabet chart or in other places around the classroom. Have them say /l/ when they point to *L* or *l*.

Blend Words

Review

To review the sound-spellings, use Alphabet Cards *Aa, Ii, Ll, Oo,* and *Tt,* and the *apple, inch, leaf, otter,* and *tiger* Picture Cards. Then use this routine for sound-by-sound blending to have children blend new words.

ROUTINE Sound-by-Sound Blending

1. **Connect** Write the letter *l*. What is the sound for this letter? The sound is /l/. Say it with me: /l/ /l/ /l/. When you see this letter in a word, what sound will you say?
2. **Model** Write *lap* on the board.
   - Touch under the letter *l*. What is the sound for this letter? Say it with me: /l/ /l/ /l/. Repeat the routine touching under *a* and *p*.
   - Let's blend the sounds together. Listen as I blend the sounds: /l/ /a/ /p/. Say it with me: *lap*. Now say it without me.
   - Listen as I use *lap* in a sentence: *Mom holds the baby on her lap*. Say it with me. Then have children use *lap* in their own sentences.

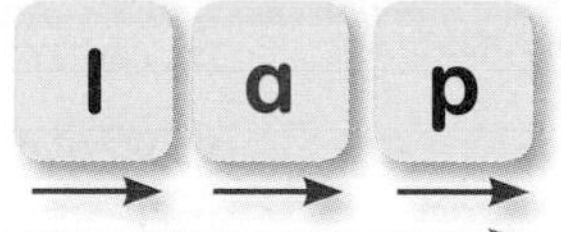

3. **Guide Practice** Continue the routine established in step 2 with the words below:

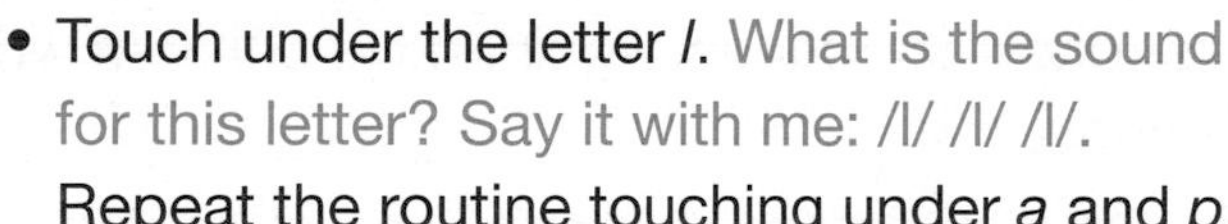

Lad	cat	can	sit	in	lot	hop	on	lid

Children should successfully read these words before reading Decodable Story 20 on p. 255 of *Reader's and Writer's Notebook.*

Corrective Feedback If children have trouble reading a word, model blending the sounds to read the word. Then have children say it with you.

Routines Flip Chart

Differentiated Instruction

 Advanced

Blend Words Display the *bat, cap,* and *fan* Picture Cards. Write *bat* on the board. Have children whisper to blend the word. Then have them point to the Picture Card that shows the word on the board. Continue the routine with *cap* and *fan*.

Teacher Tip

If children are having difficulty blending sounds to read the words, have them practice blending the words in chunks: /l/ *-ap*.

Objectives

- Write *L* and *l*.
- Learn high-frequency words.

Handwriting

Introduce Write *Ll* on the board. Words that begin with /l/ are written with an uppercase *L* or a lowercase *l*. Which letter is uppercase *L*? Which letter is lowercase *l*?

Model uppercase *L* Write *Lil* on the board. Point to the uppercase *L*. This is the uppercase *L*. We use uppercase letters to begin sentences and for the first letter in a name. Watch as I trace the uppercase *L* with my finger. Follow the stroke instructions pictured below.

Guide practice Have children write the uppercase *L* in the air. Use your finger to make an uppercase *L* in the air. Now write it on your hand.

Model lowercase *l* Point to the lowercase *l* in *Lil*. This is a lowercase *l*. Watch as I trace a lowercase *l* with my finger. Write another lowercase *l* on the board following the stroke instructions. Again, have children write *l* in the air and on their hands.

Guide practice Have children use their Write-On Boards to write a row of uppercase *L* and a row of lowercase *l*.

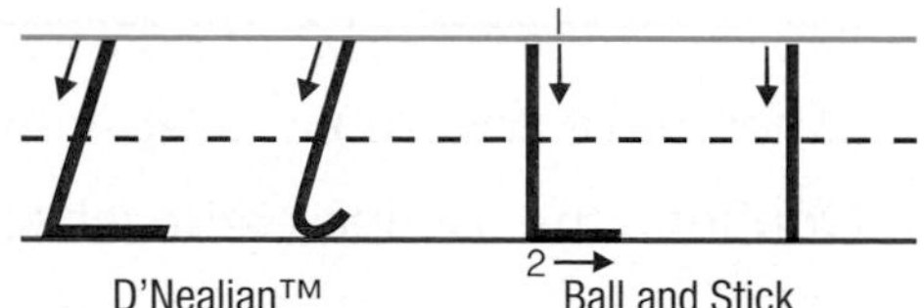

D'Nealian™ Ball and Stick

More practice Use *Reader's and Writer's Notebook,* pp. 253, 254, for additional practice with initial *l*.

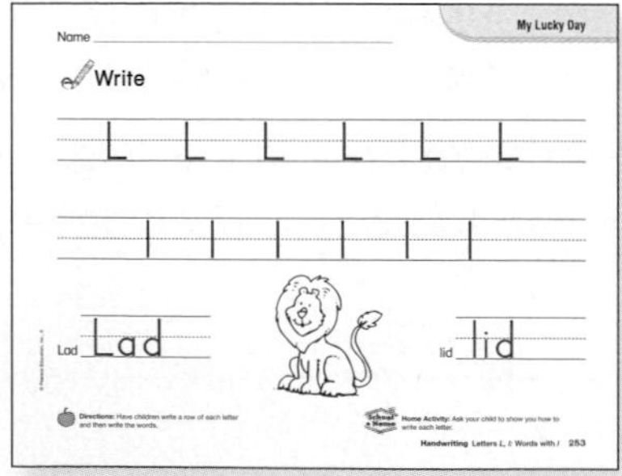

Reader's and Writer's Notebook, p. 253

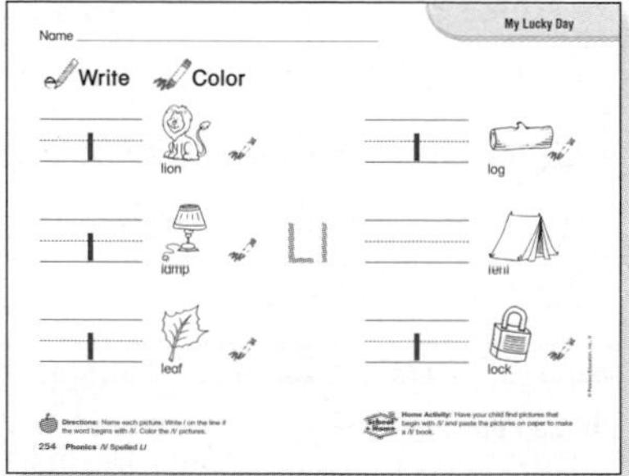

Reader's and Writer's Notebook, p. 254

High-Frequency Words

Introduce Use the routine below to teach high-frequency words *are, that,* and *do*.

Nondecodable Words

1. **Say and Spell** Some words we must learn by remembering the letters rather than saying the sounds. We will say and spell the words to help learn them. Write *do* on the board. This is the word *do*. It has two letters. The letters in the word *do* are *d* and *o*. Have children say and spell the word, first with you and then without you.
2. **Demonstrate Meaning** I can use the word *do* in lots of sentences. Here is one sentence: *She can do anything*. Now you use the word in a sentence.

Repeat the routine with the words *are* and *that*.

Routines Flip Chart

Academic Vocabulary

Write the following words on the board:

cause	**effect**
action part	**compare and contrast**
poem	**table**

Point to the list. This week we are going to learn these important words. They are tools for learning. As we work this week you will hear them many times. Read the words. Preteach the Academic Vocabulary at point-of-use by providing a child-friendly description, explanation, or example that clarifies the meaning of each term. Then ask children to restate the meaning of the Academic Vocabulary in their own words.

Differentiated Instruction

 Strategic Intervention

Support High-Frequency Words Say these sentences one at a time: *They are very funny. That window is open. Do you want to try?* After each sentence, have children tell you the high-frequency words. Then have them tell you the letters in the word.

English Language Learners

Extend Language Explain that when talking about two similar objects, we use *this* to refer to the closer object and *that* to refer to the object that is farther away. Have children practice using the words *this* and *that* to point out objects in the classroom.

Objectives

- Read high-frequency words.
- Decode and read words in context and isolation.

Decodable Story 20
/l/ Spelled *Ll* and High-Frequency Words

Review Review the following high-frequency words by having children read each word as you point to it on the Word Wall.

is my little do you like I are that a the we

Read Decodable Story 20

Display Decodable Story 20, *Lad and Me*. Today we will read a story about a boy and his cat. Point to the title of the story. What is the title of the story? *Lad and Me* is the title of the story. We will read lots of words that begin with /l/ in this story. Have children read Decodable Story 20 on pp. 255–256 in *Reader's and Writer's Notebook*.

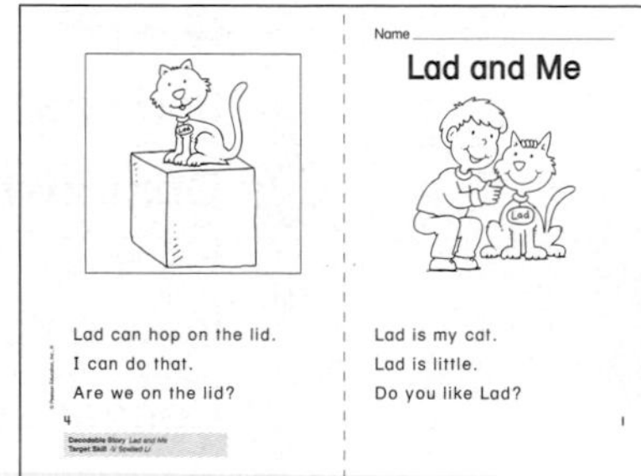

Reader's and Writer's Notebook, pp. 255–256

Use the routine for reading decodable books to read Decodable Story 20.

ROUTINE Reading Decodable Books

1. **Read Silently** Have children whisper read the story page by page as you listen in.
2. **Model Fluent Reading** Have children finger point as you read a page. Then have children reread the page without you.
3. **Read Chorally** Have children finger point as they chorally read the page. Continue reading page by page, repeating steps 1 and 2.
4. **Read Individually** Have children take turns reading aloud a page.
5. **Reread and Monitor Progress** As you listen to individual children reread, monitor progress and provide support.
6. **Reread with a Partner** Have children reread the story page by page with a partner.

Routines Flip Chart

Differentiated Instruction

Strategic Intervention

/l/ Spelled *Ll* Have children look over *Lad and Me*. Circle any words you see that begin with /l/. What letter is at the beginning of these words? (*Ll*)

A Advanced

Decodable Reader Have children list high-frequency words as they read *Lad and Me*. Then have them read their lists aloud.

Small Group Time

DAY 1 **Break into small groups after reading the Decodable Story and before the comprehension lesson.**

Teacher-Led

 Strategic Intervention	OL On-Level	A Advanced
Teacher-Led Page DI•18 • Phonemic Awareness and Phonics • **Reread** Decodable Story 20	**Teacher-Led** Page DI•23 • Phonemic Awareness and Phonics • **Reread** Decodable Story 20	**Teacher-Led** Page DI•26 • Phonemic Awareness and Phonics • **Reread** Decodable Story 20 for Fluency

Place English language learners in the groups that correspond to their reading abilities in English.

Practice Stations
- Visit the Listen Up! Station
- Visit the Word Work Station

Independent Activities
- Read independently
- Concept Talk Video
- *Reader's and Writer's Notebook*

Objectives

- Identify and describe cause and effect.

Skills Trace

◎ **Cause and Effect**

Introduce U3W3D1; U4W2D1; U5W2D1

Practice U3W3D2; U3W3D3; U3W3D4; U4W2D2; U4W2D3; U4W2D4; U5W2D2; U5W2D3; U5W2D4

Reteach/Review U3W3D5; U4W2D5; U5W2D5; U5W5D4; U6W3D4

KEY:
U=Unit W=Week D=Day

My Skills Buddy, pp. 34–35

Listening Comprehension
Cause and Effect

Introduce Many times we see or read about something that happened and we wonder why it happened. This is called **cause and effect.** A cause is why something happens. An effect is what happens.

Have children turn to pp. 34–35 in *My Skills Buddy* and look at the two pictures. These pictures tell a story.

- What happens in the second picture? (The paint is spilled on the floor.)
- Why does it happen? (The dog pushes on the table.)

Model Today I will read you a selection about a duck that has a lucky day. Read "Lucky Ducky" and model how to identify cause and effect.

When I read a story, I think about what happens and why it happens. This story is called **"Lucky Ducky."** As I read, I learn that Ducky is having a very lucky day. I wonder what is causing Ducky to have a lucky day. Let's listen to find out.

Guide practice After reading, have children identify examples of cause and effect.

- Why does Ducky go to the pet store, the bakery, and the park? (Grandpa asks him to go.)
- Why are Ducky's family and friends at the park? (to surprise him for his birthday)

More practice Display the Trade Book *The Lion and the Mouse*. Page through the story. Help children retell events in the story. Have them identify the causes of these events.

- A lion cub wakes up from his nap. Why? (A mouse runs over his paw.)
- The lion needs help. Why? (He gets stuck in a trap.)
- The lion and the mouse become friends. Why? (The mouse frees the lion from the trap.)

Connect to everyday life Invite children to sit in a circle and think about why things happen. Ask a volunteer to stand and finish the thought when you say a phrase, such as *Because I forgot my lunch one day...* or *Because I ran really fast...*

Academic Vocabulary

cause why something happens

effect what happens as the result of a cause

English Language Learners

Oral Comprehension To prepare English learners for the Read Aloud, use the modified Read Aloud in the ELL Support lesson on p. DI•30.

Lucky Ducky

Ducky woke up early. He thought it would be a lucky day. After breakfast, Grandpa asked Ducky to come to the pet store with him.

That was lucky. Ducky loved to watch fish in the aquarium. Grandpa picked up a package while Ducky counted the fish. Next, Grandpa wanted to go to the bakery.

That was lucky. Ducky loved the smell of the fresh baked bread. Grandpa picked up a box while Ducky stared at the muffins. Then Grandpa wanted to go to the park.

That was lucky too. Ducky loved to wade in the pond at the park.

At the pond Ducky saw Mom, Dad, and his friends. They had balloons and presents. They cried, "Happy birthday, you lucky Ducky!"

Objectives

- Identify and use action parts.
- Write or dictate a sentence about feelings.

Conventions
Action Parts

Teach action parts Introduce the action parts of sentences by saying the sentence: *I write.* Which word tells you what I am doing, or my action? The word *write* tells what I am doing. *Write* is the action part of the sentence. An action part is the part of a sentence that tells what someone or something is doing.

Model Write these sentences on the board: *The cat sat. The dog ran.* Read the sentences together, pointing to the action part of each sentence. Which word tells what the cat is doing? *Sat* is the action part of this sentence because it tells what the cat is doing. It is the part of the sentence that tells the action of the cat. Continue with the second sentence. Repeat with other sentences that children dictate.

Guide practice Have children sit in a circle. Act out various actions and have children guess the words. Have children dictate complete sentences about the actions you demonstrate. Remind them to speak in complete sentences.

Team Talk Pair children and have them take turns acting out various actions. Have children guess the words acted out by their partners. Then have the pairs tell the class about their actions in complete sentences.

Daily Fix-It Use the Daily Fix-It for more conventions practice.

Writing
Wonderful, Marvelous Me!
Today I Feel...

Introduce Talk with children about feelings. Think about all the ways we can feel. We may feel *excited* when we visit friends. We may feel *nervous* when we meet new people. We may feel *surprised* when we get a special treat. Display the following list of emotion words and review it with children.

silly	tired	afraid	lonely	sad	proud	curious
happy	surprised	angry	scared	shy	nervous	excited

Model Today we are going to share how we feel. I'm going to close my eyes and look inside at my feelings. When I got to school this morning, I looked around at our beautiful classroom. I saw the excellent work we have done and thought about all the new things we have learned together. Today I feel *proud* because we have learned so much!

Guide practice Encourage children to help you come up with other things that make people feel proud. Have them complete the sentence *I feel proud when...* Write down their ideas and draw pictures when appropriate.

Independent writing Now you're going to share how you feel today. Close your eyes and look inside at your wonderful, marvelous feelings. What do you see? How do you feel? Why do you feel that way? Have children write or dictate their ideas in complete sentences. Then have them illustrate the sentences.

Daily Handwriting

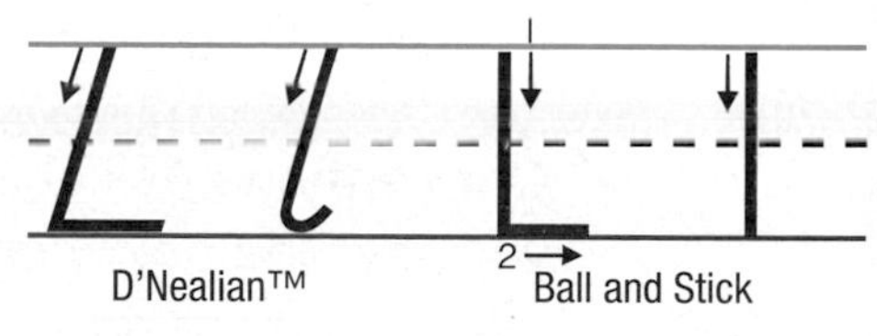

Write *Lil* and *lap* on the board. Review correct letter formation of uppercase *L* and lowercase *l*.

Have children write *Lil* and *lap* on their Write-On Boards. Remind them to use proper left-to-right and top-to-bottom progression and proper spacing between letters when writing *L* and *l*.

Write Guy
Jeff Anderson

Writing to Learn

When a child writes a sentence, she is writing to learn. Let's provide her with at least one reader so that she learns how her language communicates. That reader may be a partner, a family member, the teacher, or a group of classmates. Writing comes alive and has a purpose when it has an audience. Young writers do as well.

Daily Fix-It

nan had a lucky day
<u>N</u>an had a lucky day<u>.</u>

This week's practice sentences appear on Teacher Resources DVD-ROM.

Writing Routine

Day 1 Wonderful, Marvelous Me!
Day 2 Respond to Literature
Day 3 Genre Writing
Day 4 Extend the Concept
Day 5 This Week We . . .

English Language Learners

Conventions In English action parts (predicates), verbs are often followed by objects, as in *drank the water.* Korean- and Hindi-speaking children, however, may place the verb at the end of the sentence. Provide opportunities for children to practice building English sentences.

DAY 1 Language Arts

Objectives

- Practice compare and contrast.
- Face the speaker when listening.
- Take turns speaking aloud.

Listening and Speaking
Compare and Contrast

Teach Today we are going to compare and contrast things. When we *compare* things, we tell how things are alike, or the same. When we *contrast* things, we tell how things are different, or not the same.

Model I want to tell how a book and a magazine are alike and how they are different. Display a book and a magazine. A book and a magazine are both things we read. They both have covers, pages, and words. A book is usually smaller, has a hard cover, and may not have pictures. A magazine is larger, has a soft cover, and usually has many pictures.

Guide practice Display the cover of *My Lucky Day*. Have children use the cover illustration to tell how the fox and the pig are alike and how they are different. Refer children to the Rules for Listening and Speaking on pp. 1–2 of the *Reader's and Writer's Notebook*. Remind children to be good speakers by speaking one at a time during classroom discussions. Then remind them to be good listeners by facing the speaker.

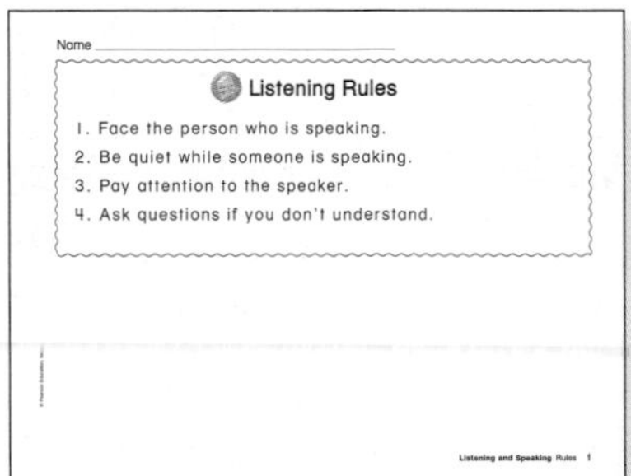
Name

Listening Rules

1. Face the person who is speaking.
2. Be quiet while someone is speaking.
3. Pay attention to the speaker.
4. Ask questions if you don't understand.

Listening and Speaking Rules 1

Reader's and Writer's Notebook, p. 1

Wrap Up Your Day

✔ **Oral Language** Today we talked about adventures. Let's say the Amazing Words again: *piglet, fox, lucky, filthy, cook, scrubber.*

✔ **Conventions** Ask children to identify the action part in each sentence you say. *The boys play. My teacher reads a book. My mom drives home.*

✔ **Homework Idea** Send home the Family Times Newsletter on Let's Practice It! TR DVD•39.

Science
Our Senses

Introduce the Five Senses Every day we smell, taste, feel, see, and hear many things. The things that help us smell, taste, feel, see, and hear are called the five senses. Point to your eyes. What do you do with your eyes? How do your eyes help you? Continue with ears, nose, mouth, and hands. Review "Lucky Ducky," pointing out the senses Ducky uses. (eats breakfast: taste; watches fish: sight; smells bread: smell; wades in the pond: feel; guests say "Happy birthday!": hear)

Materials: crayons, construction paper

Ask children to name the five senses again. Write each one on the board. Have children choose a sense and write the word on their paper. Then have them draw items that the particular sense helps them experience. Pages can be combined into class or individual sense books.

Conventions
Action Parts

Materials: paper, drawing tools

Write Action Parts Write this sentence frame on the board: I ______. Have children brainstorm a list of action parts they can use in this sentence. Have them divide a paper into four sections. In each section, have them illustrate and write an action part. Have volunteers act out one of their action parts.

Math
Make a Guess

Materials: balance, paper cups, small classroom objects

Estimate Weight In our story today, Ducky's grandpa picks up a package at the pet store and a box at the bakery. Which package do you think weighs more? How could you check your guess? Show children a pencil and a highlighter. Ask them to tell which is heavier. Help children place one piece on each pan of the balance. Explain that the heavier item will make that end of the balance go lower than the other. Continue to compare other items.

Objectives

- Discuss the concepts to develop oral language.
- Build oral vocabulary.

Today at a Glance

Oral Vocabulary
piglet, fox

Phonemic Awareness
◎ Final /l/

Phonics
◎ /l/ Spelled *Ll*

Handwriting
Words with *Ll*

Comprehension
◎ Cause and Effect

Conventions
Action Parts

Writing
Respond to Literature

Vocabulary
Words for Textures

TRUCKTOWN on Reading Street

Start your engines! Display p. 5 of *Truckery Rhymes.* Point to "Jack Be Nimble." Who remembers which truck this rhyme is about? Yes, it's about Jack. Let's read the rhyme together. Have a child touch under the rhyming words as the class reads the rhyme again. Give additional children the opportunity to say the rhyme aloud and track the print.

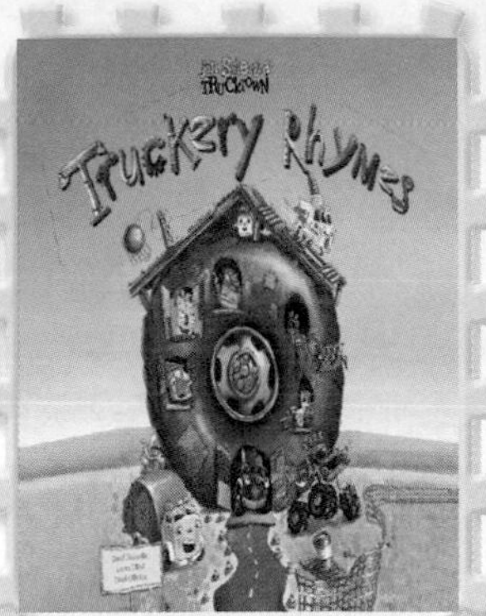

Truckery Rhymes

Concept Talk

Question of the Week
What is a lucky adventure?

Build concepts Write the question of the week on the board and track the print as you read it aloud. Have children answer the question in complete sentences. Remind children to speak loudly and clearly when sharing their ideas. To reinforce the concept and focus children's attention, display Sing with Me Chart 20B. We are going to sing a song about a piglet that wants to play.

Sing with Me Audio

Talk with Me/Sing with Me Chart 20B

Listen for Amazing Words The Amazing Words *piglet* and *fox* are in the song "It's My Lucky Day." Ask children to listen for those words as you sing the song to the tune of "Baby Bumble Bee." Sing the song several times until children become familiar with the words and can sing along. Have children clap when they hear the words *piglet* and *fox.*

ELL Reinforce Vocabulary Use the Day 2 instruction on ELL Poster 20 to reinforce the meanings of high-frequency words.

ELL Poster 20

Oral Vocabulary
Amazing Words

Amazing Words Oral Vocabulary Routine

Teach Amazing Words

1. **Introduce the Word** In this song, the animal that walks through the woods looking for a friend is a *piglet*. A *piglet* is a young pig. What's our new Amazing Word for a young pig? Say it with me: *piglet.*
2. **Demonstrate** Provide examples to show meaning. *A piglet has a curly, pink tail.* Have you ever seen a *piglet?*

Repeat steps 1 and 2.

Introduce the Word A medium-sized furry animal with a bushy tail and a pointed snout is a *fox*. What's our new Amazing Word for an animal with a bushy tail and a pointed snout? Say it with me: *fox.*

Demonstrate *Sometimes a fox acts sneaky.* Smaller or slower animals must hide from a *fox*. What does the *fox* in the song want to eat?

3. **Apply** Tell children to use *piglet* and *fox* in complete sentences. Have them tell about a piglet or a fox from another story.

Routines Flip Chart

Use Amazing Words

To reinforce the concept and the Amazing Words, have children supply the appropriate Amazing Word for each sentence.

An animal with a long, bushy tail is a _______. (fox)

A little animal with a curly, pink tail is a _______. (piglet)

Amazing Words

piglet	fox
lucky	filthy
cook	scrubber

Differentiated Instruction

Strategic Intervention

Sentence Production If children have difficulty completing a sentence, say the sentence using the words *fox* and *piglet.* Then help children decide which word is correct.

Advanced

Amazing Words Have children dictate a short story about a piglet and a fox. Have them illustrate and share their stories.

English Language Learners

Language Transfer Display pictures of a fox and a piglet. Say the animal names aloud and have children repeat. Then have them share the words for *fox* in *piglet* in their native languages. Note any similarities between the English and non-English words.

ELL Support For additional support for language transfer, see Linguistic Contrastive Analysis in the *ELL Handbook*.

DAY 2 Get Ready to Read

Objectives

- ◎ Practice initial /l/.
- ◎ Introduce final /l/.
- • Practice segmenting words.

Phonemic Awareness

◎ Final /l/

Picture Card

Isolate /l/

Display the *lamp* Picture Card. This is a *lamp*. *Lamp* begins with /l/. What is this? What sound does it begin with? Continue the routine with the *ladybug, lake, leaf, lemon,* and *loaf* Picture Cards.

Picture Card

Teach final /l/

Display the *doll* Picture Card. This is a *doll*. Listen as I say the sounds: /d/ /o/ /l/. I hear /l/ at the end of the word: /d/ /o/ /l/, *doll.* Say it with me: /d/ /o/ /l/, *doll;* /l/ is at the end. Let's try some more. Continue with the following words: *call, fall, ball, tall, bill, fill, hill.*

Guide practice

Have children look at the picture on *My Skills Buddy* pp. 32–33. Let's look for words that end with /l/. I see a waitress filling water glasses. *Fill* ends with /l/. What other things in the picture end with /l/? Discuss with children those bulleted items on p. 32 not discussed on Day 1.

My Skills Buddy, pp. 32–33

Corrective feedback

If... children cannot discriminate final /l/,
then... have them say /l/ several times as they segment final /l/ words.

Listen as I say the parts of a word: /h/ /i/ /l/, *hill.* Say it with me: /h/ /i/ /l/, *hill.* What sound do you hear at the end of *hill?* I hear /l/ at the end. Continue with the following words: *mall, hall, sill, dill.*

On their own Display Phonics Songs and Rhymes Chart 20, "Lucy Leopard Loves Her Lunch." Remind children of the tune "Twinkle, Twinkle, Little Star." Play the CD or sing the song several times. Raise your hand with your fingers in an *L* shape each time you hear a word that begins with /l/. Identify *Lucy, Leopard, loves, lunch, lettuce, limes, licks, lemonade,* and *likes.*

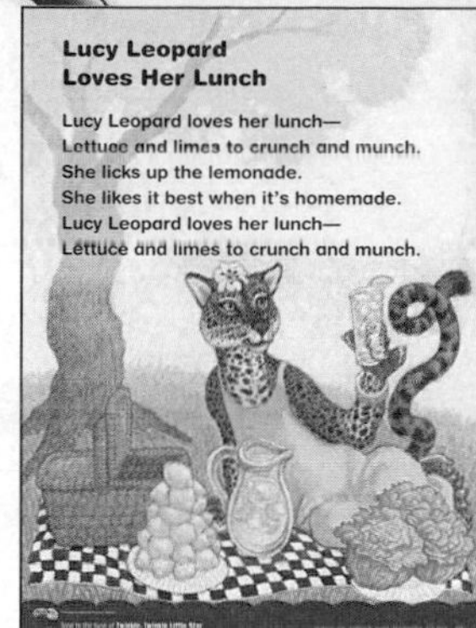

Phonics Songs and Rhymes Chart 20

Review **Substitute Phonemes** Listen as I say the sounds in a word: /p/ /i/ /l/, *pill.* What sound do you hear at the beginning? I hear /p/ at the beginning. Let's say another sound at the beginning. Listen: /d/ /i/ /l/, *dill.* What sound do you hear at the beginning now? I hear /d/. Continue the substitution routine for initial sounds with the words *bill, fill, gill,* and *hill* and for final sounds with the words *lap, lad, lag,* and *lab.*

Differentiated Instruction

Advanced

Segment Words Write *lit* on the board. Have children segment the word *lit*. Then have them change the first sound to a different sound to make a new word. Have them write and share their new words.

ELL

English Language Learners

Support Phonemic Awareness In Spanish, the letters *ll* represent another letter of the alphabet, pronounced like /y/ in *yes* or /zh/ in *measure.* Children may need extra practice with words ending in *ll.*

DAY 2 Get Ready to Read

Objectives

- ◎ Practice /l/ spelled *Ll*.
- Blend /l/ words.

Check Sound-Spelling
SUCCESS PREDICTOR

Phonics—Teach/Model

◎ /l/ Spelled *Ll*

Review /l/*Ll* Display the *Ll* Alphabet Card and point to the uppercase *L*. What is the name of this letter? What is the sound for this letter? Point to the lowercase *l*. What is the name of this letter? What is the sound for this letter?

Point to the *lemon* on the Alphabet Card. What is this? What sound does *lemon* begin with? *Lemon* begins with /l/. Write *lemon* on the board and point to the letter *l*. The letter for /l/ is *l*. What letter does *lemon* begin with?

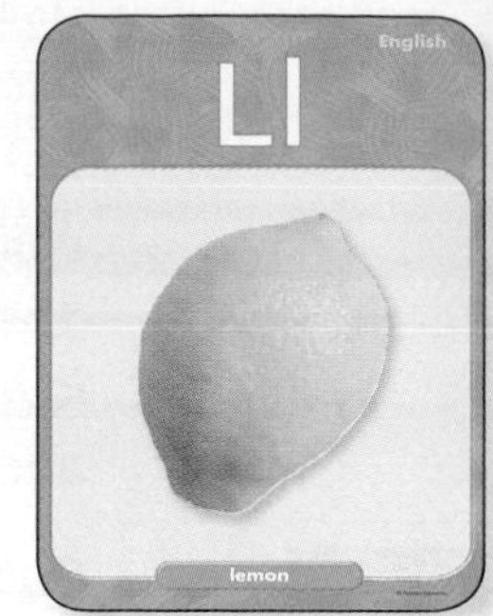

Alphabet Card

Model Display the *woman* Picture Card. This is a woman. Her name is Lil. Say the sounds in *Lil* with me: /l/ /i/ /l/. Where do you hear /l/ in *Lil*? (at the beginning and at the end) Write *Lil* on the board. Point to each letter as you say the sound: /l/ /i/ /l/, *Lil*. Continue the routine with the following names: *Hal, Sal, Lin.*

Picture Card

Guide practice Have children open *My Skills Buddy* to p. 36. Demonstrate blending using the blending arrows on *My Skills Buddy* p. 36 as you model blending the first word. Put your finger on the red arrow below the *l*. Say the sound that *l* stands for: /l/. Continue with the letters *a* and *d*. Now I run my finger along the blue arrow as I blend the letters quickly to read *lad*. Repeat with the word *lid*. Have children work with a partner to blend the rest of the words on the page.

Envision It!

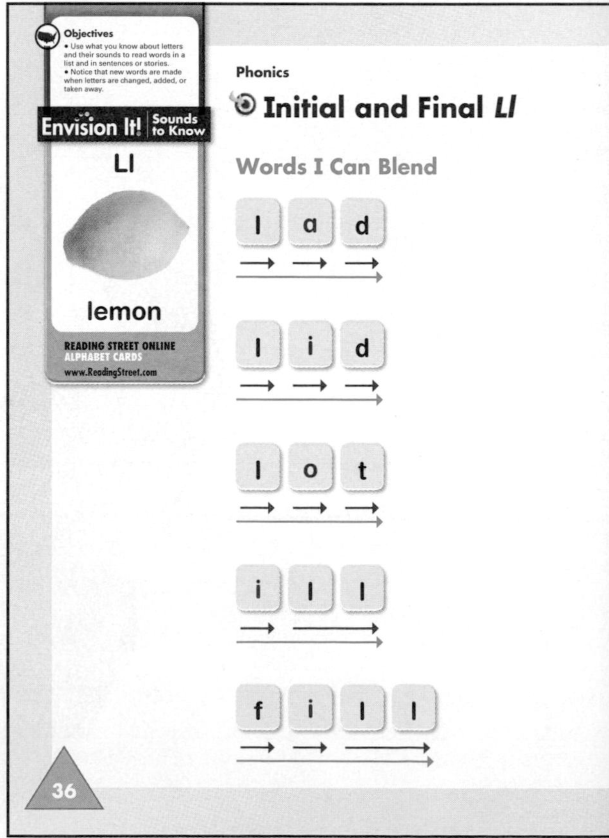

My Skills Buddy, p. 36

Blend Use the following routine to review blending *l* words.

ROUTINE Sound-by-Sound Blending

1. **Connect** Write the letter *l*. What is the sound for this letter? The sound is /l/. Say it with me: /l/ /l/ /l/. When you see this letter in a word, what sound will you say?
2. **Model** Write *lad* on the board.
   - Touch under the *l* and ask: What is the sound for this letter? Say it with me: /l/ /l/ /l/. Repeat the routine for *a* and *d*.
   - Let's blend the sounds together. Listen as I blend the sounds: /l/ /a/ /d/. Say it with me: /l/ /a/ /d/, *lad*. Now say it without me.
   - Listen as I use *lad* in a sentence: *The lad had a cat*. Say it with me. Have children use *lad* in a sentence.
3. **Guide Practice** Continue the routine established in step 2 with these words:

lap **Lil** **lit** **doll** **lid**

Have children successfully read all of the words before reading Decodable Reader 20 on pp. 38–45 of *My Skills Buddy.*

Corrective Feedback If children have difficulty blending words, model blending the sounds to read the word. Then have children say it with you.

Routines Flip Chart

Don't Wait Until Friday MONITOR PROGRESS Check Sound-Spelling /l/ Spelled *Ll*

Give each child a blank card. Have children write the letters *Ll* on the card. I am going to read some words. When you hear a word that begins with /l/, hold up your *Ll* card. Say: *lady, man, back, lucky, lamb, road, mom, large, lost, coat, foot*.

If... children cannot discriminate initial /l/,

then... use the small-group Strategic Intervention lesson, pp. DI•19, to reteach /l/.

Continue to monitor children's progress using other instructional opportunities during the week so that children can be successful with the Day 5 Assessment.

Day 1	**Day 2**	**Day 3**	**Day 4**	**Day 5**
Check Phonemic Awareness	Check Sound-Spelling/ Retelling	Check Word Reading	Check Phonemic Awareness	Check Oral Vocabulary

Success Predictor

Differentiated Instruction

SI Strategic Intervention

/a/ Spelled *Aa* Display the *Aa* Alphabet Card. Have children name the letter and the sound it makes. Repeat this routine with the *Dd* Alphabet Card.

A Advanced

Blending Sounds Have children write the word *tab* on their Write-On Boards. Then have them explain how to blend *tab* in their own words.

Objectives

- Write *L* and *l*.
- Read high-frequency words.

Handwriting

Write Words with *Ll*

Review Write *Lin* on the board. This is the name *Lin*. I use an uppercase *L* for the first letter in the name *Lin* because all names start with uppercase letters. Watch me make an uppercase *L*. Write another uppercase *L* on the board using the instructional strokes indicated in the model.

Write *lip* on the board. This is the word *lip*. I use a lowercase *l* at the beginning of *lip*. See how I make a lowercase *l*. Write another *l* on the board using the proper instructional strokes.

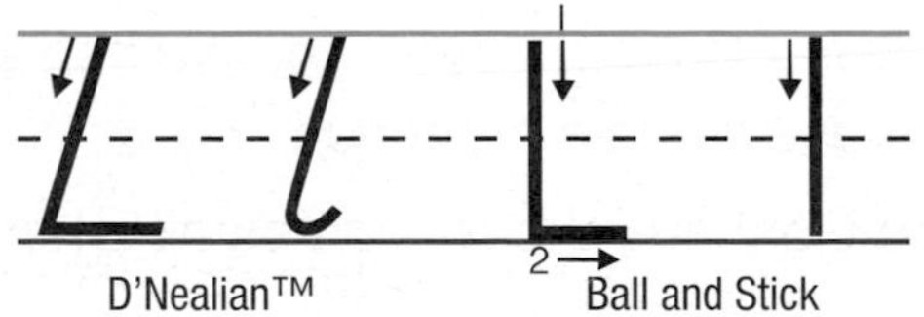

Guide practice Have children use their Write-On Boards to make a row of uppercase *L* and a row of lowercase *l*. Circulate around the room, assisting children as necessary. Have children then write the following words: *lid, Lil, lap, lit, lad, lot, Sal, pal.*

High-Frequency Words

Model reading

Have children turn to p. 37 of *My Skills Buddy.* Read the high-frequency words *are, that,* and *do* together. Then have children point to each word and read it themselves. Read the sentences on the *My Skills Buddy* page together to read the new high-frequency words in context.

Team Talk Pair children and have them take turns reading each of the sentences aloud.

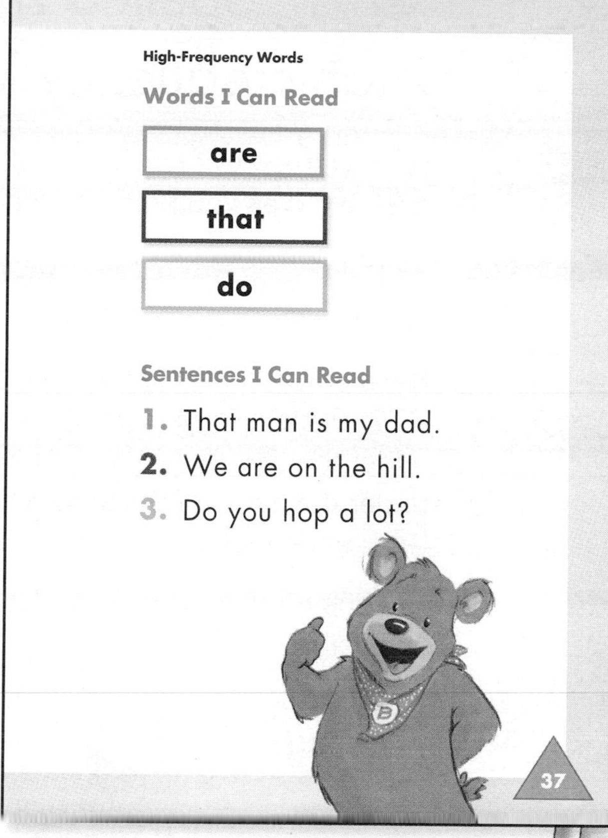

High-Frequency Words

Words I Can Read

are

that

do

Sentences I Can Read

1. That man is my dad.
2. We are on the hill.
3. Do you hop a lot?

37

My Skills Buddy, p. 37

On their own

Use *Reader's and Writer's Notebook,* p. 257, for additional practice with this week's high-frequency words.

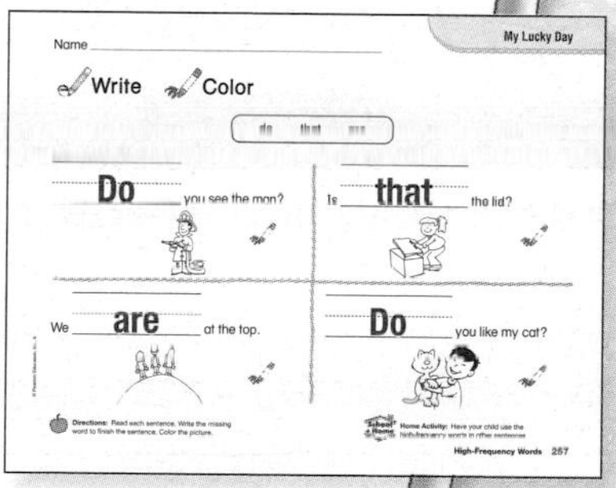

Reader's and Writer's Notebook, p. 257

Differentiated Instruction

 Strategic Intervention

Handwriting Practice writing the other letters needed to complete the Guide Practice section. Have children write the uppercase and lowercase form of each of these letters on their Write-On Boards: *Aa, Dd, Ii, Oo, Pp, Ss, Tt.*

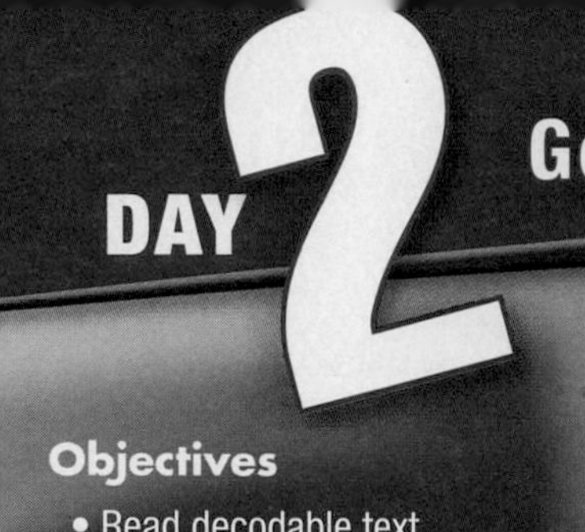

Objectives

- Read decodable text.
- Read high-frequency words.

Decodable Reader 20

/l/ Spelled *Ll* and High-Frequency Words

Review

Review the previously taught high-frequency words. Have children read each word as you point to it on the Word Wall.

a	you	the	that	do	see	they	are

Have children turn to Decodable Reader 20, *Can It Fit?,* on p. 38 of *My Skills Buddy*. Today we will read a story about two cats and a girl. Touch under the title. The title of the story is *Can It Fit?* What is the title? Touch under the name of the author. The author's name is Myleen Rush. What does an author do?

Use the routine for reading decodable books to read Decodable Reader 20.

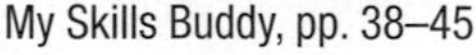
My Skills Buddy, pp. 38–45

ROUTINE Reading Decodable Books

1. **Read Silently** Have children whisper read the book page by page as you listen in.
2. **Model Fluent Reading** Have children finger point as you read a page. Then have children reread the book without you.
3. **Read Chorally** Have children finger point as they chorally read the page. Continue reading page by page, repeating steps 1 and 2.
4. **Read Individually** Have children take turns reading aloud a page.
5. **Reread and Monitor Progress** As you listen to individual children reread, monitor progress and provide support.
6. **Reread with a Partner** Have children reread the book page by page with a partner.

Routines Flip Chart

Differentiated Instruction

SI Strategic Intervention

Review Vowels Before children read *Can It Fit?,* review the letters *Aa* and *Ii* and their sounds with the words *can* and *fit*.

Small Group Time

DAY 2 Break into small groups after reading the Decodable Reader and before the comprehension lesson.

Teacher-Led

SI Strategic Intervention	OL On-Level	A Advanced
Teacher-Led Page DI•19 • Phonemic Awareness and Phonics • **Reread** Decodable Reader 20	**Teacher-Led** Page DI•23 • Phonemic Awareness and Phonics • **Reread** Decodable Reader 20	**Teacher-Led** Page DI•26 • Phonics and Spelling • **Reread** Decodable Reader 20 for Fluency

ELL Place English language learners in the groups that correspond to their reading abilities in English.

Practice Stations
- Visit the Word Work Station
- Visit the Words to Know Station

Independent Activities
- Read independently
- Background Building Audio
- *Reader's and Writer's Notebook*

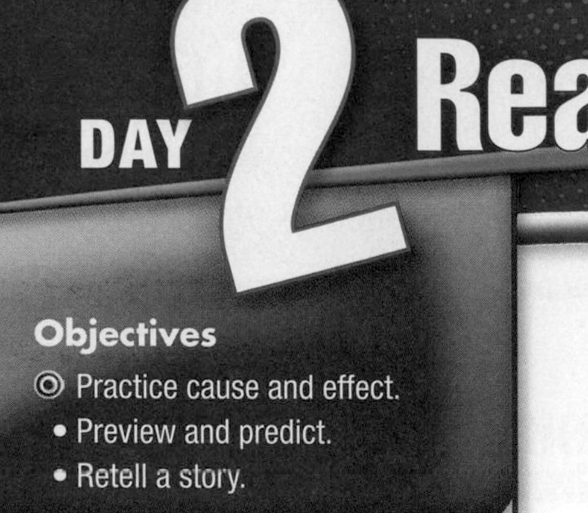

Read and Comprehend

20–25 mins.

Objectives

- ◎ Practice cause and effect.
- Preview and predict.
- Retell a story.

Check Retelling
SUCCESS PREDICTOR

Listening Comprehension
◎ Cause and Effect

Review

Envision It!

Have children turn to p. 34 of *My Skills Buddy*. Remind children that things usually happen because something else made them happen. As they read, good readers ask why things happen because it helps them understand the story.

My Skills Buddy, pp. 34–35

First Read—Trade Book
My Lucky Day

Concepts of print Display the cover of *My Lucky Day*. Explain that printed words tell us the title of the story and who wrote the story.

Preview and predict **Think Aloud** Display *My Lucky Day*. The title of this book is *My Lucky Day*. Tell me what you see on the cover. I see a piglet and a fox. They look like they are talking to each other. What do you think this book will be about? Let's read to find out.

Use pictures Take children on a picture walk through the book. Have children tell about what they see in each picture.

Introduce genre An animal fantasy is a story about animal characters that talk and act like people. We will read about an animal that has a lucky adventure.

Set purpose Remind children of the question of the week: *What is a lucky adventure?* Have children listen as you read to see how the piglet has a lucky adventure.

Model Read *My Lucky Day* with expression for enjoyment.

Retell

Check retelling

Envision It!

Have children turn to p. 46 of *My Skills Buddy.* Walk through the retelling boxes as children retell *My Lucky Day.* Let's retell what happens in the first box and why it happens. The piglet looks afraid and surprised. Why? The fox opens the door. Continue with the rest of the boxes. Then have children draw a picture of a cause-and-effect relationship from the story. Have them write or dictate a sentence to go with their picture.

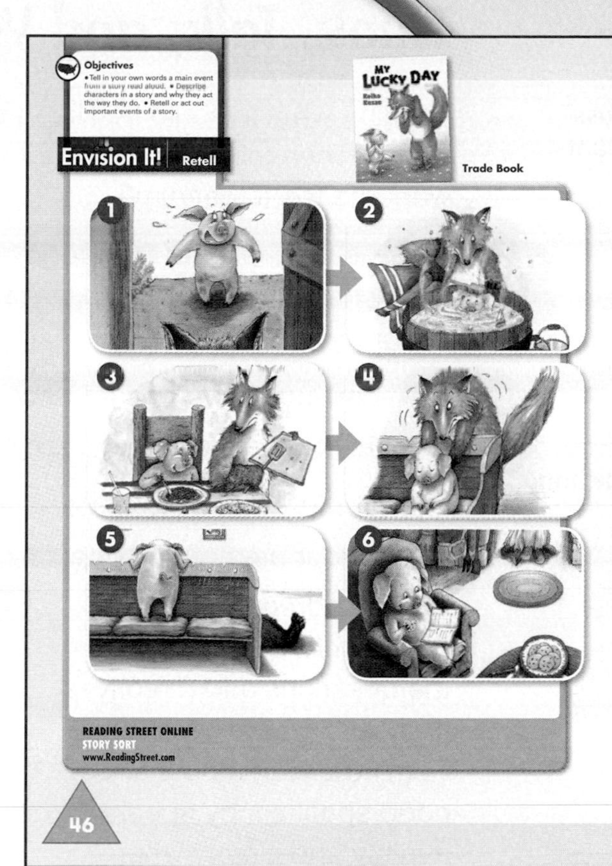

My Skills Buddy, p. 46

Top-Score Response A top-score response describes events in sequence with details.

Don't Wait Until Friday

MONITOR PROGRESS Check Retelling

Grade K Retelling Cards

If... children have difficulty retelling the story,
then... go through the story one page at a time, and have children tell what they learn on each page.

Day 1	Day 2	Day 3	Day 4	Day 5
Check Phonemic Awareness	Check Sound-Spelling/ Retelling	Check Word Reading	Check Phonemic Awareness	Check Oral Vocabulary

Success Predictor

Differentiated Instruction

SI Strategic Intervention

Build Background Review the word *piglet* with children. Explain that a piglet is a young or baby pig.

A Advanced

Cause and Effect Assign partners. Have children take turns pointing to an event in the retelling boxes and asking their partners to explain the cause of the event.

Retelling Plan

- [x] **Week 1** Assess Advanced students.
- [x] **This week assess On-Level students.**
- [ ] **Week 3** Assess Strategic Intervention students.
- [ ] **Week 4** Assess Advanced students.
- [ ] **Week 5** Assess On-Level students.
- [ ] **Week 6** Assess Strategic Intervention students.

Objectives

- ◎ Practice cause and effect.
- Confirm predictions.
- Practice action parts.

Think, Talk, and Write

Discuss concept

Imagine what it would be like to be the fox, who wants to eat the piglet for dinner. Then think about what it would be like to be the piglet, who doesn't want the fox to eat him!

- At the beginning of the story, did you feel sorry for the piglet? Why or why not?
- The piglet gets what he wants. Why?
- Whose lucky day was it? Why?

Confirm predictions

Ask children to recall their predictions before you read *My Lucky Day.*

- What did you think the story would be about?
- Was your prediction correct?

Have children turn to p. 47 of *My Skills Buddy.* Read the questions and directives and have children respond. Remind children how to be good speakers by speaking audibly and clearly when sharing ideas.

Think, Talk, and Write

1. Tell about a lucky adventure you have had.
Text to Self

2. What does the fox do to the piglet? Why does he do this?

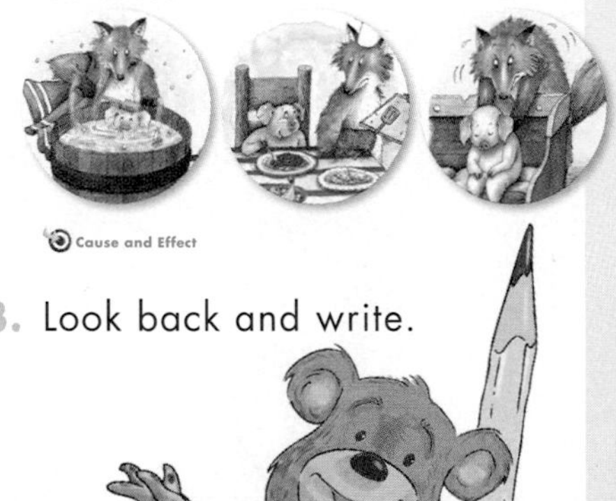

◎ Cause and Effect

3. Look back and write.

47

My Skills Buddy, p. 47

Text to self

1. Tell about a lucky adventure you have had. Who came with you on your adventure? What was lucky about your adventure?

◎ Cause and Effect

2. Touch under the first picture of the fox washing the piglet. What does the fox do to the piglet? Why does he do this? (The fox washes the piglet because the piglet says he is dirty.) Continue this routine with other pictures in the story.

Look back and write

3. Let's look back at our story and write about it. Remember that the fox does many things to make a dinner for the piglet. Listen for what he does. Read pp. 16–17 of *My Lucky Day*. Now let's write our ideas. Discuss with children the things that kept the fox busy preparing the meal. Record children's responses on chart paper. When you are finished, track the print as you read the list together. (Possible responses: He picked tomatoes. He made spaghetti. He baked cookies. He set the table.)

Conventions
Action Parts

Review Remind children that the action part is the part of a sentence that tells what something or someone does.

Write the following sentence on the board: *The piglet knocks loudly*. Read aloud the sentence. *Knocks loudly* is the action part of this sentence. It tells what the piglet does.

Guide practice Write this sentence on the board: *The fox grabs the piglet*. Read aloud the sentence. What is the action part? *(grabs the piglet)* How do you know? (It tells what the fox does.) Have children identify action parts in these sentences:

> **The fox opens the door.** (opens the door)
>
> **The piglet walks in.** (walks in)

On their own Use *Reader's and Writer's Notebook,* p. 258, for more practice with action parts.

Daily Fix-It Use the Daily Fix-It exercise for more conventions practice.

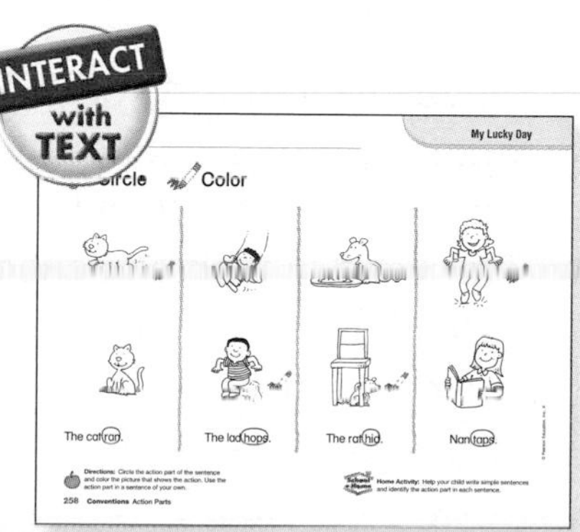

Reader's and Writer's Notebook, p. 258

Differentiated Instruction

 Strategic Intervention

Physical Response To help them understand how the animals might think and feel, have children pretend to be the animals as they answer the questions.

Academic Vocabulary

action part a word or group of words that tells what the naming part (subject) in a sentence does

Daily Fix-It

will Linda eat her lunch

Will Linda eat her lunch?

This week's practice sentences appear on Teacher Resources DVD-ROM.

DAY 2 Language Arts

15–20 mins.

Objectives

- Identify and use words for textures.
- Write *L* and *l*.

Writing
Respond to Literature

Discuss Display *My Lucky Day*. What does the fox do to prepare to eat the piglet? You may wish to write labels or draw simple illustrations for each response.

Model I am going to write a sentence about one of the things the fox does for the piglet:

The fox gives the piglet a bath.

Guide practice Invite children to help you write more sentences about what the fox does for the piglet.

The fox cooks dinner for the piglet.

The fox gives the piglet a massage.

Independent writing Have children write or dictate sentences about what the fox does in *My Lucky Day*. Remind children to capitalize the first word in their sentence and end it with a period. Then have them illustrate their sentences.

Daily Handwriting

Write *Lon* and *lid* on the board. Review correct letter formation of uppercase *L* and lowercase *l*.

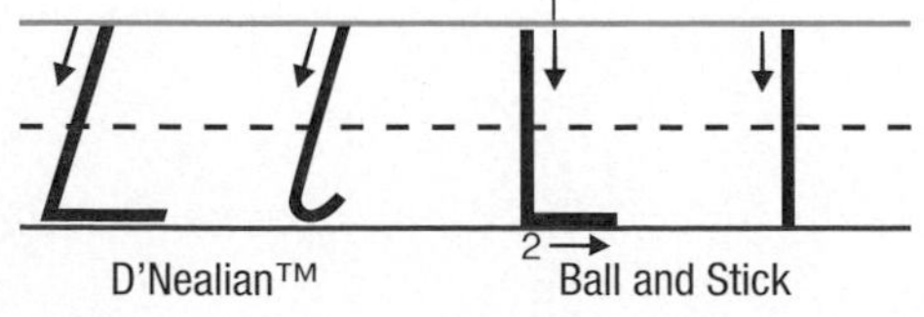

Have children write *Lon* and *lid* on their Write-On Boards. Remind children to use proper left-to-right and top-to-bottom progression when writing *L* and *l*.

Vocabulary
Words for Textures

Model Have children turn to p. 48 of *My Skills Buddy* and use the first Vocabulary bullet to guide the discussion. Direct children to the picture of the pickle. *Texture* is the way something feels when we touch it. If we could touch this pickle, it would feel *bumpy*. This pickle has a bumpy texture. Direct children to the picture of the pencil. Does this pencil look like it would feel *bumpy*? Show children a real sharpened pencil and point to the tip. No, the tip of a pencil is not bumpy. We use a different word to tell about it. The tip of a pencil is *sharp*. Direct children to the remaining pictures. Living things have *textures* too. Touch under the caterpillar picture. This animal is *fuzzy*. Touch under the dog picture. This animal is *furry*.

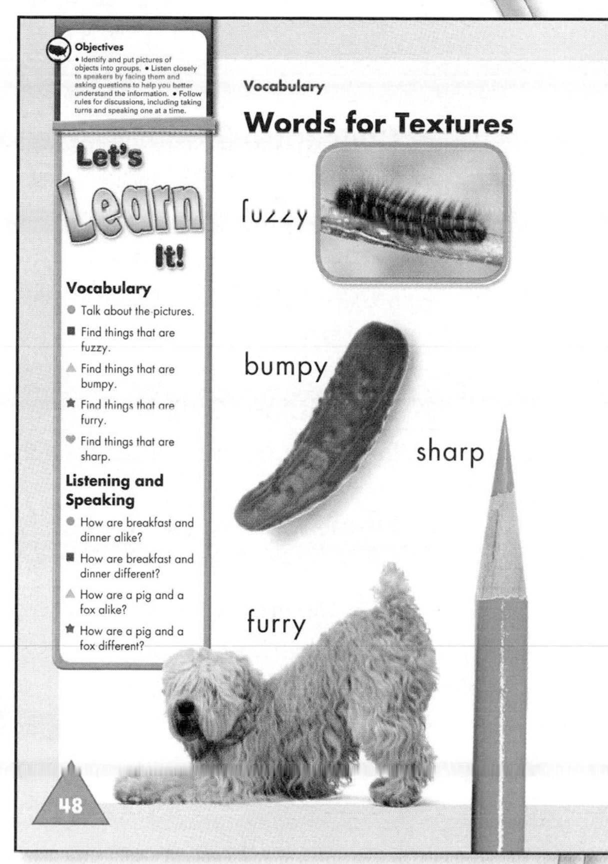

My Skills Buddy, p. 48

Guide practice Write the words *fuzzy, bumpy, furry,* and *sharp* on the board. Point to each word as you read it.

fuzzy **bumpy** **furry** **sharp**

Let's practice our new words. Have children look at the pictures on p. 48 of *My Skills Buddy*. Point to the picture of something fuzzy. What is fuzzy? (caterpillar) The caterpillar is fuzzy. Continue with the remaining pictures and textures.

On their own Have children find things around the room that are fuzzy, bumpy, furry, or sharp. Have them share their findings with the class.

Differentiated Instruction

 Strategic Intervention

Physical Response To demonstrate the difference between *fuzzy* and *furry,* bring the following items to class: a peach and a stuffed animal with thick fur. Give children the opportunity to touch each item as you identify the item as *fuzzy* or *furry*.

A Advanced

Vocabulary Ask children to think of an item from home that feels fuzzy, bumpy, furry, or sharp. Then have them draw a picture of that item and label the picture with the correct texture word.

English Language Learners

Professional Development
Using Visuals "Visuals enable students to 'see' the basic concepts we are trying to teach much more effectively than if we rely only on words. Among the visuals we can use are: pictures/diagrams, vocabulary cards, real objects, graphic organizers, [and] maps."—Dr. Jim Cummins, the University of Toronto

Objectives

- Review skills learned and practiced today.

Wrap Up Your Day

✔ **Concept Talk** Today we read about a piglet's lucky day. What happened to the piglet that was lucky?

✔ **Phonemic Awareness** I am going to say some words. Say the word *lunch* if the word begins with /l/: *latch, late, morning, dinner, listen, fun, lots, little*.

✔ **Vocabulary Skill** Today we talked about words that name textures. Can you name something that *feels fuzzy, bumpy, furry,* or *sharp?*

✔ **Homework Idea** Have children draw a picture of something in their home that begins with /l/. Then have them write or dictate a label for it.

Preview DAY 3

Tomorrow we will read more about the fox and the piglet.

Social Studies
Consequences

Materials: *My Lucky Day;* Patterns Book in the TR•DVD: fox, piglet; craft sticks; crayons; glue

Discuss the Story Events What did the piglet do to save himself from the fox? Discuss how the story would have been different if the fox was not hungry or if the piglet was not very clever. Remind children that each character's actions caused the story to turn out the way it did.

Put on a Puppet Play Divide the group into pairs. Have each pair make simple puppets by coloring and cutting out the fox and piglet patterns and gluing them onto craft sticks. Challenge each pair to create a skit telling how the story would have been different if the fox was not hungry or the piglet was not clever. Have each pair of children present their puppet play to the class.

Conventions
Adventures of the Fox and the Piglet

Materials: paper, crayons, markers

Discuss Adventures What do you think a fox might like to do? What might a piglet like to do? What if the fox and the piglet were friends who had an adventure together? Have children work together to draw the two animals having adventures. Have children dictate or write labels below each action they draw. If children need help, suggest that the animals could play, work, read, or laugh together.

Phonics
/l/ Spelled *Ll*

Materials: *L*-shaped paper, crayons, markers

Imagine Lucky Adventures Give each child a large sheet of paper in the shape of the letter *L*. Imagine you have been given three wishes for a lucky adventure. You may wish for three exciting things as long as they begin with the letter *L*. Have children write the names or draw pictures of the three things on their *L*-shaped paper. Display them on a "Lucky *L*" bulletin board.

Objectives

- Share information and ideas about the concept.
- Build oral vocabulary.

Today at a Glance

Oral Vocabulary
lucky, filthy

Phonemic Awareness
◉ Initial and Final /l/

Phonics
◉ /l/ Spelled *Ll*

Comprehension
◉ Cause and Effect

Conventions
Naming Parts

Writing
Poem

Listening and Speaking
Compare and Contrast

TRUCKTOWN on Reading Street

Start your engines! Display p. 5 of Truckery Rhymes. Do you know the original "Jack Be Nimble"? Recite it first, and then have children repeat it with you:

Jack be nimble,
Jack be quick.
Jack jump over the candlestick.

Truckery Rhymes

Concept Talk

Question of the Week
What is a lucky adventure?

Write the question of the week on the board. Read the question as you track the print. Ask children to identify the word in the question that begins with /l/. Remind children to speak loudly and clearly and to take turns speaking.

Listen for Amazing Words

Let's Sing Display Sing with Me Chart 20B. Remind children that yesterday they sang "It's My Lucky Day" and learned the Amazing Words *piglet* and *fox*. Today we are going to listen for the Amazing Words *lucky* and *filthy*. Sing the song again. Ask children to pretend to brush dirt off of themselves when they hear the Amazing Words *lucky* and *filthy.*

Sing with Me Audio

Talk with Me/Sing with Me Chart 20B

Oral Vocabulary
Amazing Words

Amazing Words Oral Vocabulary Routine

Teach Amazing Words

1. **Introduce the Word** In the story *My Lucky Day,* the piglet is lucky because the fox does so many nice things for him. *Lucky* means having good things happen. What's our new Amazing Word for having good things happen? Say it with me: *lucky.*

2. **Demonstrate** Provide examples to show meaning. *The fox thinks he is lucky to have a piglet come to his house.*

   Repeat steps 1 and 2.

   Introduce the Word The piglet was very dirty from being outside in the mud. He told the fox that he was *filthy.* What's our new Amazing Word for very dirty? Say it with me: *filthy.*

   Demonstrate *If you play soccer on a muddy field, you will probably get filthy.*

3. **Apply** Tell children to use *lucky* and *filthy* in complete sentences. Have them illustrate their sentences.

Routines Flip Chart

Use Amazing Words

To reinforce the concept and the Amazing Words, have children supply the appropriate Amazing Word for each sentence.

Mom was ________ when she found her lost keys. (lucky)

The puppy was ________ after he ran through the mud. (filthy)

ELL Expand Vocabulary
Use the Day 3 instruction on ELL Poster 20 to help children expand vocabulary.

ELL Poster 20

Amazing Words

piglet	fox
lucky	filthy
cook	scrubber

Differentiated Instruction

SI Strategic Intervention

Connect /l/ to *Ll* Write the Amazing Words *lucky* and *filthy* on the board. Touch under each word as you read it aloud. Ask children which word begins with /l/. Have children name the letter that makes /l/.

A Advanced

Amazing Words Have children use the two Amazing Words they learned earlier this week (*piglet, fox*) in sentences with the two Amazing Words from today (*lucky, filthy*). Have them dictate and illustrate their sentences.

English Language Learners

Access Content Have children tell what words in their home languages are used for *lucky* and *filthy*.

Objectives

- ◎ Isolate final /l/.
- Segment words.
- Substitute initial and final sounds.

Phonemic Awareness

◎ Initial and Final /l/

Picture Card

Review **Initial /l/** Display the *lamp* Picture Card. Listen as I say this word: *lamp*. What is the first sound in *lamp?* Say it with me: /l/ /l/ /l/, *lamp.* Today we will also listen for /l/ at the ends of words.

Review **Final /l/** Use the *doll* Picture Card to isolate final /l/. This is a *doll*. I hear /l/ at the end of *doll.* Display the *bubble* Picture Card. This is a *bubble*. Where do you hear /l/ in *bubble?* Yes, /l/ is at the end of *bubble*. Continue the routine with the following Picture Cards: *pail, puzzle, seal.*

Picture Card

Discriminate sounds Tell children you will say two words. Ask them to tell you which word ends in /l/. Which word has the same last sound as *doll: full* or *lap?* Say the words with me: *full* and *lap.* I hear /l/ at the end of *doll* and *full*. Continue the routine with the following pairs of words: *all, top; big, bowl; add, squeal; pole, desk.*

On their own Display the *pail*, *seal*, *leaf*, and *lemon* Picture Cards. Have children choose one of the pictures to draw. Have them write an *l* on their paper if the word ends with /l/.

Segment Listen to the sounds in the word *bill:* /b/ /i/ /l/. Say them with me: /b/ /i/ /l/. How many sounds do you hear? There are three sounds in *bill.* Let's try more. Continue with the following words: *lip, doll, lid, hill, log.*

Corrective feedback **If...** children cannot segment the words into sounds, **then...** provide practice segmenting the words into chunks, such as /l/ *-id* or *hi-* /l/.

Substitute final sounds Let's make some new words. Listen to this word again: *bill.* Instead of /b/, I'll say /d/: /d/ /i/ /l/, *dill.* Continue the routine with the following words: *fill, hill, will; call, fall, ball.* Now let's make some new words by changing the sound at the end of the words. Instead of /b/ /i/ /l/, I'll say /b/ /i/ /t/, *bit.* Continue the routine with the following words: *bib, big, bin; doll, dog, dot, dock.*

Differentiated Instruction

Strategic Intervention

Final /l/ Spelled *ll* Write *bill* on the board. Segment the word and draw a line under *ll* as you say /l/. Remind children that final /l/ is sometimes spelled *ll.*

Teacher Tip

Use sound discrimination activities that focus on words with final /l/ to check children's ability to discriminate sounds in the final position.

Get Ready to Read

Objectives

- Practice /l/ spelled *Ll*.
- Substitute phonemes.
- Read /l/ words.
- Read high-frequency words.

Check Word Reading
SUCCESS PREDICTOR

Phonics—Teach/Model

/l/ Spelled *Ll*

Review

/l/Ll Display the *Ll* Alphabet Card and point to the uppercase *L*. What is the name of this letter? What is the sound for this letter? Point to the lowercase *l*. What is the name of this letter? What is the sound for this letter? Explain that sometimes final /l/ is spelled *ll.*

Alphabet Card

Review

Letter Names and Sounds Use Alphabet Cards to review the following letter names and sounds: *Aa, Bb, Dd, Ff, Ii, Mm, Pp.*

Blend sounds Write *mill* on the board. Point to each letter as you say the sound: /m/ /i/ /l/. When I blend these sounds together, I make the word *mill.* Say the sounds with me: /m/ /i/ /l/. Now blend the sounds together: /m/ /i/ /l/, *mill.* Point to each letter as children identify the sounds.

Change the *m* to *p* to write *pill*. Now we have a new word. Let's blend the sounds to read the word. Say them with me: /p/ /i/ /l/. What is the new word? The new word is *pill*. Continue practice with the following pairs of words: *lab, lap; Lill, Bill; dill, fill.*

More practice Use *Reader's and Writer's Notebook,* p. 259, for additional practice with initial and final /l/.

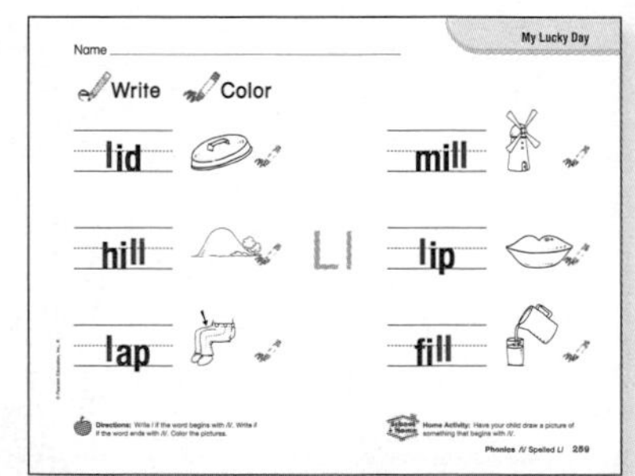

Reader's and Writer's Notebook, p. 259

Review **Sound-Spelling** Display the *Hh* Alphabet Card. What sound do you hear at the beginning of *helicopter?* What letter spells that sound? Yes, the letter *H* spells /h/. Review the following sounds and letters with Alphabet Cards: *Mm, Tt, Ss, Cc, Nn, Rr*.

Review **High-Frequency Words** Write *do* on the board. This is the word *do*. What is this word? Continue this routine with *you, we, that, the, are, like,* and *a*.

Alphabet Card

Don't Wait Until Friday

MONITOR PROGRESS Check Word Reading High-Frequency Words

Write *do, you, we, that, the, are, like,* and *a* on the board. Have children take turns reading the words.

Practice reading these words from Kindergarten Student Reader K.4.2, *Our Musical Adventure.*

Nat	**tap**	**Lin**	**rap**	**Rob**
pot	**bam**	**lid**	**hit**	**Dad**

If... children cannot read the high-frequency words,
then... write the words on cards for them to practice at home.

If... children cannot blend sounds to read the words,
then... provide practice blending the words in chunks, /l/ *-in.*

If... children can successfully blend sounds to read the words,
then... have them read Kindergarten Student Reader K.4.2, *Our Musical Adventure.*

Day 1	Day 2	Day 3	Day 4	Day 5
Check Phonemic Awareness	Check Sound-Spelling/ Retelling	Check Word Reading	Check Phonemic Awareness	Check Oral Vocabulary

Success Predictor

Differentiated Instruction

SI Strategic Intervention

High-Frequency Words Ask children to name each letter in *do.* Then have them write each of these lowercase letters on their Write-On Boards.

ELL

English Language Learners

Spell English Words Have children spell familiar English words that begin with *Ll*. Say the words *let, lot, lip,* and *lap*. Have children write the words as you say them. Then have them read the words by blending the sounds. Children should write other familiar words with *Ll* as well.

Get **Ready** to **Read**

Objectives

- Read /l/ words.
- Read high-frequency words.

Kindergarten Student Reader K.4.2

/l/ Spelled *Ll* and High-Frequency Words

Review

High-Frequency Words Review the previously taught high-frequency words. Have children read each word as you point to it on the Word Wall.

you	**do**	**we**	**that**
the	**are**	**like**	**a**

Read Kindergarten Student Reader K.4.2

Display Kindergarten Student Reader K.4.2, *Our Musical Adventure.* Today we are going to read a new story. Point to the title of the story. What is the title of this story? The title of this story is *Our Musical Adventure.* The author's name is Ann Rossi. The book was illustrated by Jaime Smith.

Use the reading decodable books routine to read the Kindergarten Student Reader.

ROUTINE **Reading Decodable Books**

Small Group

1. **Read Silently** Have children whisper read the book page by page as you listen in.
2. **Model Fluent Reading** Have children finger point as you read a page. Then have children reread the page without you.
3. **Read Chorally** Have children finger point as they chorally read the page. Continue reading page by page, repeating steps 1 and 2.
4. **Read Individually** Have children take turns reading aloud a page.
5. **Reread and Monitor Progress** As you listen to individual children reread, monitor progress and provide support.
6. **Reread with a Partner** Have children reread the book page by page with a partner.

Routines Flip Chart

Go Digital!

eReaders 

Can you do it, Nat?
Can you tap, Lin?
Can you rap, Rob?
2

We can do that.
We can rap on the pot.
3

We can bam on the lid.
We can rap, tap, tap.
4

Kindergarten Student Reader K.4.2

We are tops.
We can rap, tap, tap.
5

Nat can hit the lid.
Lin can bam on the can.
6

Nan can hit the pot.
Lin can tap, tap, tap.
7

Do you like that, Dad?
We can tap, tap, bam.
Dad did like it a lot!
8

Small Group Time

DAY 3 **Break into small groups to read the Kindergarten Student Reader before the comprehension lesson.**

Teacher-Led

SI Strategic Intervention	OL On-Level	A Advanced
Teacher-Led Page DI•20 • Phonemic Awareness and Phonics • **Read** Concept Literacy Reader K.4.2 or Kindergarten Student Reader K.4.2	**Teacher-Led** Page DI•24 • Phonemic Awareness and Phonics • **Read** Kindergarten Student Reader K.4.2	**Teacher-Led** Page DI•27 • **Read** Independent Reader K.4.2 or Kindergarten Student Reader K.4.2

Place English language learners in the groups that correspond to their reading abilities in English.

Practice Stations
- Visit the Words to Know Station
- Visit the Let's Write! Station

Independent Activities
- Read independently
- Audio Text of Trade Book
- *Reader's and Writer's Notebook*

Differentiated Instruction

Strategic Intervention

Support Phonemic Awareness Display the *Aa* Alphabet Card. Have children name the letter on this card. Then have them tell what sound this letter makes.

Advanced

/a/ Spelled *Aa* Display the second page of *Our Musical Adventure*. Have children copy words that contain *Aa* on their Write-On Boards. (*can, Nat, tap, rap*) Then have them blend these words.

Teacher Tip

You may wish to have children use the high-frequency words in sentences so that they may better understand the words.

Read and Comprehend

Objectives

- Recall and retell a story.
- ◎ Practice cause and effect.
- Develop and use vocabulary.
- Develop and use comprehension skills.

Comprehension

Retell the story

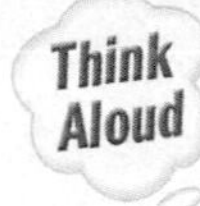

Have children turn to p. 46 of *My Skills Buddy* and use the retelling boxes to retell the story *My Lucky Day.*

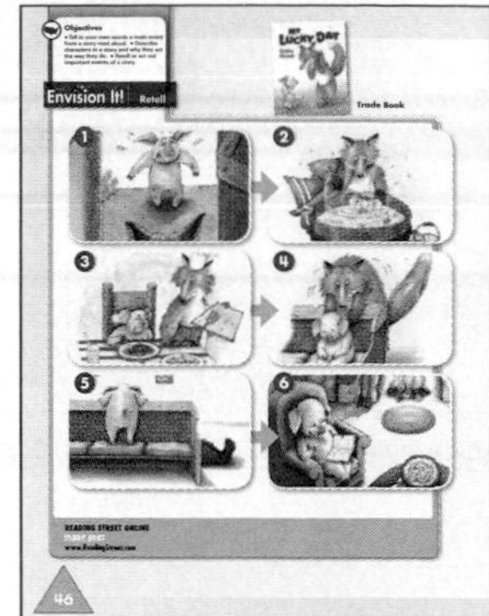

My Skills Buddy, p. 46

Think Aloud Direct children to the first retell box. This is when the piglet arrives at the fox's door. Tell me about why the piglet looks surprised.

Continue reviewing the retelling boxes and having children retell the selection.

Review

Cause and Effect Display illustrations in *My Lucky Day*. Remind children that characters in the story do or say things that cause other things to happen.

- What happens after the piglet tells the fox he is filthy? (The fox washes him.)
- What causes the fox to fall down and let the piglet go free? (He falls asleep.)
- What does the piglet do to try to have another lucky day? (He goes to a bear's house.)

More practice

Use *Reader's and Writer's Notebook,* p. 260, for additional practice with cause and effect.

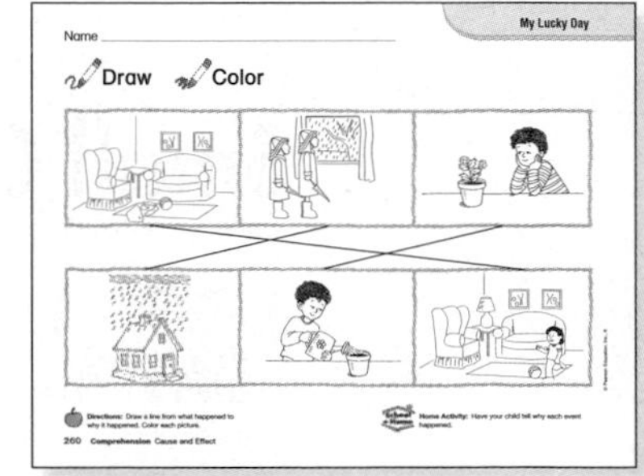

Reader's and Writer's Notebook, p. 260

Second Read—Trade Book
My Lucky Day

Reread *My Lucky Day.* Follow the Day 3 arrow beginning on p. 156, and use the Develop Vocabulary notes to prompt conversations about the selection.

Have children use the Amazing Words *piglet, fox, lucky, filthy, cook,* and *scrubber* to talk about the selection.

DAY 2 Read for enjoyment

DAY 3 Reread using Develop Vocabulary notes

DAY 4 Reread using Guide Comprehension notes

Differentiated Instruction

Strategic Intervention

Vocabulary Write the Amazing Words *piglet, fox, lucky, filthy, cook,* and *scrubber* on the board. Review the definitions of these words and remind children to listen for them in the story.

DAY 3

Develop Vocabulary

***Wh-* question**
What kind of animal is this? (a fox)
- This is a fox. What is the fox doing?

Develop Vocabulary dinner

Expand Vocabulary startled

One day, a hungry fox was preparing to hunt for his dinner. As he polished his claws, he was startled by a knock at the door.

Trade Book, p. 3

Guide Comprehension

Cause and Effect
Why is the fox sharpening his claws? (He will need them to hunt for his dinner.)

***Wh-* question**

What is the fox looking at? (the door)

- The fox is looking at the door because someone is knocking. Who is the "someone" at the door asking for?

Develop Vocabulary rabbit

Trade Book, pp. 4–5

Inferential

Is the someone at the door at the wrong house? How do you know? (Yes, whoever is at the door thinks this is the rabbit's house, but this is really the fox's house.)

Develop Vocabulary, continued

DAY 3

Open-ended

Who is standing there when the fox opens the door? (a piglet)

- A piglet is standing at the door. How can you tell the piglet is afraid when he sees the fox?

Expand Vocabulary delicious

When the fox opened the door, there stood a delicious-looking piglet.

"Oh, no!" screamed the piglet.

"Oh, yes!" cried the fox. "You've come to the right place."

He grabbed the piglet and hauled him inside.

Trade Book, pp. 6–7

Guide Comprehension, continued

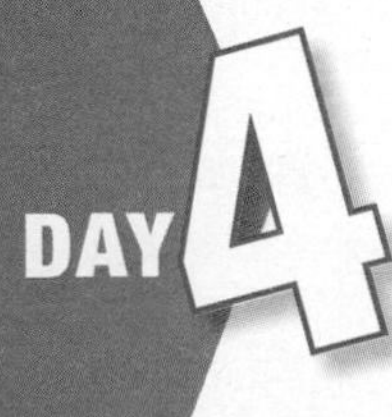

Inferential

The piglet realizes he has come to the wrong house. Why does the fox say that the piglet has come to the right place? (The fox thinks it's the right place because he wants to eat the piglet for dinner.)

Wh- question

What does the fox do? (picks up the piglet)

- The fox picks up the piglet. What is the fox going to do with the roasting pan?

Trade Book, pp. 8–9

Cause and Effect

The fox thinks this is his lucky day. Why? (The piglet is at his house and he won't have to hunt.)

- Do you think this is why the title of the story is *My Lucky Day?* Why or why not? (It really isn't the fox's lucky day, because at the end of the story the piglet gets away from the fox. It is really the piglet's lucky day.)

Develop Vocabulary, continued

Distancing

What does the piglet tell the fox to do before he eats him? (wash him)

- The piglet tells the fox he is filthy, so he needs to be washed. Do you wash your food before you eat it?

It was useless to struggle. "All right," sighed the piglet. "I will. But there is just one thing."

"What?" growled the fox.

"Well, I am a pig, you know. I'm filthy. Shouldn't you wash me first? Just a thought, Mr. Fox."

"Hmmm . . ." the fox said to himself, "he is filthy."

Trade Book, pp. 10–11

Guide Comprehension, continued

Inferential

Why do you think the piglet is so filthy? (He has probably been playing in the mud and dirt.)

Recall

What is the fox doing? (giving the piglet a bath)

- The fox is giving the piglet a bath. What does the fox do before he can give the piglet a bath?

Develop Vocabulary bath

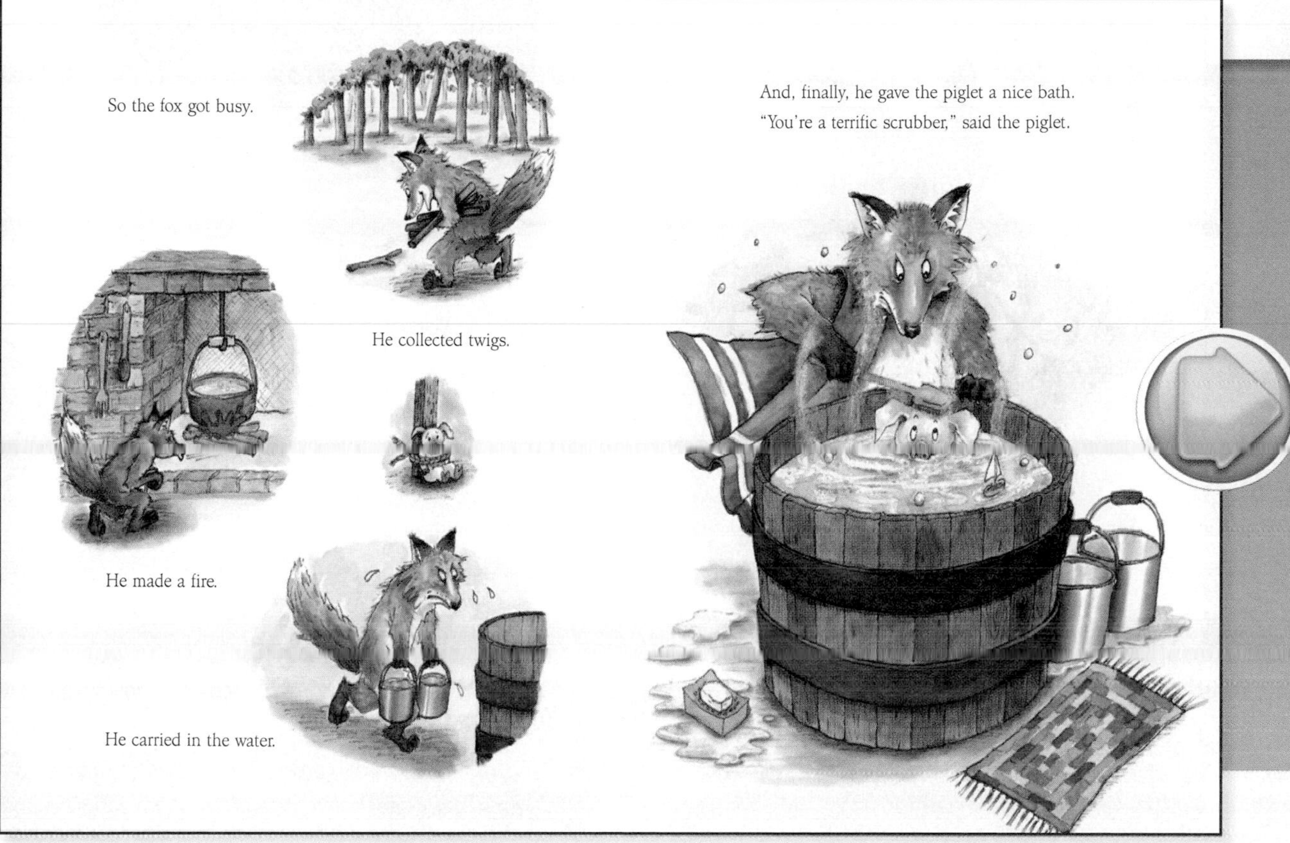

Trade Book, pp. 12–13

Cause and Effect

The fox ties up the piglet while he is getting the bath ready. Why? (to keep the piglet from escaping)

Develop Vocabulary, continued

DAY 3

Recall

Where is the piglet now? (in the pan)

- The piglet is in the roasting pan. What does the piglet tell the fox to do?

"There," said the fox. "Now you're the cleanest piglet in the county. You stay still, now!"

"All right," sighed the piglet. "I will. But . . ."

"But what?" growled the fox.

"Well, I am a very small piglet, you know. Shouldn't you fatten me up to get more meat? Just a thought, Mr. Fox."

"Hmmm . . ." the fox said to himself, "he is on the small side."

Trade Book, pp. 14–15

Guide Comprehension, continued

DAY 4

Cause and Effect

Why do you think the piglet keeps telling the fox things to do before he cooks the piglet? (The piglet does not want to be cooked, so he is trying everything he can to stop the fox.)

Distancing

What does the fox do to fatten up the piglet? (make dinner for him)

- The fox makes the piglet a nice dinner to fatten him up. What is your favorite dinner?

Trade Book, pp. 16–17

Cause and Effect

Why does the piglet tell the fox that the fox is a terrific cook? (He probably means it, but he might also be trying to be so friendly that the fox will decide not to eat him.)

Develop Vocabulary, continued

DAY 3

***Wh-* question**

Where is the fox going to put the piglet? (in the oven)

- The fox is putting the piglet in the oven. What other foods is the fox going to cook when he roasts the piglet?

"There," said the fox. "Now you're the fattest piglet in the county. So get into the oven!"

"All right," sighed the piglet. "I will. But . . ."

"What? What? WHAT?" shouted the fox.

"Well, I am a hardworking pig, you know. My meat is awfully tough. Shouldn't you massage me first to make a more tender roast? Just a thought, Mr. Fox."

"Hmmm . . ." the fox said to himself, "I do prefer tender meat."

Trade Book, pp. 18–19

Guide Comprehension, continued

DAY 4

Recall

What does the piglet think up to stop the fox from cooking him? (He thinks the fox should massage him to make him tender.)

Open-ended

What does the fox do to make the piglet tender? (He pushes, pulls, squeezes, and pounds on the piglet.)

- The fox pushes, pulls, squeezes, and pounds to give the piglet a massage. Why does the piglet have the fox give him a bath, make dinner, and now massage him?

Trade Book, pp. 20–21

Inferential

How do you think the fox is feeling? (He's probably frustrated, tired, and annoyed with the piglet.)

Develop Vocabulary, continued

Open-ended

How does the fox look now? (tired)

- The fox looks very tired. Why does the fox look tired?

Trade Book, pp. 22–23

Guide Comprehension, continued

Inferential

Do you think that the piglet is still scared of the fox? What makes you think so? (He doesn't act scared anymore. He seems to be enjoying his massage the way he enjoyed his spaghetti dinner.)

Open-ended

What is the fox doing? (falling down)

- The fox is falling down. Why do you think the fox is falling down? Why is he so tired?

Trade Book, pp. 24–25

Inferential

How do you think the piglet is feeling now? (He looks as if he is feeling very relaxed, and maybe even a little sleepy.)

Develop Vocabulary, continued

DAY 3

***Wh-* question**

Where is the fox? (on the floor)

- The fox is lying down on the floor. Have you ever worked so hard that you were too tired to do anything else?

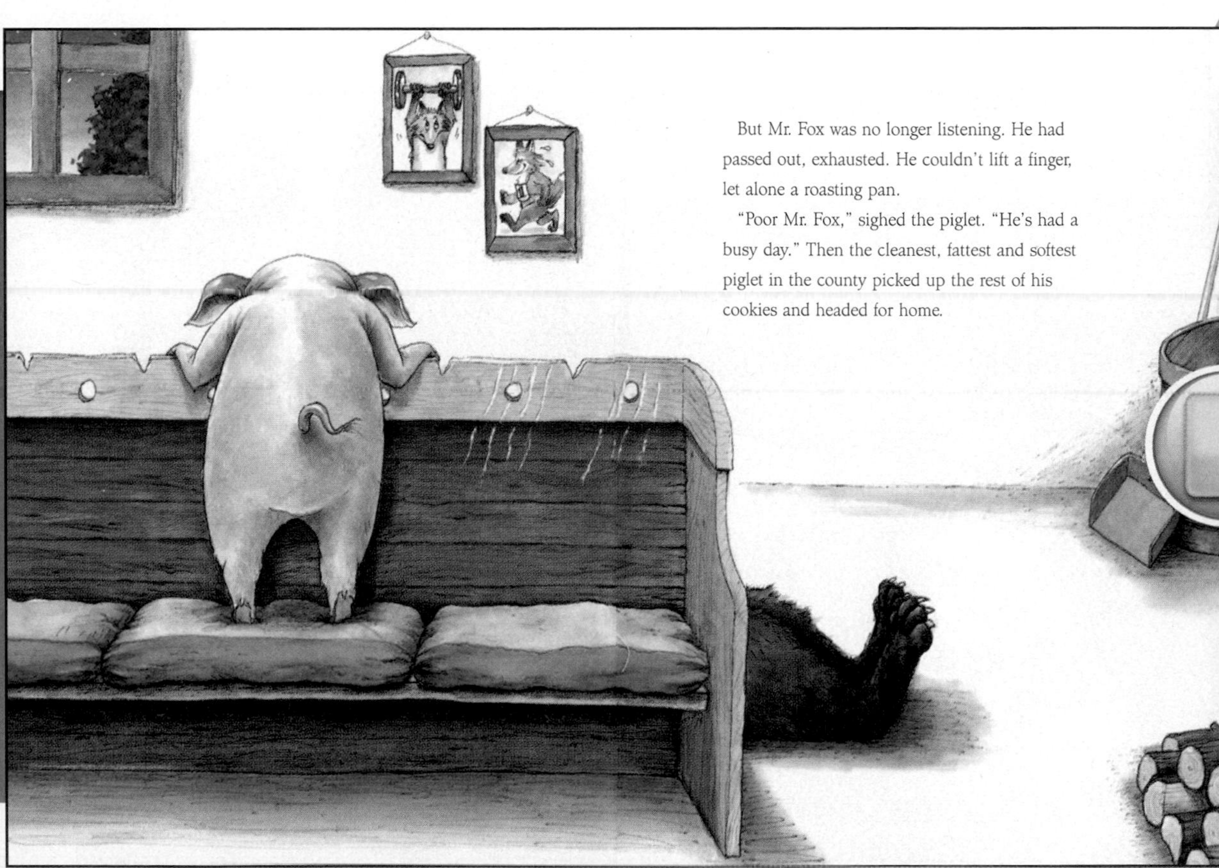

Trade Book, pp. 26–27

Guide Comprehension, continued

Compare and Contrast

How is the way the fox is feeling different from the way the piglet is feeling? (The fox is very tired, but the piglet is feeling great after his bath, dinner, and massage.)

Open-ended

What is the piglet doing? (running away)

- The piglet is running away happy after his bath, dinner, and massage. Do you think the piglet has had a lucky day? Why?

Trade Book, pp. 28–29

Main Idea

Are you surprised that it was the piglet's lucky day instead of the fox's lucky day? Why or why not? (At the beginning of the story, it seems to be the fox's lucky day because the piglet comes to his house. But the piglet changes it into his lucky day.)

DAYS 3 & 4 Read and Comprehend

Develop Vocabulary, continued

DAY 3

***Wh-* question**

What does the piglet do when he gets home? (sits in a chair)

- The piglet is sitting in a chair relaxing after his lucky day. Why is the piglet relaxing?

When he got home, the piglet relaxed before a warm fire. "Let's see," he wondered, looking at his address book. "Who shall I visit next?"

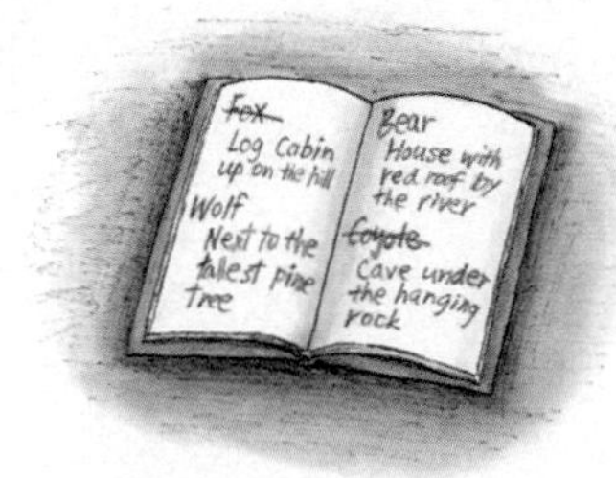

Trade Book, pp. 30–31

Guide Comprehension, continued

DAY 4

***Wh-* question**

What makes you think that maybe the piglet planned to visit the fox, after all? (The piglet is planning whom else to visit, so it seems that maybe he did plan to visit the fox.)

Open-ended

Who does the piglet visit next? (the bear)

- The piglet is standing at the bear's door. Do you think the piglet is surprised?

Conventions p. 172

Trade Book, p. 32

Predict

Do you think the piglet will do to the bear the same things he did to the fox? What makes you think so? (Maybe he will. It seems that perhaps he planned to visit the fox, and now he is at the bear's house.)

Conventions p. 186

Objectives

- Review naming parts.
- Dictate or write poems.

Conventions
Naming Parts

Review What do you remember about the part of a sentence that names something? Write this sentence on the board: *The teacher talks*. If *talks* is the action part of the sentence, what is the naming part of the sentence? *The teacher* is the naming part of the sentence.

Continue to remind children of what they learned about naming parts in sentences. The naming part is the part of a sentence that tells who or what does something. Have children make up sentences using people and animals you have learned about in the selections. Have children tell you the naming parts and action parts of their sentences.

Guide practice Write this sentence on the board: *Tom goes to school.* Touch under the words as you read the sentence aloud. Help children identify the subject. Touching under *Tom,* say: *Tom* is the naming part. Touching under *goes to school,* say: *goes to school* is the action part. Continue practice with the following sentences:

The girls ride their bikes.

Mom drives the car.

I ride the school bus.

Team Talk Pair children and have them take turns saying, writing, and illustrating simple sentences. Have each child identify the naming part and action part of his or her partner's sentence and picture.

On their own Use *Reader's and Writer's Notebook,* p. 261, for more practice with naming parts.

Daily Fix-It Use the Daily Fix-It for more conventions practice.

Reader's and Writer's Notebook, p. 261

Writing
Poem

Teach Talk about poems with children. A poem is a type of writing that has short lines. Poems have rhythm and sometimes rhyme. We write poems to share experiences, feelings, and ideas. Poems can be about anything we want.

Model Display the *fox* Picture Card. Today I am going to write a poem about a fox, like the fox in our story. My poem will have two lines. The two lines will end in rhyming words. What words rhyme with *fox?* The word *box* rhymes with *fox*. I will write this poem:

I see a fox.
It fits in a box.

Reread the poem with children. Have children identify the rhyming words.

Guide practice What kinds of things can we write poems about? Let's use our imaginations. Write children's suggestions on the board and select one topic for the class poem. Then have children suggest rhyming words for the poem. Write their rhyming words on the board.

Independent writing With children, write a class poem on the board. Use the selected topic and one of the suggested rhyming words. Have children copy the class poem on p. 262 of *Reader's and Writer's Notebook*. Then have them draw a picture about the poem.

Reader's and Writer's Notebook, p. 262

Daily Handwriting

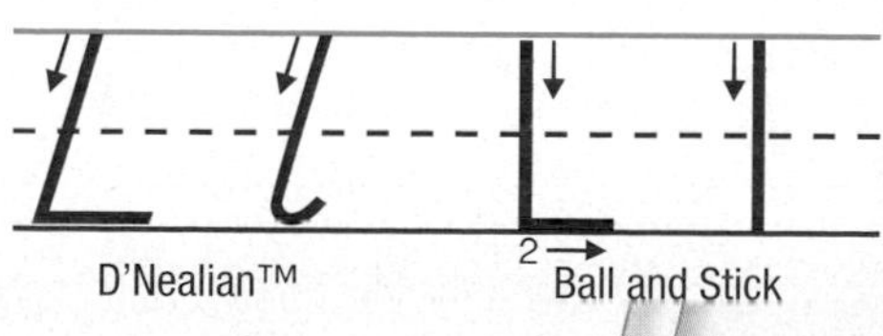

Write *Lib* and *lag* on the board. Review correct letter formation of uppercase *L* and lowercase *l*.

Have children write *Lib* and *lag* on their Write-On Boards. Remind children to use proper left-to-right and top-to-bottom progressions and proper spacing between letters when writing *L* and *l*.

Differentiated Instruction

SI Strategic Intervention

Academic Vocabulary Review the definition of *rhyme:* When words rhyme, they end in the same sound. Write *cat* and *hat* on the board. Say the words as you underline the rhyming parts. *Cat* and *hat* rhyme because they both end with /a/ /t/.

Academic Vocabulary

poem an imaginative piece of writing often arranged in lines having rhythm and rhyme

Daily Fix-It

the piglet had a lucky day
The piglet had a lucky day.

This week's practice sentences appear on Teacher Resources DVD-ROM.

ELL

English Language Learners

Support Phonemic Awareness English language learners may find it difficult to distinguish certain ending sounds in words, especially if the sounds do not exist in their home language. If children make mistakes when identifying rhyming words, provide extra practice.

DAY 3 Language Arts

Objectives

- Practice compare and contrast.
- Face the speaker when listening.
- Ask the speaker questions to clarify information.
- Speak one at a time.

Listening and Speaking
Compare and Contrast

Review Remind children that they can learn more about things by thinking about how they are the same or not the same. When you think about how things are the same, or alike, you are comparing. When you think about how things are not alike, or different, you are contrasting.

Model Have children turn to p. 49 of *My Skills Buddy.* I see a picture of an apple and an orange. Let's play "Alike and Different" with the apple and the orange. I will name a way the apple and orange are alike: the apple and the orange are both fruit. Can you name ways they are different? (They have different tastes and smells; they are different colors; they grow on different trees.) Repeat the routine to compare breakfast and dinner and a fox and a pig.

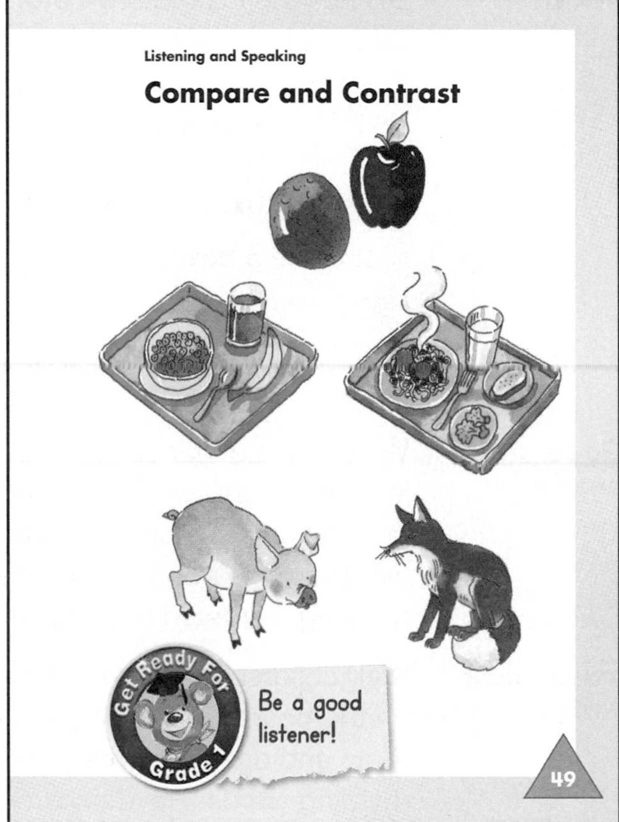

My Skills Buddy, p. 49

Independent practice You know that comparing and contrasting two things teaches us more about both things. When we do this with things from a story, we learn more about the story. Ask children to think about the fox and the piglet from the story. Have each child take turns telling how the fox and piglet from the story are alike or different. Or, if they prefer, have children tell how the fox or piglet from the story is different from an animal from a different story. Remind children that good listeners face the speaker and ask questions if they need the speaker to retell or explain information. Refer children to their Rules for Listening and Speaking on pp. 1–2 of the *Reader's and Writer's Notebook.*

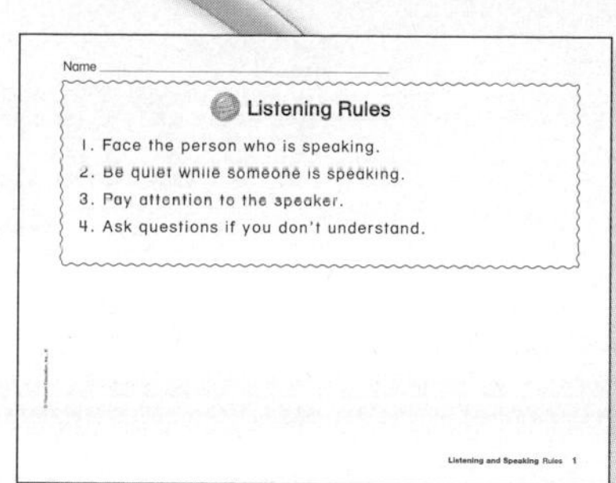
Name

Listening Rules

1. Face the person who is speaking.
2. Be quiet while someone is speaking.
3. Pay attention to the speaker.
4. Ask questions if you don't understand.

Listening and Speaking Rules 1

Reader's and Writer's Notebook, pp. 1–2

Be a Good Listener

1. Face the person who is speaking.
2. Be quiet while someone is speaking.
3. Pay attention to the speaker.
4. Ask questions if you don't understand.

English Language Learners

Access Content Ask children to tell about what is the same and different about the names of two objects that sound similar in English and their home language.

Objectives
- Review skills learned and practiced today.

Wrap Up Your Day

- ✔ **Concept Talk** Today we read more about having a lucky day. How was the piglet lucky? What would you do on a lucky day?
- ✔ **Respond to Literature** Today we read about a musical adventure. Have you ever played a musical instrument? What did it sound like?
- ✔ **Conventions** Ask children to tell you the naming parts and action parts of these sentences: *The cat runs fast. The toy makes noise. The children play ball.*

Preview DAY 4

Tell children that tomorrow they will read a story about their Trucktown friend, Gabriella Garbage Truck.

Science
Real or Make-Believe?

Materials: photographs of a real fox and a real pig, paper, crayons or markers

Show and Tell Remind children that sometimes the animals we read about in stories act and talk like people but that real animals do not do that. Show children photographs of a real fox.

This is a real fox. What does the make-believe fox in the story *My Lucky Day* do that this real fox does not do? (talk and act like a person) What does the real fox do that the make-believe fox in the story does? (try to get something to eat) Would a real fox use a stove? (no) Continue with the photograph of the real pig.

Give children paper and crayons or markers. Divide the group into pairs. Have one child in each pair draw a picture of a fox and the other child draw a pig. Have the pairs take turns showing their pictures and acting out something a real fox and pig would do and then acting out something a make-believe fox and pig might do.

Vocabulary Skill
Same and Different

Materials: various small classroom objects

Colors, Sizes, Shapes Scatter the objects in random order on a large table. Let volunteers take turns choosing items that are alike in some way and putting them in a separate pile. Have children discuss ways in which the items in the pile are alike. Continue similarly to have a second pile made. How are the things in these two piles different? Are they alike in any way? Have children put the objects in the two piles back into the main collection, and then continue the game.

Phonics
Letter and People Names

Materials: drawing paper, crayons or markers

What Letter Are You? Have children write the first letter of their first name as a large uppercase letter on drawing paper. Then have them recite the alphabet with you slowly. As each letter is named, have children whose name begins with that letter stand up and gather in a group. Ask what letters are not represented. Write each of those uppercase letters on separate sheets of drawing paper and tack them to the bulletin board in alphabetical order.

DAY 4 Get Ready to Read

20–25 mins.

Objectives

- Discuss the concept to develop oral language.
- Build oral vocabulary.

Today at a Glance

Oral Vocabulary
cook, scrubber

Phonemic Awareness
Review /h/

Phonics
Review /h/ spelled *Hh*
Spell Words

Comprehension
◉ Cause and Effect

Conventions
Action Parts

Writing
Extend the Concept

Vocabulary
Words for Textures

TRUCKTOWN on Reading Street

Start your engines!

- Display "Jack Be Nimble" and lead the group in saying the rhyme a few times.
- Have the group clap the rhythm as they recite the rhyme.
- When children master the rhythm, have them skip in place as they say the rhyme.

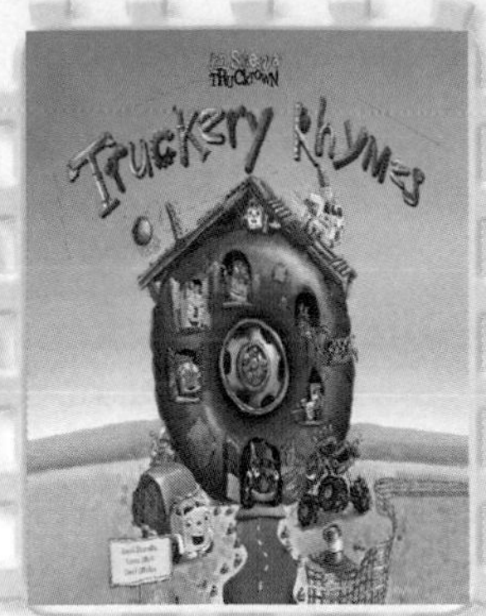

Truckery Rhymes

Concept Talk

Question of the Week

What is a lucky adventure?

Build concepts Write the question of the week on the board. Read the question as you track the print. Remind children to respond in complete sentences and to take turns speaking. Display Sing with Me Chart 20B.

Listen for Amazing Words We are going to sing this song again. Listen for the Amazing Words *cook* and *scrubber.* Sing the song with children to the tune of "Baby Bumble Bee." Ask children to clap when they hear *cook* and *scrubber.*

Sing with Me Audio

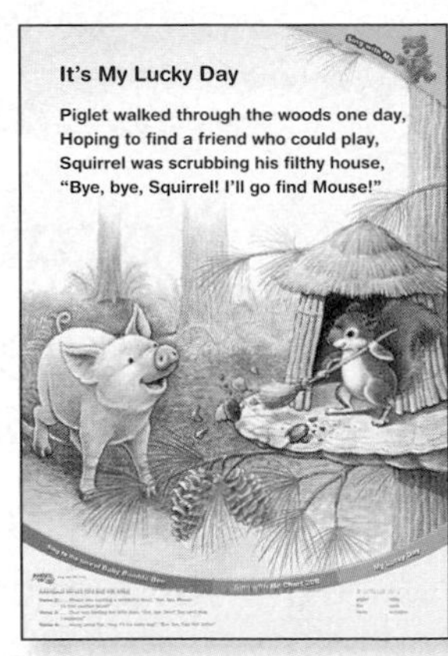

Talk with Me/Sing with Me Chart 20B

ELL Produce Oral Language Use the Day 4 instruction on ELL Poster 20 to extend and enrich language.

ELL Poster 20

Oral Vocabulary
Amazing Words

Teach Amazing Words

Amazing Words Oral Vocabulary Routine

1. **Introduce the Word** A *cook* is the person who prepares our meals. In our story, the fox is the *cook*. What's our new Amazing Word for a person who prepares meals? Say the word with me: *cook.*
2. **Demonstrate** *The cook makes spaghetti for the piglet.* What else can a *cook* make?

Repeat steps 1 and 2.

Introduce the Word A *scrubber* is someone who works hard to clean something dirty. What's our new Amazing Word for a person who works hard to wash something? Say it with me: *scrubber.*

Demonstrate *When something dirty needs cleaning, we might need a scrubber.* The piglet said fox was a good *scrubber.*

3. **Apply** Have children act out the Amazing Words *cook* and *scrubber*.

Routines Flip Chart

Use Amazing Words

To reinforce the concept and the Amazing Words, have children supply the appropriate Amazing Word for each sentence.

The ________ made a big dinner. (cook)

I am the ________ of the pots and pans. (scrubber)

Amazing Words

piglet	fox
lucky	filthy
cook	scrubber

Differentiated Instruction

Advanced

Amazing Words Tell children that the Amazing Word *cook* can be a naming part and an action part. Write this sentence on the board: *The cook makes lunch.* In this sentence, *cook* is the naming part. Then write this sentence on the board: *I cook eggs*. In this sentence, *cook* is part of the action part, *cook eggs*. Have children dictate two sentences using *cook* as a naming part and as an action part.

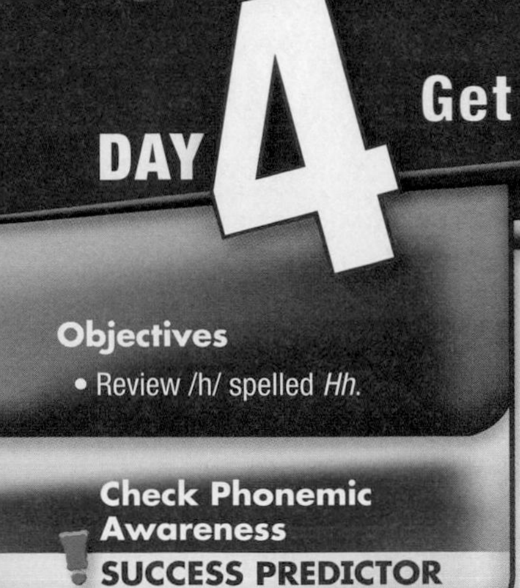

Objectives

- Review /h/ spelled *Hh.*

Check Phonemic Awareness
SUCCESS PREDICTOR

Phonemic Awareness
Review /h/

Review Display the *hat* Picture Card. This is a *hat. Hat* begins with /h/. What sound does *hat* begin with? Continue the routine with the following Picture Cards: *hose, hen, hammer, house*.

I am going to say three words. Tell me which two words begin with /h/. Listen carefully: *hop, has, doll*. *Hop* and *has* begin with /h/. *Doll* begins with /d/. Continue the activity with the following sets of words: *hair, tall, how; mat, half, horse; tip, hold, hum; pink, house, him.*

Corrective feedback

If... children cannot discriminate /h/,
then... have them say /h/ several times, /h/ /h/ /h/.

When you say /h/, your lips are open. You say /h/ by blowing air out from your throat. Have children practice saying /h/ and then repeat the discrimination activity.

Picture Card

Picture Card

Picture Card

Phonics
/h/ Spelled *Hh*

Review

Display the *Hh* Alphabet Card. This is a *helicopter. Helicopter* begins with /h/. What letter spells the sound /h/? Yes, the letter *h*.

Alphabet Card

Write the word *hat* on the board. Help me blend this word. Listen as I say each sound: /h/ /a/ /t/. Say it with me: /h/ /a/ /t/. Now let's blend the sounds together to read the word: /h/ /a/ /t/, *hat*. What is the word? (*hat*) Let's try one more. Write *hip* on the board and repeat the routine.

Don't Wait Until Friday

MONITOR PROGRESS Check Phonemic Awareness

Phoneme Segmentation I am going to say a word. Tell me all the sounds you hear in the word.

Tab	**bat**	**lid**	**fit**	**Lil**	**lit**
doll	**lap**	**did**	**not**	**it**	**kit**

If... children cannot segment the sounds in words,

then... use the small-group Strategic Intervention lesson, p. DI•21, to reteach segmentation skills.

Continue to monitor children's progress using other instructional opportunities during the week so that they can be successful with the Day 5 Assessment. See the Skills Trace on p. 116.

Day 1	Day 2	Day 3	Day 4	Day 5
Check Phonemic Awareness	Check Sound-Spelling/ Retelling	Check Word Reading	Check Phonemic Awareness	Check Oral Vocabulary

Success Predictor

Differentiated Instruction

SI Strategic Intervention

Sound Game Pair children and have them each look around the room or think of something that begins with /h/. Then tell them to draw a picture of the object. Have each child show the drawing to his or her partner to guess the /h/ word. If the partner can't guess, tell the illustrator to provide clues. Then have partners switch roles.

Objectives
- Spell words.
- Blend and segment words.
- Read decodable text.
- Read high-frequency words.

Spelling
/l/ Spelled *Ll*

ROUTINE Spell Words

Spell words

1. **Review Sound-Spellings** Display the *Ll* Alphabet Card. This is a *lemon. Lemon* begins with /l/. What is the letter for /l/? (*l*) Continue the routine with the following Alphabet Cards: *Aa, Hh, Ii, Pp, Dd, Mm, Oo, Cc, Tt.*
2. **Model** Today we are going to spell some words. Listen to the three sounds in *lap:* /l/ /a/ /p/.

   l a p

   - What is the first sound in *lap?* (/l/) What is the letter for /l/? (*l*) Write *l* on the board.
   - What is the middle sound you hear? (/a/) What is the letter for /a/? (*a*) Write *a* on the board.
   - What is the last sound you hear? (/p/) What is the letter for /p/? (*p*) Write *p* on the board.
   - Point to *lap.* Help me blend the sounds of each letter together to read this word: /l/ /a/ /p/. The word is *lap.* Repeat the modeling with *hill.*
3. **Guide Practice** Now let's spell some words together. Listen to this word: /l/ /i/ /d/. What is the first sound in *lid?* (/l/) What is the letter for /l/? (*l*) Write *l* on the board. Now you write *l* on your paper. What is the middle sound in *lid?* (/i/) What is the letter for /i/? (*i*) Write *i* on the board. Now you write *i* on your paper. What is the last sound in *lid?* (/d/) What is the letter for /d/? (*d*) Write *d* on the board. Now you write *d* on your paper. Now we can blend the sound of each letter together to read the word: /l/ /i/ /d/. What is the word? (*lid*) Continue spell and blend practice with the following words: *cat, doll, mop, lit.*
4. **On Your Own** This time I am going to say a word. I want you to write it on your paper. Remember, first, say the word slowly in your head and then write the letter for each sound. Listen carefully: *pin.* Write the word *pin.* Give children time to write the word. How do you spell the word *pin?* Listen to the sounds: /p/ /i/ /n/. The first sound is /p/. What is the letter for /p/? Did you write *p* on your paper? What is the letter for /i/? Did you write *i* on your paper? What is the letter for /n/? Did you write *n* on your paper? Name the letters in *pin. Pin* is spelled *p, i, n.* Continue the activity with the following words: *hat, fill, top, cab, sob.*

Routines Flip Chart

Get Set, Roll! Reader 20

Practice /l/ Spelled *Ll*

Review Review the high-frequency words *I, have, a, to, the,* and *is.* Have children find each word on the Word Wall.

Teach rebus words Write the word *garbage* on the board. This is the word *garbage*. Name the letters with me: *g, a, r, b, a, g, e; garbage.* Continue with the words *Gabriella* and *yard*. Look for the words *garbage, Gabriella,* and *yard* in the story we read today.

Read Get Set, Roll! Reader 20 Display Get Set, Roll! Reader 20. Today we will read a story about our friend Gabriella Garbage Truck. Point to the title of the story. What is the title of the story? (*Are You Like Gabriella?*) We will read several /l/ words in this story.

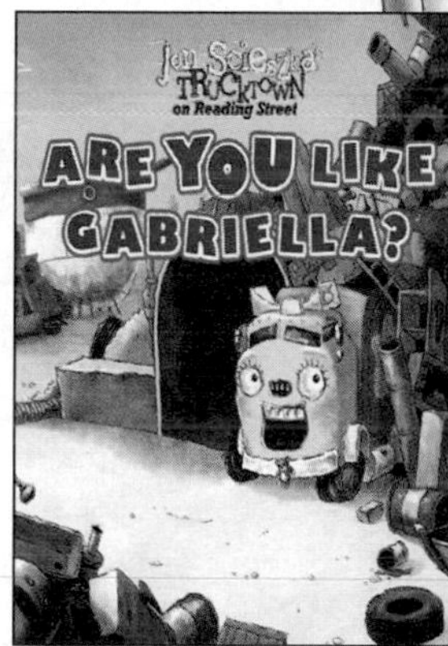

Get Set, Roll! Reader 20

Differentiated Instruction

 Strategic Intervention

Build Background Ask children if they have ever seen a garbage truck in real life. Have them share what they know about garbage trucks. Define *garbage* and describe what happens to garbage after it is thrown away. Explain the difference between garbage and recyclables.

Small Group Time

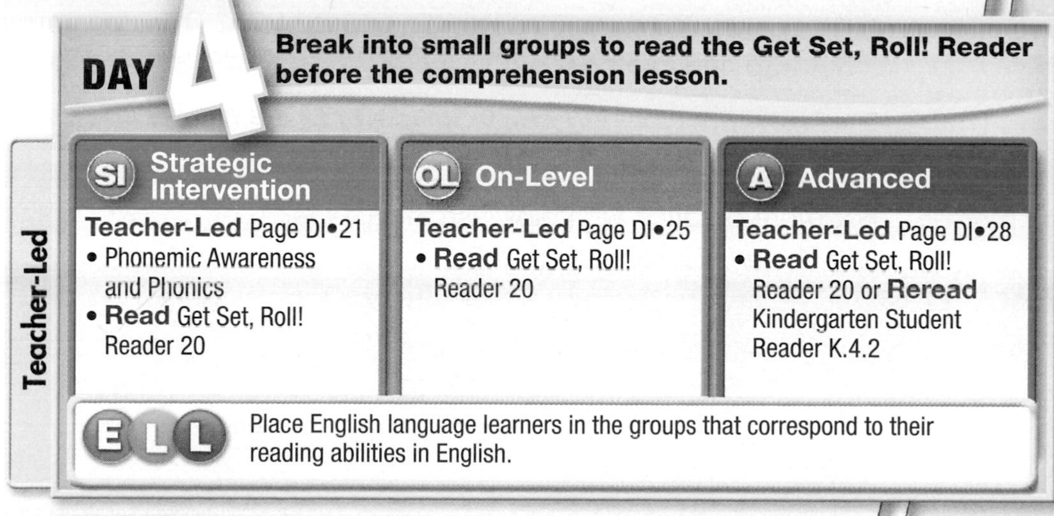

DAY 4 **Break into small groups to read the Get Set, Roll! Reader before the comprehension lesson.**

Teacher-Led

SI Strategic Intervention	OL On-Level	A Advanced
Teacher-Led Page DI•21 • Phonemic Awareness and Phonics • **Read** Get Set, Roll! Reader 20	**Teacher-Led** Page DI•25 • **Read** Get Set, Roll! Reader 20	**Teacher-Led** Page DI•28 • **Read** Get Set, Roll! Reader 20 or **Reread** Kindergarten Student Reader K.4.2

ELL Place English language learners in the groups that correspond to their reading abilities in English.

Practice Stations
- Visit the Let's Write! Station
- Visit the Read for Meaning Station

Independent Activities
- Read independently
- Audio Text of the Trade Book
- *Reader's and Writer's Notebook*

DAY 4 Read and Comprehend 20–25 mins.

Objectives

- Practice cause and effect.
- Review plot.

Comprehension
Cause and Effect

Practice cause and effect

Have children turn to pp. 34–35 of *My Skills Buddy.* Remind children that many things happen because something else makes them happen. What happens is called an *effect*. Why it happens is called a *cause*.

My Skills Buddy, pp. 34–35

Team Talk Pair children and have them take turns describing examples of cause and effect from their day.

Plot

Review

Review plot with children. All stories have a beginning, a middle, and an end. Together, these parts make a story's plot. Display *The Lion and the Mouse* and review the plot with children.

- What happens at the beginning of this story? (The mouse offers to help the lion, but the lion laughs at him.)
- What happens during the middle of this story? (The lion gets caught in a net trap and can't get out.)
- What happens at the end of this story? (The mouse chews a hole in the net and frees the lion.)

More practice

For more practice with plot, use the *Reader's and Writer's Notebook*, p. 263.

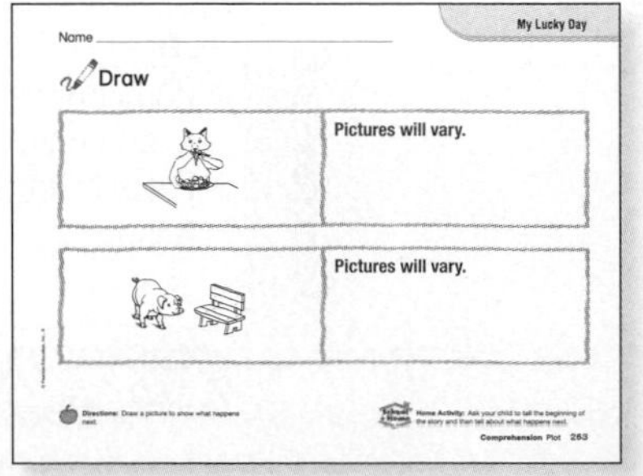

Reader's and Writer's Notebook, p. 263

Third Read—Trade Book
My Lucky Day

Guide comprehension

Display *My Lucky Day*. This story has a beginning, a middle, and an end.

- What happens at the beginning of the story? (The piglet knocks on the fox's door.)
- What happens in the middle of the story? (The piglet gets the fox to do nice things for him.)
- What happens at the end of the story? (The fox is too tired to cook the piglet, so the piglet gets away.)

Reread *My Lucky Day.* Return to p. 156. Follow the Day 4 arrow and use the Guide Comprehension notes to give children the opportunity to gain a more complete understanding of the story.

Read for enjoyment

Reread using Develop Vocabulary notes

DAY 4
Reread using Guide Comprehension notes

Objectives
- Identify action parts.
- Practice action parts.
- Write or dictate ideas about lucky adventures.

Conventions
Action Parts

Review Remind children of what they learned about action parts. Remember that sentences have naming parts and action parts. The naming part tells who or what does something. The action part tells the action the naming part is doing. Listen for the action part in this sentence: *Judy runs fast.* In this sentence, *Judy* is the naming part. *Runs fast* is the action part. It tells what Judy is doing.

Guide practice I am going to say a sentence. Listen for the action part: *Tom hits the ball. Tom* is the naming part. What does Tom do? (hits the ball) What part of the sentence is this? (action part) What are some different actions you can do? Write children's suggestions on the board. Have children say a complete sentence with their names as the naming part and an action part from the board.

On their own Use *Reader's and Writer's Notebook,* p. 264, for more practice with action parts.

Daily Fix-It Use the Daily Fix-It for more conventions practice.

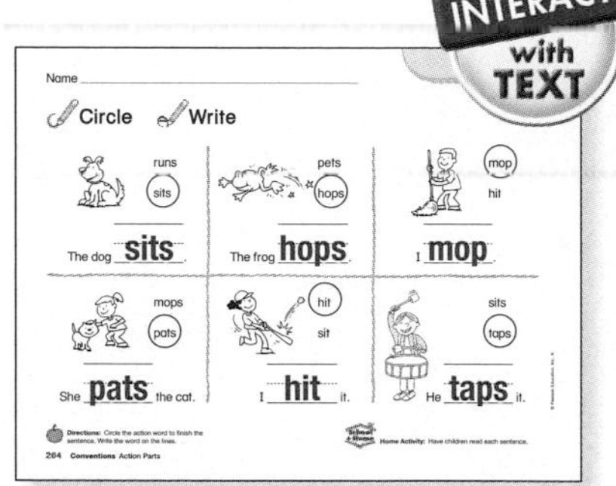

Reader's and Writer's Notebook, p. 264

Writing
Extend the Concept: Text to Self

Discuss lucky adventures

We just read a story about a piglet's lucky day. At the beginning of the story, the fox thinks it is his lucky day. When the piglet gets the fox to do nice things for him, we find out it is actually the piglet's lucky day! Sometimes our adventures may be lucky, like the piglet's adventure.

Ask children to think about lucky adventures they have had. Have children talk about how surprises can make an adventure lucky. Remind them to speak in complete sentences. List some of their adventures on the board.

Guide practice

Use children's contributions to the discussion to write sentences.

We are lucky when...	**we get surprises.** **we find new friends.**
We have adventures when...	**we make believe.** **we take trips.**

Encourage children to help you write more sentences. Have them read the sentences with you.

Independent writing

Have children write or dictate their own complete sentences about a lucky adventure, or they may copy a sentence from the board. Then have them illustrate one of the sentences and share their drawings with the class.

Daily Handwriting

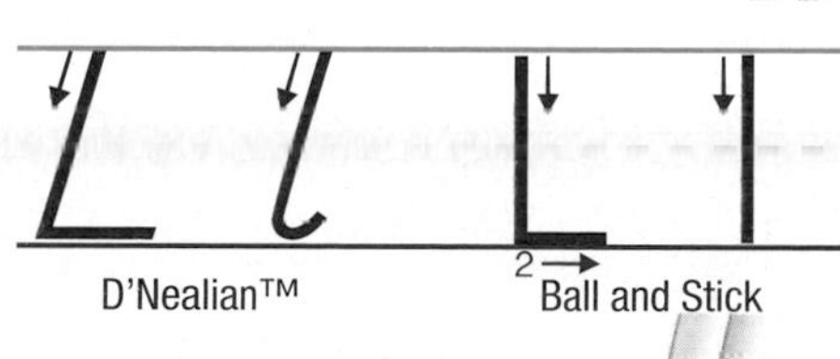

Write uppercase *L* and lowercase *l* on the board. Review correct letter formation with children.

Have children write a row of uppercase *L* and a row of lowercase *l* on their Write-On Boards. Remind them to use proper left-to-right and top-to-bottom progression when writing *L* and *l*.

Differentiated Instruction

Strategic Intervention

Guide Writing Brainstorm lucky adventures with children in order to help them write or dictate their sentences.

Daily Fix-It

the duck will fix it

<u>T</u>he duck will fix it<u>.</u>

This week's practice sentences appear on Teacher Resources DVD-ROM.

DAY 4 Language Arts

Objectives

- Practice using words for textures in sentences.
- Identify words that begin with /l/.

Vocabulary
Words for Textures

fuzzy **bumpy** **furry** **sharp**

Teach

Write the words *fuzzy*, *bumpy*, *furry*, and *sharp* on the board. Point to each word as you read it. These words show how something feels if you touch it. Have children turn to p. 48 of *My Skills Buddy*. Direct them to the picture of the dog. Is the dog *fuzzy* or *furry?* Then direct them to the picture of the caterpillar. Is the caterpillar *fuzzy* or *furry?* Have children point to the picture of the bumpy object (pickle) and then to the picture of the sharp object (pencil). Discuss the second through fifth Vocabulary bullets on the page.

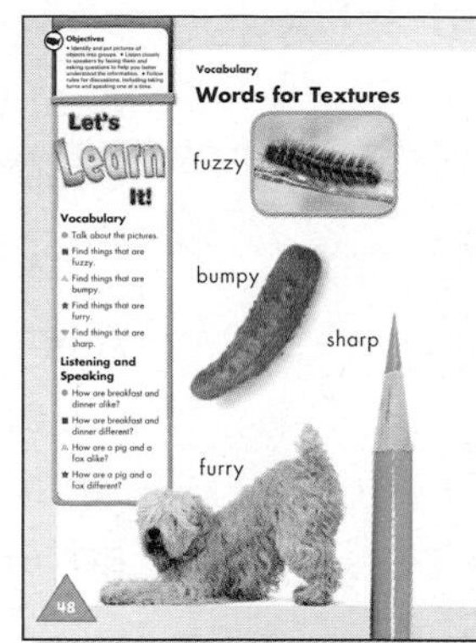

My Skills Buddy, p. 48

Team Talk Pair children and have them take turns using the texture words *fuzzy, bumpy, furry,* and *sharp* in sentences. Remind children to use complete sentences.

Wrap Up Your Day

- ✔ **Oral Language** Sing "It's My Lucky Day" with me. Clap when you hear these Amazing Words: *piglet, fox, lucky, filthy, cook, scrubber.*
- ✔ **Phonemic Awareness** I am going to read some sentences. Clap when you hear words that begin with /l/: *Leah has a loud laugh. Larry is a little lad.*
- ✔ **Homework Idea** Have children ask a family member to help them make a list of things that feel fuzzy, bumpy, furry, or sharp. Allow time for children to share their lists.

Tell children that tomorrow they will review some of the books and stories they have read this week.

Science
Water, Water, Everywhere

Materials: clear plastic pitcher, clear plastic cups, tablespoon, water, ice cubes, Trade Book *My Lucky Day*.

How Much Water? Display pp. 12–13 of *My Lucky Day*. The fox carries buckets of water to fill the tub for the piglet's bath. What else do we use water for?

What Kind of Water? Put two ice cubes in a clear plastic cup. Fill another cup about one-third full with water. Use a marker to show the water level on the outside of the cup. What will happen to the ice and the water if we let them sit on a table? Let's see what happens if we leave them on the table for a while. After a period of time, have children check the ice cubes. What happened to the ice cubes? Point out the forms of water: It is solid when it is ice but becomes a liquid when it melts. After several days, check the water level in the cup. What happened to the cup of water? Point out that water can evaporate, or go into the air, when it is left in an open cup.

Have children draw pictures to show what happened to the ice cubes and to the cup of water.

Comprehension
Follow the Plot

Materials: Trade Book *My Lucky Day*, paper, crayons or markers

Then What Happened? Divide a paper into 3 panels, labeling them *Beginning, Middle,* and *End*. Reread pp. 3–5 of *My Lucky Day* aloud to children, showing the illustrations as you read. What happened at the beginning of this story? Let's draw the beginning of the story. Indicate the word *Beginning* on the paper. Let children work together to draw the scene. Have them dictate or write a sentence about it. Continue with the rest of the story.

Conventions
Action Parts

Materials: two small pieces of paper for each child, crayons or markers

Illustrate Parts of a Sentence Give each child two small pieces of paper. On one paper, children will write their names to serve as the naming part of your sentences. On the other piece of paper, they will draw an action that is fun and easy to act out to serve as the action part of your sentences.

Put all naming parts in one basket and all action parts in a separate basket. Have children sit in a circle. Randomly choose one paper from each basket. The child called will act out the action selected. Assist children by listing possible actions they can draw.

Objectives

- Review the concepts.
- Build oral vocabulary.

Today at a Glance

Oral Vocabulary
piglet, fox, lucky, filthy, cook, scrubber

Phonemic Awareness
◉ Initial and Final /l/

Phonics
◉ /l/ Spelled *Ll*

Comprehension
◉ Cause and Effect

Conventions
Action Parts

Writing
This Week We…

Check Oral Vocabulary
SUCCESS PREDICTOR

TRUCKTOWN on Reading Street

Start your engines!

- Display "Jack Be Nimble" and lead the group in saying the rhyme a few times.
- Have half the group recite the rhyme while the other half acts it out.
- Then have the groups change roles.

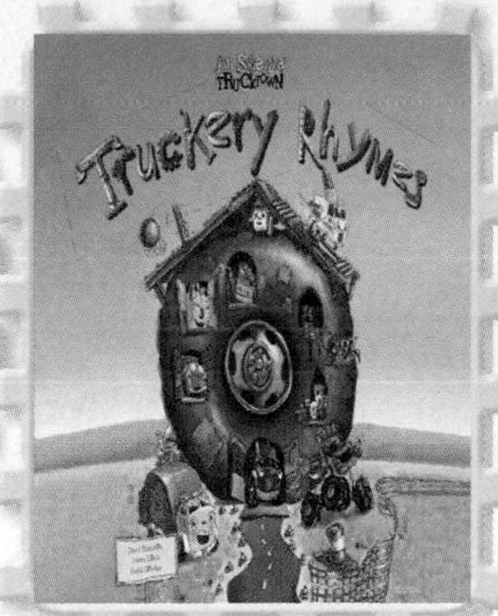

Truckery Rhymes

Concept Wrap Up

Question of the Week

What is a lucky adventure?

Listen for Amazing Words

Write the question of the week on the board. Track the print as you read it to children. Ask them to answer the question in complete sentences, using as many of the Amazing Words as possible (*piglet, fox, lucky, filthy, cook, scrubber*). Display Sing with Me Chart 20B. Let's sing "It's My Lucky Day" again. Remind children that the Amazing Words *piglet, fox, lucky, filthy, cook,* and *scrubber* are in the song. Sing the song again with them. Discuss how the piglet in the song is similar to and different from the piglet in *My Lucky Day*. Remind children to speak one at a time.

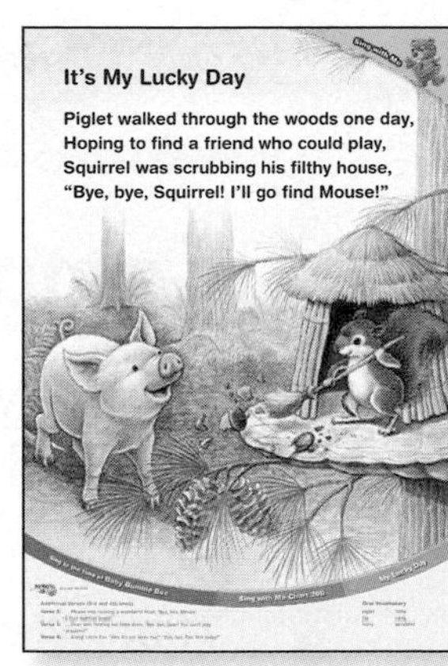

Sing with Me Chart 20B

Sing with Me Audio

ELL Check Concepts and Language Use Day 5 instruction on ELL Poster 20 to monitor children's understanding of the lesson concept.

ELL Poster 20

Oral Vocabulary
Amazing Words

Review

Let's Talk Display Talk with Me Chart 20A. We learned six new Amazing Words this week: *piglet, fox, lucky, filthy, cook, scrubber*. Let's say the Amazing Words as we look at the pictures on the chart. Touch under each picture and give children the chance to say the appropriate Amazing Word before offering it.

A ________ has a curly tail. (piglet)
The ________ washes a mug. (scrubber)
The animal with orange fur is a ________. (fox)
Kim's hands are ________ from painting. (filthy)
The school ________ makes lunch. (cook)
Sam is ________ to win a prize. (lucky)

It's Friday

MONITOR PROGRESS

Check Oral Vocabulary

Demonstrate Word Knowledge Monitor the Amazing Words by asking the following questions. Have children use the Amazing Word in their answer.

- **What do you call the kind of day when everything good happens?** (lucky)
- **What is a small pig called?** (piglet)
- **What other animal was in the story *My Lucky Day?*** (fox)
- **When you are really dirty, what are you?** (filthy)
- **What do we call a person who prepares food?** (cook)
- **If you scrub something very hard, what are you?** (scrubber)

If... children have difficulty using the Amazing Words,
then... reteach unknown words using the Oral Vocabulary Routine on the Routines Flip Chart.

Day 1	Day 2	Day 3	Day 4	Day 5
Check Phonemic Awareness	Check Sound-Spelling/ Retelling	Check Word Reading	Check Phonemic Awareness	Check Oral Vocabulary

Success Predictor

Amazing Words

piglet	fox
lucky	filthy
cook	scrubber

Differentiated Instruction

Strategic Intervention

Amazing Words Some children may have trouble remembering the six Amazing Words. After you read each question, offer two or three of the Amazing Words for children to choose from.

Talk with Me/Sing with Me Chart 20A

DAY 5 Wrap Up your Week

Objectives

- ◎ Review initial and final /l/.
- ◎ Review /l/ spelled *Ll*.

Phonemic Awareness Review

/l/

Isolate initial and final /l/

Display the *lake* Picture Card. What is the first sound in *lake?* Say the word with me: /l/ /l/ /l/, *lake.* Review initial /l/ with these Picture Cards: *loaf, ladybug, lemon, leaf, lamp.*

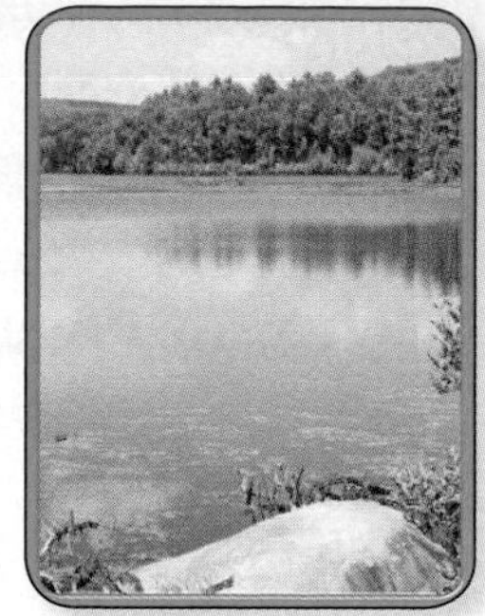

Picture Card

Display the *doll* Picture Card. What is the last sound in *doll?* Say it again: *doll,* /l/ /l/ /l/. Continue isolating final /l/ with these Picture Cards: *pail, seal, snail*.

Discriminate initial and final /l/

Listen as I say the sounds in a word: /l/ /a/ /b/. Say the sounds with me: /l/ /a/ /b/. What is the word? (*lab*) Where do you hear /l/ in the word *lab?* (at the beginning of the word) Repeat the steps with the word *pal* as children identify /l/ at the end of the word. Continue with these words: *lid, lap, Sal, lot, ball, mill, let, lad*.

Picture Card

Phonics Review
/l/ Spelled *Ll*

Teach /l/*Ll* Display the *Ll* Alphabet Card. This is a *lemon*. What sound do you hear at the beginning of *lemon*? What letter spells that sound?

High-frequency words Write the word *are* on the board. What is this word? Repeat the routine with *that* and *do*.

Apply phonics in familiar text **Let's Reread** Have children reread one of the books specific to the target letter sound. You may wish to review the decodable words and high-frequency words that appear in each book prior to rereading.

Alphabet Card

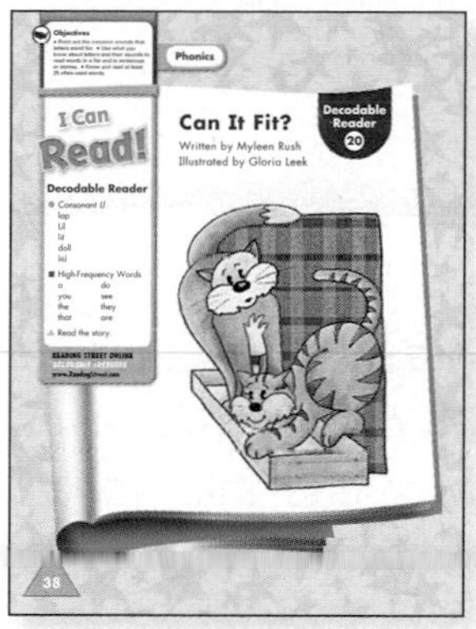

Decodable Reader 20
My Skills Buddy, p. 38

Kindergarten Student
Reader K.4.2

Get Set, Roll!
Reader 20

Differentiated Instruction

 Strategic Intervention

Practice Reading Have children reread the books with a partner. Tell children to alternate sentences. If one child has difficulty, encourage his or her partner to help.

Small Group Time

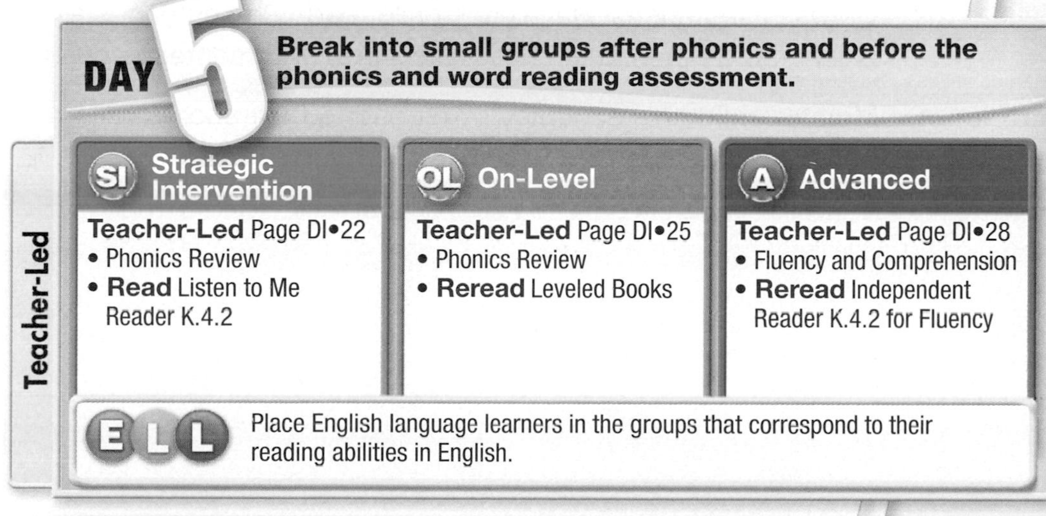

DAY 5 **Break into small groups after phonics and before the phonics and word reading assessment.**

Teacher-Led

SI Strategic Intervention	OL On-Level	A Advanced
Teacher-Led Page DI•22 • Phonics Review • **Read** Listen to Me Reader K.4.2	**Teacher-Led** Page DI•25 • Phonics Review • **Reread** Leveled Books	**Teacher-Led** Page DI•28 • Fluency and Comprehension • **Reread** Independent Reader K.4.2 for Fluency

ELL Place English language learners in the groups that correspond to their reading abilities in English.

Practice Stations
- Visit the Read for Meaning Station
- Visit the Let's Make Art Station

Independent Activities
- Read independently
- Story Sort
- Concept Talk Video

Assess

- ◎ Read words with /l/.
- Read high-frequency words.
- Read sentences.

Assessment
Monitor Progress

/l/ Spelled *Ll* **Whole Class** Have children fold a sheet of paper to make four sections. Ask them to draw a picture of something whose name begins or ends with /l/ in each section. Then ask them to label each picture with the word with the letter *l*.

MONITOR PROGRESS **Check Word and Sentence Reading**

If... children cannot complete the whole-class assessment, **then...** use the Reteach lesson in *First Stop.*

If... you are unsure of a child's grasp of this week's skills, **then...** use the assessment below to obtain a clearer evaluation of the child's progress.

/l/ Spelled *Ll* and high-frequency words **One-on-One** To facilitate individual progress monitoring, assess some children on Day 4 and the rest on Day 5. While individual children are being assessed, the rest of the class can reread this week's books and look for words with /l/.

Word reading Use the reproducible word list on reproducible p. 195 to assess each child's ability to read words that begin and end in /l/. We're going to read some words. I'll read the first word, and you read the rest. The first word is *lip,* /l/ /i/ /p/. For each child, record any decoding problems.

Sentence reading Use the reproducible sentences on p. 195 to assess a child's ability to read words in sentences. Have each child read two sentences aloud. Have each child read different sentences. Start over with sentence one if necessary.

Record scores Monitor children's accuracy by recording their scores using the Word and Sentence Reading Chart for this unit in *First Stop*.

Name ______________________________

Read the Words

lip	☐	that	☐
lad	☐	hill	☐
do	☐	lit	☐
lap	☐	are	☐
lid	☐	doll	☐
fill	☐	Bill	☐

Read the Sentences

1. That little lad is sad.
2. That is my doll.
3. Are you Bill?
4. Do they have a doll?
5. Are they in the lab?

Note to Teacher: Children read each word. Children read two sentences.

Scoring for Read the Words: Score 1 point for each correct word.

/l/*Ll* (*lip, lad, lap, lid, fill, hill, lit, doll, Bill*) _______ / 9

High-Frequency Words (*do, that, are*) _______ / 3

MONITOR PROGRESS

- /l/ Spelled *Ll*
- High-frequency words

DAY 5 Wrap Up your Week

Objectives

- Identify a fable.
- Identify the moral or lesson in a fable.

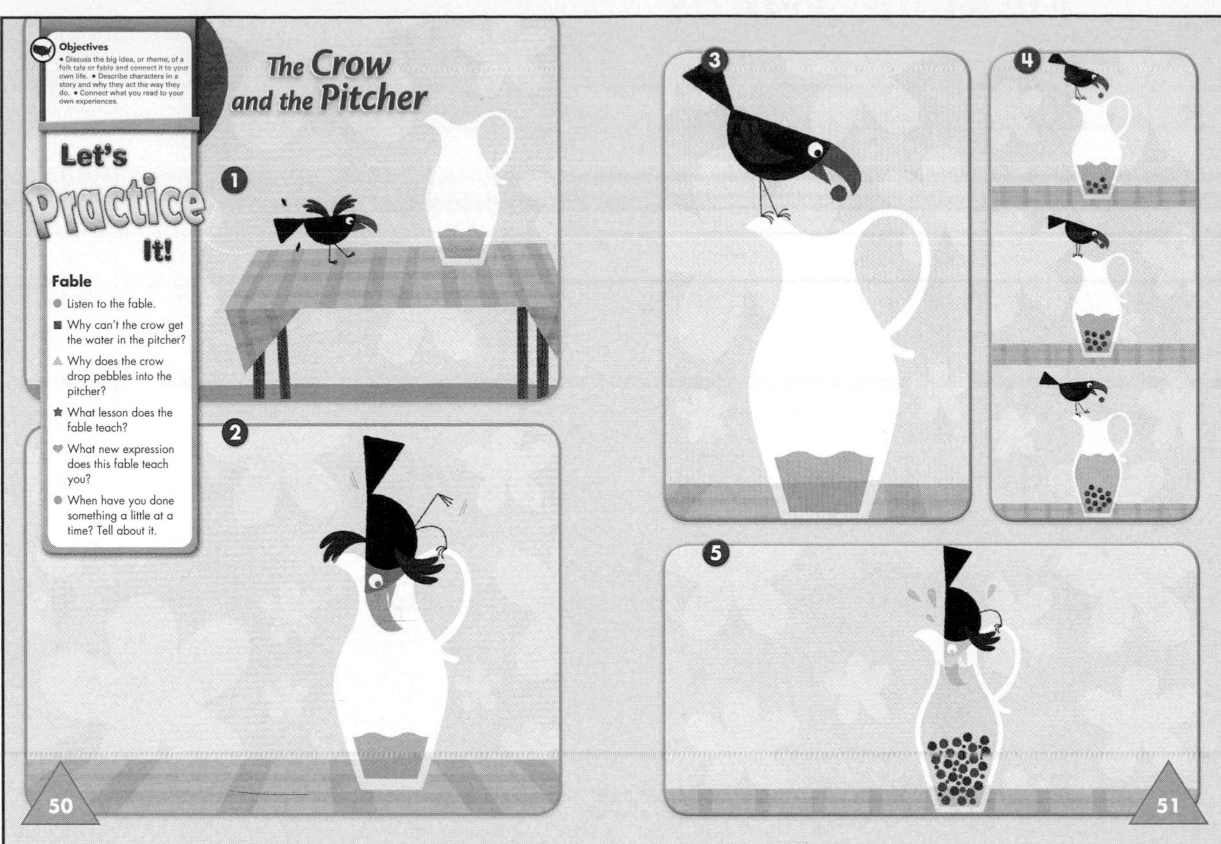

My Skills Buddy, pp. 50–51

Let's Practice It!
Fable

Teach

Tell children that today they will listen to a well-known fable. A fable is a type of story. Review the features of a fable with children.

- A fable usually has animal characters.
- A fable teaches a moral, or lesson.

Have children turn to pp. 50–51 of *My Skills Buddy*. I am going to read a fable called "The Crow and the Pitcher." Look at the pictures as I read. Read the text of "The Crow and the Pitcher." As you read, direct children to look at the appropriate picture.

Guide practice

Discuss the features of the fable with children and the bulleted text on *My Skills Buddy* p. 50.

- A fable usually has animal characters. What animal is the character in this fable? (a crow) Why does the crow drop pebbles into the pitcher? (There is a little bit of water in the pitcher, and the crow can't reach it. He is using pebbles to make the water rise up.)
- A fable teaches a moral, or lesson. What big idea, or lesson, does the fable teach? (The lesson is stated in the last sentence. Little by little does the trick.)
- What does "little by little does the trick" mean? (Sometimes it takes a little at a time to get things done.) When have you done something a little at a time? (Possible answer: When I was learning to write my name. I had to learn one letter at a time.)

Academic Vocabulary

fable a story, usually with animal characters, that is written to teach a moral, or lesson

English Language Learners

Frontload Read Aloud Display Read Aloud art from *My Skills Buddy* to children. Touch under the *pitcher* and the *crow* as you define these words for English language learners.

The Crow and the Pitcher

A very thirsty crow came upon a pitcher. She hoped it would be full of water. But, alas, when the crow stuck her beak into the pitcher, she found there was only a little water left at the bottom. She could not reach far enough to get the water. The crow tried and tried, poking her beak into the pitcher this way and that. But at last she had to give up.

Then the crow had an idea. She flew away, picked up a pebble, flew back, and dropped the pebble into the pitcher.

She picked up another pebble and dropped it into the pitcher.

She picked up another pebble and dropped it into the pitcher.

She picked up yet another pebble and dropped it into the pitcher.

Each time the crow dropped a pebble into the pitcher, the water rose a little higher. At last, after dropping in many pebbles, the crow was able to reach the water and drink her fill. The crow learned that little by little does the trick.

Objectives

◎ Review cause and effect.

Assess

◉ Identify cause and effect.

Comprehension Assessment
Monitor Progress

Review

◎ **Cause and Effect** Remember, most things in stories happen because something else has made them happen. The thing or event that happens is called the *effect*. Why this happens is called the *cause*.

Good readers look for causes and effects to help them better understand the story.

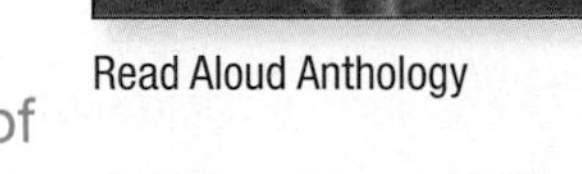

Read Aloud Anthology

Read "The Three Billy Goats Gruff"

Tell children you are going to read them a story about three goats who trick a troll into letting them cross his bridge. Listen carefully. I am going to read you a story, and then I will ask you to tell me some of the things that happened and why they happened. Read "The Three Billy Goats Gruff" on p. 46 of the *Read Aloud Anthology.*

Check cause and effect

After you read the story, ask children to tell you about cause and effect.

- Why did the troll let the first goat cross? (The littlest goat said he could catch a bigger goat if he waited.)
- Why was the second goat allowed to cross? (He told the troll that he could catch a very large goat if he waited.)
- Why didn't the biggest goat get caught? (He was so big that he could easily butt the troll away.)

Corrective feedback

If... children cannot identify cause and effect,
then... reteach cause and effect using the Reteach lesson in *First Stop*.

Assess cause and effect

Use the blackline master on p. 199. Make one copy for each child. Have children color the top picture and then one other picture that caused the top picture to happen.

Name ___________________________

Cause and Effect

Look at the top picture. Choose and color another picture that caused it to happen.

Note to Teacher: Have children look at the top picture. Then have them choose and color another picture that caused the top picture to happen.

MONITOR PROGRESS

- Cause and Effect

Objectives

- Review action parts.
- Write or dictate sentences about lucky feelings.

Conventions
Action Parts

Review Remind children of what they learned about action parts. The part of a sentence that tells what someone or something is doing is called the action part of the sentence.

Model Draw a box on the board. As you draw, say: *I draw a box*. What do I do? Right, I *draw a box*. *Draw a box* is the action part in the sentence *I draw a box*. Write your name on the board. As you write, say: *I write my name*. What is the action part of the sentence *I write my name? Write my name* is the action part.

Guide practice Have children demonstrate an action and say a complete sentence that tells about the action. Ask others to identify the action part of each sentence.

On their own Have children write or dictate a complete sentence about something they can do and then circle the action part in the sentence.

Daily Fix-It Use the Daily Fix-It exercise for more conventions practice.

Writing
This Week We...

Review Display *My Lucky Day,* Sing With Me Chart 20B, Phonics Songs and Rhymes Chart 20, Decodable Reader 20 from *My Skills Buddy,* Kindergarten Student Reader K.4.2, and Get Set, Roll! Reader 20. This week we learned about lucky adventures. We read new books, and we sang new songs. Which book or song told your favorite adventure? Let's share our ideas with each other.

Team Talk Pair children and have them take turns telling which book or song told their favorite adventure and why.

Model Today let's write about something we feel lucky about. I'll write about something lucky I did. I will write these sentences:

I went on a trip.

I saw a big dog.

Guide practice Have children dictate several complete sentences about something that makes them feel lucky. Write the sentences on the board.

Bret saw an owl.

Jade got a cat.

On their own Have children copy the sentence they dictated and illustrate it.

Daily Handwriting

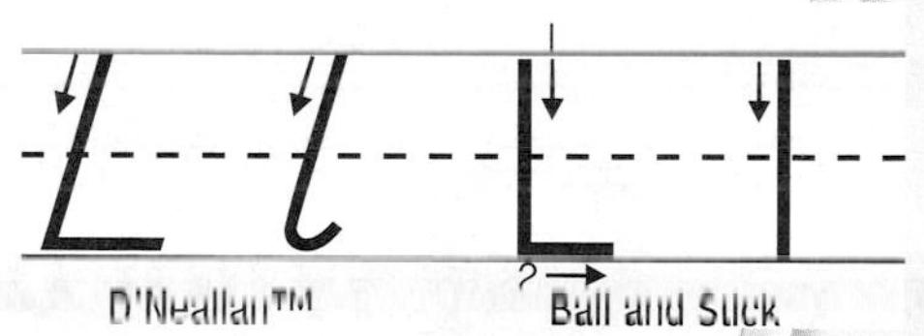

Write uppercase *L* and lowercase *l* on the board. Review correct letter formation with children.

Have children write a row of uppercase *L* and a row of lowercase *l* on their Write-On Boards. Remind them to use proper left-to-right and top-to-bottom progression.

Differentiated Instruction

 Advanced

Naming Parts and Action Parts Pair children and have one child explain naming parts in his or her own words. Then have the other partner explain action parts in his or her own words.

Daily Fix-It

i am lucky

I am lucky.

This week's practice sentences appear on Teacher Resources DVD-ROM.

English Language Learners

Poster Preview Prepare children for next week by using Week 3 ELL Poster number 21. Read the Poster Talk-Through to introduce the concept and vocabulary. Ask children to identify and describe objects and actions in the art.

Objectives
- Review weekly concept.
- Review cause and effect.

Wrap Up Your Week!

Question of the Week
What is a lucky adventure?

Illustrate cause and effect

This week we talked about adventures and what makes them lucky.

- Make a Cause and Effect chart like the one shown or use Graphic Organizer 29.
- Have children suggest events that happen in "Three Billy Goats Gruff." Write their responses in the *Effect* circle.
- Then have children identify what caused each event to happen and write their responses in the *Cause* circle.
- Have them draw their favorite cause and effect from the chart.
- Have children write or dictate a phrase or sentence about their picture.

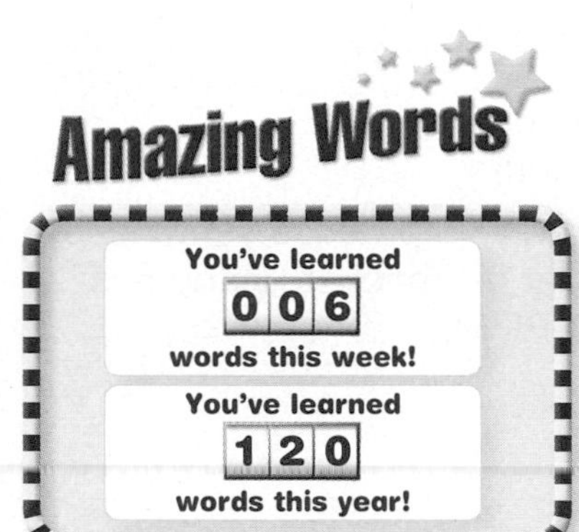

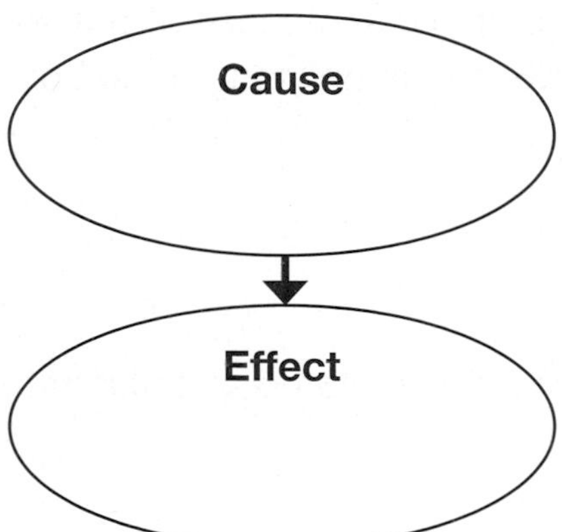

Next Week's Question
What adventures can animals have?

Discuss next week's question. Guide children in making connections between lucky adventures and animal adventures.

Tell children that next week they will read about animal adventures.

Science

Comparing Animals

Materials: *My Lucky Day,* drawing paper, crayons or markers

Compare and Contrast Piglets and Foxes Discuss with children how the piglet and the fox look alike and different. Show them pictures of both animals in *My Lucky Day* and draw attention to their features.

Look at the piglet's nose. Now compare it to the fox's nose. How are they alike? How are they different? Let's draw their noses. Have children draw the fox's nose and the piglet's nose on a sheet of paper. Write *noses* on the board and have children copy it to label their pictures. Continue the procedure with other features of the two animals, such as ears, feet, and tails.

Conventions

Adventure Charades

Imaginary Adventures Have children tell about adventures they would like to have. Make a list on the board. Assign partners and give each pair an adventure to act out. Have groups present their skits. Let the class identify each group's adventure. Then have children write or dictate a sentence describing an adventure. Have them identify the action part in each sentence.

Art

My Lucky Day

Materials: construction paper, crayons, glitter, glue

Draw Lucky Pictures Have children think of a day when good things happened to them. Have them draw a picture that shows what happened. After they are done, have them outline one special thing in their pictures with glue. Sprinkle glitter over their pictures to make that thing stand out. Have children share their pictures with the group and explain why the part they chose is special.

Assessment Checkpoints for the Week

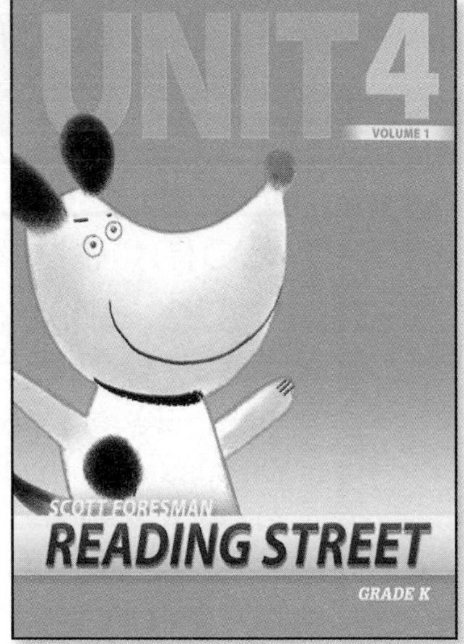

Teacher's Edition, Day 5

Weekly Assessment

Use the whole-class assessment on pages 194–195 and 198–199 in this Teacher's Edition to check:

- ✔ **/l/ Spelled *Ll***
- ✔ **Comprehension Skill** *Cause and Effect*
- ✔ **High-Frequency Words** *are* *that* *do*

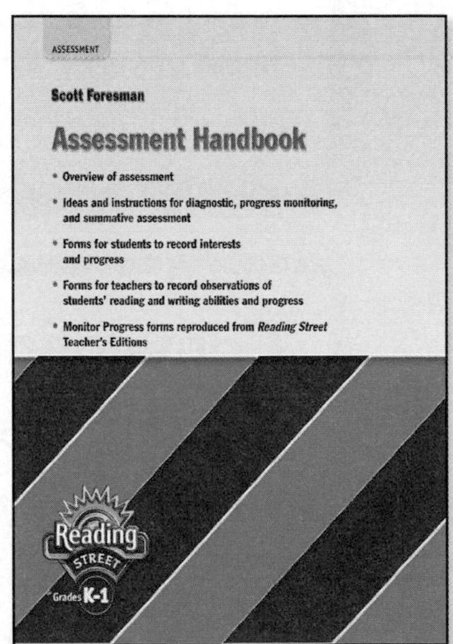
ASSESSMENT

Scott Foresman

Assessment Handbook

- Overview of assessment
- Ideas and instructions for diagnostic, progress monitoring, and summative assessment
- Forms for students to record interests and progress
- Forms for teachers to record observations of students' reading and writing abilities and progress
- Monitor Progress forms reproduced from *Reading Street* Teacher's Editions

Reading Street Grades K-1

Assessment Handbook

Managing Assessment

Use the Assessment Handbook for:

- ✔ **Observation Checklists**
- ✔ **Record-Keeping Forms**
- ✔ **Portfolio Assessment**

Teacher Notes

Pacing Small Group Instruction

5 Day Plan

DAY 1	• Phonemic Awareness/ Phonics • Decodable Story 20
DAY 2	• Phonemic Awareness/ Phonics • Decodable Reader 20
DAY 3	• Phonemic Awareness/ Phonics • Concept Literacy Reader K.4.2 or Kindergarten Student Reader K.4.2
DAY 4	• Phonemic Awareness/ Phonics • Get Set, Roll! Reader 20
DAY 5	• Phonics Review • Listen to Me Reader K.4.2

3 or 4 Day Plan

DAY 1	• Phonemic Awareness/ Phonics • Decodable Story 20
DAY 2	• Phonemic Awareness/ Phonics • Decodable Reader 20
DAY 3	• Phonemic Awareness/ Phonics • Concept Literacy Reader K.4.2 or Kindergarten Student Reader K.4.2
DAY 4	• Phonemic Awareness/ Phonics • Get Set, Roll! Reader 20

3 Day Plan: Eliminate the shaded box.

DAY 1

Phonemic Awareness • Phonics

- **Isolate /l/** Display the *ladybug* Picture Card. This is a *ladybug. Ladybug* begins with /l/. Say it with me: /l/ /l/ /l/, *ladybug.* Repeat with the *lake, lamp,* and *leaf* Picture Cards.
- **Connect /l/ to *Ll*** Write *Ll* on the board. This is uppercase *L* and lowercase *l.* When I see these letters, I will say /l/. Say the sound with me: /l/ /l/ /l/. I am going to say three words. I want you to tell me which word begins with /l/. Listen carefully: *lick, eat, bite.* Say the words with me: *lick, eat, bite.* Which words begins with /l/? *Lick* begins with /l/. *Eat* and *bite* do not begin with /l/. Continue discriminating /l/ with the following sets of words: *lily, daisy, rose; grin, laugh, smile; iguana, snake, lizard.*

Decodable Story 20

- **Review** Review the high-frequency words *is, my, little, do, you, like, my, a, I, that, we,* and *are.* Write each word on the board and have children read the word with you.

  If... children have difficulty reading the words,
  then... say a word and have children point to the word. Repeat several times, giving assistance as needed.

- **Read** Have children read the story orally. Then have them reread the story several times individually.

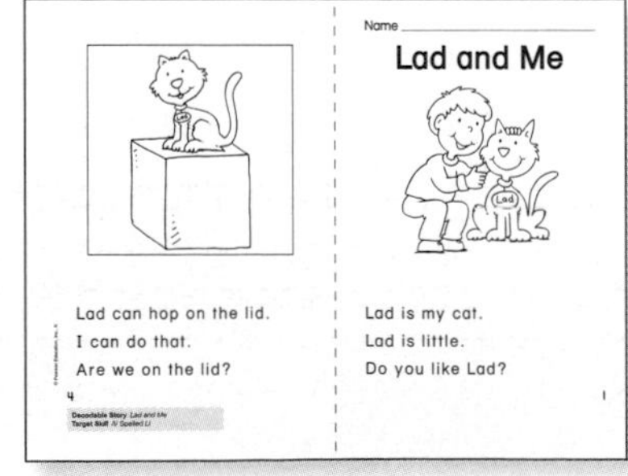
Name

Lad and Me

Lad can hop on the lid.
I can do that.
Are we on the lid?

Lad is my cat.
Lad is little.
Do you like Lad?

Reader's and Writer's Notebook, pp. 255–256

Objectives

- Isolate the initial sound in spoken one-syllable words.
- Identify the common sounds that letters represent.
- Read at least 25 high-frequency words from a commonly used list.

DAY

More Reading

Use Leveled Readers or other text at children's instructional level.

Phonemic Awareness • Phonics

- **Isolate /l/** Display the *leaf* Picture Card. This is a *leaf.* Do you hear /l/ in *leaf?* Say it with me: /l/ /l/ /l/, *leaf. Leaf* begins with /l/. Repeat with the words *lake, lamp,* and *loaf.*
- **Connect /l/ to *Ll*** Display the *lemon* Picture Card. This is a *lemon. Lemon* begins with /l/. Say it with me: /l/ /l/ /l/, *lemon.* Write the letters *Ll* on the board. The letter *L* or *l* spells /l/. Another word that begins like *lemon* is *laugh.* When you hear a word that begins with /l/, I want you to laugh. Use the following words: *lock, luck, duck, land, water, found, lost.*

Decodable Reader 20

- **Review** Review the high-frequency words by writing *are* on the board. This is the word *are.* What word is this? Continue with the following words: *a, you, the, that, do, see, they.*

  If... children have difficulty reading the words,
  then... say a word and have children point to the word. Repeat several times, giving assistance as needed.

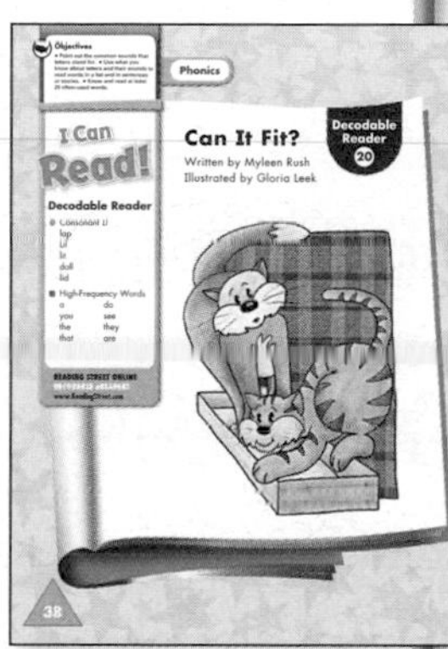

My Skills Buddy

- **Read** Display the cover of *Can It Fit?* on p. 38 of *My Skills Buddy.* Ask a volunteer to read the first page of the story. Have children tell what each cat is doing in each picture. Continue through the story in this manner.

Objectives

- Identify the common sounds that letters represent.
- Read at least 25 high-frequency words from a commonly used list.
- Retell a main event from a story read aloud.

Phonemic Awareness • Phonics

- **Isolate Final /l/** Display the *doll* Picture Card. This is a *doll.* Say it with me: *doll.* Do you hear /l/ in *doll? Doll* has /l/ at the end. Repeat with the following words: *pail, seal, snail.*
- **Connect /l/ to *Ll*** Display the *seal* Picture Card. This is a *seal. Seal* has /l/ at the end. Say it with me: *seal,* /l/ /l/. Write *Ll* on the board. These are the letters *Ll.* At the end of a word *l* or *ll* spells /l/. Who can show me how a seal acts? When I say a word that has /l/ at the end, I want you to pretend be a seal. Use the following words: *doll, pull, put, run, roll, feel, when, wheel, cool.*
- **Blend Sounds** Write *lid* on the board. Have children blend the sound of each letter to read the word. Repeat the routine with the words *lap* and *lot.*
- **Review High-Frequency Words** Write *that* on the board. Have volunteers say the word and use it in a sentence. Continue with the word *do* and *are.*
- To practice phonics and high-frequency words, have children read Kindergarten Student Reader K.4.2. Use the instruction on pp. 152–153.

For a complete lesson plan and additional practice, see the **Leveled Reader Teaching Guide**.

Concept Literacy Reader K.4.2

- **Preview and Predict** Display the cover of the Concept Literacy Reader K.4.2. Point to the title of the book. The title of the book is *My Lucky Day.* What do you think the book is about? What can make a day lucky? Have children tell about the picture and what they think the book might be about.
- **Set a Purpose** We talked about the title of the book. Let's read the book to find out about what can make a day lucky. Have children read the Concept Literacy Reader.
- **Read** Provide corrective feedback as children read the book orally. During reading, ask them if they were able to confirm any of the predictions they made prior to reading.

If... children have difficulty reading the book individually,
then... read a sentence aloud as children point to each word. Then have the group reread the sentences as they continue pointing to the words.

- **Retell** Have children retell the content as you page through the book. Help them identify what the book is about. Ask children to discuss how finding something new can make a day lucky.

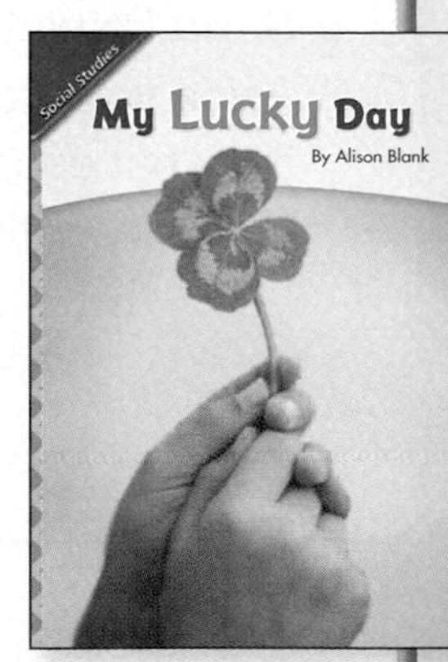

Concept Literacy Reader K.4.2

Objectives

- Identify the common sounds that letters represent.
- Predict what might happen next based on the title.

Strategic Intervention

DAY 4

Phonemic Awareness • Phonics

- **Sing a Song** Teach children the following song sung to the tune of "London Bridge":

  Lions like to live by lakes,
  Live by lakes, live by lakes.
  Lions like to live by lakes
  And seals like it too.

  Have children sing the song several times. Have children clap when they hear a word that begins with /l/. The letters *L* and *l* each stand for /l/. Write the letters on the board.

- **Segmenting** Say *lad.* I hear three sounds in *lad,* /l/ /a/ /d/. How many sounds do you hear in *lab?* What are they? (three, /l/ /a/ /b/) Continue with *lot, hit, Lin, pill, lip,* and *lox.*

Get Set, Roll! Reader 20

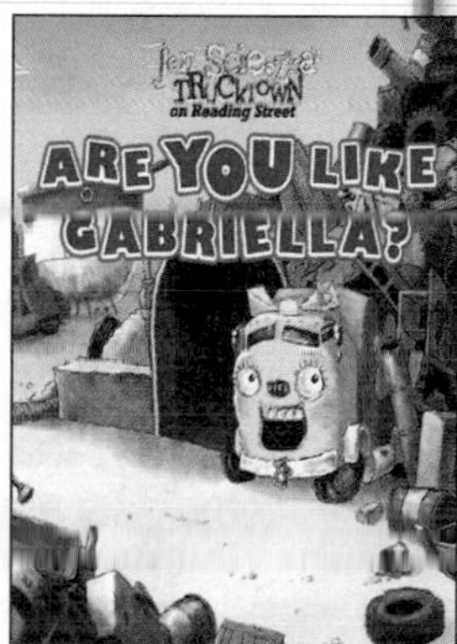

Get Set, Roll! Reader 20

- **Review** Review the following high-frequency words with children prior to reading the story: *I, have, a, to, the, is.*

- **Teach Rebus Words** Write the word *yard* on the board. This is the word yard. Say the letters with me: *y, a, r, d, yard.* What can you do in a yard? Repeat the routine with the words *Gabriella* and *garbage.* Look for these words in the story today. A picture above the word will help you read it.

- **Preview and Predict** Display Get Set, Roll! Reader 20, *Are You Like Gabriella?* Point to the title of the story. What is the title of the story? *Are You Like Gabriella?* Is the title of the story. Look at the picture and think about the title. What do you think this story will be about?

  If... children have difficulty reading the story individually,
  then... read a sentence aloud as children point to each word. Then have the group reread the sentences as they continue pointing to the words.

- **Reread** Use echo reading of Get Set, Roll! Reader 20 to model fluent reading. Use your oral reading to model for children where to pause, when to change pitch, and which words to stress. Then have children reread orally three to four times, or until they can read with few or no mistakes.

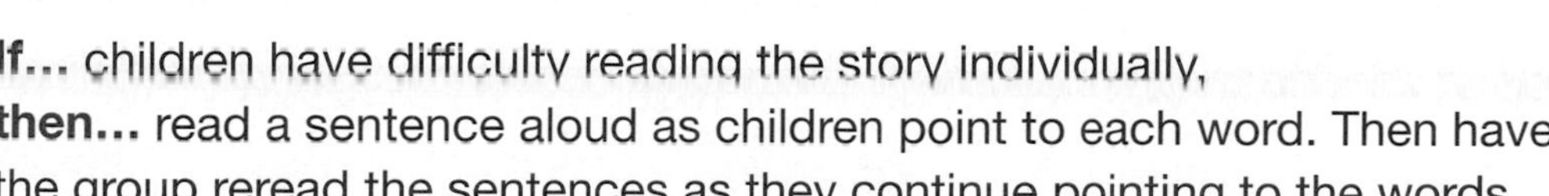

Objectives

- Identify the common sounds that letters represent.
- Predict what might happen next based on the title.

More Reading

Use Leveled Readers or other text at children's instructional level.

More Reading

Use Leveled Readers or other text at children's instructional level.

Phonics Review

- **Connect *Ll* to /l/** Write a lowercase *l* on the board. Name the letter. The letter *l* stands for the sound /l/. Have children make the letter in the air as you trace the letter. Next, write an uppercase letter *L* on the board. Name the letter and the sound it represents as you write it several times. Then give each child two strips of paper to set into the shape of an uppercase *L*.
- **Make Large Letters** We are going to make some large letters. The words *large* and *letters* both begin with /l/. Provide each child with a large piece of construction paper. Demonstrate how to draw and cut out a large *L*-shape. Have children draw and color pictures of things that begin with /l/ inside the letter.

Listen to Me Reader K.4.2

- **Preview and Predict** Display the cover of the book. The title of this story is *The Rainy Day.* It is written by Donna Latham. It is illustrated by Aleksey Ivanov. What do you think this story will be about? Tell me your ideas.
- **Set a Purpose** Review children's ideas. Point out that after they read, they will know if they predicted correctly. Tell children that you will read the story with them. Follow along with your finger as I read. Then we will take turns reading this page. Repeat this routine through all of the pages. Guide children to decode words.

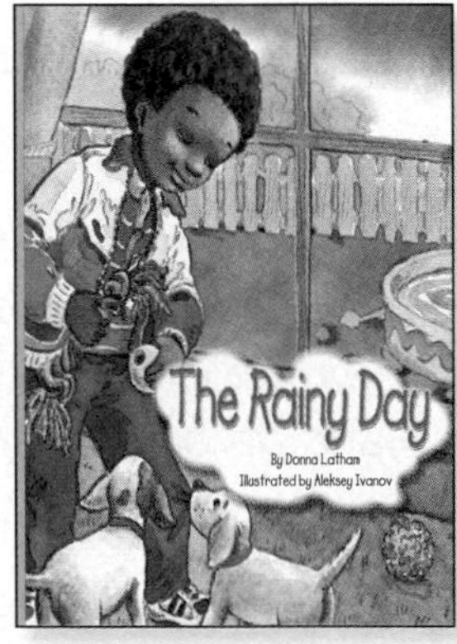

Listen to Me Reader K.4.2

- **Reread for Fluency** Use echo reading of Listen to Me Reader K.4.2 to model reading fluently. Use your oral reading to model for children when to pause, when to change pitch, and which words to stress. Then have children reread orally three to four times, or until they can read with few or no mistakes.

Objectives

- Identify the common sounds that letters represent.
- Predict what might happen next based on the title.

eReaders

DAY 1

Phonemic Awareness • Phonics

- **Recognize *Ll*** Ask children to name words that begin with /l/. List the words on the board as they say them. Have children echo read the list of words. Then ask children to take turns circling *l* in the words.

Objectives

- Identify the common sounds that letters represent.

Pacing Small Group Instruction

20–30 mins.

5 Day Plan

DAY 1	• Phonemic Awareness/ Phonics • Decodable Story 20
DAY 2	• Phonemic Awareness/ Phonics • High-Frequency Words • Decodable Reader 20
DAY 3	• Phonemic Awareness/ Phonics • Kindergarten Student Reader K.4.2
DAY 4	• Get Set, Roll! Reader 20
DAY 5	• Phonics Review • Reread Leveled Books

DAY 2

Phonemic Awareness • Phonics

- **Listen for /l/** Tell children you will tell them a story and they should listen for /l/ as in *leg.* When you say a word that begins with /l/, the children should pat their legs and repeat the word. Tell a simple story, emphasizing the initial /l/ words and pausing to give children a chance to pat their legs and repeat the word. *Lucy likes lemons.* She *loves* to *lick lots* of *lemons* by the *lake.* With a *little luck,* she can *lick lemons* for her entire *life. Lucy* really *likes lemons!*
- **Connect /l/ to *Ll*** Write several sentences from the story from the previous activity on the board. The letters *L* and *l* stand for the sound /l/. Have children circle the letters *L* and *l* as you read the words.
- **High-Frequency Words** Display the following word cards: *do, that, are, of, they, you.* Say the word *are* and select a child to point to the word. Have children say the word and use it in a sentence. Continue with the other words.

Objectives

- Isolate the initial sound in spoken one-syllable words.
- Read at least 25 high-frequency words from a commonly used list.

3 or 4 Day Plan

DAY 1	• Phonemic Awareness/ Phonics • Decodable Story 20
DAY 2	• Phonemic Awareness/ Phonics • High-Frequency Words • Decodable Reader 20
DAY 3	• Phonemic Awareness/ Phonics • Kindergarten Student Reader K.4.2
DAY 4	• Get Set, Roll! Reader 20

3 Day Plan: Eliminate the shaded box.

More Practice

For additional practice with this week's phonics skills, have children reread the Decodable Story (Day 1) and the Decodable Reader (Day 2).

Phonemic Awareness • Phonics

- **Discriminate /l/** Draw five leaves on the board. Collect ten Picture Cards, including the following *Ll* cards: *ladybug, lake, lamp, lemon, loaf.* Mix the cards and display them one at a time. Have a child name the picture. If the name has initial /l/, have the child write a lowercase *l* in a leaf.

Kindergarten Student Reader K.4.2

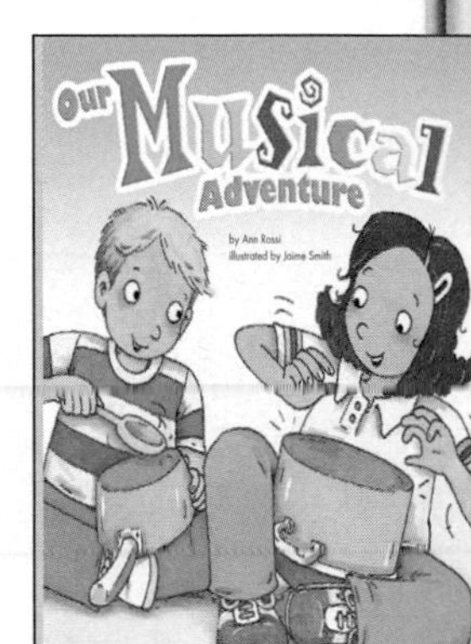

Kindergarten Student Reader K.4.2

- **Preview and Predict** Display the cover of the book. The title of this story is *Our Musical Adventure.* Look at the cover. What do you think this story is about? What kinds of instruments are the children playing? Tell me your ideas.
- **Set a Purpose** Review the list of things children think might happen in the story. Remind children that setting a purpose for reading can help them better understand the story. Tell children to pay attention to how the children play their instruments.
- **Read** Have children follow along as they read the story with you. After reading p. 3, ask children to tell about what Nan and Nat do. Continue with each page. Ask the following questions:
  - What do the children use as instruments?
  - How do the children play the instruments?
- **Summarize** Have children retell the story to a partner and tell who listens to the music at the end.
- **Text to Self** Help children make personal connections to the story as they tell which instrument they would like to play and why.

Objectives

- Identify the common sounds that letters represent.
- Predict what might happen next based on the title.
- Make connections to own experiences.

On-Level DAY 4

Get Set, Roll! Reader 20

- **Review** Review the words *is, the, to, a, have,* and *I* by writing each word on the board and saying the word with children. Then give clues to a word and have children tell which word it is.
- **Review Rebus Words** Write *garbage* on the board and read the word with children. This is the word *garbage.* What kind of truck comes to take garbage away? Continue with the words *yard* and *Gabriella.* Remember, there will be a picture above the words to help us read them.
- **Read** Display Get Set, Roll! Reader 20, *Are You Like Gabriella?* Point to the title of the story. What is the title of the story? *Are You Like Gabriella?* is the title of the story. Let's read the story together.

Objectives

- Read at least 25 high-frequency words from a commonly used list.

More Reading

Use Leveled Readers or other text at children's instructional level.

On-Level DAY 5

Phonics Review

- **Clap for Letters** Have children stand in a circle. Tell them you are going to play a musical game with the letter *Ll.* We are going to make music with our hands. We will clap slowly to make the rhythm for our game. When it is your turn, say a word that begins with *Ll*. Start a simple, slow clapping rhythm with the children. Once all of the children are clapping in rhythm, say a word like *leaf.* Go around the circle, having children say words that begin with *Ll* in rhythm. Repeat the game with final /l/.

Objectives

- Identify the common sounds that letters represent.

Pacing Small Group Instruction

5 Day Plan

DAY 1	• Phonemic Awareness/ Phonics • Decodable Story 20
DAY 2	• Phonics • Spelling • Decodable Reader 20
DAY 3	• Independent Reader K.4.2 or Kindergarten Student Reader K.4.2
DAY 4	• Get Set, Roll! Reader 20 or Kindergarten Student Reader K.4.2
DAY 5	• Fluency/Comprehension • Independent Reader K.4.2

3 or 4 Day Plan

DAY 1	• Phonemic Awareness/ Phonics • Decodable Story 20
DAY 2	• Phonics • Spelling • Decodable Reader 20
DAY 3	• Independent Reader K.4.2 or Kindergarten Student Reader K.4.2
DAY 4	• Get Set, Roll! Reader 20 or Kindergarten Student Reader K.4.2

3 Day Plan: Eliminate the shaded box.

More Practice

For additional practice with this week's phonics skills and to develop fluency, have children reread the Decodable Story (Day 1) and the Decodable Reader (Day 2).

A Advanced — DAY 1

Phonemic Awareness • Phonics

- **Words with *Ll*** Write *map* on the board. Read the word with the class. Ask a volunteer to change the beginning letter to *l* and write the new word. Have children read the new word *lap.* Continue with these words: *bid (lid), rip (lip), sad (lad), hit (lit), cab (lab).*

Objectives

- Isolate the initial sound in spoken one-syllable words.

A Advanced — DAY 2

Phonics • Spelling

- **Connect /l/ to *Ll*** Display the *Ll* Alphabet Card. What sound does *lamb* begin with? What letter spells that sound?
- **Spell Sounds** Give each child the following letter tiles: *a, d, f, i, l, p.* Listen to the sounds in the word *lip:* /l/ /i/ /p/, *lip.* What is the letter for /l/? It is *l.* Place your *l* tile in front of you. Continue with the remaining sounds.

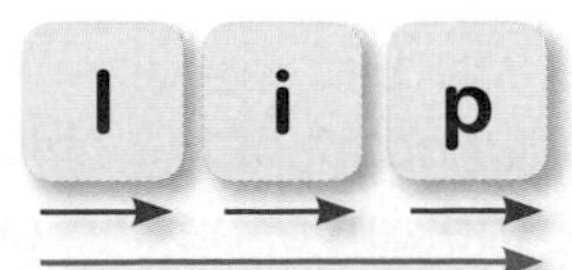

Let's blend the sounds to read the word: /l/ /i/ /p/, *lip.* Continue with the words *lad, lap,* and *fill.*

Objectives

- Identify the common sounds that letters represent.
- Use letter-sound correspondences to spell consonant-vowel-consonant (CVC) words.

DAY 3

For a complete lesson plan and additional practice, see the **Leveled Reader Teaching Guide**.

Independent Reader K.4.2

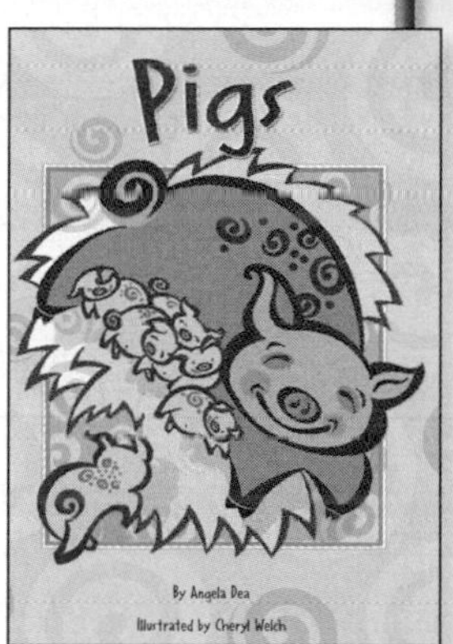
Independent Reader K.4.2

- **Practice High-Frequency Words** Write *are* on the board. Have volunteers say the word and use it in a sentence. Continue with the words *that* and *do*.
- **Activate Prior Knowledge** Have children read the title and look at the picture. What animal is this? Remind children that a pig is a farm animal that often lives in a pen. Pigs take mud baths to keep them cool in the hot sun. Encourage children to act out sniffing for food with their "snouts" and shaking off after taking a mud bath. After children discuss what they know about pigs, have them take turns reading *Pigs* for their group.
- **Cause and Effect** After reading the book, have children draw a picture that shows why pigs take mud baths. What causes the pigs to take mud baths?
- **Reread for Fluency** After rereading with children, model reading fluently for them. I am going to read this book aloud. I will read the words with no mistakes. I want you to read it aloud with me. Try to read the words just as I do.
    - Use echo reading of Independent Reader K.4.2 to model reading fluently. Use your oral reading to model for children where to pause, when to change pitch, and which words to stress. Then have children reread orally three to four times, or until they can read with few or no mistakes.
- For more practice with phonics and high-frequency words and to develop fluency, have children read Kindergarten Student Reader K.4.2. Use the instruction pp. 152–153.

Objectives
- Read at least 25 high-frequency words from a commonly used list.

More Reading

Use Leveled Readers or other text at children's instructional level.

More Reading

Use Leveled Readers or other text at children's instructional level.

Kindergarten Student Reader K.4.2

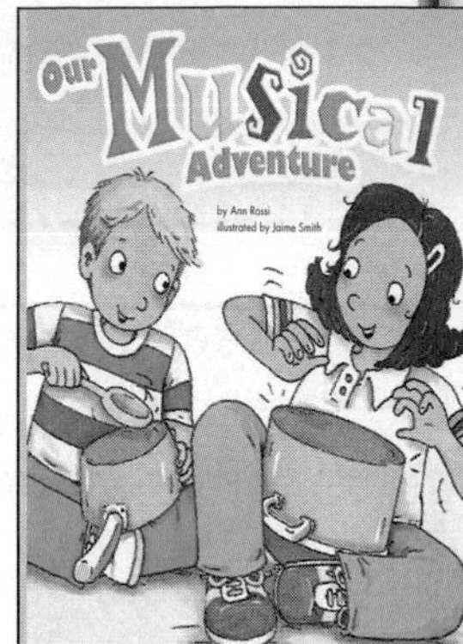

Kindergarten Student Reader K.4.2

- **Revisit Prior Knowledge** Have children discuss what they know about musical instruments. What kinds of musical instruments do you know? How do you play those musical instruments?
- **Reread** Kindergarten Student Reader K.4.2 to practice reading fluently.
- **Text to World** Ask children to describe the instruments in the story. Then have children find things in the classroom that they can use as instruments.
- **Read** Have children read Get Set, Roll! Reader 20, *Are You Like Gabriella?* Use the instruction on p. 183.

Objectives

- Read at least 25 high-frequency words from a commonly used list.
- Make connections to the larger community.

Fluency•Comprehension

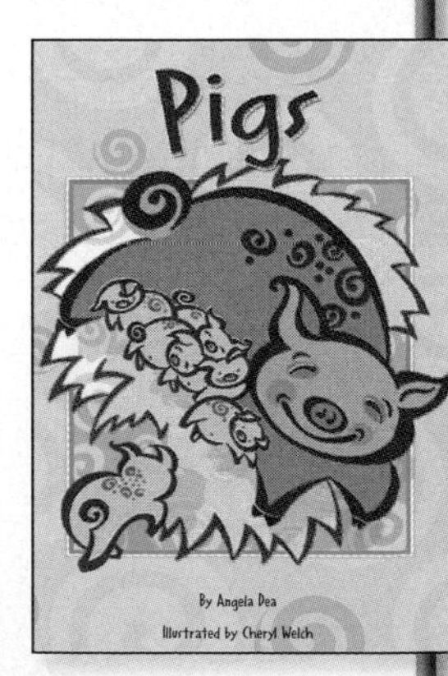

Independent Reader K.4.2

- **Reread for Fluency** Use the Independent Reader K.4.2 to model reading fluently for children. I am going to read this selection aloud. I will read the words with no mistakes. I want you to read it aloud with me. Try to read the words just as I do.
- **Comprehension** After children have finished reading, have them retell what happens in the selection. Then have children write about why pigs take mud baths.

Objectives

- Read at least 25 high-frequency words from a commonly used list.

ELL English Language Learners DAY 1

Concept Development

- **Read the Concept Literacy Reader** To build background and vocabulary, read *My Lucky Day* with children. Begin by reading the title and author's name. Have children describe what they see on the cover. Then have children look at the pictures in the book. What things do you see? Where could you find each object? Read the book aloud, pausing to discuss each page. Model sentence patterns and vocabulary that describe the objects on the page. This is a penny. It is worth one cent. He found one penny. Have you ever found any money? On a second reading, invite children to talk about the pictures on each page.
- **Develop Oral Language** Revisit *My Lucky Day*, pointing out that you can find a lot of lucky treasures on any given day. Then have children sing the following song with you to the tune of "Bingo":

> I walked around and found a nest,
> Today's my lucky day-O.
> L-U-C-K-Y, L-U-C-K-Y, L-U-C-K-Y,
> Today's my lucky day-O.

Repeat the song with other objects from the selection.

Phonemic Awareness/Phonics

- **Frontload Words with /l/** Have children look at the picture on pp. 32–33 of *My Skills Buddy*. The children in the picture are eating lunch. Listen to the word *lunch*. What sound does *lunch* begin with? *Lunch* begins with /l/; /l/, *lunch*. Then use a chant to introduce picture words beginning with /l/. For example, for *lunch* you can say:

  In this picture they eat lunch. Crunchy lettuce goes munch, munch.

  Have children point to the lettuce in the picture. Make up a chant for other words in the picture that begin with /l/, including *log, lobster, lemonade, leg, lid,* and *lap*.
- **Connect /l/ to *Ll*** Use letter tiles to display the word *lip* or write it on the board. This word is lip: /l/ /i/ /p/, *lip*. Say the word with me. Have children write the word *lip* and circle the letter that makes /l/. Write and read aloud the following sentence: *We ate a late lunch at Len's house.* Point to the letter *l* in *late* and ask: What letter is this? Yes, this is *l*. Repeat with the *l* in *lunch* and *Len's*.

Objectives

- Distinguish sounds of English with increasing ease. • Distinguish intonation patterns of English with increasing ease. • Recognize elements of the English sound system in newly acquired vocabulary. • Learn relationships between sounds and letters of the English language.

Content Objective

- Develop content knowledge related to luck and lucky adventures.

Language Objectives

- Understand and use grade-level content area vocabulary.
- Recognize the sounds of English.

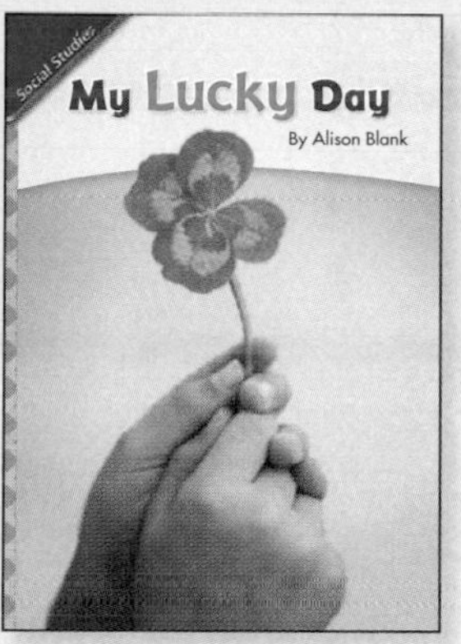

Concept Literacy Reader K.4.2

Daily Lesson Planner

DAY 1	• Concept Development • Phonemic Awareness/ Phonics • Listening Comprehension
DAY 2	• Comprehension • Vocabulary
DAY 3	• Phonemic Awareness/ Phonics • Conventions
DAY 4	• Phonemic Awareness/ Phonics • Concepts and Oral Language
DAY 5	• Language Workshop • Writing

Content Objective

- Understand cause and effect.

Language Objective

- Learn and use academic vocabulary.

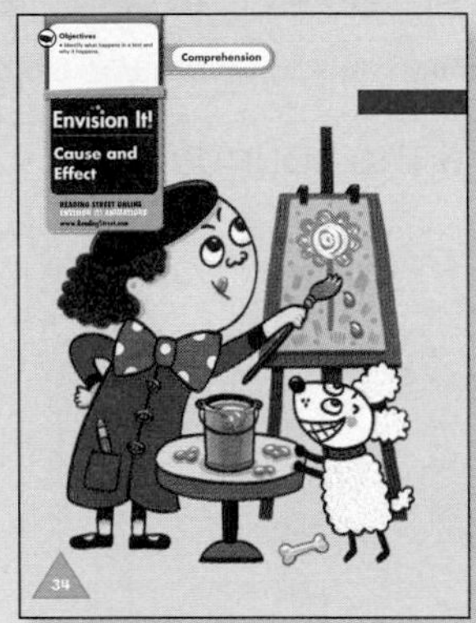

My Skills Buddy, pp. 34–35

DAY 1

Listing Comprehension: Cause and Effect

- **Provide Scaffolding** Discuss the illustrations on pp. 34–35 in *My Skills Buddy* to frontload vocabulary. Explain what is happening in each illustration. Help children understand that these drawings show cause and effect. Explain that a cause is a reason that something happens. Explain that an effect is a result of something happening. Clap once for the class. I just clapped my hands. That was the cause. Clap again. What is the effect? (It makes a sound.) The sound is the effect of me clapping my hands. Point to the first illustration. The dog is trying to get on the table. This is the cause. Point to the second illustration. The paint is knocked over. This is the effect. Support your words with gestures or simple drawings.
- **Prepare for the Read Aloud** The modified Read Aloud below prepares children for listening to the oral reading "Lucky Ducky" on p. 83.

Read Aloud

Lucky Ducky

Ducky wakes up. He thinks it will be a lucky day. Grandpa takes Ducky to the pet store. That is lucky. Ducky likes to watch the fish. He counts them.

Grandpa takes Ducky to the bakery. That is lucky. Ducky likes the smell. Grandpa takes Ducky to the park. That is lucky. Ducky likes the pond.

Ducky sees his family and friends at the pond. They have presents. They yell, "Happy birthday, you lucky Ducky!"

- **First Listening** Write the title of the Read Aloud on the board. This is about a duck named Ducky. He wakes up feeling lucky. Listen to find out what happens during his day. After reading, ask children to recall the events. Where does Ducky go? Why is the day extra special for Ducky?
- **Second Listening** Write the words *pet store, bakery,* and *puppy* on the board. Point to the words and ask questions. What does Ducky like about the pet store? What does Ducky like about the bakery? What does Ducky like about the park? Explain that Ducky's family and friends are waiting at the park to celebrate his birthday. How do you celebrate your birthday?

Objectives

- Expand and internalize initial English vocabulary by retelling simple stories and basic information represented or supported by pictures. • Use visual and contextual support to enhance and confirm understanding needed to comprehend increasingly challenging language.

English Language Learners

DAY 2

Comprehension

- **Provide Scaffolding** Display *My Lucky Day*. Lead a picture walk through the story, naming what you see in the illustrations and describing what is happening.
  - **Set the Scene** Use the cover to help children understand that this story is about a fox and a pig. In the wild, a fox would eat a pig. In this story, the fox wants to eat the pig. Explain that the pig outsmarts the fox. He tricks the fox into feeding him. Have you had to think your way out of a problem?
  - **Frontload Vocabulary** As you lead the picture walk, use the illustrations to introduce unfamiliar words in the text, including descriptive words. Look at the picture on page 10. The piglet is filthy. What does *filthy* mean? Can you name other things that are filthy? Have you ever been filthy? Why? Include some of the following words from the story: *hungry* (p. 3); *terrific* (p. 13); *tough* (p. 19); *stiff* (p. 23); *exhausted* (p. 27).

Vocabulary: Words for Textures

- **Frontload Vocabulary** Have children turn to p. 48 of *My Skills Buddy*. Talk about the texture in each picture, using the words *fuzzy, bumpy, sharp*, and *furry*. For example, point to the caterpillar. What would it feel like to touch a caterpillar? Explain that the caterpillar is fuzzy. Would it hurt to touch something fuzzy? Then invite children to talk about the pictures using the texture words.
- **Provide Scaffolding** Write the words *fuzzy, bumpy, sharp*, and *furry* on the board. These words tell us about the way things feel. Point to the word *furry*. What things are furry? (animals, hairy things) Point to the word *sharp*. What things are sharp? (claws, a dart, a saw) What would you rather rub, something furry or something sharp? Ask more questions with the other words about texture.
- **Practice** Show the class four (or more) images or objects: a hairy animal, a golf ball, a pair of scissors, a cotton ball. Ask the children textural questions about each object using the words on the board.

Objectives

- Use prior experiences to understand meanings in English. • Speak using learning strategies. • Learn new basic and academic vocabulary heard during classroom instruction and interactions.

Content Objective

- Develop background knowledge.

Language Objective

- Learn and use words for textures.

Use Learning Strategies

Remind children that if they have trouble naming an item in their pictures, they can ask their group members for help.

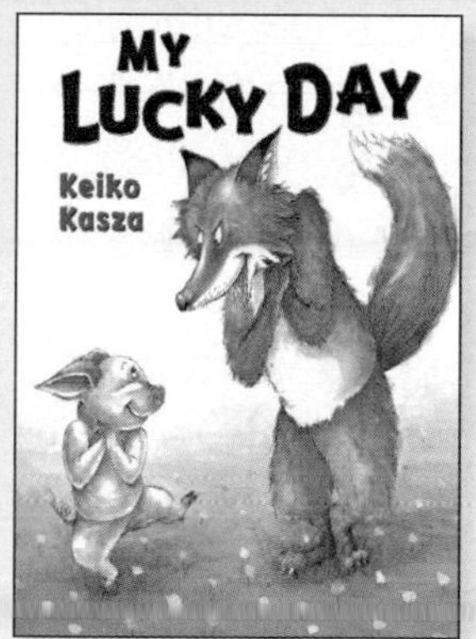

Trade Book

Support for English Language Learners

Content Objective

- Use learning strategies.

Language Objectives

- Connect /l/ and *Ll*.
- Use action parts.

Transfer Skills

Pronouncing /l/ The /l/ sound in Cantonese, Japanese, and Korean closely resembles /r/. Children who speak these languages may have difficulty differentiating between the /l/ and /r/ sounds in English. Model pronouncing each sound. Then have children practice repeating word pairs like *rock, lock; ray, lay; row, low;* and *rid, lid.*

Use Learning Strategies

Help children understand that in English, the action part is usually listed after the naming part. For example, *The fox makes the spaghetti.* In many foreign languages, the action part, or verb, is listed at the beginning of a sentence.

ELL English Language Learners — DAY 3

Phonemic Awareness/Phonics

- **Isolate Initial and Final /l/** Say *lap*, and then model segmenting sounds by saying /l/ /a/ /p/. Emphasize the initial sound in the word. Repeat with *lip* and *lot*. Help children identify the initial sound in each word. Say *mill*, and then model segmenting sounds by saying /m/ /i/ /l/. Emphasize that the double *ll* makes the final /l/ sound in the word. Repeat with *bill*. Help children identify the final sound in the word.
- **/l/ Spelled *Ll*** Write the words *lid, lad*, and *fill* on the board. As you read them aloud, track the sounds and letters with your fingers. Help children recognize that these words either begin or end with /l/.

Conventions: Action Parts

- **Provide Scaffolding** Point to the image on pp. 8–9 of *My Lucky Day*. The piglet kicked and squealed. Tell children to kick and squeal like the piglet. Kicking and squealing are actions. The action part of the sentence tells what happens. *Kicked and squealed* is the action part of the sentence.
- **Practice** What are some other action parts in this story? Page through the Trade Book and have children name the action parts of sentences: He *collected twigs* (p. 12); He *picked tomatoes* (p. 16); He *pushed* and he *pulled* (p. 20); the piglet *relaxed* (p. 31).

Leveled Support

Beginning/Intermediate Find examples of action parts that students can act out from the story. While the child is acting out the action, say a sentence with the child's name and the action part: (Child's name) carries the water. Have children repeat the sentence.

Advanced/Advanced-High Help a child pick out an action from the story to act out. Have the rest of the children try to guess the action the child is acting out. Have children guess their answers in sentence form: *(Child's name) makes a fire.*

Objectives

- Develop repertoire of learning strategies commensurate with grade-level learning expectations. • Speak using a variety of grammatical structures with increasing accuracy and ease as more English is acquired. • Learn relationships between sounds and letters of the English language.

DAY 4

Phonemic Awareness/Phonics

- **Review /h/** To review /h/, ask a question with a word that contains an initial /h/: Can you hop with a hat? Then remind children that *h* sounds like /h/ at the beginning of words. Repeat the question a few words at a time, and have children chorally repeat after you. Listen to these words: *hop, hat*. What sound do they both start with?
- **/h/ Spelled *Hh*** Write the letters *Hh*. What letter is this? Yes, this letter is *Hh*. Use word tiles to form these words: *hid, ham, hot, his, hit, had.* Model reading each word, isolating /h/. Show all the sound-letter correspondences (for example, /h/ /i/ /d/ = *hid*).

Concepts and Oral Language

- **Revisit Talk with Me Chart 20A** Display the chart. Have children describe the people, animals, or objects in the photos. Then say a sentence for each picture. Have children identify the action part in each sentence. For example, *The fox hunts for food. Hunts for food* is the action part in the sentence.
- **Develop Oral Language** Introduce language patterns that help describe the pictures on Talk with Me Chart 20A. Use the Amazing Word associated with each picture. This is the *piglet*. A *piglet* is a young pig. A *piglet* has four legs and a squiggly tail. Then ask questions about the pictures, such as: Which picture shows a birthday present? Have children point to the correct picture and answer your questions with complete sentences.

Beginning Have children point to each picture on the chart and use the Amazing Word to describe the picture.

Intermediate Ask questions to help children notice more details about the people, animals, and objects in the pictures, such as Does the lucky girl look happy or sad? Does the scrubber look fuzzy and soft? Is the piglet furry? Is the fox?

Advanced/Advanced-High Encourage children to think about their own experiences with the actions and objects in the pictures. For example, *The girl is lucky. I was lucky when…* or *The people cook food. The food I cooked was…*

Objectives

- Use support from peers and teachers to read grade-appropriate content area text needed to comprehend increasingly challenging language.
- Demonstrate comprehension of increasingly complex English by participating in taking notes commensurate with content area and grade level needs.

Content Objectives

- Develop oral language.
- Use learning strategies.

Language Objectives

- Connect /h/ with *Hh*.
- Learn English language patterns.

Use Learning Strategies

Draw a two-column chart on the board titled *Vocabulary*. On the left side write the Amazing Words from this week. Ask children to assist you in defining each term with words or pictures on the right side of the chart. Encourage students to copy the words and make notes or drawings that define each term on their own paper.

Talk with Me Chart 20A

Content Objectives

- Understand *My Lucky Day*.
- Practice cause and effect.

Language Objectives

- Retell a selection through speaking and writing.
- Write using grade-level vocabulary.

Monitor and Self-Correct

Remind children that if they don't know how to say a word, they can ask other students or their teacher for help.

Home Language Support

Invite children to share ideas in their home languages before creating their poems.

Language Workshop: Talk About Poems

- **Introduce and Model** Display pp. 8–9 of *My Lucky Day*. Look at the animals. Who are they? (a fox and a piglet) What does the fox want to do to the piglet? (eat him) Ask students more questions about the story: What does the piglet do to tire out the fox? (He gets the fox to clean him, cook for him, and massage him.) Explain that the piglet tricks the fox into treating him like a king.
- **Practice** A poem has short lines that sound like a song. It has rhythm, like clapping to a beat. The words at the end of the lines may rhyme, but they don't have to. Explain that you will be writing a poem together about *My Lucky Day.* Write the poem below on the board:

  Piglet knocked on fox's door,
  And let out a big squeal.
  "Come right on in, Mr. Pig,
  You'll be my next meal!"

  Point out that the second half of the poem is in quotes. That means it is something being said. In this case, it is being said by the fox. Read the poem with the proper intonation several times to help children hear the rhythm. Then have children say the poem with you. Encourage them to march to the beat to help them hear the rhythm. Then ask them which words rhyme. (*squeal* and *meal*)

Writing: Write a Poem

- **Prepare for Writing** We read a poem about *My Lucky Day*. Now let's write our own poem. Have each child fold a piece of paper in half to create two sections.
- **Create Poems About *My Lucky Day*** Write the following poem frame on a sheet of paper and make a copy for each child.

  The fox smiled when he opened the _____,
  "With you I'll have my _____."
  But hours later a clean, full _____,
  Said "It's my lucky _____."

  Have children complete the poem by writing or dictating words in the blanks. (Possible answers: *door, way, pig, day*) Then have children illustrate their poems.

Objectives

- Use support from peers and teachers to enhance and confirm understanding needed to comprehend increasingly challenging language. • Write using a variety of grade-appropriate sentence lengths in increasingly accurate ways as more English is acquired.

One Little Mouse

Grade K • Unit 4 • Week 3
One Little Mouse
204–303

Common Core Standards
Weekly Planning Guide

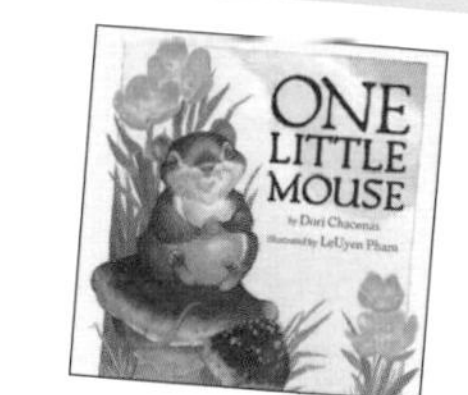

Selection: One Little Mouse
Genre: Animal Fantasy

Alignment of the Common Core Standards with This Week's Skills and Strategies

This Week's Common Core Standards for English Language Arts	Instructional Summary
Reading Standards for Literature	
Literature 1. With prompting and support, ask and answer questions about key details in a text. **Literature 2.** With prompting and support, retell familiar stories, including key details. **Literature 9.** With prompting and support, compare and contrast the adventures and experiences of characters in familiar stories.	The lesson focuses on the **sequence** of events in a story, helping children identify what happens first, next, and last in a story. The lesson instruction for **predict** and **set a purpose** teaches children to look at the selection to predict what the selection might be about and to set a purpose to help them understand what they read.
Foundational Skills Standards	
Foundational Skills 2.c. Blend and segment onsets and rimes of single-syllable spoken words. **Foundational Skills 3.c.** Read common high-frequency words by sight. (e.g., *the, of, to, you, she, my, is, are, do, does*).	The lesson works with consonant blends to **decode words.** The lesson provides instruction for combining the sounds of two letters to make the blended sound at the beginning of a word. Children also learn **high-frequency words** to identify words that are irregularly spelled.
Writing Standards	
Writing 2. Use a combination of drawing, dictating, and writing to compose informative/explanatory texts in which they name what they are writing about and supply some information about the topic. **Writing 8.** With guidance and support from adults, recall information from experiences or gather information from provided sources to answer a question.	Writing activities include **sharing** ideas about why something happens. Group activities for writing include a **response** to the literature, a **description,** and **sentences** about animal adventures. The wrap-up activities ask children to write about their favorite topic in this week's lesson.
Speaking and Listening Standards	
Speaking/Listening 1. Participate in collaborative conversations with diverse partners about *kindergarten topics and texts* with peers and adults in small and larger groups.	This lesson's activities focus on listening for **sequence** when children listen to a story. Children identify relevant details to identify the sequence of events in the story. The lesson reinforces the skills of being a good listener.
Language Standards	
Language 1.d. Understand and use question words (interrogatives) (e.g., *who, what, where, when, why, how*). **Language 2.** Demonstrate command of the conventions of standard English capitalization, punctuation, and spelling when writing. **Language 5.a.** Sort common objects into categories (e.g., shapes, foods) to gain a sense of the concepts the categories represent.	The Conventions section concentrates on the study of **sentences.** Children learn that a sentence is a group of words that tells a complete thought with a naming part and an action part. Children also learn that a sentence begins with a capital letter and ends with a punctuation mark.

Additional Support for a Common Core Standard This Week

Use the following instruction to supplement the teaching of one of this week's Common Core Standards.

Common Core Standard: Foundational Skill 3.c.
In each lesson, children are introduced to a set of High-Frequency Words that will be used in the selections in the lesson.

- Display *My Skills Buddy,* page 57. Read the words together and have children find the word in the I Can Read sentences.
- After children are introduced to the words, have them write one of the words or a sentence with the word and draw a picture about the word.
- Ask children to show their page and read and tell about the word and the picture they made.

ISBN-13 978-0-328-64357-8 ISBN-10: 0-323-64357-2

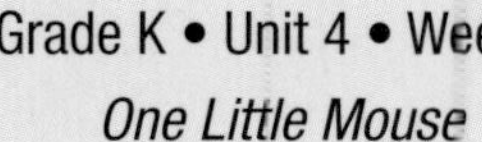

Unit 4
Where will our adventures take us?

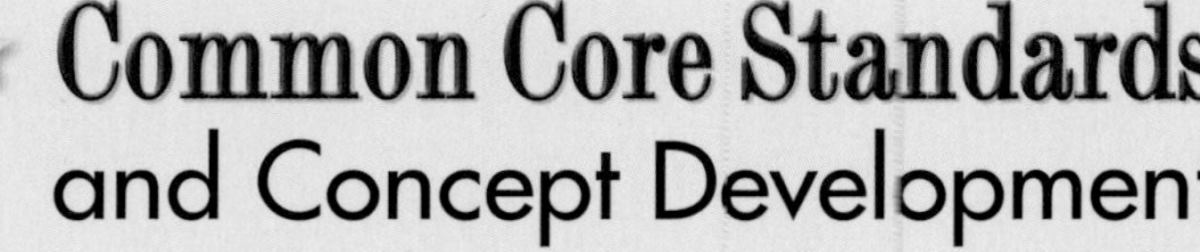

Common Core Standards and Concept Development

- Introduce and explore this unit's weekly concepts through rich, structured conversations
- Develop complex content knowledge and vocabulary
- Expand on a single concept with engaging literature and nonfiction
- Build better readers in all content areas

Align instruction to **Common Core Anchor Standards**

Week 1

Rooster's Off to See the World

Question of the Week
What can we learn from our adventures?

Concept Talk Guide children as they discuss questions such as:

- What things does the child see?

Writing Have children turn to p. 250 of *Reader's and Writer's Notebook.* Explain that the pictures show how the boy gets from his house to the mailbox around the corner. Tell children that they will give the boy directions. Have them write words to tell the boy how to get to the mailbox.

Week 2

My Lucky Day

Question of the Week
What is a lucky adventure?

Concept Talk Guide children as they discuss questions such as:

- Why is the boy lucky? Does he know he is lucky at first? How can you tell?

Writing Have children write a class poem on the board. Use the selected topic and one of the suggested rhyming words. Have children copy the class poem on p. 262 of *Reader's and Writer's Notebook*. Then have them draw a picture about the poem.

You Are Here: Week 3

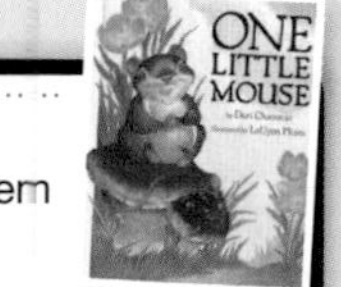

One Little Mouse

Question of the Week
What adventures can animals have?

As children answer this unit's Big Question and this week's Question of the Week, they will address:

Reading 1. Read closely to determine what the text says explicitly and to make logical inferences from it; cite specific textual evidence when writing or speaking to support conclusions drawn from the text. **(Also Reading 2.)**

Concept Talk Guide children as they discuss questions such as:

- What would a small animal's adventure be like?

As children answer this week's Concept Talk question, they will address:

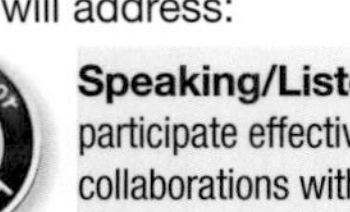

Speaking/Listening 1. Prepare for and participate effectively in a range of conversations and collaborations with diverse partners, building on others' ideas and expressing their own clearly and persuasively.

Writing Have children turn to p. 274 of *Reader's and Writer's Notebook*. Have them draw a picture of the mouse in the selection. Then have children write or dictate a sentence on the line that tells about the mouse.

As children write this week, they will address:

Writing 2. Write informative/explanatory texts to examine and convey complex ideas and information clearly and accurately through the effective selection, organization, and analysis of content.

Listening and Speaking On page 69, children learn to listen for sequence. By doing so, they address:

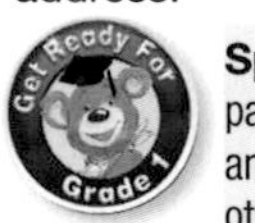

Speaking/Listening 1. Prepare for and participate effectively in a range of conversations and collaborations with diverse partners, building on others' ideas and expressing their own clearly and persuasively.

Week 4

Goldilocks and the Three Bears

Question of the Week
How can an adventure cause trouble?

Concept Talk Guide children as they discuss questions such as:

- Are these real or make-believe bears? What do real bears do? What do make-believe bears do?

Writing Have children turn to p. 286 of *Reader's and Writer's Notebook.* Have them write or dictate a list of things found in *Goldilocks and the Three Bears.*

Week 5

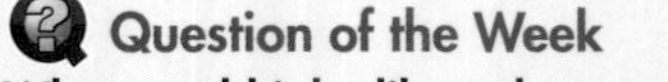

If You Could Go to Antarctica

Question of the Week
What would it be like to have an Antarctic adventure?

Concept Talk Guide children as they discuss questions such as:

- What would you ask the explorer?
- Would you like to be an explorer?

Writing Have children turn to p. 298 of *Reader's and Writer's Notebook.* Have them write or dictate a letter to someone by finishing the sentence that tells what they like to read about. Then have them write their name at the end of the letter.

Week 6

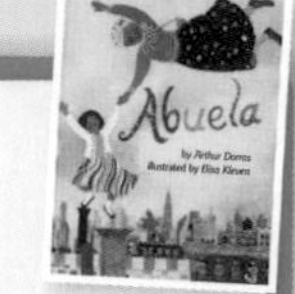

Abuela

Question of the Week
What kind of adventures can you have in the city?

Concept Talk Guide children as they discuss questions such as:

- How do the children feel about their grandmothers? What do they like best about spending time with their grandmothers?

Writing Reread and discuss your list of things to do in the community, underlining key words in your draft. Have children write or dictate the group draft or copy the underlined key words on p. 314 in *Reader's and Writer's Notebook.* Then have them draw pictures to go with their list.

This Week's ELL Overview

Grade K • Unit 4 • Week 3
One Little Mouse
205–304
and DI•46–DI•51

ELL Handbook

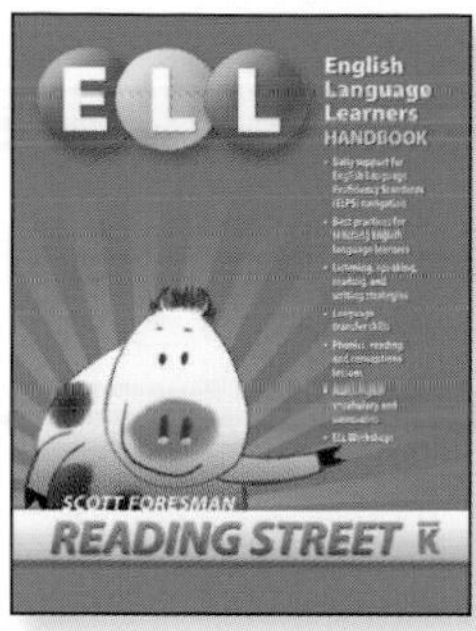

- Maximize Literacy and Cognitive Engagement
- Research Into Practice
- Full Weekly Support for Every Selection

  One Little Mouse
  - Routines to Support Instruction
- Transfer Activities
- Professional Development

Daily Leveled ELL Notes

ELL notes appear throughout this week's instruction and ELL Support is on the DI pages of your Teacher's Edition. The following is a sample of an ELL note from this week.

English Language Learners

Beginning Listening Comprehension English learners will benefit from additional visual support to understand words in the song. For example, point to the *woodland* and *nest* on the Talk with Me chart to scaffold meaning.

Intermediate Support Blending Spanish does not have initial *s*- blends, so Spanish speakers may add a short *e* sound at the beginning of words such as *slap.* Help children practice blending the sounds in words with initial *s*- blends.

Advanced Complete Sentences Remind children that sentences begin with uppercase letters and end with periods or other ending punctuation marks. The Spanish word for *uppercase letter* is *mayúscula.* The Spanish word for period is *punto.*

Advanced High Complete Sentences Help children see that word order affects meaning in English. For example, *Ty ate the pickle* is not the same as *The pickle ate Ty.* Remind children that the naming part often comes before the action part in English sentences.

ELL by Strand

The ELL lessons on this week's Support for English Language Learners pages are organized by strand. They offer additional scaffolding for the core curriculum. Leveled support notes on these pages address the different proficiency levels in your class. See pages DI•46–DI•51.

	The Three Pillars of ELL Instruction		
ELL Strands	**Activate Prior Knowledge**	**Access Content**	**Extend Language**
Vocabulary p. DI•48	Frontload Vocabulary	Provide Scaffolding	Provide Scaffolding
Reading Comprehension p. DI•48	Provide Scaffolding	Set the Scene	Frontload Vocabulary
Phonics, Spelling, and Word Analysis pp. DI•46, DI•49–DI•50	Frontload Consonant Blends with /l/	Isolate Final Blends	Review Initial and Final /l/
Listening Comprehension p. DI•47	Prepare for the Read Aloud	First Listening	Second Listening
Conventions and Writing pp. DI•49, DI•51	Provide Scaffolding/ Introduce and Model	Practice	Leveled Practice Activities/ Leveled Writing Activities
Concept Development p. DI•46	Read the Concept Literacy Reader	Read the Concept Literacy Reader	Develop Oral Language

This Week's Practice Stations Overview

Grade K • Unit 4 • Week 3
One Little Mouse
205–304

Six Weekly Practice Stations with Leveled Activities can be found at the beginning of each week of instruction. For this week's Practice Stations, see pp. 212–213.

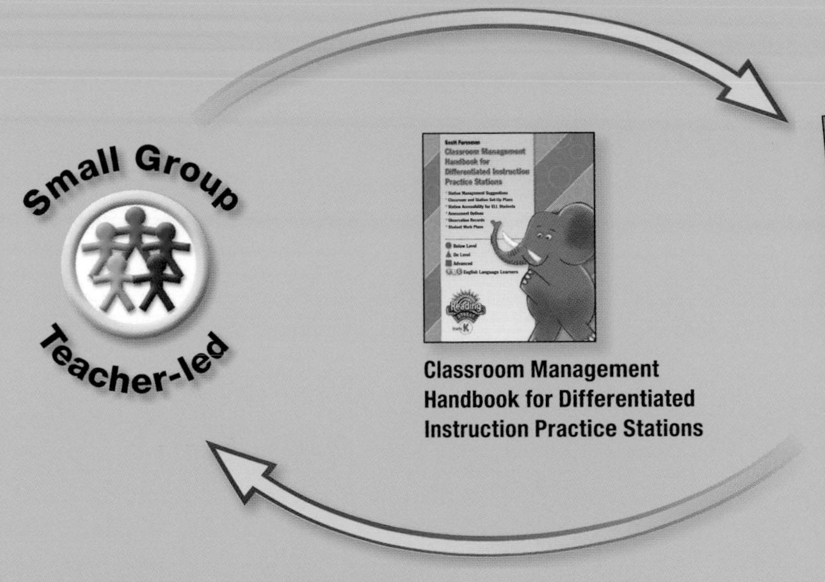

Classroom Management Handbook for Differentiated Instruction Practice Stations

Practice Stations

Daily Leveled Center Activities

 Below
 Advanced
 On-Level
 ELL

Practice Stations Flip Charts

	 Listen Up	 Word Work	 Words to Know	 Let's Write	 Read for Meaning	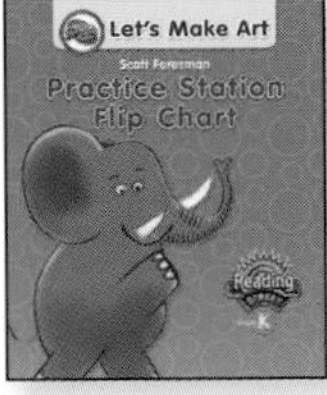 Let's Make Art
Objectives	• Identify words with /l/.	• Identify words with /l/ spelled *Ll*.	• Identify and use words for textures.	• Write a poem.	• Identify cause and effect.	• Paint a picture.
Materials	• *Listen Up* Flip Chart Activity 21 • Picture Cards: *cap, lake, leaf, loaf, soap, yo-yo* • paper, crayons	• *Word Work* Flip Chart Activity 21 • Alphabet Card: *Ll* • Picture Cards: *bag, egg, hen, ladybug, lamp, lemon* • Letter Tiles	• *Words to Know* Flip Chart Activity 21 • Teacher-made Word Cards: *fuzzy, bumpy, furry, sharp* • objects: a piece of fuzzy fabric, a bumpy rock, a piece of furry fabric or a furry stuffed animal, a sharpened pencil • paper, pencils	• *Let's Write* Flip Chart Activity 21 • copies of poem starter: One little mouse Looks for a ____. • paper, pencils, crayons	• *Read for Meaning* Flip Chart Activity 21 • Trade Book *My Lucky Day* • pencil, crayons, paper	• *Let's Make Art* Flip Chart Activity 21 • yarn • construction paper scraps • paper, crayons, pencils, glue, scissors

This Week on Reading Street!

Question of the Week

What adventures can animals have?

Daily Plan

Whole Group

- ◎ Consonant Blends
- ◎ Sequence
- Vocabulary

MONITOR PROGRESS **Success Predictor**

Day 1	Day 2	Day 3	Day 4	Day 5
Check Phonemic Awareness	Check Sound Spelling/ Retelling	Check Word Reading	Check Phonemic Awareness	Check Oral Vocabulary

Small Group

Teacher-Led

- Reading Support
- Skill Support
- Fluency Practice

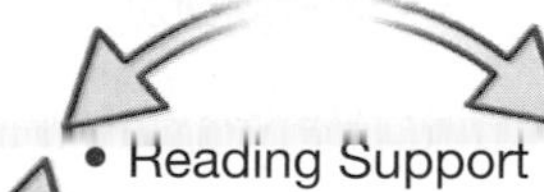

Customize Literacy More support for a Balanced Literacy approach, see pp. CL•1–CL•31.

Whole Group

- Writing
- Conventions: Complete Sentences
- Listening and Speaking

Assessment

- Day 5 Assessment for Phonics
- Day 5 Assessment for Comprehension

You Are Here! Unit 4 Week 3

This Week's Reading Selections

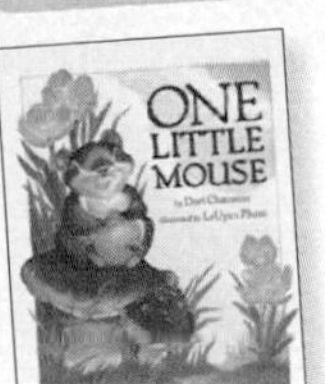

Big Book
Genre: **Animal Fantasy**

Decodable Reader 21

Leveled Readers

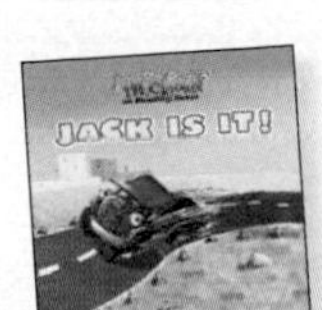

Get Set Roll! Reader 21

Resources on Reading Street!

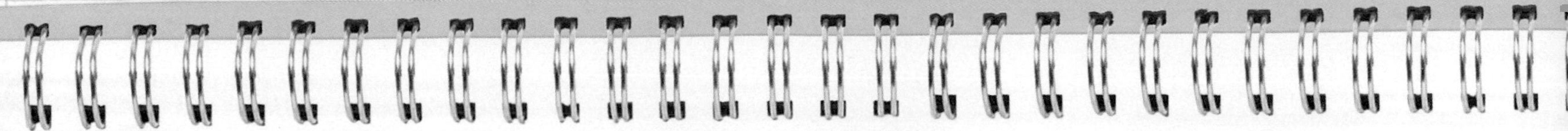

	Build Concepts	Phonemic Awareness and Phonics	Vocabulary
Whole Group	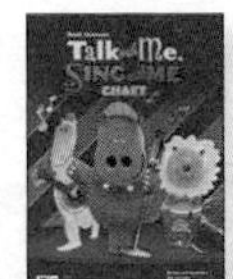 Talk With Me/ Sing With Me	 Student Edition pp. 52–53;  Student Edition p. 56	 Student Edition p. 57; 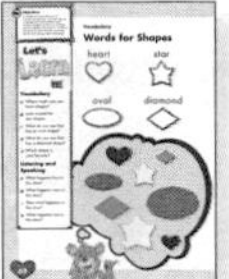 Student Edition p. 68
  Go Digital	• Concept Talk Video • Sing with Me Animations	• eReaders	
Small Group and Independent Practice	 Practice Station Flip Chart;  Leveled Readers	 Practice Station Flip Chart;  Decodable Reader 21;  Leveled Readers;  Get Set, Roll! Reader 21	 Practice Station Flip Chart; 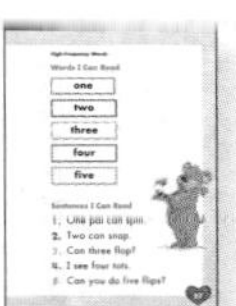 Student Edition p. 57
 Go Digital	• eReaders	• eReaders • Letter Tile Drag and Drop	
Customize Literacy	• Leveled Readers	• Decodable Reader	• High-Frequency Word Cards
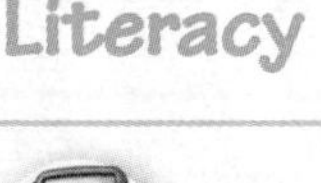 Go Digital	• Concept Talk Video • Big Question Video • eReaders	• eReaders	• Sing with Me Animations

Question of the Week

What adventures can animals have?

Comprehension	Fluency	Conventions and Writing
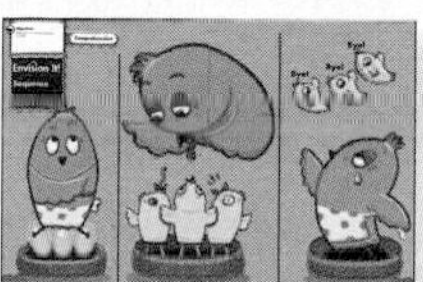  Student Edition pp. 54–55  Big Book	 Decodable Reader 21  Kdg. Student Reader K.4.3 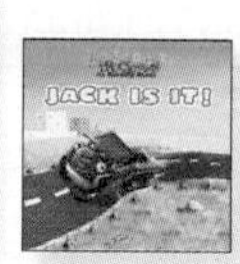 Get Set, Roll! Reader 21	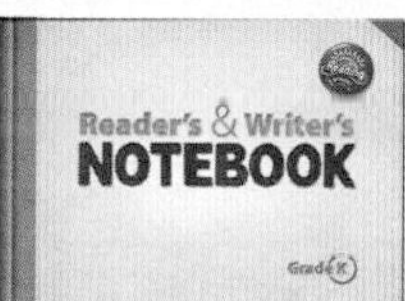 Reader's and Writer's Notebook
• Envision It! Animations	• eReaders	• Grammar Jammer
 Practice Station Flip Chart  Leveled Readers 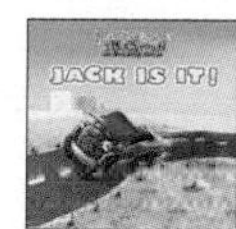 Get Set, Roll! Reader 21	 Practice Station Flip Chart  Leveled Readers	 Practice Station Flip Chart 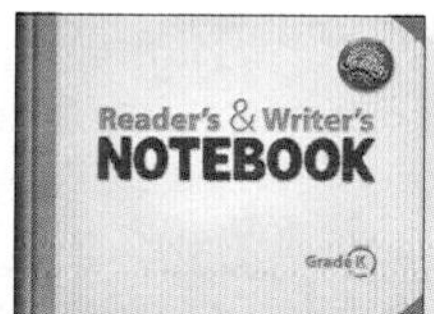 Reader's and Writer's Notebook
• Envision It! Animations • eReaders	• eReaders	• Grammar Jammer • Online Journal
• Leveled Readers	• Leveled Readers	• *Reader's and Writer's Notebook*
• Envision It! Animations • eReaders	• eReaders	• Grammar Jammer

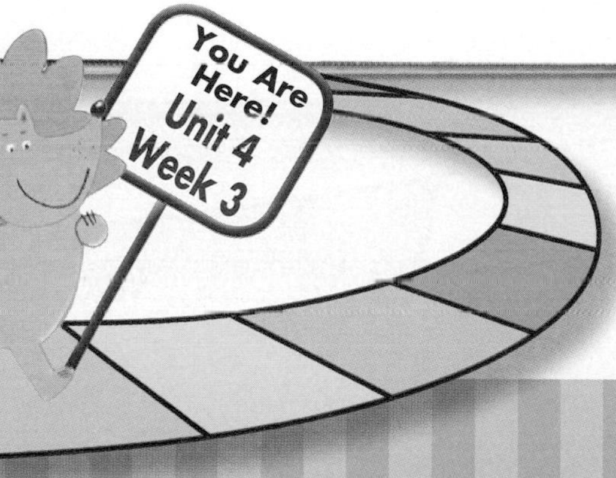

Week 3

My 5-Day Planner for Reading Street!

Don't Wait Until Friday MONITOR PROGRESS

	Check Phonemic Awareness **Day 1** pages 214–229	Check Sound-Spelling Check Retelling **Day 2** pages 230–247
Get Ready to Read	**Concept Talk,** 214 **Oral Vocabulary,** 215 *woodland, nest, vale, hollow, comfortable, shadows* **Phonemic Awareness,** 216–217 ◉ Consonant Blends with *l* **Phonics,** 218–219 ◉ Consonant Blends **Handwriting,** 220 Write Numerals and Number Words **High-Frequency Words,** 221 Introduce *one, two, three, four, five* **READ Decodable Story 21,** 222–223	**Concept Talk,** 230 **Oral Vocabulary,** 231 *woodland, nest* **Phonemic Awareness,** 232–233 ◉ Consonant Blends **Phonics,** 234–235 ◉ Consonant Blends **Handwriting,** 236 Write Numerals and Number Words **High-Frequency Words,** 237 *one, two, three, four, five* **READ Decodable Reader 21,** 238–239
Read and Comprehend	**Listening Comprehension,** 224–225 ◉ Sequence	**Listening Comprehension,** 240 ◉ Sequence **READ Big Book—First Read,** 240 One Little Mouse **Retell,** 241 **Think, Talk, and Write,** 242
Language Arts	**Conventions,** 226 Complete Sentences **Writing,** 227 Wonderful, Marvelous Me! **Daily Handwriting,** 227 Write Numerals and Number Words **Listening and Speaking,** 228 Listen for Sequence **Wrap Up Your Day,** 228 **Extend Your Day!,** 229	**Conventions,** 243 Complete Sentences **Writing,** 244 Respond to Literature **Daily Handwriting,** 244 Write Numerals and Number Words **Vocabulary,** 245 Words for Shapes **Wrap Up Your Day,** 246 **Extend Your Day!,** 247

You Are Here! Unit 4 Week 3

Question of the Week

What adventures can animals have?

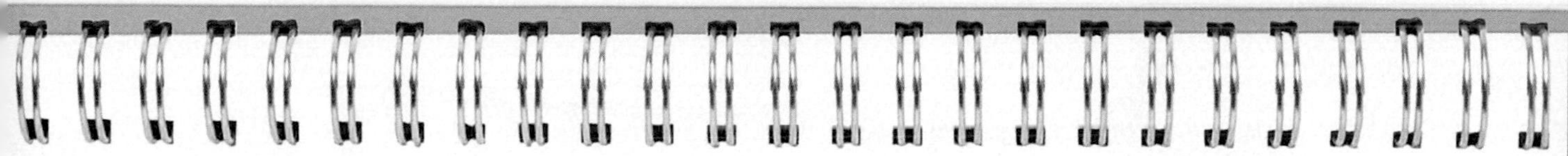

Check Word Reading	Check Phonemic Awareness	Check Oral Vocabulary
Day 3 pages 248–277	**Day 4** pages 278–289	**Day 5** pages 290–303
Concept Talk, 248 **Oral Vocabulary,** 249 *vale, hollow* **Phonemic Awareness,** 250–251 ◉ Final Blends **Phonics,** 252–253 ◉ Consonant Blends **READ Kindergarten Student Reader K.4.3,** 254–255	**Concept Talk,** 278 **Oral Vocabulary,** 279 *comfortable, shadows* Review **Phonemic Awareness,** 280 /l/ Review **Phonics,** 281 /l/ Spelled *Ll* **Spelling,** 282 ◉ Consonant Blends **READ Get Set, Roll! Reader 21,** 283	**Concept Wrap Up,** 290 **Oral Vocabulary,** 291 *woodland, nest, vale, hollow, comfortable, shadows* Review **Phonemic Awareness,** 292 ◉ Sounds for Blends Review **Phonics,** 293 ◉ Consonant Blends **Assessment,** 294–295 Monitor Progress
Comprehension, 256 ◉ Sequence **READ Big Book—Second Read,** 257–271 One Little Mouse	**Comprehension,** 284 ◉ Sequence Review Draw Conclusions **READ Big Book—Third Read,** 285 One Little Mouse	**Let's Practice It!,** 296–297 Directions **Assessment,** 298–299 Monitor Progress
Conventions, 272 Action Parts **Writing,** 273 Genre: Description **Daily Handwriting,** 273 Write Numerals and Number Words **Listening and Speaking,** 274–275 Listen for Sequence **Wrap Up Your Day,** 276 **Extend Your Day!,** 277	**Conventions,** 286 Complete Sentences **Writing,** 287 Extend the Concept **Daily Handwriting,** 287 Write Numerals and Number Words **Vocabulary,** 288 Words for Shapes **Wrap Up Your Day,** 288 **Extend Your Day!,** 289	Review **Conventions,** 300 Complete Sentences **Writing,** 301 This Week We... **Daily Handwriting,** 301 Write Numerals and Number Words **Wrap Up Your Week!,** 302 What adventures can animals have? **Extend Your Day!,** 303

Week 3

Grouping Options for Differentiated Instruction
Turn the page for the small group time lesson plan.

Planning Small Group Time on Reading Street!

SMALL GROUP TIME RESOURCES

DAY 1 **Look for this Small Group Time box each day to help meet the individual needs of all your children. Differentiated instruction lessons appear on the DI pages at the end of each week.**

Teacher-Led

SI Strategic Intervention	OL On-Level	A Advanced
Teacher-Led • Phonemic Awareness and Phonics **Reread** Decodable Story	**Teacher-Led** • Phonemic Awareness and Phonics **Reread** Decodable Story	**Teacher-Led** • Phonemic Awareness and Phonics **Reread** Decodable Story for Fluency

ELL Place English language learners in the groups that correspond to their reading abilities in English.

Practice Stations
- Listen Up
- Word Work

Independent Activities
- Read Independently
- *Reader's and Writer's Notebook*
- Concept Talk Video

ELL

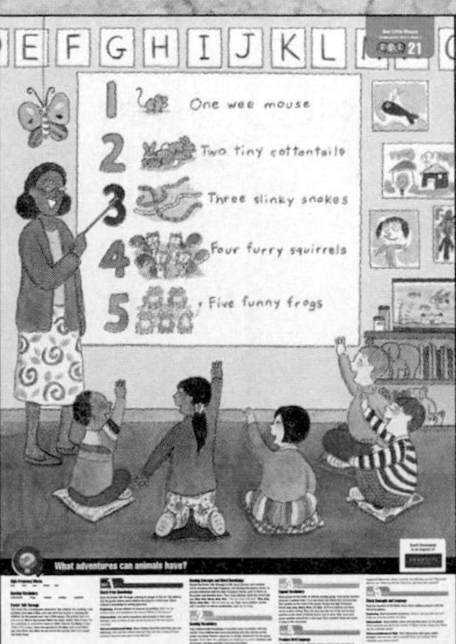

ELL Poster 21

Day 1

 Strategic Intervention	**Phonemic Awareness and Phonics,** DI•35 **Reread** Decodable Story 21, DI•35
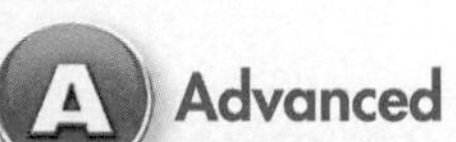 On-Level	**Phonemic Awareness and Phonics,** DI•40 **Reread** Decodable Story 21, DI•40
A Advanced	**Phonemic Awareness and Phonics,** DI•43 **Reread** Decodable Story 21 for Fluency, DI•43
 English Language Learners	DI•46–DI•47 Frontload Concept Phonemic Awareness and Phonics Comprehension Skill

You Are Here! Unit 4 Week 3

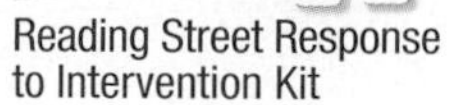

Reading Street Response to Intervention Kit

Reading Street Leveled Practice Stations Kit

Question of the Week

What adventures can animals have?

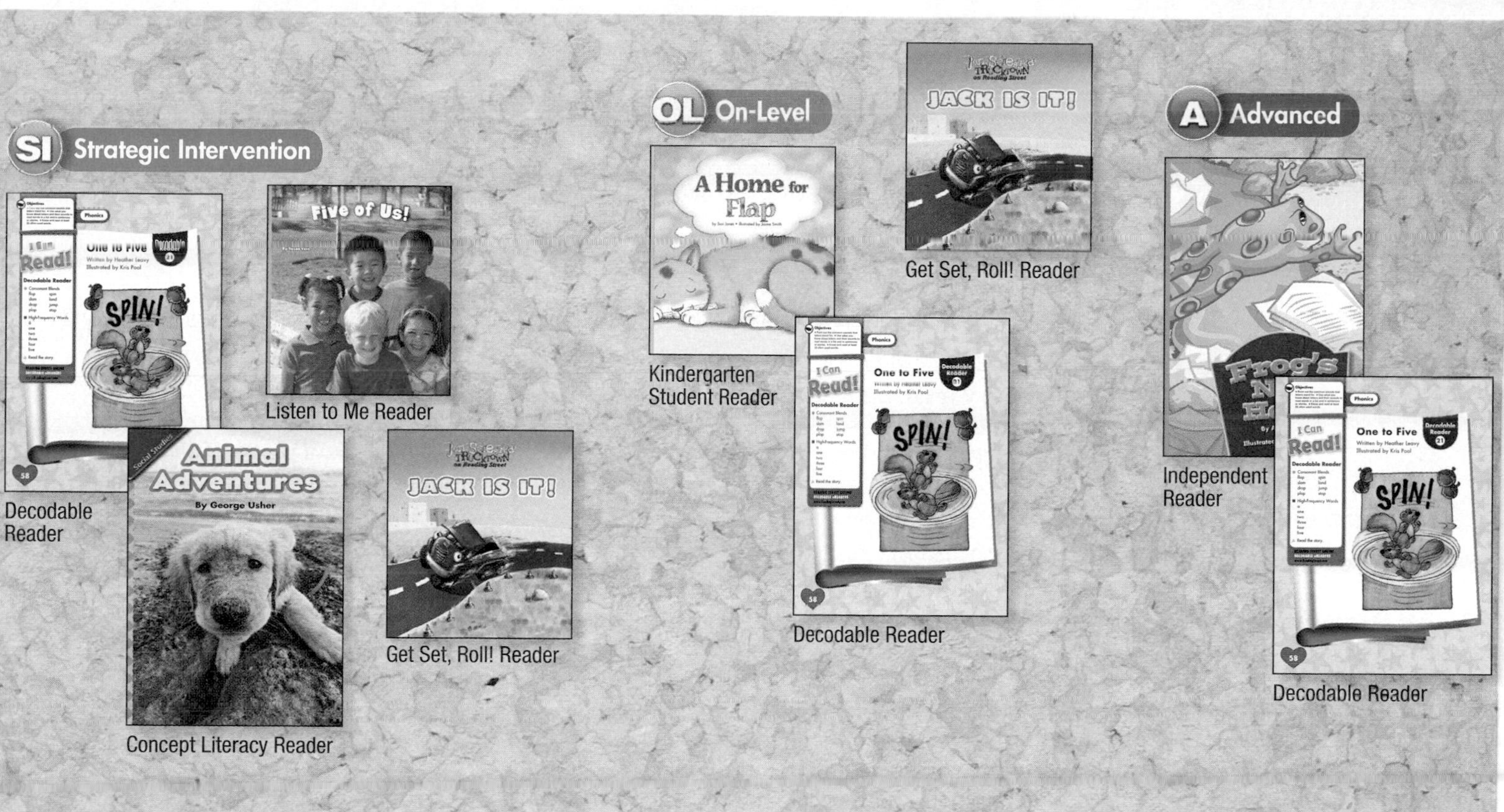

Week 3

Small Group Weekly Plan

Day 2	Day 3	Day 4	Day 5
Phonemic Awareness and Phonics, DI•36 **Reread** Decodable Reader 21, DI•36	**Phonemic Awareness and Phonics,** DI•37 **Read** Concept Literacy Reader K.4.3, DI•37	**Phonemic Awareness and Phonics,** DI•38 **Read** Get Set, Roll! Reader 21, DI•38	**Phonics Review,** DI•39 **Read** Listen to Me Reader K.4.3, DI•39
Phonemic Awareness and Phonics, DI•40 **Reread** Decodable Reader 21, DI•40	**Phonemic Awareness and Phonics,** DI•41 **Read** Kindergarten Student Reader K.4.3, DI•41	Review Phonics and High-Frequency Words **Read** Get Set, Roll! Reader 21, DI•42	**Phonics Review,** DI•42 **Reread** Leveled Books
Phonics and Spelling, DI•43 **Reread** Decodable Reader 21 for Fluency, DI•43	**Read** Independent Reader K.4.3 or Kindergarten Student Reader K.4.3, DI•44	**Read** Get Set, Roll! Reader 21 or **Reread** Kindergarten Student Reader K.4.3, DI•45	**Fluency and Comprehension,** DI•45 **Reread** Independent Reader for Fluency, DI•45
DI•48 Comprehension Skill Frontload Vocabulary	DI•49 Review Phonemic Awareness and Phonics Scaffold Conventions	DI•50 Review Phonemic Awareness and Phonics Revisit Concepts and Oral Language	DI•51 Language Workshop Writing

Practice Stations for Everyone on Reading Street!

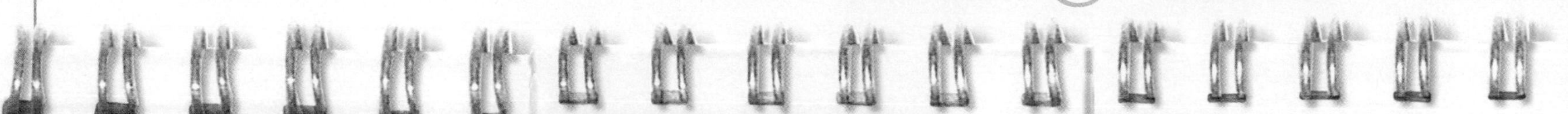

Listen Up!
Words with /l/

Objectives
- Identify words with /l/.

Materials
- *Listen Up!* Flip Chart Activity 21
- Picture Cards: *cap, lake, leaf, loaf, soap, yo-yo*
- paper, crayons

Differentiated Activities

● Find the Picture Card for *leaf*. Say the sound you hear at the beginning. Find another Picture Card with the same sound at the beginning.

▲ Find the Picture Card for *leaf*. Say the sound you hear at the beginning. Find all the Picture Cards with the same sound at the beginning.

■ Find the Picture Card for *leaf*. Find all the Picture Cards with the same sound at the beginning. Draw pictures of other things whose names begin like *leaf*.

Word Work
/l/ Spelled *Ll*

Objectives
- Identify words with /l/ spelled *Ll*.

Materials
- *Word Work* Flip Chart Activity 21
- Alphabet Card: *Ll*
- Picture Cards: *bag, egg, hen, ladybug, lamp, lemon*
- Letter Tiles

Differentiated Activities

● Find the Alphabet Card for *Ll*. Look for Picture Cards whose names begin with *Ll* like *lamb*.

▲ Find the Alphabet Card for *Ll*. Find Picture Cards whose names begin with *Ll* like *lamb*. Look around the room. Find other objects whose names begin with *Ll* like *lamb*.

■ Find the Alphabet Card for *Ll*. Find Picture Cards whose names begin with *Ll* like *lamb*. Look around the room. Find other objects whose names begin with *Ll* like *lamb*. Use the Letter Tiles to spell other words that begin with *Ll*.

Technology
- Letter Tiles Drag and Drop

Words To Know
Words for textures

Objectives
- Identify and use words for textures.

Materials
- *Words to Know* Flip Chart Activity 21
- Teacher-made word cards: *fuzzy, bumpy, furry, sharp*
- objects: a piece of fuzzy fabric, a bumpy rock, a piece of furry fabric or a furry stuffed animal, a sharpened pencil
- paper, pencils

Differentiated Activities

● Find objects that are *fuzzy, bumpy, furry, sharp*. Tell a partner how each feels.

▲ Find the objects that are *fuzzy, bumpy, furry, sharp*. Match each object with a word card.

■ Match the Word Cards with the objects that are *fuzzy, bumpy, furry, sharp*. Write sentences to tell about things that are *fuzzy, bumpy, furry,* and *sharp*.

You Are Here! Unit 4 Week 3

Use this week's materials from the Reading Street Leveled Practice Stations Kit to organize this week's stations.

Key

Below-Level Activities

On-Level Activities

Advanced Activities

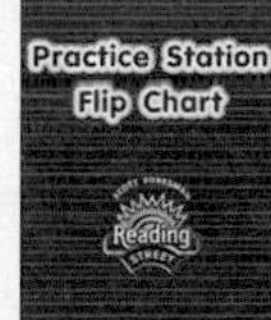

Practice Station Flip Chart

Let's Write!

Poem

Objectives

• Write a poem.

Materials

• *Let's Write!* Flip Chart Activity 21
• copies of poem starter:
  One little mouse
  Looks for a ______.
• paper, pencils, crayons

Differentiated Activities

With a partner, finish the poem. Write a rhyming word. Draw a picture to go with your poem.

With a partner, finish the poem. Together think of another line for the poem. Draw a picture to go with it.

Finish the poem. Write two more rhyming lines for the poem. Draw a picture to go with it.

Read For Meaning

Cause and effect

Objectives

• Identify cause and effect.

Materials

• *Read for Meaning* Flip Chart Activity 21
• Trade Book *My Lucky Day*
• pencil, crayons, paper

Differentiated Activities

Look at the book. Choose an event that happened in the story. Tell a partner why it happened.

Look at the book. Choose an event that happened in the story. Tell a partner why it happened. Draw a picture of the event.

Look at the book. Choose an event that happened in the story. Draw a picture of the event. Write a sentence that tells the cause, or why it happened.

Let's Make Art!

Objectives

• Create a picture.

Materials

• *Let's Make Art!* Flip Chart Activity 21
• yarn
• construction paper scraps
• paper, crayons, pencils, glue, scissors

Differentiated Activities

Think about *One Little Mouse*. Draw a picture of Mouse in his house. Then glue scraps of yarn around Mouse to show he is sleeping in his nest.

Think about *One Little Mouse*. Draw a picture of Mouse in his house or another animal in its house. Then glue scraps of yarn or pieces of construction paper to your picture to show the animal's nest or home.

Think about *One Little Mouse*. Draw a picture of Mouse or another animal in its house. Then glue scraps of yarn or pieces of construction paper to your picture to show the animal's nest or home. Write something about your picture.

Week 3

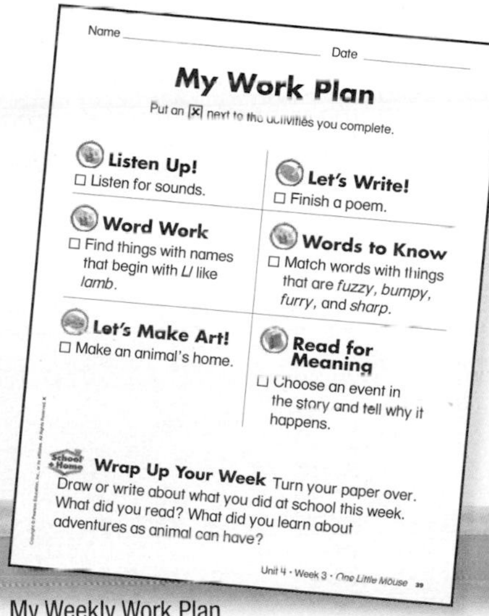
Name ______ Date ______

My Work Plan

Put an [X] next to the activities you complete.

Listen Up!
☐ Listen for sounds.

Let's Write!
☐ Finish a poem.

Word Work
☐ Find things with names that begin with *L/* like *lamb*.

Words to Know
☐ Match words with things that are *fuzzy, bumpy, furry,* and *sharp*.

Let's Make Art!
☐ Make an animal's home.

Read for Meaning
☐ Choose an event in the story and tell why it happens.

Wrap Up Your Week Turn your paper over. Draw or write about what you did at school this week. What did you read? What did you learn about adventures as animal can have?

Unit 4 • Week 3 • One Little Mouse

My Weekly Work Plan

30–35 mins.

Objectives

- Share information and ideas about the concept.

Today at a Glance

Oral Vocabulary
woodland, nest, vale, hollow, comfortable, shadows

Phonemic Awareness
⊙ Consonant Blends with *l*

Phonics
⊙ Consonant Blends with *l*

Handwriting
Numerals and Number Words

High-Frequency Words
one, two, three, four, five

Comprehension
⊙ Sequence

Conventions
Complete Sentences

Writing
Wonderful, Marvelous Me!

Listening and Speaking
Listen for Sequence

TRUCKTOWN on Reading Street

Start your engines! Display p. 7 of *Truckery Rhymes*.

- Read aloud "Three Loud Trucks" and track the print.
- Reread the rhyme and have children chime in as they wish.
- Ask children to identify the rhyming words. (*goo, blew, crew*)

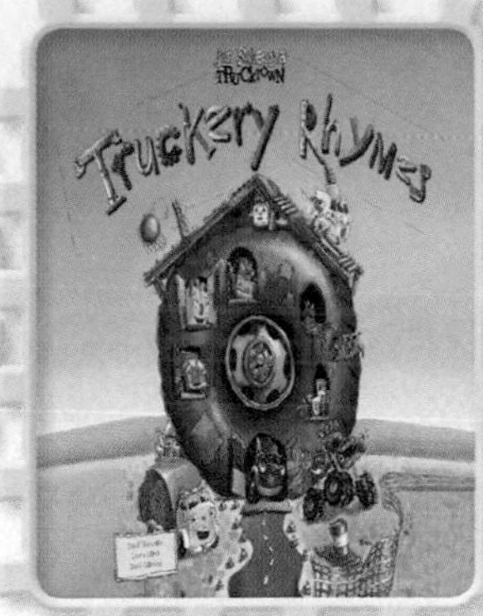

Truckery Rhymes

Concept Talk

Question of the Week

What adventures can animals have?

Introduce the concept

To build concepts and to focus their attention, tell children that this week they will have an opportunity to talk, sing, read, and write about **animal adventures.** Track each word as you read the question of the week.

Play the CD that features an adventure that a small animal could have. What would a small animal's adventure be like?

Background Building Audio

ROUTINE Activate Prior Knowledge — Team Talk

1. **Think** Have children think for a minute about what they know about animal adventures.
2. **Pair** Have pairs of children discuss the question of the week. Remind them to take turns speaking. Have children use complete sentences in their discussions about adventures animals can have.
3. **Share** Call on a few children to share their ideas with the group. Guide discussion and encourage elaboration with prompts such as: What adventure have you had?

Routines Flip Chart

Anchored Talk

Develop oral language

Display Talk with Me Chart 21A. Have children look at the forest. Read the question together. This week we will be talking about adventures that animals can have. Look at the pictures. What adventures could an animal have in these places?

We are going to learn six new Amazing Words. Listen as I say the Amazing Words: *woodland, nest, vale, hollow, comfortable, shadows*. Have children say each word as you point to the picture.

Display Sing with Me Chart 21B. Today we are going to sing a song about a mouse looking for a new house. Listen for the Amazing Words *woodland, nest, vale, hollow, comfortable,* and *shadows.* Read the title and have children describe the pictures. Sing the song several times to the tune of "Hickory, Dickory, Dock." Have children stand up and sing with you.

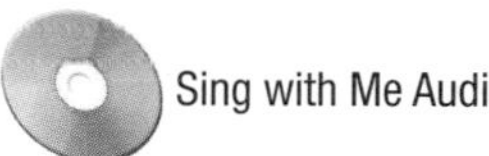
Sing with Me Audio

Talk with Me/Sing with Me Chart 21A

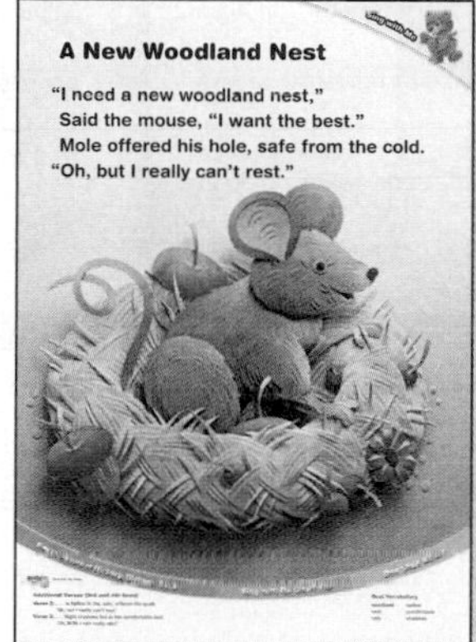

Talk with Me/Sing with Me Chart 21B

ELL Preteach Concepts Use the Day 1 instruction on ELL Poster 21 to assess and build background knowledge, develop concepts, and build oral vocabulary.

ELL Poster 21

Amazing Words

woodland	nest
vale	hollow
comfortable	shadows

Differentiated Instruction

SI Strategic Intervention

Build Background To help children understand words in the story such as *vale* and *hollow,* use the art and make sure they know what animals might live there.

English Language Learners

Listening Comprehension English learners will benefit from additional visual support to understand words in the song. For example, point to the *woodland* and *nest* on the Talk with Me chart to scaffold meaning.

ELL Support Additional ELL support and modified instruction is provided in the *ELL Handbook* and in the ELL Support Lessons on pp. DI•46–51.

Objectives

- Learn consonant blends with *l*.
- Recognize words with initial consonant blends with *l*.
- Discriminate words with initial consonant blends with *l*.
- Segment and blend words that begin with consonant blends with *l*.

Check Phonemic Awareness
SUCCESS PREDICTOR

My Skills Buddy, pp. 52–53

Phonemic Awareness

Consonant Blends with *l*

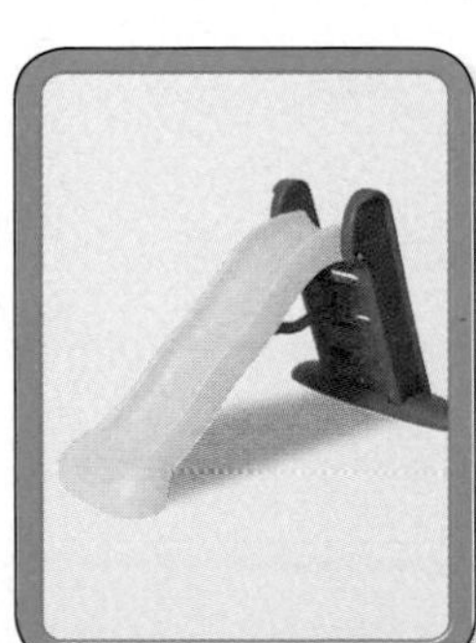

Picture Card

Introduce Two sounds are put together to make a consonant blend. Display the *slide* Picture Card. Listen to the beginning sounds of the word *slide*. Two sounds blend together at the beginning: /s/ /l/, /sl/ /sl/, *slide*. Continue the routine with the *clock, blue, playground, glove,* and *flashlight* Picture Cards.

Model Have children look at the picture on pp. 52–53 of *My Skills Buddy*. I see an ice skater slipping in the picture. What sounds do you hear at the beginning of *slipping?* I hear /s/ /l/, /sl/ at the beginning of *slipping*. The first sound in *slipping* is the blend /sl/. What other things do you see that begin with blends? Look for words that begin with the blends /sl/, /pl/, /bl/, /gl/, /fl/, and /kl/.

Guide practice As children name example words from the picture, guide them in stating the beginning blend. Discuss with children some of the bulleted items on p. 52 of *My Skills Buddy*. Save the other bulleted items for discussion on Day 2.

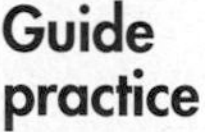

Corrective feedback **If...** children have difficulty recognizing words with initial consonant blends, **then...** have them repeat /sl/, /pl/, /bl/, /gl/, /fl/, and /kl/.

Discriminate blends with *l*

Display the *slide, clock,* and *flashlight* Picture Cards around the classroom. I will say a word. Listen to the first sound. Does it start like *slide, clock,* or *flashlight?* Go stand by the Picture Card that begins with the same sound. I will do the first one: *flip*. I hear /f/ /l/, /fl/ at the beginning of *flip*. *Slide. Clock. Flashlight*. I hear /fl/ at the beginning of *flashlight*. *Flip* and *flashlight* begin the same. Continue with the words *slam, clip, flag, clap,* and *sled*.

Repeat the routine with the *block, glove,* and *playground* Picture Cards. Say the words *plan, black, glue, glide, blow,* and *plod*.

Corrective feedback

If... children cannot blend spoken phonemes to form words,
then... have them segment the two sounds before blending them together.

Blend

Review blending sounds. We have learned how to blend sounds together to say words with blends. Listen as I say the sounds and then blend them together to make a word: /fl/ /a/ /p/, *flap*. Say it with me: /fl/ /a/ /p/, *flap*. Continue the blending practice with *slim, slab, plot, plug, club, click, flop,* and *flat.*

MONITOR PROGRESS — Check Phonemic Awareness — Consonant Blends

Say *slip* and *sip*. Have children identify the word that begins with a blend. Continue with *flip, lip; cap, clap; lap, flap;* and *play, pay*.

If... children cannot discriminate initial consonant blends,
then... use the small-group Strategic Intervention lesson, p. DI•35, to reteach blends.

Day 1	Day 2	Day 3	Day 4	Day 5
Check Phonemic Awareness	Check Sound-Spelling/ Retelling	Check Word Reading	Check Phonemic Awareness	Check Oral Vocabulary

Success Predictor

Differentiated Instruction

Advanced

Support Consonant Blends
Have children tell silly sentences using multiple words that begin with initial blends, such as *Slippery slithering snakes slide down sloping hills*.

Academic Vocabulary

consonant blend two or more consecutive consonants, each of which is pronounced and blended with the other, such as *cl* in *clock*

ELL

English Language Learners

Phonemic Awareness The consonant blends /pl/, /kl/, and /fl/ exist in both English and Spanish. Help Spanish speakers discover the similarity by comparing the beginning sounds in cognates such as *planta* (plant), *clase* (class), and *flor* (flower).

Phonemic Awareness

Success Predictor

Objectives

- Recognize consonant blends with *l*.
- ◎ Associate the sounds in each consonant blend with letters.
- Blend and read words with consonant blends with *l*.

Skills Trace

◎ Consonant Blends
Introduce U4W3D1
Practice U4W3D2; U4W3D3
Reteach/Review U4W3D5; U4W4D4
Assess/Test Benchmark Assessment U4

KEY:
U=Unit W=Week D=Day

Phonics—Teach/Model
◎ Consonant Blends with *l*

Introduce Display the *clock* Picture Card. What is this? This is a *clock*. What are the first two sounds in *clock?* *Clock* begins with /k/ /l/, /kl/. Say it with me: /kl/ /kl/ /kl/, *clock*. Write *clock* on the board and point to *cl*. The letter we learned for /k/ is *c,* and the letter for /l/ is *l*. Put the sounds together to make /kl/. *Clock* begins with a consonant blend. Continue the routine with the *slide, playground, block, glove,* and *flashlight* Picture Cards for the sound-spellings of *sl, pl, bl, gl*, and *fl*.

Picture Card

Model Write "Sliding Down the Slippery Slope" on the board. Point to *Sl* in *Sliding*. When I see these letters together, I know it is a blend. I blend the sounds /s/ and /l/ to get /sl/. The first word is *Sliding*—/sl/, *Sliding*. Point to *Slippery*. This word begins with *Sl* too. I know that when I see *Sl* the sound will be the blend /sl/. This word is /sl/, *Slippery*. Repeat with the word *Slope*. The song we will sing is "Sliding Down the Slippery Slope." It has lots of blends with the letter *l*. You can make blends with other letters too. We will learn about those blends later.

Guide practice Display Phonics Songs and Rhymes Chart 21. Teach children the song "Sliding Down the Slippery Slope" to the tune of "Jack and Jill Went Up the Hill." Play the CD and sing the song several times. When children are familiar with the song, have them clap when they hear words with /sl/, /pl/, /kl/, or /fl/. Have volunteers come up and point to words that begin with *sl, pl, cl,* or *fl*. I will do the first one. I see a consonant blend at the beginning of the word *sliding*. *Sliding* begins with *sl*.

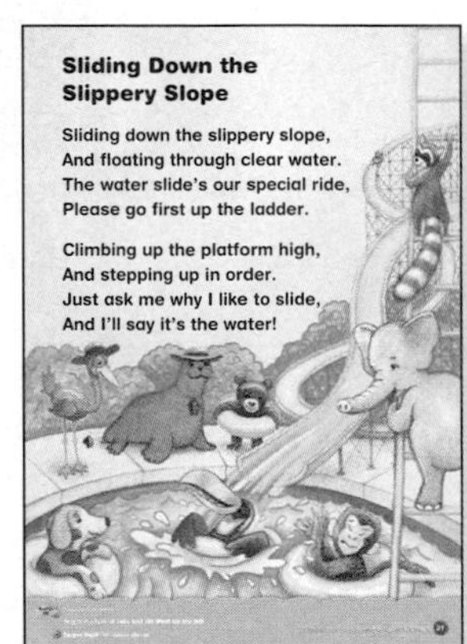

Phonics Songs and Rhymes Chart 21

Phonics Songs and Rhymes Audio

On their own Have children choose a Picture Card whose name begins with one of the target consonant blends, say the name of the picture, and tell the two letters that make up the initial blend. Then ask children to look around the room and find things whose names begin with that blend.

Blend Words

Review

To review sound-spellings, use Alphabet Cards *Aa, Ff, Cc, Oo, Ll, Pp,* and *Tt* and the *ant, flag, cloud, lake, otter, pail,* and *tent* Picture Cards. Then use this routine for sound-by-sound blending to have children blend new words.

ROUTINE Sound-by-Sound Blending

1. **Connect** Write the letters *fl* on the board. What are the sounds for these letters? The sounds are /fl/. Say it with me: /fl/ /fl/ /fl/. When you see these letters in a word, what will you say?

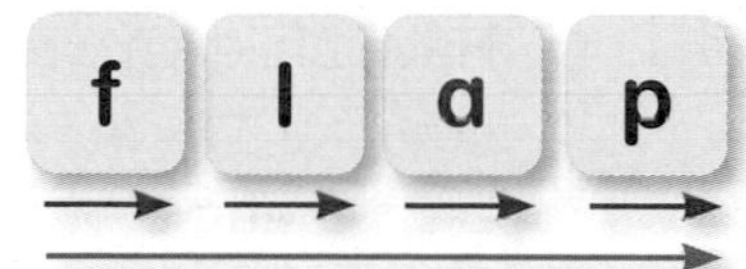

2. **Model** Write *flap* on the board.
   - Touch under the letters *fl*. What are the sounds for these letters? Say them with me: /fl/ /fl/ /fl/. Repeat the routine touching under *a* and *p*.
   - Let's blend the sounds together. Listen as I blend the sounds: /fl/ /a/ /p/. Say it with me: *flap*. Now say it without me.
   - Listen as I use *flap* in a sentence. *A bird can flap its wings.* Say it with me. Then have children use *flap* in their own sentences.
3. **Guide Practice** Continue the routine established in step 2 with the words below:

clap	flat	blot	plan	plot	slap	glob

Children should successfully read these words before reading Decodable Story 21 on p. 267 of *Reader's and Writer's Notebook.*

Corrective Feedback If children have trouble reading a word, model blending the sounds to read the word. Then have children say it with you.

Routines Flip Chart

Differentiated Instruction

 Strategic Intervention

Support Blending If children are having difficulty blending sounds to read the words, have them practice blending the words in chunks: /f/ /l/ *-at*.

Teacher Tip

Use pairs of words such as *slip* and *sip* to help children hear and understand the importance of each letter in a word that contains a blend. Other pairs: *flame, fame; clash, cash; place, pace.*

English Language Learners

Support Blending Spanish does not have initial *s*- blends, so Spanish speakers may add a short *e* sound at the beginning of words such as *slap*. Help children practice blending the sounds in words with initial *s*- blends.

Objectives

- Write numerals and number words.
- Learn high-frequency words.

Handwriting

Introduce Explain to children the difference between numerals and number words. Numbers can be written as numerals or as words. Write the numeral 1 and the number word *one* on the board. This is the numeral 1. This is the number word *one*. They mean the same thing.

Model numerals Write the numerals 1, 2, 3, 4, and 5 in a column on the board. These are numerals. Numerals sometimes have periods after them, such as when we use them to make a list. Write a period after each numeral on the board. Watch as I trace the numerals with my finger.

Guide practice Have children write the numeral 1 in the air. Use your finger to make the numeral 1 in the air. Now write it on your hand. Repeat with the numerals 2, 3, 4, and 5.

Model number words Write the number words *one, two, three, four,* and *five* in a column next to the numerals. These are number words. They mean the same things as the numerals 1, 2, 3, 4, and 5. Point to *one*. This is the word *one*. Say the letters with me: *o, n, e*. Write the number word slowly, describing each stroke. Have children write the number word in the air and on their hands. Continue with the other number words.

Guide practice Have children use their Write-On Boards to write a row of each numeral: 1, 2, 3, 4, and 5.

More practice Use *Reader's and Writer's Notebook,* p. 265, for additional practice with numerals and number words.

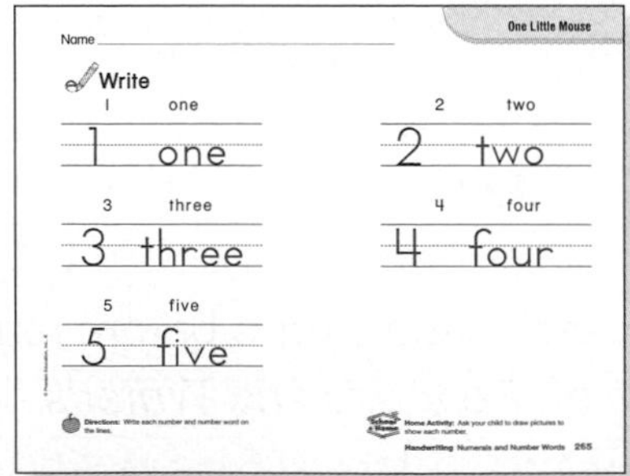
Name
One Little Mouse
Write
1 one — 1 one
2 two — 2 two
3 three — 3 three
4 four — 4 four
5 five — 5 five

Reader's and Writer's Notebook, p. 265

High-Frequency Words

Introduce Use the routine below to teach high-frequency words *one, two, three, four,* and *five*.

Nondecodable Words

1. **Say and Spell** Some words we must learn by remembering the letters rather than saying the sounds. We will say and spell the words to help learn them. Write *one* on the board. This is the word *one*. It has three letters. The letters in the word *one* are *o, n,* and *e*. Have children say and spell the word with you and then without you.
2. **Demonstrate Meaning** I can use the word *one* in lots of sentences. Here is a sentence: *I have one nose.* Now you use the word in a sentence.

Repeat the routine with the words *two, three, four,* and *five*.

Add the words *one, two, three, four,* and *five* to the Word Wall.

Routines Flip Chart

Academic Vocabulary

Write the following terms on the board:

consonant blend	**description**
complete sentence	**number word**
numeral	**sequence**

Point to the list. This week we are going to learn these important terms. They are tools for learning. As we work this week you will hear them many times. Read the terms. Preteach the Academic Vocabulary at point-of-use by providing a child-friendly description, explanation, or example that clarifies the meaning of each term. Then ask children to restate the meaning of the Academic Vocabulary in their own words.

Differentiated Instruction

A Advanced

Words in Context Have children look through a book or children's magazine for a numeral or number word in context.

Academic Vocabulary

number word the word form of a number, such as *one*

numeral the digit form of a number, such as 1

ELL

English Language Learners

Professional Development
Academic Vocabulary
According to Dr. Lily Wong Fillmore of the University of California at Berkeley, "The most important way to help ELLs perform well in mandated reading assessments is by giving them the instructional support they need to become successful readers. This involves help in learning English, discovering the purpose of reading, becoming active learners, [and] gaining access to academic language."

Objectives

- Read high-frequency words.
- Decode and read words in context and isolation.

Decodable Story 21

Consonant Blends and High-Frequency Words

Review Review the following high-frequency words by having children read each word as you point to it on the Word Wall.

do **have** **I** **is** **like** **see** **you**

Read Decodable Story 21

Display Decodable Story 21. Today we will read a story about a boy and words he can make with blends. Point to the title of the story. The title of this story is *My Words*. We will read lots of words with blends in this story. Have children read Decodable Story 21 on pp. 267–268 in *Reader's and Writer's Notebook*.

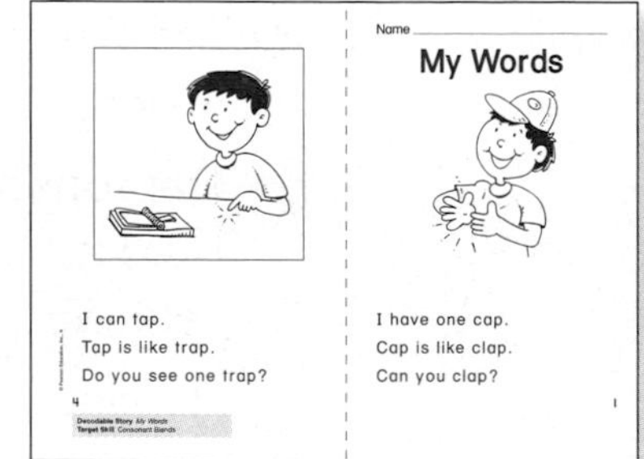

Reader's and Writer's Notebook, pp. 267–268

Use the routine for reading decodable books to read Decodable Story 21.

ROUTINE Reading Decodable Books

1. **Read Silently** Have children whisper read the story page by page as you listen in.
2. **Model Fluent Reading** Have children finger point as you read a page. Then have children reread the page without you.
3. **Read Chorally** Have children finger point as they chorally read the page. Continue reading page by page, repeating steps 1 and 2.
4. **Read Individually** Have children take turns reading aloud a page.
5. **Reread and Monitor Progress** As you listen to individual children reread, monitor progress and provide support.
6. **Reread with a Partner** Have children reread the story page by page with a partner.

Routines Flip Chart

Small Group Time

DAY 1 Break into small groups after reading the Decodable Story and before the comprehension lesson.

Teacher-Led

SI Strategic Intervention	OL On-Level	A Advanced
Teacher-Led Page DI•35 • Phonemic Awareness and Phonics • **Reread** Decodable Story 21	**Teacher-Led** Page DI•40 • Phonemic Awareness and Phonics • **Reread** Decodable Story 21, DI•40	**Teacher-Led** Page DI•43 • Phonemic Awareness and Phonics • **Reread** Decodable Story 21 for Fluency, DI•43

Place English language learners in the groups that correspond to their reading abilities in English.

Practice Stations
- Visit the Listen Up! Station
- Visit the Word Work Station

Independent Activities
- Read independently
- Concept Talk Video
- *Reader's and Writer's Notebook*

Differentiated Instruction

Strategic Intervention

Decodable Story Before children read *My Words,* review the consonant blends *cl, fl, pl,* and *sl* with the following Picture Cards: *cloud, flag, playground, slide*.

Advanced

Support Decoding Display the *Ll* Alphabet Card. Have children name the sound and then the letter. Repeat the routine with the *Cc, Ff, Pp,* and *Ss* Alphabet Cards. Then have children practice saying the sounds then the letters in *l* blends: *sl, fl, cl, pl*.

DAY 1

Read and Comprehend

10–15 mins.

Objectives

◎ Identify and describe sequence.

Skills Trace

◎ **Sequence**

Introduce U1W3D1; U2W5D1; U4W1D1; U4W3D1

Practice U1W3D2; U1W3D3; U1W3D4; U2W5D2; U2W5D3; U2W5D4; U4W1D2; U4W1D3; U4W1D4; U4W3D2; U4W3D3; U4W3D4

Reteach/Review U1W3D5; U1W5D4; U2W5D5; U2W2D4; U4W1D5; U2W6D4; U4W3D5; U5W2D4

Assess/Test Benchmark Assessment U4

KEY:

U=Unit W=Week D=Day

My Skills Buddy, pp. 54–55

Listening Comprehension

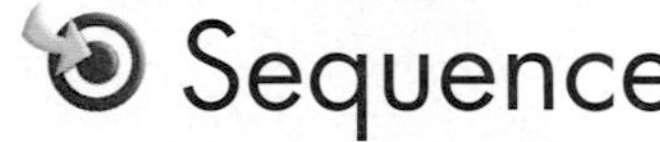

◎ Sequence

Introduce

In most stories, things happen in a certain order: first, next, last. The order in which things happen is called the **sequence.** Good readers pay attention to the sequence, or order, in which things happen because it helps them understand the story. What do good readers do?

Envision It!

Have children turn to pp. 54–55 in *My Skills Buddy* and look at the three pictures. These pictures show three events in order.

- What happens first? (The mother bird has three eggs in her nest.)
- What happens next? (She feeds the baby birds.)
- What happens last? (The baby birds fly away.)

Model

Today I will read aloud a story about a salmon that has an adventure. Read **"Swimming Sally"** and model how to identify sequence.

Think Aloud

When I read a story, I pay attention to the order in which things happen. I think about what happens first, next, and last. In "Swimming Sally," first, a salmon named Sally lives at the top of a stream. Next, she swims down the stream to the ocean. Last, Sally swims back up to her home at the top of the stream.

Guide practice After reading, ask children questions about the story's sequence.

- Where does Sally swim first? (She swims in the stream first.)
- Where does Sally swim next? (She swims in the river next, then the ocean.)
- Where does Sally swim last? (She swims in the stream last.)

More practice Display the Trade Book *My Lucky Day*. In *My Lucky Day*, we read about a piglet's adventure. What does the piglet do first, next, and last? Page through the story. Have children identify the sequence of events. First, the fox gives the piglet a bath. What does the fox do next? What does the fox do last?

Connect to everyday life When you get ready for school, you usually do things in a certain order. What do you do first, next, and last?

Academic Vocabulary

sequence the order of events in a selection

Teacher Tip

To familiarize children with the concept of sequence, use a simple graphic organizer with the word *first, next,* or *last* in each of three boxes vertically arranged. Use arrows to indicate the sequence.

English Language Learners
Oral Comprehension To prepare English learners for the Read Aloud, use the modified Read Aloud in the ELL Support lesson on p. DI•47.

Swimming Sally

Sally Salmon was born at the top of a stream. She swam in the clear, cold water and grew bigger every day. One day, Sally felt restless.

"Time to go!" she said. Sally swam down the stream. The stream got bigger and became a river. Sally kept swimming. The river flowed into the ocean.

"This is huge!" said Sally when she saw the ocean. "Too huge for me. I want to go home!"

Sally turned around. She splashed, leaped, and swam out of the ocean, up the river, and into her clear, cold stream.

"It's good to be home!" said Sally.

DAY 1 Language Arts 20–25 mins.

Objectives

- Identify parts of complete sentences.
- Speak in complete sentences.
- Use proper capitalization and punctuation to write complete sentences.
- Write or dictate a question about animals.

Conventions
Complete Sentences

Teach complete sentences A complete sentence has a naming part and an action part. Remember, a naming part is who or what the sentence is about, and the action part is what the naming part is or does. A complete sentence begins with an uppercase letter and ends with a punctuation mark.

Model Write the following sentence on the board: *The dog runs.* Is this a complete sentence? *The dog* is the naming part. *Runs* is the action part. Point to the uppercase *T.* This sentence begins with an uppercase *T.* Point to the period. This sentence ends with a period, which is a punctuation mark. This is a complete sentence.

Guide practice Write the complete sentences below on the board. Have children circle the naming part and underline the action part. Then have them identify the uppercase letter and the end punctuation in each sentence.

- Matt walks to the bus. (circle *Matt,* underline *walks to the bus*)
- The baby swings in the park. (circle *The baby,* underline *swings in the park*)
- I go home after school. (circle *I,* underline *go home after school*)
- The big boy jumps. (circle *The big boy,* underline *jumps*)

Have children copy one of the sentences on their Write-On Boards. Remind them to capitalize the sentence's first word and to end the sentence with a punctuation mark.

Team Talk Pair children and have them take turns talking about their favorite animals in complete sentences. Have them name the naming part and action part in each sentence they say.

Daily Fix-It Use the Daily Fix-It for more conventions practice.

Writing
Wonderful, Marvelous Me!
I Wonder About ...

Introduce Talk with children about the question, "Why?" Do you ever ask why something happens? Asking a *why* question is one way we can wonder about something. The question word *why* helps us get more information. If I ask you to put on your coat, you may wonder why. I could answer, "Because we are going outside, and it is cold." The word *why* helped you get more information about putting on your coat. What other *why* questions might you ask during the school day? Encourage children to share their thoughts.

Model Today we are going to ask *why* questions. I am going to close my eyes and think of a *why* question that will help me get more information. I know that beavers use sticks and mud to build dams in rivers and streams. I wonder why beavers build dams. Show a picture of a beaver dam and write *Why do beavers build dams?*

Guide practice Encourage children to help you come up with possible reasons why beavers build dams. Write their ideas on the board and draw pictures when appropriate. Then read from a reference source about why beavers build dams. (Beavers build dams to create a relatively safe body of water to swim and build their homes in. They often build their homes, called lodges, near the dams.)

Independent writing Now you are going to share something you wonder about animals. Close your eyes and ask a wonderful, marvelous *why* question about an animal. What do you wonder about? What *why* question can you ask about it? Have children write or dictate their ideas and then illustrate them.

Daily Handwriting

Write *1* and *one* on the board. Review correct formation of the numeral *1* and the lowercase letters *o, n,* and *e.*

Have children write *1* and *one* on their Write-On Boards. Remind them to use proper left-to-right and top-to-bottom progression and proper spacing between letters when writing *1* and *one.*

Write Guy
Jeff Anderson

The Sunny Side

I like to look for what's *right* in children's writing rather than focusing on things I can edit or fix. Most children don't write flawlessly—who does? However, they will learn what they are doing well if we point it out.

Academic Vocabulary

complete sentence a sentence that has a naming part and an action part, begins with an uppercase letter, and has end punctuation

Daily Fix-It

i sat in the car
I sat in the car.

This week's practice sentences appear on Teacher Resources DVD-ROM.

Writing Routine

Day 1 Wonderful, Marvelous Me!
Day 2 Respond to Literature
Day 3 Genre Writing
Day 4 Extend the Concept
Day 5 This Week We...

English Language Learners
Complete Sentences Remind children that sentences begin with uppercase letters and end with periods or other ending punctuation marks. The Spanish word for *uppercase letter* is *mayúscula.* The Spanish word for period is *punto.*

Objectives

- Practice listening for sequence.
- Face the speaker when listening.
- Speak loudly and clearly.
- Take turns when speaking.

Listening and Speaking
Listen for Sequence

Teach Today we are going to listen for sequence, or the order of events. When you listen for sequence, you pay attention to what happens first, next, and last.

Model Listen carefully as I tell you a story. Remind children how to be good listeners by facing the speaker and raising their hands if they have questions. First, Molly wants her dad to teach her how to ride her new bike. Then she falls off her bike and skins her knee. Last, she gets back on her bike and rides it all the way down the driveway. Who can tell me what happens first? next? last? Remind children to speak loudly and clearly.

Guide practice Have children take turns telling simple three-step stories. Then have other children identify the sequence of events in the stories. Refer children to the Rules for Listening and Speaking on pp. 1–2 of *Reader's and Writer's Notebook.* Remind them to speak loudly and clearly when telling their story and to speak one at a time when identifying the sequence of events.

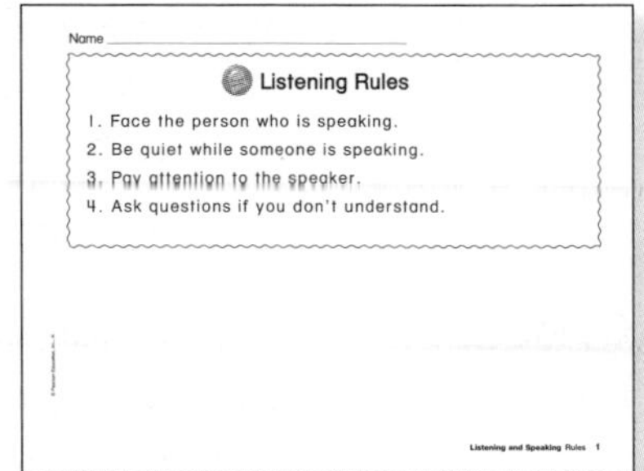
Name
Listening Rules
1. Face the person who is speaking.
2. Be quiet while someone is speaking.
3. Pay attention to the speaker.
4. Ask questions if you don't understand.

Reader's and Writer's Notebook, p. 1

Wrap Up Your Day

✔ **Concept Talk** This week we will talk about adventures an animal can have. Today we read about a salmon that had an adventure. What adventures have you had?

✔ **Conventions** Today we talked about making complete sentences. Who can tell me what parts we need to make a complete sentence?

✔ **Homework Idea** Send home the week's Family Times Newsletter, Let's Practice It! TR DVD•41.

Social Studies

How Maps Help

Materials: chart paper, markers or crayons

Draw a Classroom Map Tell children that people use a map to help them find their way around a place they have never been before. Have children look around the classroom. Ask them what kind of map they could make of the room that would help a stranger get around.

- How would we draw the room?
- Where would we put the windows and the door?
- What would we draw in the corners and in the center of the room?

As children answer the questions, have them suggest symbols (little pictures) to represent parts of the room. Fill in the chart paper to make a map of the room. Discuss the chart with children once it is completed.

Conventions

Complete Sentences

Materials: sentence strips, paper

Put Parts Together On strips of paper, write short sentences about things children can do. Cut the sentences into naming parts and action parts. Show children the naming part of one sentence strip.

- Is this a complete sentence?
- What does it need to be complete?

Once children have identified and discussed each part, lay out all the parts and have children combine them.

Comprehension

Steps in Sequence

The Animal Dance Today I am going to teach you an animal dance. The dance has four steps that you must follow in order, so listen and watch carefully as I tell and show you what to do. Model each step as you describe it. First, open and close your hands like a duck's bill. Second, fold your arms under and flap them like a chicken's wings. Third, bend your knees and walk like a monkey. Fourth, clap your hands four times and start all over again. Who remembers the steps I just told you? Let's do the steps in order. Review all of the steps with children.

Objectives

- Discuss the concept to develop oral language.
- Build oral vocabulary.

Today at a Glance

Oral Vocabulary
woodland, nest

Phonemic Awareness
◉ Consonant Blends with *r, t,* and *p*

Phonics
◉ Consonant Blends with *r, t,* and *p*

Handwriting
Write Numerals and Number Words

Comprehension
◉ Sequence

Conventions
Complete Sentences

Writing
Respond to Literature

Vocabulary
Shape Words

TRUCKTOWN on Reading Street

Start your engines! Display p. 7 of *Truckery Rhymes.* Point to "Three Loud Trucks." Who remembers how many trucks are in this rhyme? Yes, there are three trucks. Let's read the rhyme together. Have a child point to the rhyming words as the class reads the rhyme again. Give additional children the opportunity to point to the rhyming words as you repeat the rhyme.

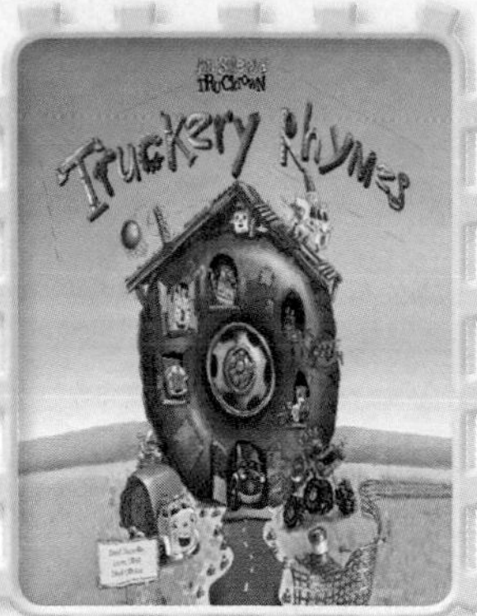

Truckery Rhymes

Concept Talk

Question of the Week

What adventures can animals have?

Build concepts Write and read the question of the week as you track the print. Have children answer the question in complete sentences. To reinforce the concept and focus children's attention, display Talk with Me/Sing with Me Chart 21B. Tell children that they are going to sing about woodland homes.

Sing with me Audio

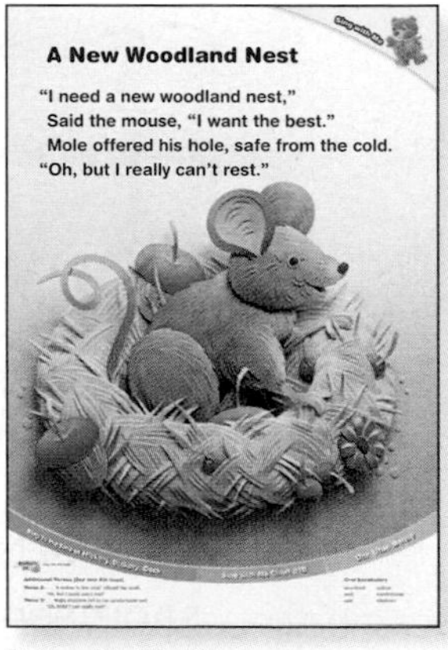

Talk with Me/Sing with Me Chart 21B

Listen for Amazing Words The Amazing Words *woodland* and *nest* are in the song "A New Woodland Nest." Read the title and tell children to describe the picture. Sing the song several times to the tune of "Hickory, Dickory, Dock" until children become familiar with the words and can sing along. Have children clap when they hear *woodland* and *nest.*

ELL Reinforce Vocabulary Use the Day 2 instruction on ELL Poster 21 to reinforce the meanings of high-frequency words.

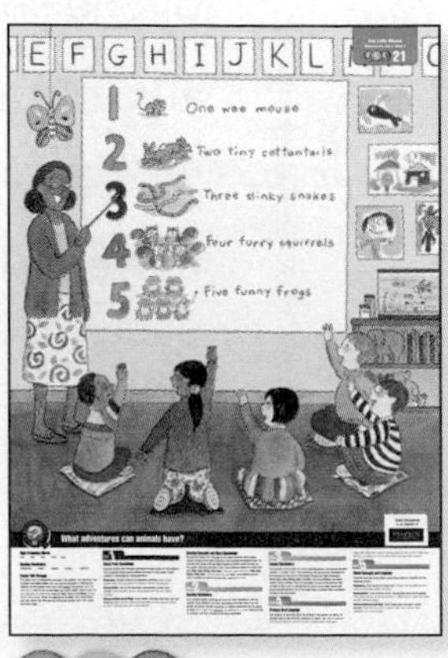

ELL Poster 21

Oral Vocabulary
Amazing Words

Amazing Words

woodland, nest
vale, hollow
comfortable, shadows

Teach Amazing Words

Amazing Words Oral Vocabulary Routine

1. **Introduce the Word** The selection *One Little Mouse* that we will read this week takes place in a woodland. *Woodland* is another name for a forest, or a place with many trees. What's our new Amazing Word for a forest? Say it with me: *woodland.*

2. **Demonstrate** Provide examples to show meaning. *Deer and foxes live in a woodland.*

   Repeat steps 1 and 2.

   Introduce the Word In the beginning of the selection *One Little Mouse,* the mouse lives in a small nest. A *nest* is a place some animals build to live in. What's our new Amazing Word for an animal's home? Say it with me: *nest.*

   Demonstrate A mother bird builds a *nest.*

3. **Apply** Tell children to use *woodland* and *nest* in complete sentences. Have them use the words to tell about an animal they have seen living outside.

Routines Flip Chart

Use Amazing Words To reinforce the concept and the Amazing Words, have children supply the appropriate missing Amazing Word for each sentence.

Many animals live in a ________. (woodland)
A bird made a ________ in the tree. (nest)

Differentiated Instruction

Strategic Intervention

Sentence Production If children have difficulty completing the sentences, model saying a complete sentence and have them repeat it.

English Language Learners

Access Content Have children tell what words in their home languages are used for *woodland* and *nest.*

Objectives

- ◎ Learn consonant blends with *r, t,* and *p.*
- Practice consonant blends with *l.*

Phonemic Awareness
◎ Consonant Blends

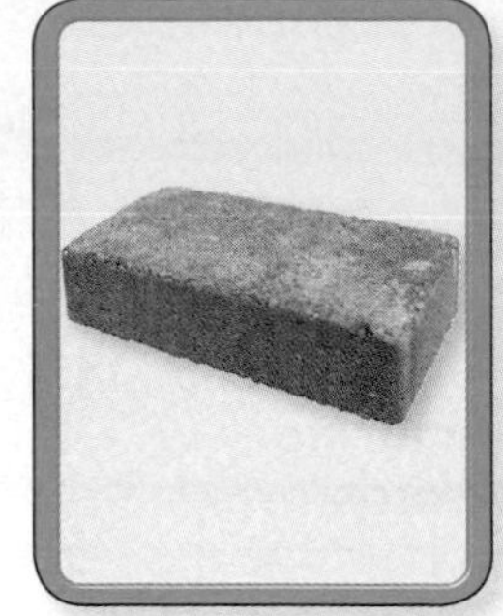
Picture Card

Isolate consonant blends Today we will learn some more consonant blends. Display the *brick, crab, dress, frog, grapes, spider, stamp,* and *train* Picture Cards. Listen to the beginning of the word *brick:* /b/ /r/, /br/ /br/, *brick.* Two sounds blend together at the beginning. Say the sounds with me: /b/ /r/, /br/ /br/, *brick.* Repeat the routine with the other Picture Cards.

Model Display the *brick, crab, dress,* and *frog* Picture Cards. I will say a word. Tell me whether the word begins like *brick, crab, dress,* or *frog.* I will do the first one: *crop.* I hear /k/ /r/, /kr/ at the beginning of *crop.* I hear /k/ /r/, /kr/ at the beginning of *crab. Crop* and *crab* begin the same. Continue the routine with the words *drag, crib, brown, frown, brag, drop,* and *fry.*

Picture Card

Repeat the routine with the *grapes, spider, stamp,* and *train* Picture Cards. Say the words *trap, grow, step, spin, grandma, trip, stem,* and *spell.*

Guide practice Have children look at the picture on *My Skills Buddy* pp. 52–53. Remember that we saw an ice skater slipping in the picture. *Slipping* starts with a consonant blend. Let's look for other things that begin with consonant blends. Look for things that begin like *brick, crab, dress, frog, grapes, spider, stamp,* and *train.* Discuss with children those bulleted items on p. 52 not discussed on Day 1.

My Skills Buddy, pp. 52–53

Corrective feedback **If...** children have difficulty with blends,
then... have them practice saying the sounds one at a time and then sliding the sounds together to form the blend.

On their own Display Phonics Songs and Rhymes Chart 21, "Sliding Down the Slippery Slope." Remind children of the tune "Jack and Jill Went Up the Hill." Sing the song several times. When you hear a word that begins with a consonant blend, clap your hands. Identify *Sliding, slippery, slope, floating, clear, special, please, climbing, platform, stepping,* and *slide.*

Review **Consonant Blends with *l*** What sounds do you hear at the beginning of *play?* /p/ /l/, /pl/ /pl/, *play. Play* begins with the blend /pl/. Now listen as I say two words: *glow, plant.* Which word starts like *play?* Yes, *plant* starts like *play.* Repeat the routine for *flower* and say the words *flip* and *block.*

Sliding Down the Slippery Slope

Sliding down the slippery slope,
And floating through clear water.
The water slide's our special ride,
Please go first up the ladder.

Climbing up the platform high,
And stepping up in order.
Just ask me why I like to slide,
And I'll say it's the water!

Phonics Songs and Rhymes Chart 21

Differentiated Instruction

 Strategic Intervention

Support Phonemic Awareness
If children struggle to identify initial consonant blends, say the word slowly and deliberately. Help them hear each sound that makes up the consonant blend before blending the sounds together.

English Language Learners
Support Blends Since some languages do not have /r/ and other languages pronounce /r/ differently, help children practice the pronunciation of English words, saying /r/ first, then the blend, and finally the word.

Objectives

- ◎ Associate the sounds with consonant blends.
- Blend words with consonant blends with *l, r,* and *s.*

Check Sound-Spelling SUCCESS PREDICTOR

Phonics—Teach/Model

◎ Consonant Blends

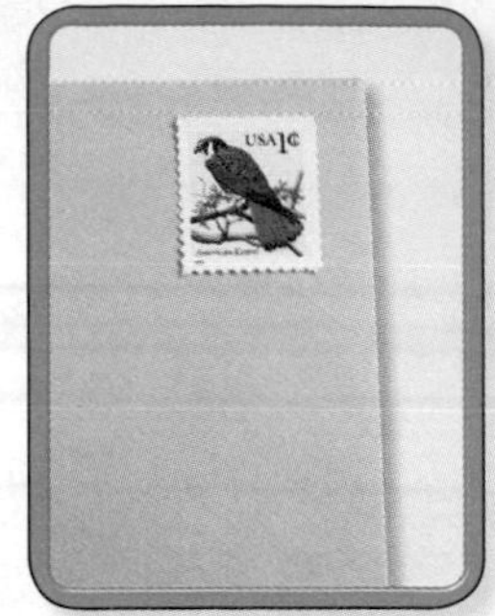
Picture Card

Teach consonant blends Display the *stamp* Picture Card. This is a stamp. What sounds does *stamp* begin with? *Stamp* begins with /s/ /t/, /st/. Write *stamp* on the board and point to the letters *st.* The letters for /st/ are *s* and *t.* Repeat the routine by writing and reviewing initial consonant blends in the words *cry, drip, tree, broom, frozen, grass,* and *spill.*

Picture Card

Model Display the *crayon* Picture Card. This is a crayon. *Crayon* begins with /k/ /r/, /kr/. Say it with me: /kr/ /kr/ /kr/, *crayon.* Write *crayon* on the board. *Crayon* begins with the blended sound /kr/. Point to the letters *c* and *r* in the word *crayon.* The letter for /k/ is *c* and the letter for /r/ is *r.* Put them together to make /kr/, *cr.* Repeat the routine with the following Picture Cards: *drum, truck, brown, frog, green, starfish, spoon.*

Guide practice

Envision It!

Have children open *My Skills Buddy* to p. 56. Demonstrate using the blending arrows on *My Skills Buddy,* p. 56, as you model blending the first word. Put your finger on the red arrow below the *c* and *r.* Say the sounds that *c* and *r* stand for: /k/ /r/, /kr/. Continue with the letters *i* and *b.* Now I run my finger along the blue arrow as I blend the letters quickly to read *crib.* Repeat with the word *drop.* Have children work with a partner to blend the rest of the words on the page.

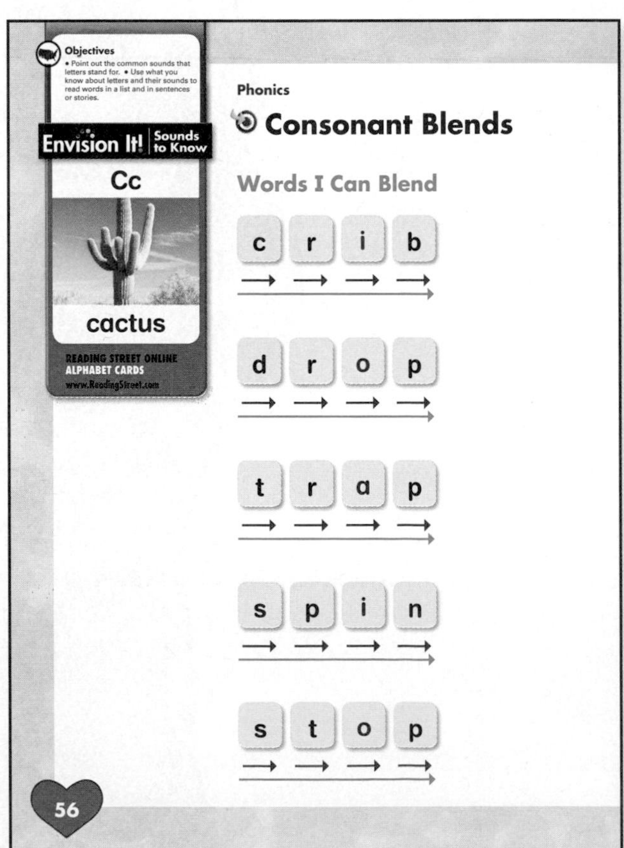

My Skills Buddy, p. 56

Blend Use the following routine to blend initial consonant blend words.

ROUTINE **Sound-by-Sound Blending**

1. **Connect** Write the letters *cr* on the board. What are the sounds for these letters? The sounds are /kr/. Say it with me: /kr/ /kr/ /kr/. When you see these letters in a word, what sounds will you say?
2. **Model** Write the word *crib* on the board.
   - Point to *cr.* What are the sounds for these letters? Say it with me: /kr/ /kr/ /kr/. Repeat the routine for *i* and *b.*
   - Let's blend the sounds together. Listen as I blend the sounds: /kr/ /i/ /b/. Say it with me: /kr/ /i/ /b/, *crib*. Now say it without me.
   - Listen as I use *crib* in a sentence: *The baby sleeps in a crib.* Say it with me. Have children use *crib* in a sentence.
3. **Guide Practice** Continue the routine in step 2 with these words:

crab drop trap grab stop spot plot slip

Have children successfully read all of the words before reading Decodable Reader 21 on pp. 58–65 of *My Skills Buddy.*

Corrective Feedback If children have difficulty blending words, model blending the sounds and have children say it with you.

Routines Flip Chart

MONITOR PROGRESS Check Sound-Spelling Consonant Blends

Give children a sheet of paper folded into fourths. Have them write one of the blends *sl, dr, cr,* and *fl* in each section. Display Picture Cards *crab, crayon, dress, drum, flag, flashlight, sled,* and *slide* in random order. Have children point to the correct blend on their papers when you show each card.

If... children cannot connect the sounds and letters in blends,
then... have them practice blending the words while seeing them in writing or print.

Continue to monitor children's progress using other instructional opportunities during the week so that children can be successful with the Day 5 Assessment.

Day 1	Day 2	Day 3	Day 4	Day 5
Check Phonemic Awareness	Check Sound-Spelling/ Retelling	Check Word Reading	Check Phonemic Awareness	Check Oral Vocabulary

Success Predictor

Differentiated Instruction

Advanced

Support Phonics Have children look around the classroom for other words that begin with consonant blends. When children name an object with an initial blend, have them name the letters that make the blend.

ELL

English Language Learners

Support Blends Initial *s-* blends do not appear in Cantonese, Hmong, Khmer, Korean, Spanish, or Vietnamese. Help children practice blending the sounds in words with initial *s-* blends.

DAY 2 Get Ready to Read

Objectives

- Write numerals and number words.
- Read high-frequency words.

Handwriting
Write Numerals and Number Words

Review Remind children that numbers can be written as numerals or as words. Write the numerals 1, 2, 3, 4, and 5 on the board. Write the words *one, two, three, four,* and *five* next to each numeral. We have learned how to write the numerals 1, 2, 3, 4, and 5 and the number words *one, two, three, four,* and *five.* Remind children that when they write, they need to move from left to right and make their letters clear and easy to read. We need to write so that our writing can be read by others.

Guide practice Have children use their Write-On Boards to write each number word: *one, two, three, four,* and *five.* Circulate around the room, assisting children as necessary. Then have children write a line of each numeral 1, 2, 3, 4, and 5.

High-Frequency Words

Model reading

Have children turn to p. 57 of *My Skills Buddy.* Read the high-frequency words *one, two, three, four,* and *five* together. Then have children point to each word and read it themselves. Read the sentences on the *My Skills Buddy* page together to read the new high-frequency words in context.

Team Talk Pair children and have them take turns reading each of the sentences aloud.

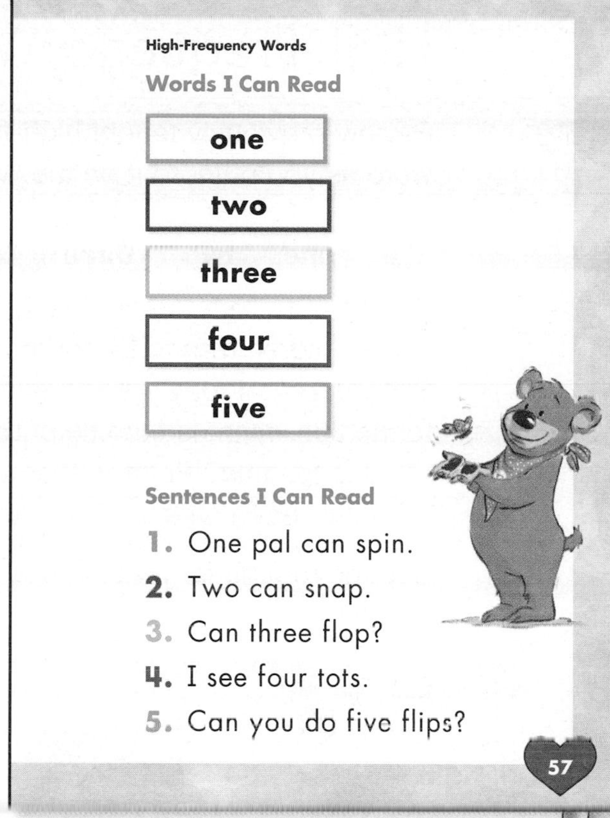

High-Frequency Words

Words I Can Read

one

two

three

four

five

Sentences I Can Read

1. One pal can spin.
2. Two can snap.
3. Can three flop?
4. I see four tots.
5. Can you do five flips?

57

My Skills Buddy, p. 57

On their own

Use *Reader's and Writer's Notebook,* p. 269, for additional practice with this week's high-frequency words.

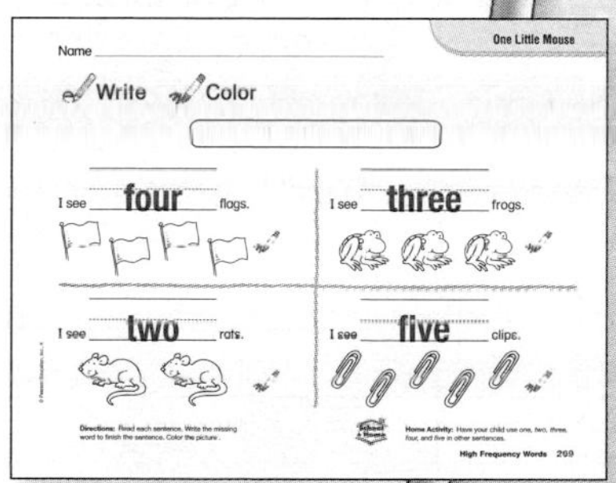

Reader's and Writer's Notebook, p. 269

Differentiated Instruction

SI Strategic Intervention

Vocabulary Write the numeral 1 and the number word *one* on a large sheet of paper. Draw one object. Repeat for 2–5. Post and review with children to help them see the numbers represented visually.

English Language Learners

Cognates Number words are similar to English and some other languages. Some cognates for number words are *tres* ("three" in Spanish) and *sis* ("six" in Haitian Creole).

DAY 2 Get Ready to Read

Objectives

- Read decodable text.
- Read high-frequency words.

Decodable Reader 21

Consonant Blends and High-Frequency Words

Review

Review previously taught high-frequency words. Have children read each word as you point to it on the Word Wall.

a **one** **two** **three** **four** **five**

Have children turn to Decodable Reader 21, *One to Five,* on p. 58 of *My Skills Buddy.* Today we will read a story about some noisy animals. Point to the title. What is the title of the story? *One to Five* is the title of the story. What is the title? Point to the name of the author. The author's name is Heather Leavy. *One to Five* was written by Heather Leavy.

Use the routine for reading decodable books to read Decodable Reader 21.

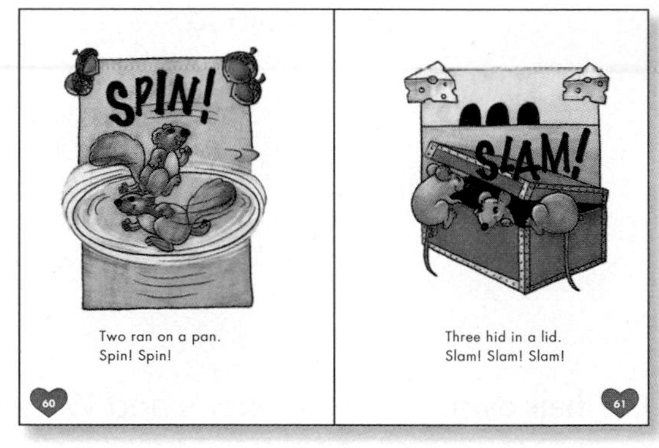

My Skills Buddy, pp. 58–65

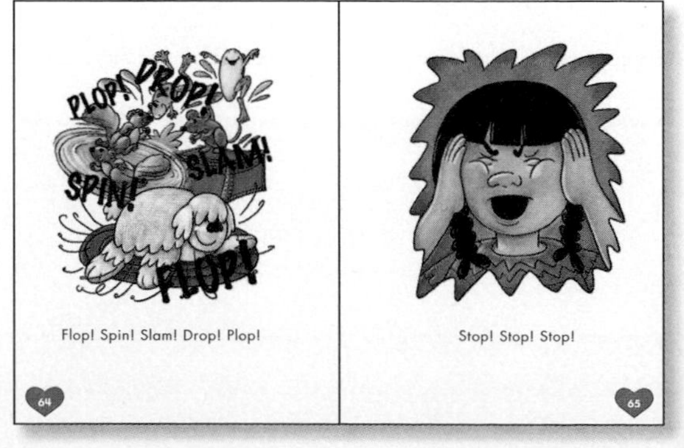

Make Connections

After children read *One to Five*, have them make connections between the ideas in the story and other texts they have read. What other stories have they read about animals? How do the actions of the animals in the other stories compare to the actions of the animals in *One to Five?* Do any of the other animal stories they've read teach numbers? How can animal stories like this one help them remember numbers?

ROUTINE Reading Decodable Books

1. **Read Silently** Have children whisper read the book page by page as you listen in.
2. **Model Fluent Reading** Have children finger point as you read a page. Then have children reread the book without you.
3. **Read Chorally** Have children finger point as they chorally read the page. Continue reading page by page, repeating steps 1 and 2.
4. **Read Individually** Have children take turns reading aloud a page.
5. **Reread and Monitor Progress** As you listen to individual children reread, monitor progress and provide support.
6. **Reread with a Partner** Have children reread the book page by page with a partner.

Routines Flip Chart

Differentiated Instruction

A Advanced

Build Background Have children explain what authors and illustrators do. Have them tell which they would rather do, write or illustrate a story.

Small Group Time

DAY 2 Break into small groups after reading the Decodable Reader and before the comprehension lesson.

Teacher-Led

SI Strategic Intervention	OL On-Level	A Advanced
Teacher-Led Page DI•36 • Phonemic Awareness and Phonics • **Reread** Decodable Reader 21	**Teacher-Led** Page DI•40 • Phonemic Awareness and Phonics • **Reread** Decodable Reader 21	**Teacher-Led** Page DI•43 • Phonics and Spelling • **Reread** Decodable Reader 21 for Fluency

Place English language learners in the groups that correspond to their reading abilities in English.

Practice Stations
- Visit the Word Work Station
- Visit the Words to Know Station

Independent Activities
- Read independently
- Background Building Audio
- *Reader's and Writer's Notebook*

English Language Learners

Access Content Have English learners share how they would say the high-frequency words *one, two, three, four,* and *five* in their home languages.

Objectives

- Practice sequence.
- Preview and predict.
- Retell a selection.

Check Retelling
SUCCESS PREDICTOR

Listening Comprehension
Sequence

Review Have children turn to p. 54 of *My Skills Buddy.* Remind them that events happen in a certain order: first, next, last. Explain that this is called the sequence. Good readers pay attention to the sequence, or order, in which things happen because it helps them understand what they are reading.

Envision It!

My Skills Buddy, pp. 54–55

First Read—Big Book
One Little Mouse

Concepts of print Display the cover of *One Little Mouse.* The printed words tell us the title. They also tell us who wrote the words and drew the pictures.

Preview and predict

Point to the title on the cover of *One Little Mouse.* The title of this book is *One Little Mouse.* On the cover, I see a little mouse sitting on a mushroom. What do you think the book will be about? Let's read to find out.

Use illustrations Take children on a picture walk through the book. As we walk through the book, tell me what you see. Have children describe the illustrations.

Introduce genre Informational texts teach readers about things in the real world. In this book, we will learn about animal homes and ways that different animals sleep.

Set purpose Remind children of the question of the week: *What adventures can animals have?* Have children listen to learn about adventures the little mouse has.

Model Read *One Little Mouse* with expression for enjoyment.

Retell

Check retelling

Envision It!

Have children turn to p. 66 of *My Skills Buddy.* Walk through the retelling boxes as children retell *One Little Mouse.* Let's retell What happens in the first box—the beginning of the story. The little mouse sits in his nest and decides it's too small. Let's retell what happens in the next box. Continue with the rest of the boxes. After children retell the story as a group, have them draw a picture to retell their favorite part of the story. Have them write or dictate a word or sentence to go with their picture.

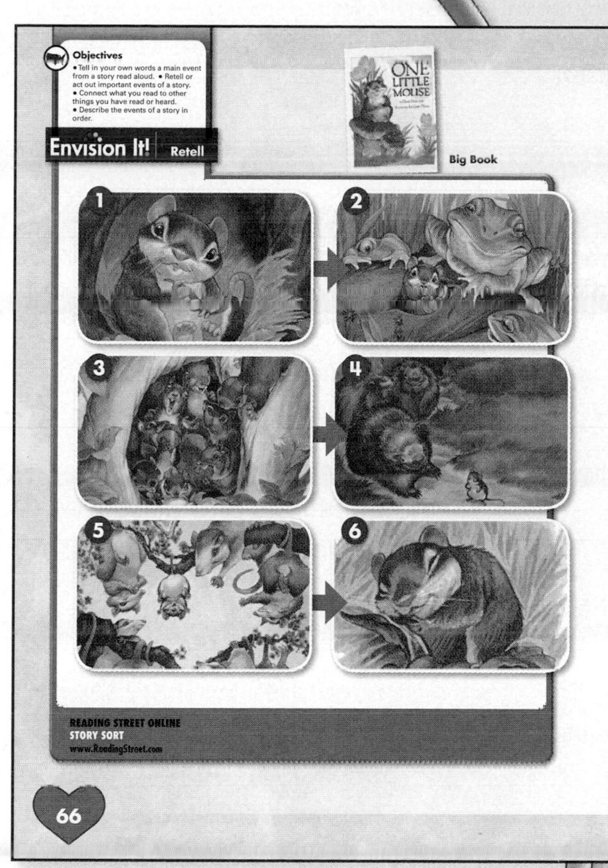

My Skills Buddy, p. 66

Top-Score Response A top-score response describes the main topic and important ideas using information from the text.

Don't Wait Until Friday **MONITOR PROGRESS** **Check Retelling**

If... children have difficulty retelling the selection,

then... use the Retelling Cards and work with children to help them move toward fluent retelling.

Day 1	**Day 2**	**Day 3**	**Day 4**	**Day 5**
Check Phonemic Awareness	Check Sound-Spelling/ Retelling	Check Word Reading	Check Phonemic Awareness	Check Oral Vocabulary

Success Predictor

Differentiated Instruction

SI Strategic Intervention

Support Retelling If children struggle to retell the selection, take a picture walk through the book. Have them use the illustrations to explain what is happening during each part of the selection.

Retelling Plan

- ☑ **Week 1** Assess Advanced students.
- ☑ **Week 2** Assess On-Level students.
- ☑ **This week assess Strategic Intervention students.**
- ☐ **Week 4** Assess Advanced students.
- ☐ **Week 5** Assess On-Level students.
- ☐ **Week 6** Assess Strategic Intervention students.

ELL

English Language Learners

Access Content Emphasize the words *first, next,* and *last* as you talk about the sequence of events in the selection.

Objectives

- ◎ Practice sequence.
- Confirm predictions.
- Practice complete sentences.

Think, Talk, and Write

Discuss concept Imagine what it would feel like to have adventures like the little mouse.

- How would it feel to hang upside down like the opossums? Why?
- What would you do if the snakes offered you a place to sleep? Why?
- How is this book similar to an earlier book we read, *A Bed for the Winter?*

Confirm predictions Have children recall their predictions before you read *One Little Mouse.*

- What did you think the selection would be about?
- Was your prediction correct?

Have children turn to p. 67 of *My Skills Buddy.* Read the questions and directives and have children respond.

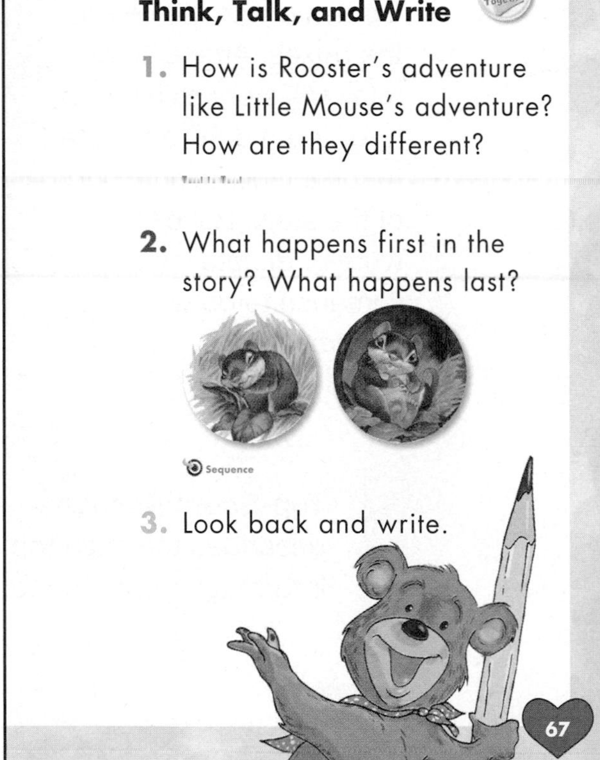

My Skills Buddy, p. 67

Text to text 1. How is Rooster's adventure like little Mouse's adventure? How are they different? Are there numbers in both stories? Do the animals all travel with the little mouse like they travel with the rooster?

◎ Sequence 2. What happens first in the story? (Mouse decides his nest is too small.) What happens last? (Mouse decides he likes his house best and goes home.)

Look back and write 3. Let's look back at our story and write about it. We remember that Mouse does not want to live in the tree with the chickadees. Listen for why Mouse doesn't want to live with in the tree. Read pp. 20–21 of *One Little Mouse.* Now let's write our ideas. Discuss with children why it would be hard to live in a tree and record children's responses on chart paper. (Possible responses: A branch is not a good pillow. You might fall out of the tree. The tree would be hard. You would not be safe from the weather.)

Conventions
Complete Sentences

Review Remind children of what they learned about complete sentences. A complete sentence has a naming part and an action part. A complete sentence begins with an uppercase letter and ends with an ending punctuation mark.

Guide practice Read the following items aloud to children. Have them identify the complete sentences. Then have them tell why the second item is not a sentence. Have children tell how to fix the second item. Tell them to rewrite it as a complete sentence.

- Mouse ran in the woods.
- Mouse the house
- Mouse saw the moles.

On their own Use the *Reader's and Writer's Notebook,* p. 270, for more practice with complete sentences.

Daily Fix-It Use the Daily Fix-It exercise for more conventions practice.

Reader's and Writer's Notebook, p. 270

Differentiated Instruction

 Strategic Intervention

Support Discussion Supply sentence starters to aid children's responses about how they would feel to have adventures like the mouse's.

 Advanced

Support Discussion Allow children to write their own responses to the question about sleeping in a tree.

Daily Fix-It

will he skip and spin
Will he skip and spin?

This week's practice sentences appear on Teacher Resources DVD-ROM.

ELL

English Language Learners
Talk About It Suggest that children pretend to be Mouse as they answer the questions.

Objectives

- Write or dictate complete sentences about animals.
- Identify and use words for shapes.

Writing
Respond to Literature

Discuss Display *One Little Mouse.* Ask children to identify how many of each animal offered Mouse their homes. List the animals on the board in order (for example, *two moles, three frogs, four quail*).

Model Many animals offered Mouse their houses. I'll write a complete sentence about the moles.

Two moles offered Mouse their house.

Guide practice Work with children to write more sentences about the other animals in the selection. Have them check each sentence to make sure it is complete.

Three frogs said Mouse could sleep on their log.

On their own Have children write or dictate and illustrate their own sentences about the animals in the selection. Remind them to write the first word with an uppercase letter and end the sentence with an ending punctuation mark. You can make a booklet out of the pages to retell the selection in sequential order.

Daily Handwriting

Write 2 and *two* on the board. Review correct formation of the numeral 2 and the lowercase letters *t, w,* and *o.*

Have children write 2 and *two* on their Write-On Boards. Remind them to use proper left-to-right and top-to-bottom progression and proper spacing between letters when writing 2 and *two.*

Vocabulary
Words for Shapes

Model Have children turn to p. 68 of *My Skills Buddy.* We are going to learn words for shapes. Look at the shapes on this page. Use the first four Vocabulary bullets on p. 68 to guide the discussion. Trace your finger around the red heart. This shape is a *heart.* Repeat for the star, oval, and diamond.

Guide practice Write the words *heart, star, oval,* and *diamond* on separate cards. Point to each word as you read it.

heart	**star**
oval	**diamond**

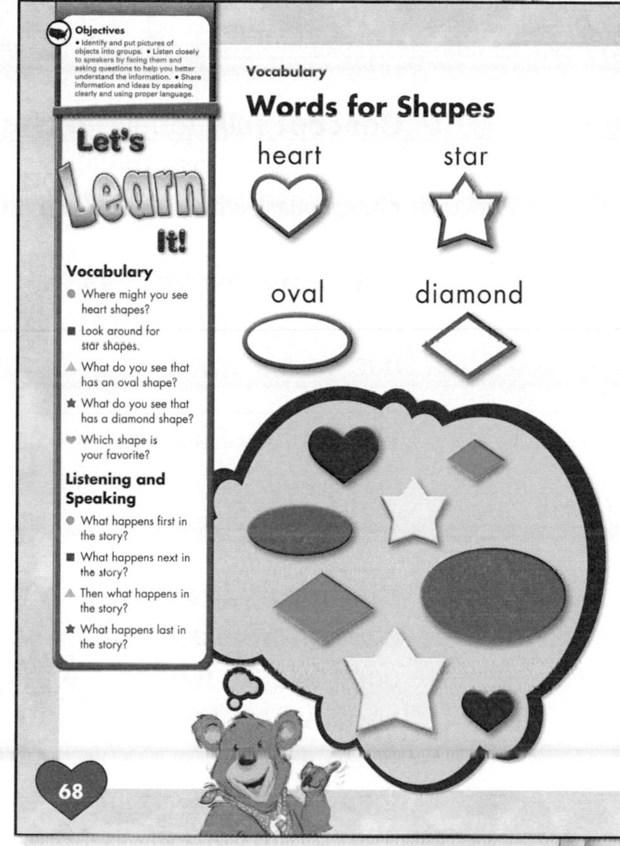

My Skills Buddy, p. 68

Display shape blocks or drawings of each shape. Have children work together to place each card next to the corresponding shape. Review the choices children made and discuss whether the cards were placed correctly.

We can find shapes all around us. I sometimes sign cards to my family with a heart. Draw a heart and write your name on the board, as though you are signing a card. I have a clock shaped like an oval. Where have you seen *heart, star, oval,* and *diamond* shapes?

On their own Distribute drawing paper. Have children fold their paper in half lengthwise. Let's draw pictures with hearts, stars, ovals, and diamonds. Have children use each half on the front and back of the paper to draw a picture for each shape. Help children label their drawings. Then have children share their drawings and explain their shape labels.

Differentiated Instruction

A Advanced

Visual Support Have children look around the classroom or in books for hearts, stars, ovals, and diamonds. Have them draw pictures of the shapes they find in real settings.

ELL

English Language Learners

Access Content Have children say the shape words in their home languages.

Objectives

- Review skills learned and practiced today.

Wrap Up Your Day

✔ **Concept Talk** Today we read about a little mouse looking for a new house. Who does the little mouse ask? What does the little mouse learn about his own house?

✔ **Phonemic Awareness** I am going to say some words. When you hear a word that starts with a consonant blend, clap your hands: *crab, drum, bat, trap, stop, see, spin, nose, bread, fruit, road, grip.*

✔ **Vocabulary Skill** Today we talked about words that name shapes: *heart, star, oval,* and *diamond.* Where might you see an oval?

✔ **Homework Idea** Have children write a complete sentence about where they sleep. Remind them to begin with an uppercase letter and end with a punctuation mark.

Preview DAY 3

Tomorrow we will read about a cat named Flap. What do you think Flap will do in the story?

Science
Compare and Contrast Animals

Materials: Big Books *Animal Babies in Grasslands* and *One Little Mouse*

Make a Comparison Chart Make a T-chart on the board or use Graphic Organizer 4. Above the left column, write *Woodland Animals.* Above the right column, write *Grassland Animals.*

Discuss the two Big Books with children and review the illustrations and photos. Let's look at the pictures in these two books. Discuss the sizes and shapes of the animals. As you talk, fill in the chart with characteristics of the animals in each place. Have children note the sizes and shapes of the animals, as well as other characteristics, such as wings or fur, two or four feet, and so on. Have them tell how the animals in the grassland and woodland are alike and different.

Woodland Animals	Grassland Animals
small	four feet
furry	live in holes
wings	tails
two feet	claws
four feet	water
nests	
tails	
live in holes	
live in trees	

Comprehension
Sequence

Neighborhood Adventure With children, pretend to take an adventure trip around the neighborhood. Have them take turns telling what they "see", repeating what the previous children said and adding something more, sequentially and numerically.

The first child might say, "I'm going on a neighborhood adventure, and I see one school." The second child might say, "I'm going on a neighborhood adventure, and I see one school and two buses," and so on until five children have added to the list. Then start over.

Math
Macaroni Math

Materials: construction paper, glue, elbow macaroni, pencils

Write and Count Have children write the words *one, two, three, four,* and *five* across the bottom of their papers, leaving space between the words. Then have children write the numerals 1–5 above the words. Instruct children to glue the correct number of macaroni noodles above each numeral.

Objectives

- Share information and ideas about the concept.
- Build oral vocabulary.

Today at a Glance

Oral Vocabulary
vale, hollow

Phonemic Awareness
◉ Initial and Final Consonant Blends

Phonics
◉ Initial and Final Consonant Blends

Comprehension
◉ Sequence

Conventions
Action Parts

Writing
Description

Listening and Speaking
Listen for Sequence

TRUCKTOWN on Reading Street

Start your engines! Display p. 7 of *Truckery Rhymes*. Read "Three Loud Trucks" to children.

Do you know the original "Three Blind Mice"? Recite it first, and then have children repeat it with you.

How are trucks different from mice?

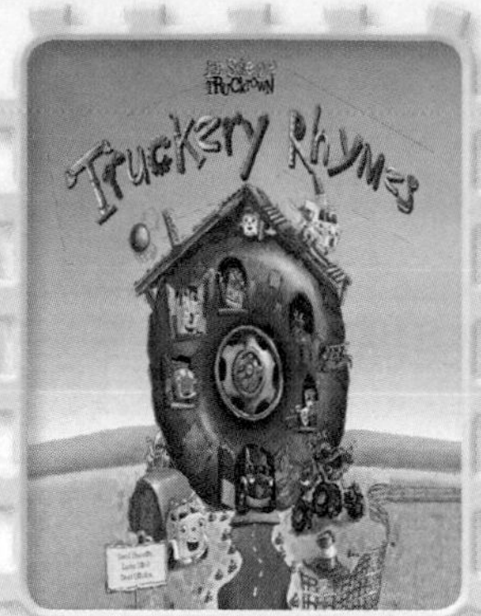

Truckery Rhymes

Concept Talk

Question of the Week

What adventures can animals have?

Write and read the question of the week on the board as you track the print. Have children take turns answering the question in complete sentences. Write their responses on the board.

Listen for Amazing Words

Let's Sing Display Sing with Me Chart 21B. Remind children that yesterday they sang "A New Woodland Nest" and learned the Amazing Words *woodland* and *nest*. Today we are going to listen for the Amazing Words *vale* and *hollow*. Sing the song several times to the tune of "Hickory, Dickory, Dock." Have children clap when they hear the Amazing Words *vale* and *hollow*.

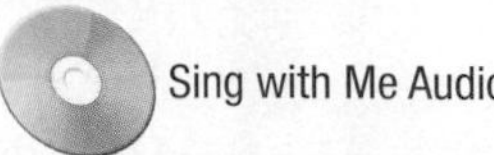
Sing with Me Audio

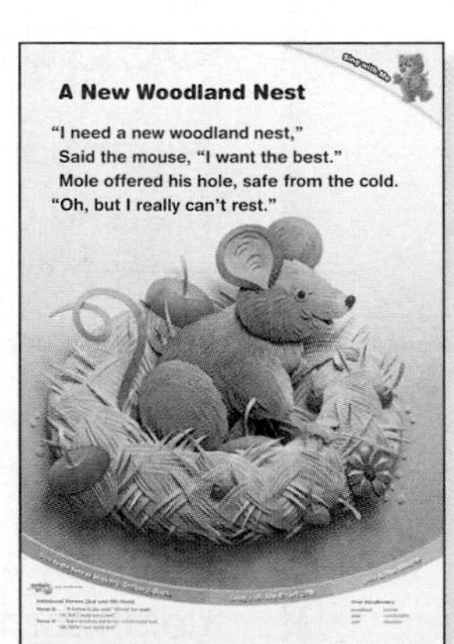

Talk with Me/Sing with Me Chart 21B

Oral Vocabulary
Amazing Words

Amazing Words Oral Vocabulary Routine

Teach Amazing Words

1. **Introduce the Word** In the selection *One Little Mouse,* some of the animals live in the vale. A valley or *vale* is a place where the ground is lower than the hills around it. What's our new Amazing Word for a valley? Say it with me: *vale*.
2. **Demonstrate** Provide examples to show meaning. *It is quiet between the hills in the vale.*

Repeat steps 1 and 2.

Introduce the Word A *hollow* is a word for an empty spot within something such as a tree. Some animals live in a *hollow*. What's our new Amazing Word for an empty place in a tree? Say it with me: *hollow*.

Demonstrate *A hollow makes a nice home for some animals.*

3. **Apply** Tell children to use *vale* and *hollow* in complete sentences. Have them illustrate the words.

Routines Flip Chart

Use Amazing Words

To reinforce the concept and the Amazing Words, have children supply the appropriate Amazing Word for each sentence.

Squirrels sometimes live in a ________ in a tree. (hollow)

The low ground between hills is called a ________. (vale)

ELL Expand Vocabulary
Use the Day 3 instruction on ELL Poster 21 to help children expand vocabulary.

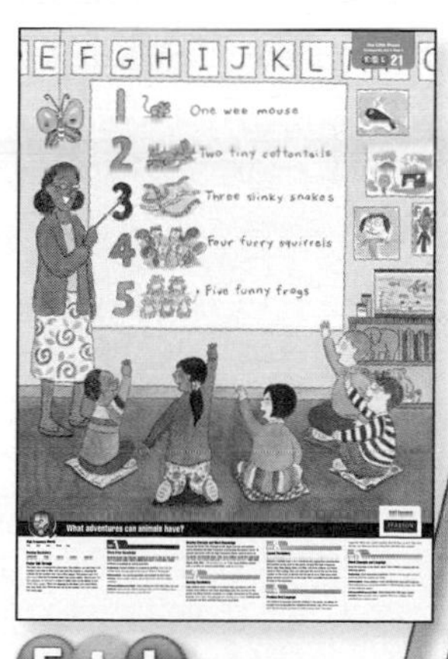

ELL Poster 21

Amazing Words

woodland	nest
vale	hollow
comfortable	shadows

Differentiated Instruction

 **Advanced**

Vocabulary Have children make up a story about an animal that lives in a vale or hollow. Have them tell the story orally or with pictures.

DAY 3 Get Ready to Read

Objectives

- ◎ Isolate final consonant blends.
- Discriminate final sounds.

Phonemic Awareness

◎ Final Consonant Blends

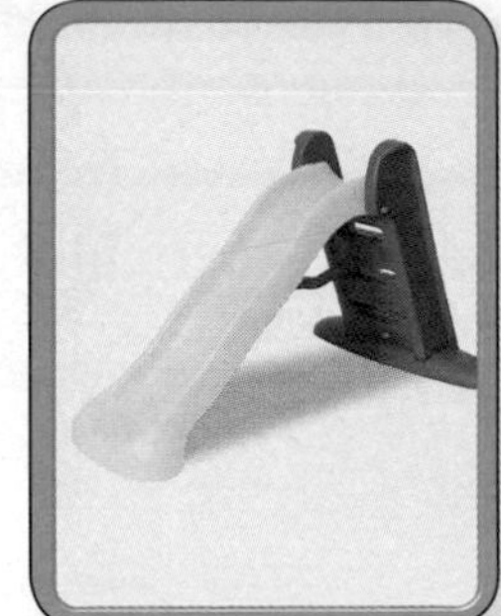
Picture Card

Review

Initial Consonant Blends Display the *slide* Picture Card. Listen as I say this word: /sl/ /sl/ /sl/, *slide*. Two sounds blend together at the beginning. Say the sounds with me: /s/ /l/, /sl/ /sl/, *slide*. Today we will hear blends at the ends of words.

Teach final blends

Write *milk* on the board. Say the word with me: /m/ /i/ /l/ /k/, *milk*. Listen carefully to the end of the word. *Milk* ends with two sounds blended together. The two sounds are /l/ /k/, /lk/ /lk/, *milk*. Continue with /ft/ (*lift, left, sift*); /nd/ (*land, band, sand*); /sk/ (*mask, task, ask*); and /st/ (*fast, list, past*).

Discriminate sounds

I will say some words. Listen for the ending sounds. If a word ends with a final blend, raise your hands and wiggle your fingers. I will do the first one: *hand*. I say the sounds in the word slowly: /h/ /a/ /n/ /d/. I hear two consonant sounds at the end. When I say them quickly, they make a blend: /n/ /d/, /nd/. *Hand* ends with a blend. Continue the routine with the following words: *gift, disk, kind, mouse, elk, sound, risk, rabbit, mole, last, silk, cost, raft.*

On their own

Display the *desk, mask, nest, playground,* and *vest* Picture Cards. Have children choose one of the words and draw a picture of it. Have them use the word on the Picture Card to label their drawing.

Picture Card

Segment words Listen to the word *nest*. What sounds do you hear? Say them with me: /n/ /e/ /s/ /t/, *nest*. There are four sounds in *nest*. The last two sounds are blended together: /n/ /e/ /st/, *nest*. Repeat the routine with the words *gift, silk, risk,* and *wind*.

Corrective feedback **If...** children cannot segment the words into sounds, **then...** provide practice segmenting the words into separate sounds, such as /m/ /i/ /l/ /k/.

Blend words Some words have more than one consonant blend. Listen to this word: *blend*. Did you hear consonant blends? *Blend* has a consonant blend at the beginning and at the end: /bl/ /e/ /nd/, *blend*. Continue the activity with the words *blast, brisk, craft, draft, frost, grind,* and *stand*.

Differentiated Instruction

Strategic Intervention

Supporting Blending Remind children to say each sound in a blend before blending them together. For example, there are four distinct sounds in *sift:* /s/ /i/ /f/ /t/.

Teacher Tip

Use sound discrimination activities that focus on blends in the final position to check children's ability to discriminate sounds in the final position.

ELL

English Language Learners

Support Phonemic Awareness For English learners, it may be difficult to identify and understand that final blends have two sounds. To help children focus on each final sound, emphasize each individual sound in the final blend, and then say the blend.

DAY 3 **Get Ready to Read**

Objectives

- ◎ Practice final consonant blends.
  - Read words with final consonant blends.
  - Read high-frequency words.

Check Word Reading
SUCCESS PREDICTOR

Phonics—Teach/Model
◎ Final Consonant Blends

Picture Card

Review **Initial Blends** Write the word *crab* on the board. This word is *crab*. It has a blend at the beginning. I am going to blend the sounds together: /kr/ /a/ /b/. What are the sounds for *c* and *r*? (/k/ /r/) Say them slowly and then faster to make a blend: /k/ /r/, /kr/ /kr/. Now do the whole word: /kr/ /a/ /b/, *crab*. What is the beginning blend in *crab*? (/kr/) Continue the routine with *flip, clip, drop, trap, stop, slam, plan,* and *spin*.

Introduce final blends Remember that a blend is two sounds put together. Today we are learning about blends at the ends of words. Display the *mask* Picture Card. What is this? What are the ending sounds in *mask*? (/s/ /k/, /sk/) Write *mask* on the board. Point to the letters *s* and *k*. What letters stand for the ending sounds? *Mask* ends with the consonant blend /sk/. Continue with these words: *lift, milk, band, land, sand, task, fast, list, past.*

Blend sounds Write the word *lift* on the board. I am going to blend the sounds of this word: /l/ /i/ /ft/. The word is *lift.* Say the sounds with me: /l/ /i/ /ft/. Now blend the sounds as I point to each letter. The word is *lift.* Continue blending with *milk, band, land, sand, mask, task, fast, list, past, skip, stop, flap, clap,* and *drop.*

More practice Use *Reader's and Writer's Notebook*, p. 271, for additional practice with final blends.

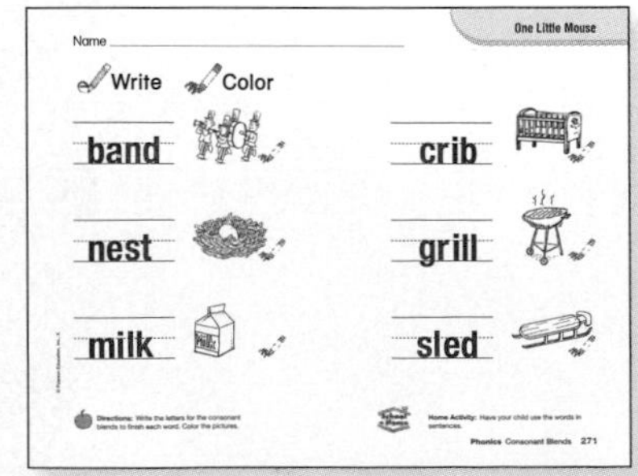
Name
One Little Mouse
Write Color
band
crib
nest
grill
milk
sled
Phonics Consonant Blends 271

Reader's and Writer's Notebook, p. 271

Review **Sound-Spelling** Display the *Ll* Alphabet Card. What sound do you hear at the beginning of *lemon?* What letter spells that sound? Yes, the letter *l* spells /l/. Review the following letters with Alphabet Cards: *Ff, Kk, Nn, Pp, Ss, Dd, Tt, Cc, Rr.*

Alphabet Card

Review **High-Frequency Words** Write *three* on the board. This is the word *three.* What is this word? Continue the routine with *one, two, four,* and *five.*

Don't Wait Until Friday

MONITOR PROGRESS Check Word Reading High-Frequency Words

Write *one, two, three, four,* and *five*. Have children take turns reading the words.

Practice reading these words from Kindergarten Student Reader K.4.3, *A Home for Flap.*

skip **stop** **Flap** **clap** **drop** **spot**

If… children cannot read the high-frequency words,
then… write the words on cards for them to practice at home.
If… children cannot blend sounds to read the words,
then… provide practice blending the words in chunks, /sk/ /i/ /p/.
If… children can successfully blend sounds to read the words,
then… have them read Kindergarten Student Reader K.4.3, *A Home for Flap.*

Day 1	Day 2	Day 3	Day 4	Day 5
Check Phonemic Awareness	Check Sound-Spelling/ Retelling	Check Word Reading	Check Phonemic Awareness	Check Oral Vocabulary

Success Predictor

Differentiated Instruction

SI Strategic Intervention

Support High-Frequency Words Remind children that high-frequency words are not words they can sound out. Children should memorize these words so they know them when they come across them in a story.

ELL

English Language Learners

Support Blends Final consonant blends do not exist in Spanish, so Spanish speakers may omit one of the sounds in a final consonant blend or add an ending vowel. Provide extra practice with hearing and pronouncing words with final consonant blends.

Objectives

- Read words with final consonant blends.
- Read high-frequency words.

Kindergarten Student Reader K.4.3

Consonant Blends and High-Frequency Words

Review Review the previously taught high-frequency words. Have children read each word as you point to it on the Word Wall.

one	two	three	four	five	for	the
I	do	you	to	my	like	

Read Kindergarten Student Reader K.4.3 Display Kindergarten Student Reader K.4.3, *A Home for Flap.* Today we are going to read a new book. Point to the title of the book. The title of the book is *A Home for Flap.* The author's name is Susi Jones. The book was illustrated by Jaime Smith.

Use the reading decodable books routine to read the Kindergarten Student Reader.

ROUTINE Reading Decodable Books

1. **Read Silently** Have children whisper read the book page by page as you listen in.
2. **Model Fluent Reading** Have children finger point as you read a page. Then have children reread the page without you.
3. **Read Chorally** Have children finger point as they chorally read the page. Continue reading page by page, repeating steps 1 and 2.
4. **Read Individually** Have children take turns reading aloud a page.
5. **Reread and Monitor Progress** As you listen to individual children reread, monitor progress and provide support.
6. **Reread with a Partner** Have children reread the book page by page with a partner.

Routines Flip Chart

Nat and Nan hop and skip.
One hop, Nan!
One skip, Nat!

2

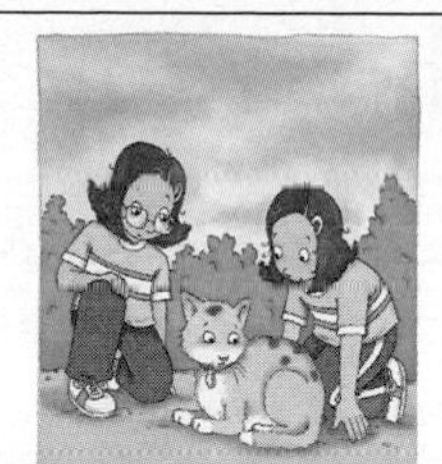

Nat and Nan stop.
Nat and Nan stop for Flap the Cat.

3

Two claps for Flap the Cat.
Clap, clap for Flap!

4

Kindergarten Student Reader K.4.3

Can Flap the Cat sip three drops?
Flap the Cat can sip three drops.
Sip, sip, sip, Flap!

5

I spot four dots on Flap the Cat.
Dot, dot, dot, dot!
Do you spot dots on him?

6

I spot one, two, three, four, five!
Dot, dot, dot, dot, dot!
Five dots on Flap the Cat.

7

Flap the Cat likes to sit on my lap!
Sit, Flap, sit!

8

Differentiated Instruction

Advanced

Support Retelling Have children retell *A Home for Flap* in front of the class to practice their retelling and speaking skills.

Small Group Time

DAY 3 **Break into small groups to read the Kindergarten Student Reader before the comprehension lesson.**

Teacher-Led

SI Strategic Intervention	OL On-Level	A Advanced
Teacher-Led Page DI•37 • Phonemic Awareness and Phonics • **Read** Concept Literacy Reader K.4.3 or Kindergarten Student Reader K.4.3	**Teacher-Led** Page DI•41 • Phonemic Awareness and Phonics • **Read** Kindergarten Student Reader K.4.3	**Teacher-Led** Page DI•44 • **Read** Independent Reader K.4.3 or Kindergarten Student Reader K.4.3

Place English language learners in the groups that correspond to their reading abilities in English.

Practice Stations
- Visit the Words to Know Station
- Visit the Let's Write! Station

Independent Activities
- Read independently
- Audio Text of Big Book
- *Reader's and Writer's Notebook*

English Language Learners

Access Content Have children name the naming part in each sentence, such as *Nat, Nan, Flap the Cat, I,* and *you*. Have children act out the action parts *hop, skip, stop, clap, sip,* and *sit*.

DAY 3 Read and Comprehend 20–25 mins.

Objectives
- Recall and retell a selection.
- ◎ Practice sequence.

Comprehension

Retell the selection Have children turn to p. 66 of *My Skills Buddy.* Using the retelling boxes, have children retell the selection *One Little Mouse.*

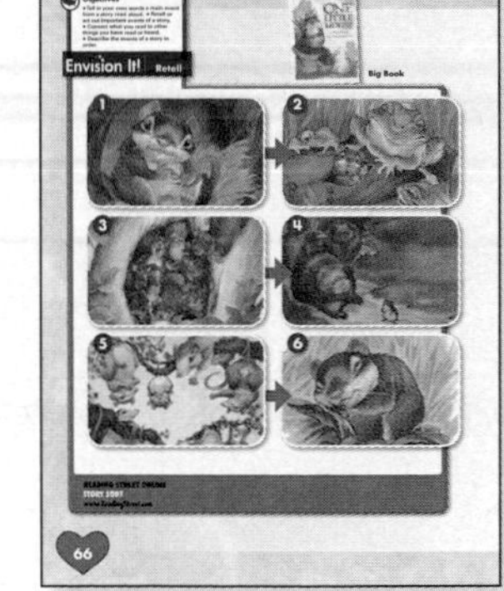

My Skills Buddy, p. 66

Direct children to the first retell box. The mouse is unhappy with his house. What will he do?

Continue reviewing the retelling boxes and having children retell the selection.

Sequence Remind children to think about what happens first, next, and last in the selection.

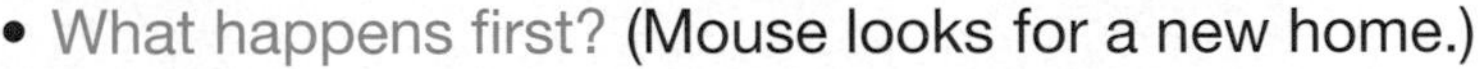

- What happens first? (Mouse looks for a new home.)
- After two moles invite Mouse to stay with them, what does Mouse do? (Mouse tries many different homes.)
- At the end of the selection, what do Mouse and all the other animals do? (They fall asleep in their own homes.)

More practice Use *Reader's and Writer's Notebook,* p. 272, for additional practice with sequence.

Reader's and Writer's Notebook, p. 272

Second Read—Big Book
One Little Mouse

Develop vocabulary

Reread *One Little Mouse.* Follow the Day 3 arrow beginning on p. 258, and use the Develop Vocabulary notes to prompt conversations about the selection.

Have children use the Amazing Words *woodland, nest, vale, hollow, comfortable,* and *shadows* to talk about the story.

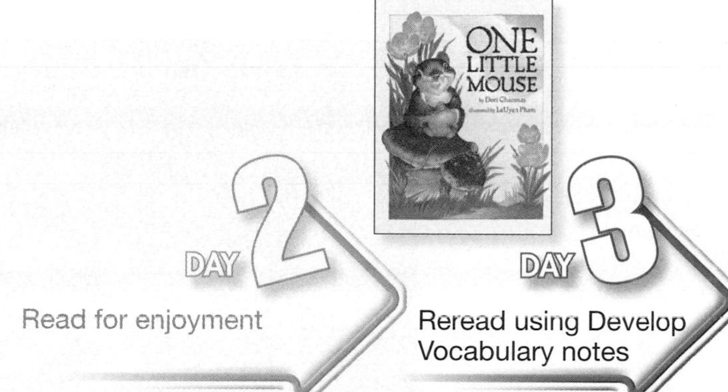

Objectives

- Develop and use vocabulary.
- Develop and apply comprehension skills.

DAY 3

Develop Vocabulary

***Wh-* question**

Why does the mouse want to look for a new house? (His nest is too small.)

- The mouse thinks his nest is too small. What things in the woodland did he use to make his nest?

Develop Vocabulary mouse

One little mouse took a look at his house
Deep in the woodland ground.
"This nest is too small! Not roomy at all!
There must be a new one around."

6

7

Big Book, pp. 6–7

DAY 4

Guide Comprehension

Open-ended

Do you think Mouse's house is too small? Why or why not? (I don't think Mouse's house is too small. It looks just right for a little mouse.)

Wh- question

Who offers the mouse their nest first? (two moles)

- Two moles offer the mouse their nest. Where do they live?

Expand Vocabulary moles

Two blackish moles peeked out of their holes
And called to the mouse passing by,
"We have a fine nest in which you can rest."
So little Mouse thought he would try.

But their diet was wormish,
And that made Mouse squirmish.
He very soon said, "Good-bye."

Big Book, pp. 8–9

Inferential

Why do you think the moles have claw-like feet? (The moles live in holes, so they probably need those claws for digging out the dirt.)

Develop Vocabulary, continued

DAY 3

***Wh-* question**

Who offers Mouse their home next? (three frogs)

- Three frogs offer Mouse their home in the logs. Where do the frogs live?

Develop Vocabulary frogs

Three meadow frogs were leaping from logs.
"You'll like sleeping here," they said.
Mouse thanked them politely, but curling up tightly
He found it too cold for a bed.

With a wheeze and a sneeze,
He was sure he would freeze.
"This never will do!" he said.

10

11

Big Book, pp. 10–11

Guide Comprehension, continued

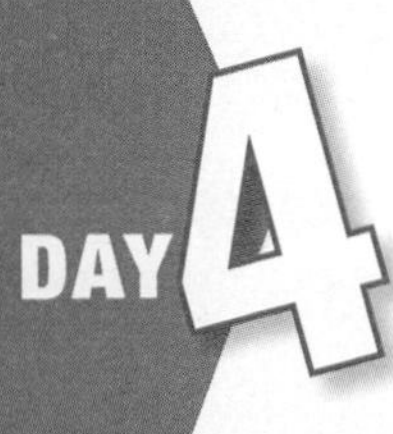

DAY 4

Draw Conclusions

When Mouse is invited to live with the frogs, what is the problem? (The cold makes Mouse wheeze, sneeze, and freeze.)

Distancing
Who offers Mouse their home next? (four bobwhite quail)

- Four bobwhite quail with eggs in their nest offer Mouse their home. What would it feel like to sleep on eggs?

Expand Vocabulary bobwhite quail

Four bobwhite quail ran up from the vale.
"If you're looking for someplace to rest,
We have a nice hollow, and if you will follow,
We think we have room for a guest."

But Mouse found it bumpy
And clumpy and lumpy,
Just too many eggs in the nest!

12 13

Big Book, pp. 12–13

Sequence
What has happened so far in the selection? (Mouse thinks his house is too small. He is looking for a new house. Two moles offered their nest. Then three frogs offered their log. Next, four bobwhite quail offer their nest.)

Develop Vocabulary, continued

DAY 3

Recall

Who wants Mouse to come home with them? (five green snakes)

- The snakes want Mouse to come home with them. Why doesn't Mouse want to go home with them?

Develop Vocabulary snakes

Big Book, pp. 14–15

Guide Comprehension, continued

DAY 4

Open-ended

Mouse comes across five greeny snakes. What would you do if you came across five snakes? (I would move away from them slowly and then run.)

Recall

Who offers Mouse their bed on this page? (six baby cottontails)

- Cottontails are one kind of rabbit. How many baby rabbits are there?

Develop Vocabulary cottontails

Six baby cottontails hopped along hilly trails.
"Come, little Mouse, share our bed."
"Oh thank you," said Mouse. "I'm in need of a house."
And he happily laid down his head.

But the cottontails bunched up
And crunched up and hunched up.
"And soon I'll be scrunched up!" Mouse said.

17

Big Book, pp. 16–17

Draw Conclusions

Why does Mouse leave the home of the cottontails? (It is too crowded and uncomfortable.)

Develop Vocabulary, continued

DAY 3

Distancing
Where do the squirrels make their nests? (in a tree)

- Squirrels make their nests in trees. Do you ever see squirrels around your home? Where do squirrels like to make their nests?

Develop Vocabulary squirrels

Seven gray squirrels
Ran in circles and swirls,
Then carried Mouse up to their nest.
"You may stay here with us
If you don't make a fuss."
And Mouse said, "I will do my best."

But the nut nest was clicky
And clacky and cracky.
He left without one bit of rest.

18

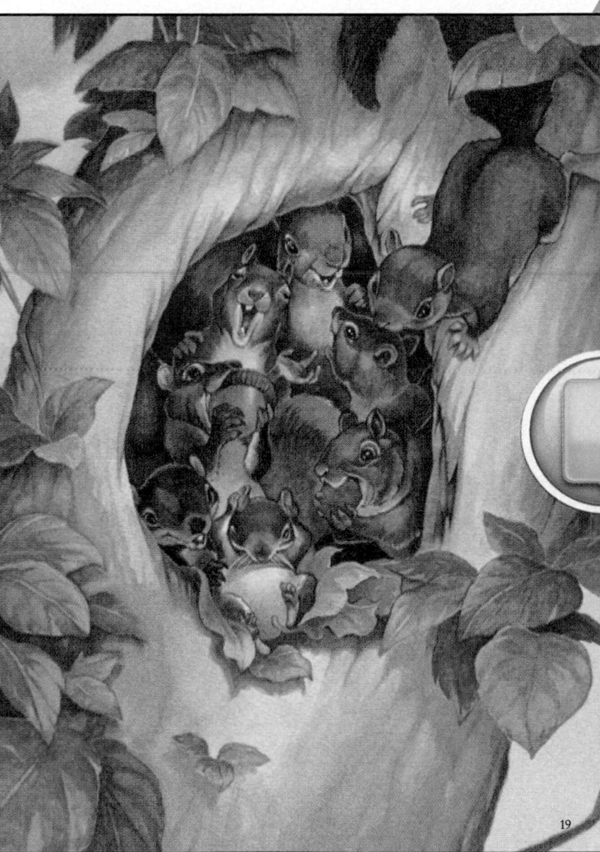

19

Big Book, pp. 18–19

Guide Comprehension, continued

DAY 4

Monitor and Fix Up
Why isn't a squirrel's nest a good home for Mouse? If you don't understand why a squirrel's nest is not a good home for a mouse, what could you do? (If I don't understand what is read, I need to raise my hand and ask if we could reread the page.)

Open-ended

Who offers Mouse their home on this page? (eight chickadees)

- Eight chickadees offer their home in the willow tree. How do you think a tree branch would feel as a pillow?

Expand Vocabulary chickadees

Eight chickadees flew in with the breeze.
"We have a fine place in the willow."
But Mouse said, "Dear me! I can't sleep in a tree!
Imagine a branch for a pillow!"

20 21

Big Book, pp. 20–21

Inferential

Besides the tree as a pillow, why else might being high up in a tree not be good for Mouse? (Mouse is very small and he has no wings. He cannot fly, and he might fall out of the birds' nest.)

Develop Vocabulary, continued

DAY 3

Open-ended
Who offers Mouse their home next?
(nine porcupine)

- Nine porcupine want Mouse to stay with them. Why doesn't Mouse want to stay with them?

Expand Vocabulary porcupine, quills

Nine porcupine waddled by in a line.
They called to the mouse, "Good day!
We have a nice den, right here in the glen."
"Thank you," Mouse answered. "I'll stay."

But their sharp quills were sticking
And picking and pricking.
So Mouse quickly went on his way.

Big Book, pp. 22–23

Guide Comprehension, continued

DAY 4

Sequence
What happens after four bobwhite quail offer their nest to Mouse?
(Five green snakes offer to have Mouse stay with them. Then six cottontails, seven squirrels, eight chickadees, and nine porcupine say Mouse can stay with them.)

Open-ended

Where do the opossums live? (in a tree)

- Ten opossums, who live in a tree, wanted Mouse to swing from his tail. How does Mouse feel about this?

Expand Vocabulary opossums

Ten small opossums were eating plum blossoms.
"Come on, sleep with us," they were singing.
They knotted his tail, and Mouse let out a wail
To find himself suddenly swinging.

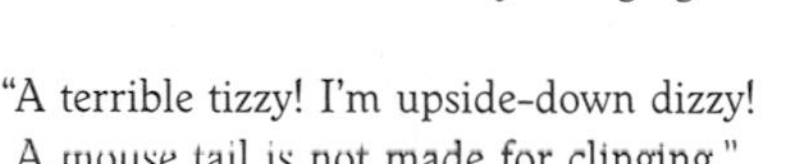

"A terrible tizzy! I'm upside-down dizzy!
A mouse tail is not made for clinging."

24 25

Big Book, pp. 24–25

Open-ended

Why do you think the opossums hang by their tails? (Opossums like to hang upside down. They like to swing by their tails. It is how they like to sleep.)

DAYS 3 & 4 Read and Comprehend

Develop Vocabulary, continued

DAY 3

Open-ended

Where does Mouse go next?
(back to his house)

- Mouse goes back home at the end of the day. Why do you think Mouse is happy with his home now?

Then Mouse turned around to the darkening wood
And scampered along just as fast as he could,
Back to his own little comfortable house
(So tiny and tidy, just right for a mouse),
And when evening shadows crept over the ground
And covered the woodland, here's what was found:

26

27

Big Book, pp. 26–27

Guide Comprehension, continued

Recall

Whom has Mouse met on his adventures in the woodland?
(Mouse has met moles, frogs, bobwhite quail, green snakes, baby cottontails, squirrels, chickadees, porcupine, and opossums.)

Distancing

What animals do we see sleeping in their beds on these pages? (ten opossums, nine porcupine, eight chickadees, and seven squirrels)

- The opossums, porcupine, chickadees, and squirrels are in bed. How do you get ready for bed?

Big Book, pp. 28–29

Distancing

Where would you sleep if you lived in the woodland? (I would sleep in a sleeping bag, a camper, or a tent.)

Develop Vocabulary, continued

DAY 3

Distancing

What animals are sleeping in their beds here? (six cottontails, five snakes, four bobwhite quail, three frogs, and two moles)

- The cottontails, snakes, quail, frogs, and moles are asleep. Why do you think people and animals need to sleep?

Big Book, pp. 30–31

Guide Comprehension, continued

Open-ended

Which animal's home would you like to sleep in? Why? (I would like to sleep in the chickadees' home in the willow tree. I think it would be fun to be up high.)

Open-ended

Who is asleep on this page? (one mouse)

- The mouse is finally asleep in his own bed. Do you think Mouse is happy to be in his own bed?

Conventions p. 272

And one little mouse,
One tired little mouse,
One content little mouse,
Sound asleep in his house.

32

Big Book, p. 32

Sequence

What happens last in the selection? (Mouse finds that his own house is the best house for him after all.)

Conventions p. 286

DAY 3 Language Arts

Objectives
- Review action parts.
- Write or dictate a description.

Conventions
Action Parts

Review Remind children of what they have learned about parts of sentences. Every sentence has an action part. It tells what someone or something is doing.

Guide practice Hold up AlphaBuddy. I will make up a sentence. Make AlphaBuddy dance. What does AlphaBuddy do? That's right. *AlphaBuddy dances.* The action part of this sentence is *dances.* It tells what AlphaBuddy is doing.

Make AlphaBuddy walk, run, twirl, and fly. Make up sentences about what AlphaBuddy is doing. Have children identify the action part of each sentence.

Team Talk Pair children. Have the first child make up a complete sentence about AlphaBuddy using the sentence frame *AlphaBuddy* ________. Have the second child name the action part in the sentence. Then have children switch roles and repeat the routine.

On their own Use *Reader's and Writer's Notebook,* p. 273, for more practice with action parts.

Daily Fix-It Use the Daily Fix-It for more conventions practice.

Reader's and Writer's Notebook, p. 273

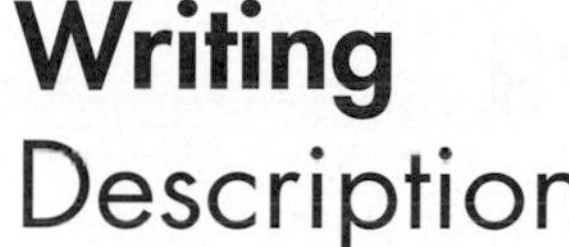

Writing
Description

Teach Display the *alligator, umbrella,* and *waffle* Picture Cards. Look at these pictures as I say a few words. Try to guess which picture I am talking about. *Small. Brown. Tastes good. Breakfast food.* Which picture am I talking about? (waffle) I used words to tell about the waffle. When we use words to tell more about something, it is called a *description.* Point to your eyes, fingers, ears, mouth, and nose as you say: A description tells how something looks, feels, sounds, tastes, or smells.

Model Display the *kite* Picture Card. This is a kite. Point to your eyes, fingers, ears, mouth, and nose as you say: I want to think about how the kite looks, feels, sounds, tastes, or smells. The kite looks colorful. I think the kite feels silky if I touch it. A kite sounds like flapping in the wind. We only taste food, so a kite does not have a taste. A kite does not have a smell, either. I think the kite is colorful, silky, and flaps in the wind. I could use any of these for my description. I like *flaps in the wind*. Write *flaps in the wind* on the board. My description of a kite is *flaps in the wind.*

Guide practice Have children provide descriptions for the *alligator, lemon,* and *mask* Picture Cards. Write their descriptions on the board.

Independent writing Have children turn to p. 274 of *Reader's and Writer's Notebook.* Have them draw a picture of the mouse in the selection. Then have children write or dictate a sentence on the line that tells about the mouse.

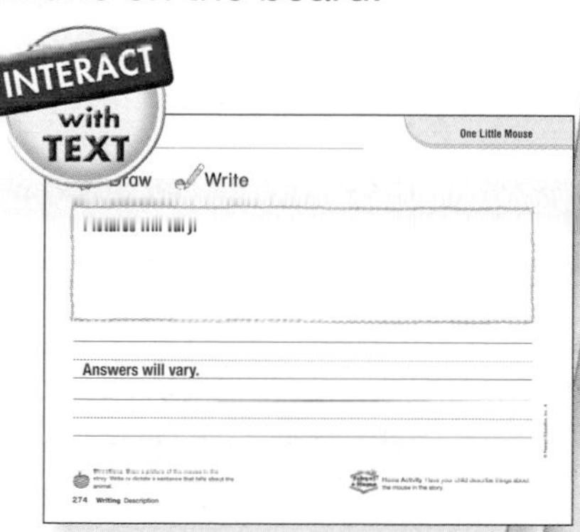

Reader's and Writer's Notebook, p. 274

Daily Handwriting

Write 3 and *three* on the board. Review correct formation of the numeral 3 and the lowercase letters *t, h, r,* and *e.*

Have children write 3 and *three* on their Write-On Boards. Remind them to use proper left-to-right and top-to-bottom progression and proper spacing between letters when writing 3 and *three.*

Differentiated Instruction

SI Strategic Intervention

Support Writing If children struggle to describe an object, ask questions about how it affects one of the senses, such as *How does it feel?* or *How does it taste?*

Academic Vocabulary

description words that tell how something looks, feels, sounds, tastes, or smells

Daily Fix-It

a mouse met a snake

A mouse met a snake.

This week's practice sentences appear on Teacher Resources DVD-ROM.

ELL

English Language Learners

Complete Sentences Help children see that word order affects meaning in English. For example, *Ty ate the pickle* is not the same as *The pickle ate Ty.* Remind children that the naming part often comes before the action part in English sentences.

DAY 3 Language Arts

Objectives

- Practice listening for sequence.
- Face the speaker when listening.
- Speak loudly and clearly.
- Speak one at a time.

Listening and Speaking
Listen for Sequence

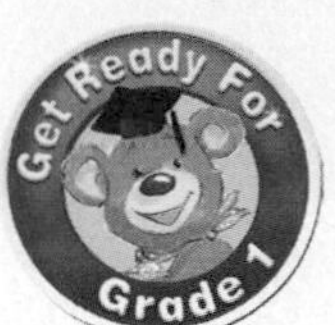

Review Remind children that when they listen to a story, they can listen for sequence, or the order in which things happen. When we listen, we should face the speaker to show we are listening. When it is time to retell the sequence we heard, we must speak loudly and clearly and speak one at a time.

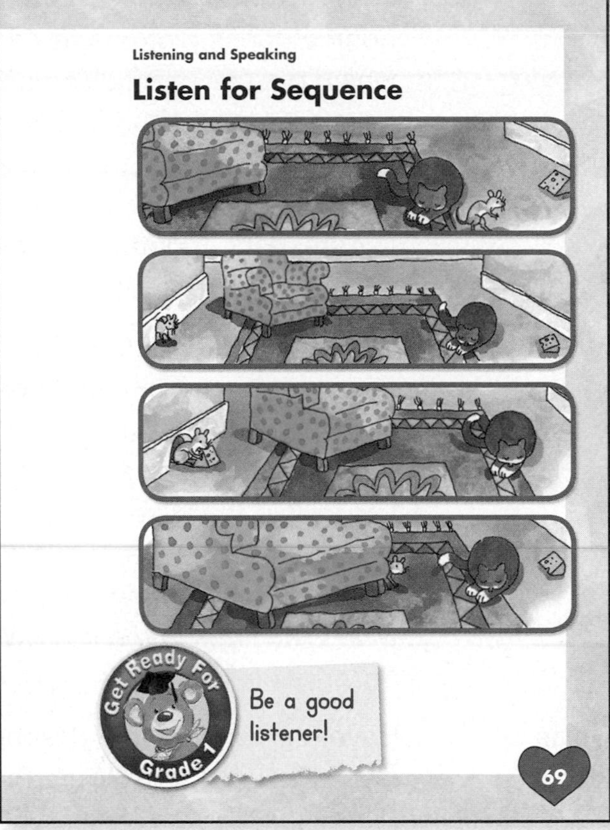

My Skills Buddy, p. 69

Model In *One Little Mouse,* first, Mouse thinks his house is too small. Next, he tries a lot of other houses. Last, Mouse decides his house is just right. That is the sequence.

AlphaBuddy is going to tell a short story. Listen carefully.

First, a mouse sees a piece of cheese all the way across the room. Next, he walks past a big chair. Then he creeps past a sleeping cat. Last, he gets the cheese and eats it back in his mouse hole.

Guide practice Have children turn to p. 69 of *My Skills Buddy.* Look at these pictures. They go along with the story AlphaBuddy just told us. As AlphaBuddy retells the story, listen for the sequence. As you listen, point to the picture that tells the part AlphaBuddy is saying. Have AlphaBuddy retell the story, pausing after each sentence. Read the Listening and Speaking bullets on p. 68 of *My Skills Buddy* with children to help them identify the sequence.

Independent practice Think about stories we have read so far. What was your favorite? Do you remember what happened first, next, then, and last? Have children take turns telling the sequence of their favorite stories. Refer to the Rules for Listening and Speaking from pp. 1–2 of *Reader's and Writer's Notebook.* Remind children to share their ideas by speaking loudly and clearly and to speak one at a time.

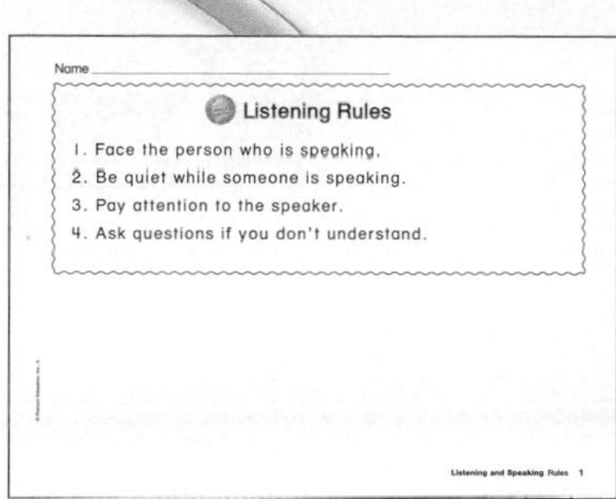
Listening Rules
1. Face the person who is speaking.
2. Be quiet while someone is speaking.
3. Pay attention to the speaker.
4. Ask questions if you don't understand.

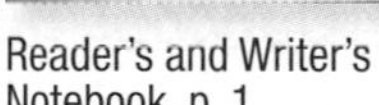
Reader's and Writer's Notebook, p. 1

Be a Good Listener

1. Face the person who is speaking.
2. Be quiet while someone is speaking.
3. Pay attention to the speaker.
4. Ask questions if you don't understand.

Differentiated Instruction

Advanced

Access Content Have children retell the story on p. 69 of *My Skills Buddy* using only the pictures. Have them first determine the order of the pictures and then retell the story.

Objectives

- Review skills learned and practiced today.

Wrap Up Your Day

✔ **Concept Talk** Today we read about a mouse looking for a house. We also read about a cat named Flap. What home did the mouse get? What kind of home did Flap get?

✔ **Respond to Literature** What would you do if you were a mouse looking for a new house?

✔ **Homework Idea** Have children make a list of words that end with *-st* or *-nd.*

Tomorrow we will read more about the little mouse's adventure.

Science
Animal Characteristics

Materials: Big Book *One Little Mouse*

Discuss Animal Differences Take a picture walk through *One Little Mouse*. Point out the differences in the animals by asking the following questions: What is their skin like? Where do they live? How do they move?

Write the following headings on chart paper: *Fur, Skin, Feathers, Quills.*

Read the headings together. Tell children to think of the animals in the selection. Have them tell which of the animals fits into each category.

Can You Guess Who? Describe an animal using the categories on the chart. Have children figure out which animal from the selection you are describing.

Conventions
Action Parts

Act Out Sentences Sentences have naming parts and action parts. The naming part is who or what the sentence is about. The action part is what a person or animal is doing. List action verbs on the board, such as *hop, skip, jump, laugh, smile, sing, bend, tap, clap,* and *wiggle.*

Now I'll choose an action word for the action part of the sentence. The naming part of my sentence is: [Name of a child in your class]. [Name] hops. Go ahead, [Name], hop! Have children make up sentences for the others to act out.

Phonics
Guess Initial Blends

Materials: list of /o/ words

Describe Words with Blends Make a list of words that begin with the consonant blends *sl, pl, bl, gl, fl, cl, cr, dr, tr, br, fr, gr, st,* and *sp* on a sheet of paper. Point to a word, showing it only to one volunteer. Have the volunteer give clues about the word or draw a picture of it and have the class guess the word.

Objectives

- Discuss the concept to develop oral language.
- Build oral vocabulary.

Today at a Glance

Oral Vocabulary
comfortable, shadows

Phonemic Awareness
Initial and Final /l/

Phonics
/l/ Spelled *Ll*

Comprehension
◉ Sequence

Conventions
Complete Sentences

Writing
Extend the Concept

Vocabulary
Words for Shapes

TRUCKTOWN on Reading Street

Start your engines!

- Display "Three Loud Trucks" and lead the group in saying the rhyme a few times.
- Next, have the group clap the rhythm as they recite the rhyme.
- When children master the rhythm, have them march around the room as they say the rhyme.

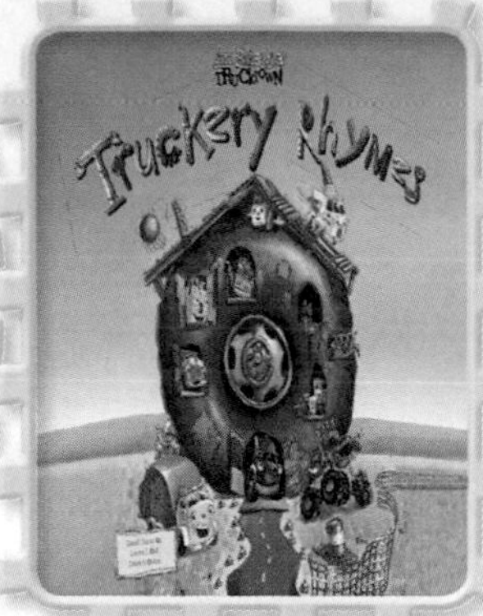

Truckery Rhymes

Concept Talk

Question of the Week

What adventures can animals have?

Build concepts Write the question of the week on the board. Read the question as you track the print. Tell children to respond in complete sentences. Display Sing with Me Chart 21B.

Listen for Amazing Words Today we are going to sing "A New Woodland Nest" again. Let's listen for the Amazing Words *comfortable* and *shadows.* Read the title. Sing the song several times with children to the tune of "Hickory, Dickory, Dock." Have children nod when they hear the Amazing Words *comfortable* and *shadows.*

Sing with Me Audio

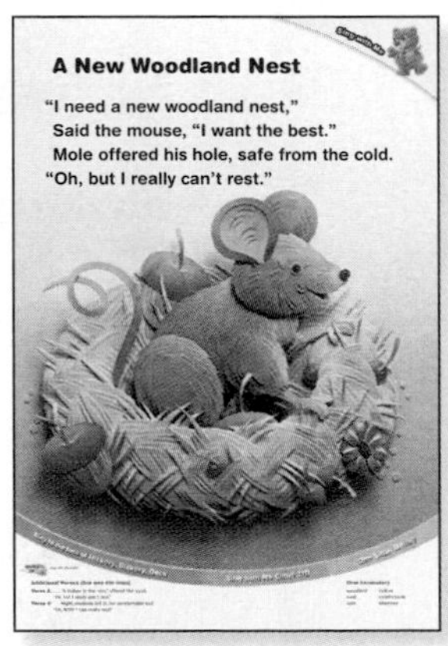

Talk with Me/Sing with Me Chart 21B

ELL Produce Oral Language Use the Day 4 instruction on ELL Poster 21 to extend and enrich language.

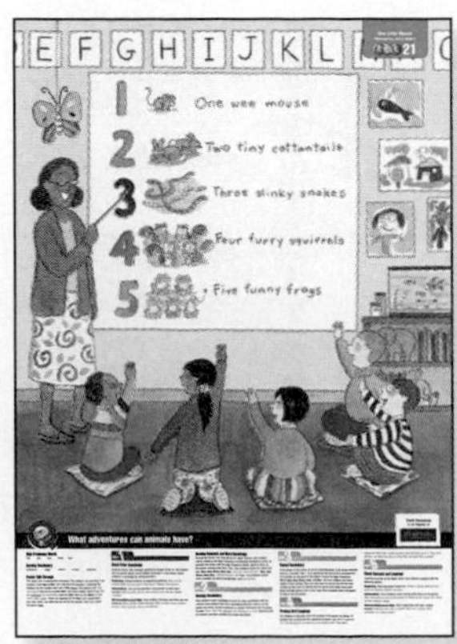

ELL Poster 21

Oral Vocabulary
Amazing Words

Teach Amazing Words

Amazing Words Oral Vocabulary Routine

1. **Introduce the Word** When you are *comfortable,* it means that your body is relaxed. You are not too cold or hot, such as when you are curled up in a blanket. What is our new Amazing Word for relaxed and cozy? Say it with me: *comfortable.*
2. **Demonstrate** *Mouse kept looking for a home that would be comfortable.* Why do we want our beds to be cozy and *comfortable?*

Repeat steps 1 and 2.

Introduce the Word *Shadows* are made when the light is blocked. When you put your hand in front of a light, you make *shadows.* What is our new Amazing Word for dark shapes when light is blocked? Say it with me: *shadows.*

Demonstrate *When we go out into the sunshine, our bodies make shadows*. Would we see *shadows* on a dark, gloomy day?

3. **Apply** Have children use *comfortable* and *shadows* in complete sentences. Have them illustrate the words.

Routines Flip Chart

Use Amazing Words

To reinforce the concept and the Amazing Words, have children supply the appropriate Amazing Word for each sentence.

When you block light, you make ________. (shadows)
My dad's big chair is cozy and ________. (comfortable)

Amazing Words

woodland	nest
vale	hollow
comfortable	shadows

Differentiated Instruction

Strategic Intervention

Sentence Production If children struggle to say sentences with correct subject-verb agreement, say each sentence correctly and have children repeat it.

English Language Learners

Practice Amazing Words Have children tell what words in their home languages are used for *comfortable* and *shadows.*

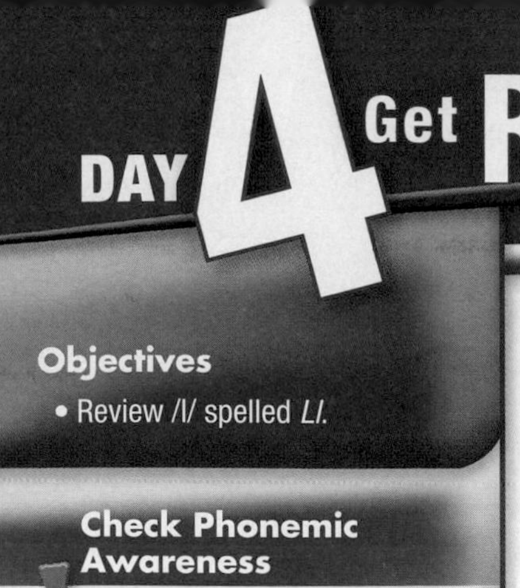

Objectives

- Review /l/ spelled *Ll.*

Check Phonemic Awareness
SUCCESS PREDICTOR

Phonemic Awareness
Review /l/

Display the *ladybug* Picture Card. This is a *ladybug*. *Ladybug* begins with /l/. What sound does *ladybug* begin with? Display the *snail* Picture Card. This is a *snail*. Where do you hear /l/ in the word *snail? Snail* ends with /l/. What sound does *snail* end with?

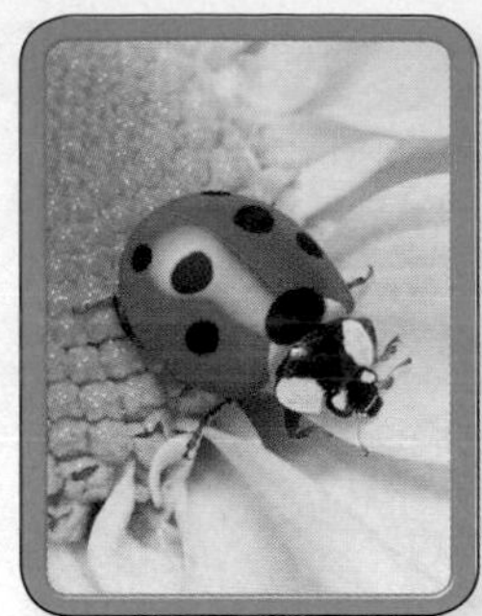
Picture Card

I am going to say some words. When you hear /l/ at the beginning, raise your hands. When you hear /l/ at the end, stomp your foot. Let's try one together: *lamp*. Good. Everyone raised his or her hands. Let's try another: *seal.* Everyone stomped his or her foot. Now listen to these words for /l/: *doll, leaf, lake, wheel, sail, lemon.*

Picture Card

Corrective feedback

If... children cannot discriminate /l/,
then... have them say /l/ several times.

When you say /l/, raise the top of your tongue and press it lightly against the ridge behind you upper teeth. Have children practice saying /l/, and then repeat the discrimination activity.

Phonics

/l/ Spelled *Ll*

Review

Display the *Ll* Alphabet Card. This is a *lemon. Lemon* begins with /l/. What letter spells /l/? Yes, the letter *l* spells /l/.

Alphabet Card

Write the word *lap* on the board. Help me blend this word. Listen as I say each sound: /l/ /a/ /p/. Now blend the sound together to read the word: /l/ /a/ /p/, *lap.* What is the word? (*lap*) Write the word *hill* on the board. Say the sounds with me: /h/ /i/ /l/. The word is *hill.* Remind children that /l/ at the end of a word is often spelled *ll.* Continue with *fill, lab, doll, pal,* and *lot.*

Don't Wait Until Friday

MONITOR PROGRESS — Check Phonemic Awareness

Phoneme Segmentation Practice segmenting sounds with these words from Decodable Reader 21, *One to Five,* after I say each word.

flop slam drop plop spin land jump stop

If... children cannot segment the sounds,

then... use the small-group Strategic Intervention lesson, p. DI•38, to reteach segmentation skills.

Continue to monitor children's progress using other instructional opportunities during the week so that they can be successful with the Day 5 Assessment. See the Skills Trace on p. 218.

Day 1	Day 2	Day 3	Day 4	Day 5
Check Phonemic Awareness	Check Sound-Spelling/ Retelling	Check Word Reading	Check Phonemic Awareness	Check Oral Vocabulary

Success Predictor

Differentiated Instruction

Advanced

Vocabulary Have children draw a collage of objects that begin or end with *Ll.* Then have them write or dictate labels for each object.

English Language Learners

Pronounce /l/ Speakers of Chinese, Japanese, Korean, and Vietnamese may confuse /l/ and /r/. Give children additional practice in producing /l/ by itself and at the beginning of words.

DAY 4 Get Ready to Read

Objectives

- Spell words.
- Blend and segment words.
- Read decodable text.
- Read high-frequency words.

Spelling

Initial and Final Blends

ROUTINE **Spell Words**

Spell Words

1. **Review Sound-Spellings** Display the *Ll* Alphabet Card. This is a *lemon. Lemon* begins with /l/. What is the letter for /l/? (*l*) Continue with the following Alphabet Cards: *Ff, Tt, Rr, Ss, Pp, Cc, Dd, Kk, Nn.*
2. **Model** Today we are going to spell some words with blends. Listen to the sounds in *flap*: /fl/ /a/ /p/.

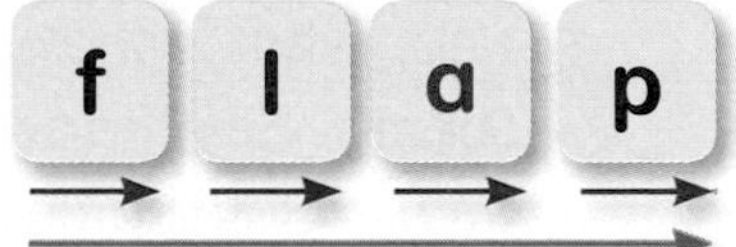

   - What are the first two sounds in *flap?* (/fl/) What are the letters for /fl/? (*fl*) Write *fl* on the board.
   - What is the middle sound you hear? (/a/) What is the letter for /a/? (*a*) Write *a* on the board.
   - What is the last sound that you hear? (/p/) What is the letter for /p/? (*p*) Write *p* on the board.
   - Point to *flap.* Help me blend the sounds of the letters together to read this word: /fl/ /a/ /p/. The word is *flap.* Repeat the modeling with the word *last.*
3. **Guide Practice** Now let's spell some words together. Listen to this word: /kr/ /i/ /b/. What are the first sounds in *crib?* (/kr/) What are the letters for /kr/? (*cr*) Write *cr* on the board. Now you write *cr* on your paper. What is the middle sound in *crib?* (/i/) What is the letter for /i/? (*i*) Write *i* on the board. Now you write *i* on your paper. What is the last sound in *crib?* (/b/) What is the letter for /b/? (*b*) Write *b* on the board. Now you write *b* on your paper. Now we can blend the sound of each letter together to read the word: /kr/ /i/ /b/. What is the word? (*crib*) Continue spell and blend practice with the following words: *drop, skip, lift, fast, plot, clap.*
4. **On Your Own** This time I am going to say a word. I want you to write it on your paper. Remember, first, say the word slowly in your head and then write the letter for each sound. Listen carefully. Say the word *sand*. Give children time to write the word. How do you spell the word *sand?* Listen to the sounds: /s /a/ /nd/. The first sound is /s/. What is the letter for /s/? Did you write *s* on your paper? What is the letter for /a/? Did you write *a* on your paper? What are the letters for /nd/? Did you write *nd* on your paper? Name the letters in *sand. Sand* is spelled *s, a, n, d.* Continue the activity with the following words: *flip, plan, trip, spat, mask, snap.*

Routines Flip Chart

Get Set, Roll! Reader 21
Practice Consonant Blends

Review Review the high-frequency words *look, is, one, two, three, four,* and *five.* Have children read each word as you point to it on the Word Wall.

Review names Write the names *Jack, Dan, Melvin,* and *Gabriella* on the board. Say each name several times. Have children say the names with you. Then point to a name and have children say the letters in the name.

Read Get Set, Roll! Reader 21 Display Get Set, Roll! Reader 21, *Jack Is It!* Today we will read a book about a game. Point to the title of the book. What is the title of the book? *Jack Is It!* is the title of the book. We will read some words with blends in this book.

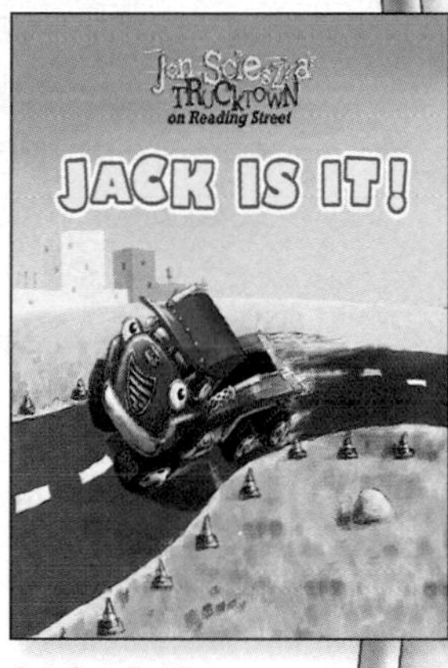

Get Set, Roll! Reader 21

Small Group Time

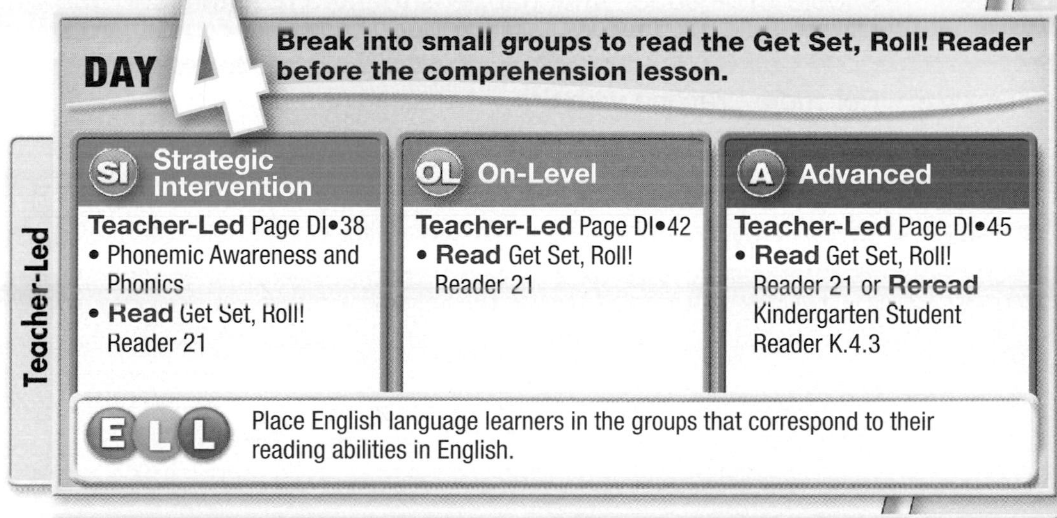
DAY 4 Break into small groups to read the Get Set, Roll! Reader before the comprehension lesson.

Teacher-Led

SI Strategic Intervention	OL On-Level	A Advanced
Teacher-Led Page DI•38 • Phonemic Awareness and Phonics • **Read** Get Set, Roll! Reader 21	**Teacher-Led** Page DI•42 • **Read** Get Set, Roll! Reader 21	**Teacher-Led** Page DI•45 • **Read** Get Set, Roll! Reader 21 or **Reread** Kindergarten Student Reader K.4.3

ELL Place English language learners in the groups that correspond to their reading abilities in English.

Practice Stations
- Visit the Let's Write! Station
- Visit the Read for Meaning Station

Independent Activities
- Read independently
- Audio Text of the Big Book
- *Reader's and Writer's Notebook*

Differentiated Instruction

SI Strategic Intervention

Spelling *sand* If children struggle to spell *sand,* point out that it is spelled like the word *and* with an *s* in front. Explain to children that knowing how to spell simple words can help them spell other words too.

ELL

English Language Learners

Frontload Reader Take a picture walk with children to preview the reader before starting the routine.

Read and Comprehend

20–25 mins.

Objectives

- ◎ Practice sequence.
- Review and practice draw conclusions.

Comprehension

Sequence

Practice sequence

Envision It!

Have children turn to the Sequence picture on p. 54 of *My Skills Buddy.* In most stories, things happen in a certain order: first, next, last. What is happening in these pictures?

My Skills Buddy, pp. 54–55

Team Talk Pair children and have them take turns describing the steps they take to get ready for school in the morning. In the morning when you get ready for school, what do you do first? What do you do next? What do you do last?

Draw Conclusions

Review Remind children that when they look at pictures and hear a story, they should think about what happens to the characters and use what they know to decide what might happen.

More practice For more practice with draw conclusions, use the *Reader's and Writer's Notebook,* p. 275.

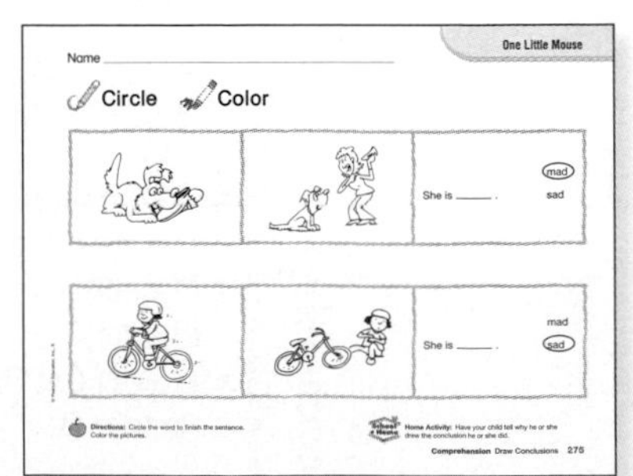

Reader's and Writer's Notebook, p. 275

Third Read—Big Book
One Little Mouse

Guide comprehension Display *One Little Mouse.* This selection is about a little mouse searching for a new home. Let's think about what happens to Mouse and use what we know to decide *why* it happens.

- Why does Mouse leave his home? (He thinks it is too small.)
- Does Mouse like the other animals' homes? (no)
- Why do you think Mouse goes back to his home? (He doesn't like other animals' homes, but his home is just right.)

Reread *One Little Mouse.* Return to p. 258. Follow the Day 4 arrow and use the Guide Comprehension notes to give children the opportunity to gain a more complete understanding of the selection.

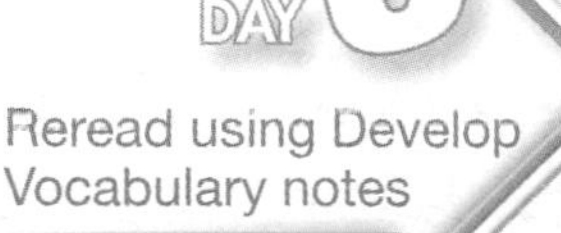

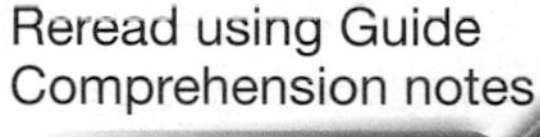

DAY 2 Read for enjoyment

DAY 3 Reread using Develop Vocabulary notes

DAY 4 Reread using Guide Comprehension notes

Differentiated Instruction

 Advanced

Support Retelling Have children explain why Mouse is happy to return to his home at the end of the story.

DAY 4 Language Arts

20–25 mins.

Objectives

- Identify complete sentences.
- Practice using complete sentences.
- Write or dictate sentences about animal adventures.

Conventions
Complete Sentences

Review Remind children that a complete sentence has a naming part and an action part. A sentence begins with an uppercase letter and ends with a punctuation mark. On the board, write *The dog barks.* Listen as I read this sentence: *The dog barks.* The naming part is *The dog.* The action part is *barks.* The sentence starts with an uppercase letter and ends with a period.

Guide practice Have children think of things they do after school. Write these actions on the board. Help children make simple sentences with children's names as the naming part, such as *Jack plays baseball* or *Molly goes to dance class.* Write the sentences children say on the board. Ask children to direct you with capitalization and punctuation.

On their own Use *Reader's and Writer's Notebook,* p. 276, for more practice with complete sentences.

Daily Fix-It Use the Daily Fix-It for more conventions practice.

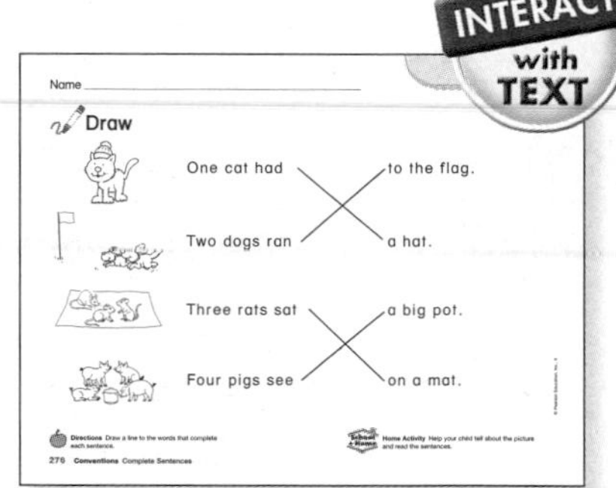

Reader's and Writer's Notebook, p. 276

Writing

Extend the Concept: Text to Text

Discuss adventures animals can have

Recall the adventures Mouse had looking for a home. Have children talk about Mouse's adventures. We have read about other animals having adventures too. Do you remember the adventures a piglet had in *My Lucky Day?* The piglet goes to the house of a fox who wants to eat him! Instead, the piglet tricks the fox into giving him a bath, cooking him dinner, and giving him a massage. After all that work, the fox falls asleep, and the piglet runs away, happy and relaxed after his big adventure.

Guide practice

Ask children to think of other stories that talk about animal adventures. Use children's suggestions to write sentences.

Animals have a party in Bear's cave.

Rooster makes new friends.

Little Quack jumps in the pond.

Have children read the sentence with you. Model writing more sentences.

Independent writing

Have children write or dictate their own sentences about animal adventures, or they may copy one of the sentences the class wrote together. Then have them illustrate their sentences.

Daily Handwriting

Write 4 and *four* on the board. Review correct formation of the numeral 4 and the lowercase letters *f, o, u,* and *r.*

Have children write 4 and *four* on their Write-On Boards. Remind them to use proper left-to-right and top-to-bottom progression and proper spacing between letters when writing 4 and *four.*

Differentiated Instruction

 Strategic Intervention

Support Writing Remind children that a complete sentence needs a naming part and an action part. Have them identify the naming part and action part of the sentences they create.

Daily Fix-It

the goose was big

The goose was big.

This week's practice sentences appear on Teacher Resources DVD-ROM.

English Language Learners

Complete Sentences Some pronouns may be omitted in Spanish and Chinese sentences when the context makes their meaning clear. Explain to children that pronouns must be included in English.

Objectives

- Practice using words for shapes.
- Identify words that begin with /f/.

Vocabulary
Words for Shapes

Teach

Write the words *heart, star, oval,* and *diamond* in a column on the board. Draw each shape next to its name. These are shapes and their names: *heart, star, oval, diamond.* Have children turn to p. 68 of *My Skills Buddy.* Which picture in your book shows a star? Repeat for the heart, oval, and diamond. Discuss the last Vocabulary bullet on the page.

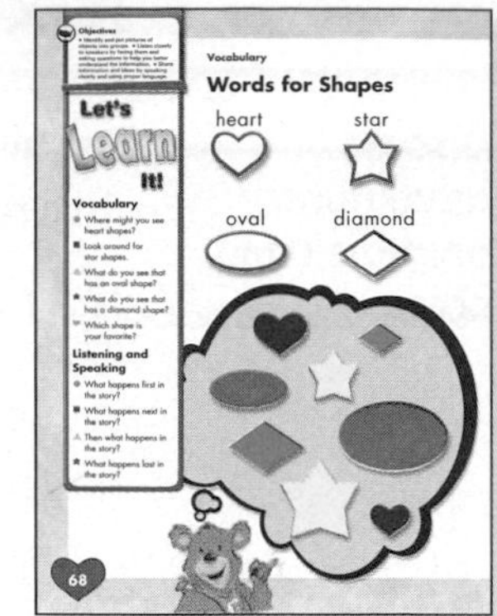

My Skills Buddy, p. 68

Team Talk Pair children and have them take turns describing items in the classroom, using the shape words *heart, star, oval,* and *diamond* in sentences.

Wrap Up Your Day

✔ **Oral Language** Sing "A New Woodland Nest" with me. Clap when you hear the Amazing Words *woodland, nest, vale, hollow, comfortable,* and *shadows.*

✔ **Phonemic Awareness** Today we practiced blends. What is a blend? Name some words that begin or end with a blend.

✔ **Homework Idea** Have children write a complete sentence about their day. Remind them to use an uppercase letter and an ending punctuation mark.

Preview DAY 5

Tell children that tomorrow they will read about Peter Rabbit. Ask what adventures they think he will have.

Science
Woodland Seasons

Materials: four pictures showing the four seasons in a woodland or forest, paper, crayons or markers

What Season Is It? Display the pictures, which should show each of the four seasons in some detail. Ask children to look at the pictures and describe what they see. Ask them how the pictures are different. Relate these differences to the changes in the seasons.

- What happens in the woods in spring? (trees get pale green leaves, small flowers grow, grass turns green, sun gets warmer)
- What happens in the woods in summer? (leaves get bigger and greener, lots of flowers grow, sun gets hot)
- What happens in the woods in fall? (leaves change colors and fall off trees, weather gets colder)
- What happens in the woods in winter? (trees are bare, weather gets cold)

Draw a Season Ask children to name their favorite season. Have them draw a picture of the woodland during that season. When children have finished, hang their drawings on a wall or bulletin board with four labels: *Spring, Summer, Fall, Winter.* Have children discuss their drawings.

Conventions
Animal Sentences

Materials: paper, writing tools, crayons

Animal Adventures As a class, discuss different adventures animals can have, such as *climb trees.* Write these phrases on the board. On a sheet of paper, have children turn the sentence parts into complete sentences. If needed, provide the sentence parts *Animals can* and *Animals like to*.

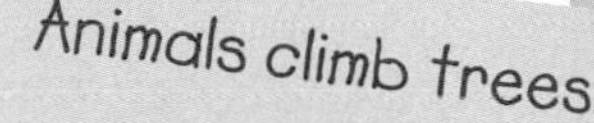

Comprehension
What Comes Next?

Sequence Have children participate in songs with actions, such as "The Hokey Pokey" or "Head, Shoulders, Knees, and Toes," that require children to follow a leader. Lead them in a round of singing and moving. Then have a child be a leader for the song and its movements. Discuss the order of the actions in the song with children and how they must match the order of the words in the song.

DAY 5 Wrap Up your Week

10–15 mins.

Objectives

- Review the concepts.
- Build oral vocabulary.

Today at a Glance

Oral Vocabulary
woodland, nest, vale, hollow, comfortable, shadows

Phonemic Awareness
◉ Initial and Final Blends

Phonics
◉ Initial and Final Blends

Comprehension
◉ Sequence

Conventions
Complete Sentences

Writing
This Week We . . .

Check Oral Vocabulary
SUCCESS PREDICTOR

TRUCKTOWN on Reading Street

Start your engines! Display "Three Loud Trucks" and lead the group in saying the rhyme a few times.

- Have half the group recite the rhyme while the other half acts it out.
- Have half the group recite the rhyme while the other half acts it out.
- Then have the groups change roles.

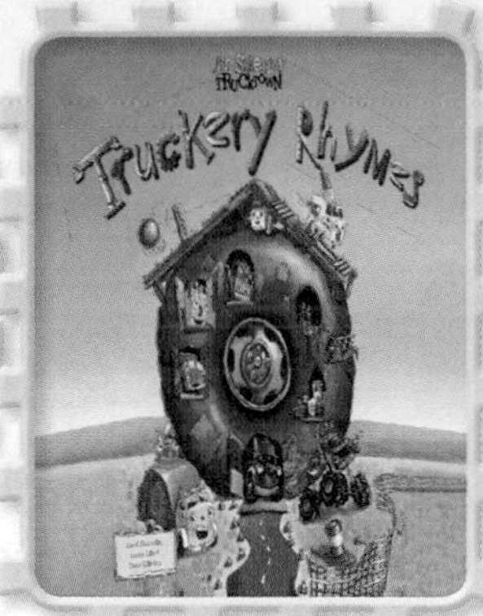

Truckery Rhymes

Concept Wrap Up

Question of the Week

What adventures can animals have?

Listen for Amazing Words

Write the question of the week on the board. Track the print as you read it to children. Have them use Amazing Words in complete sentences in their responses (*woodland, nest, vale, hollow, comfortable, shadows*). Display Sing with Me Chart 21B. Let's sing "A New Woodland Nest." I want you to listen for the Amazing Words we learned this week. Say them with me: *woodland, nest, vale, hollow, comfortable, shadows.* Sing the song several times to the tune of "Hickory, Dickory, Dock." Have children sing with you. Remind children to speak one at a time.

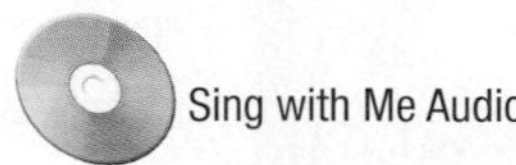
Sing with Me Audio

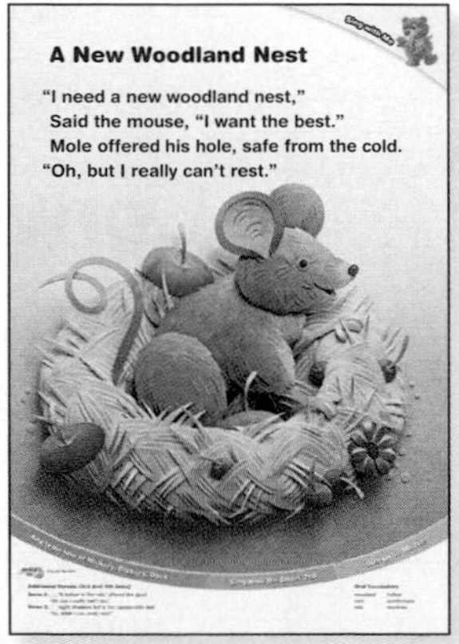

Sing with Me Chart 21B

ELL Check Concepts and Language Use the Day 5 instruction on ELL Poster 21 to monitor children's understanding of the lesson concept.

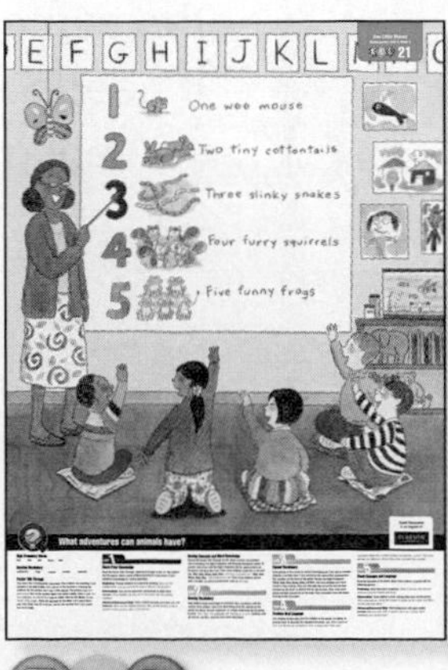
ELL Poster 21

Oral Vocabulary
Amazing Words

Talk with Me/Sing with Me Chart 21A

Review

Let's Talk Display Talk with Me Chart 21A. We learned six new Amazing Words this week, and we have learned 126 new Amazing Words this year! Let's look at the chart again. Point to each picture and give children the chance to say the appropriate Amazing Word before offering it.

Have children supply the appropriate Amazing Word to complete each sentence.

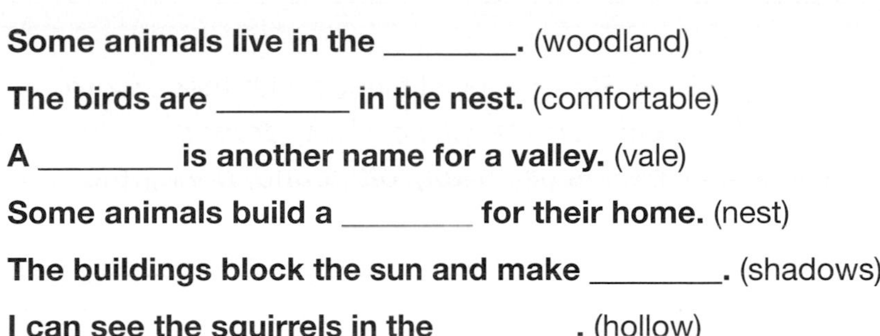
Some animals live in the ________. (woodland)

The birds are ________ in the nest. (comfortable)

A ________ is another name for a valley. (vale)

Some animals build a ________ for their home. (nest)

The buildings block the sun and make ________. (shadows)

I can see the squirrels in the ________. (hollow)

Amazing Words

woodland	nest
vale	hollow
comfortable	shadows

Differentiated Instruction

Advanced

Amazing Words Have children write or dictate their own sentence using one of this week's Amazing Words.

It's Friday

MONITOR PROGRESS Check Oral Vocabulary

Demonstrate Word Knowledge Monitor the Amazing Words by asking the following questions. Have children use the Amazing Word in their answer.

- **What kind of home do some animals build to live in?** (nest)
- **What is another name for a valley?** (vale)
- **How do you feel if you are warm and cozy?** (comfortable)
- **What is another name for a hole in a tree?** (hollow)
- **What is another name for a forest?** (woodland)
- **What do you make when light is blocked?** (shadows)

If... children have difficulty using the Amazing Words,
then... reteach the words using the Oral Vocabulary Routine on the Routines Flip Chart.

Day 1	Day 2	Day 3	Day 4	Day 5
Check Phonemic Awareness	Check Sound-Spelling/ Retelling	Check Word Reading	Check Phonemic Awareness	Check Oral Vocabulary

Objectives

- Review initial and final blends.
- Connect sounds in blends to letters.

Phonemic Awareness Review
Sounds for Blends

Isolate blends Display the *dress* Picture Card. What is the blend at the beginning of *dress?* Say the sounds with me: /d/ /r/, /dr/. Review initial blends using the words *slip, plan, clap, flip, crib, stop, trip,* and *spin.* Show the *desk* Picture Card. Say the word *desk,* emphasizing the final blend. The word *desk* ends with /s/ /k/, /sk/. Review final blends using the words *cost, lift, milk,* and *land.*

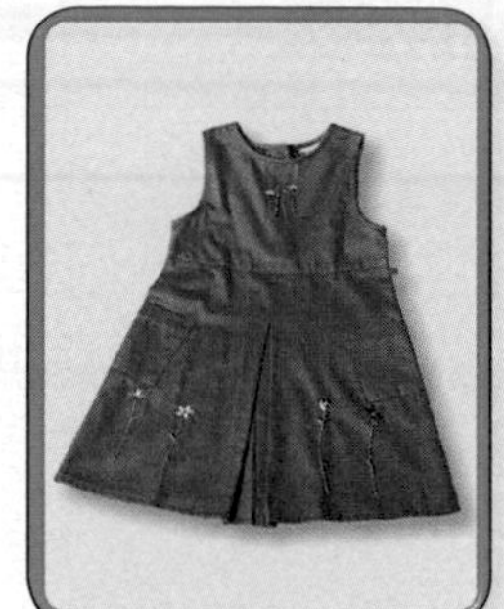

Picture Card

Discriminate blends Say the words *space* and *spoon*. Do these words begin with the same blended sound? Say the words with me: /sp/ *-ace,* /sp/ *-oon.* Yes, they begin with the same blended sound. Review initial blends with these word pairs: *cloud, clay; please, plane; draw, drop; train, truck.* Review final blends using *left, loft; round, bond;* and *last, rest.*

Picture Card

Phonics Review

Spellings for Blends

Connect sounds to blends

Display the *crab* Picture Card. What is the name of this animal? What is the blend at the beginning of the word *crab?* (/kr/) What letters stand for this blend? (*cr*) Write the letters *c* and *r.* Repeat with the following words: *drum, stand, spoon, desk, ask, trip, plan.*

Picture Card

High-frequency words

Write *five* on the board. This is the word *five.* What is this word? Repeat for *one, two, three,* and *four.*

Apply phonics to familiar text

Let's Reread Have children reread one of the books specific to the target letter sounds. Review the decodable words and high-frequency words in each book prior to rereading.

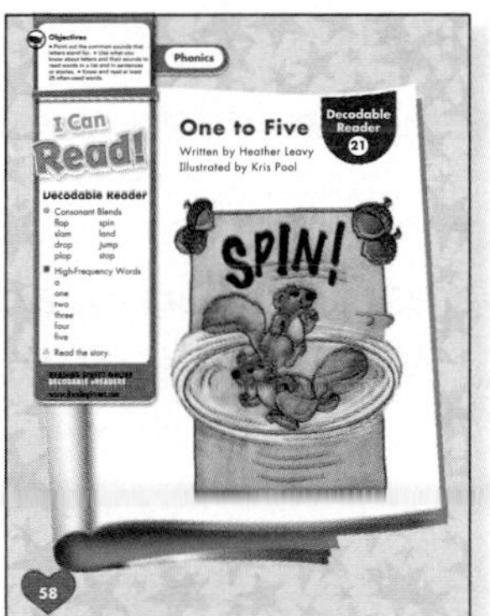

Decodable Reader 21
My Skills Buddy, p. 58

Kindergarten Student
Reader K.4.3

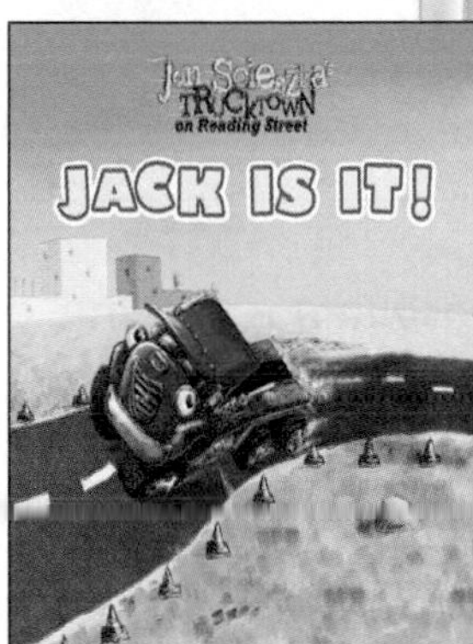

Get Set, Roll!
Reader 21

Small Group Time

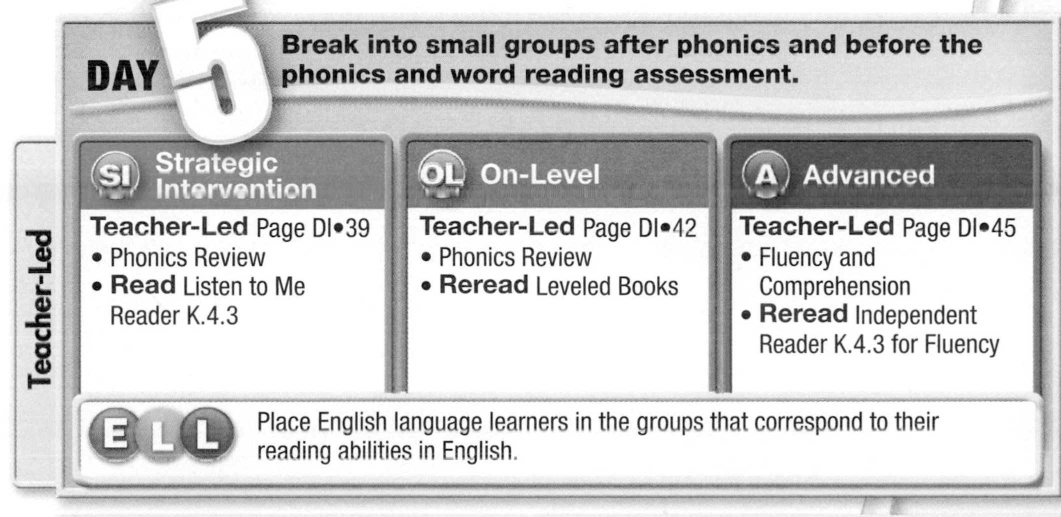

DAY 5 Break into small groups after phonics and before the phonics and word reading assessment.

Teacher-Led

SI Strategic Intervention	OL On-Level	A Advanced
Teacher-Led Page DI•39 • Phonics Review • **Read** Listen to Me Reader K.4.3	**Teacher-Led** Page DI•42 • Phonics Review • **Reread** Leveled Books	**Teacher-Led** Page DI•45 • Fluency and Comprehension • **Reread** Independent Reader K.4.3 for Fluency

ELL Place English language learners in the groups that correspond to their reading abilities in English.

Practice Stations
- Visit the Read for Meaning Station
- Visit the Let's Make Art Station

Independent Activities
- Read independently
- Story Sort
- Concept Talk Video

Differentiated Instruction

 Strategic Intervention

Sentence Production As children reread one of the books, have them identify the naming part and action part in each sentence. Have them point out the uppercase letters and ending punctuation marks.

English Language Learners

Pronounce *r* The consonant *r* is pronounced differently in English and Spanish. Help children practice the pronunciation of English words that have initial blends with *r.*

Assess

- ◎ Read words with consonant blends
- Read high-frequency words.
- Read sentences.

Assessment
Monitor Progress

Consonant blends

Whole Class Divide a paper into fourths for each child. When I say a word, write the blend you hear in that word in one of the boxes. The blends may be at the beginning or at the end of the words, so listen carefully: *stop, crab, milk, band.* Say the words slowly and repeat, emphasizing the blends.

MONITOR PROGRESS | **Check Word and Sentence Reading**

If… children cannot complete the whole-class assessment,
then… use the Reteach lesson in *First Stop*.

If… you are unsure of a child's grasp of this week's skills,
then… use the assessment below to obtain a clearer evaluation of the child's progress.

Consonant blends and high-frequency words

One-on-One To facilitate individual progress monitoring, assess some children on Day 4 and the rest on Day 5. While individual children are being assessed, the rest of the class can read this week's books and look for words with consonant blends.

Word reading

Use the word lists on reproducible p. 295 to assess a child's ability to read words with blends and high-frequency words. We're going to read some words. I'll read the first word, and you read the rest. The first word is *one.* For each child, record any decoding problems.

Sentence reading

Use the sentences on reproducible p. 295 to assess a child's ability to read words in sentences. Have each child read two sentences aloud. Have each child read different sentences. Start over with sentence one if necessary.

Record Scores

Monitor children's accuracy by recording their scores using the Word and Sentence Reading Chart for this unit in *First Stop*.

Name ______________________________

Read the Words

one	☐	trap	☐
spot	☐	four	☐
two	☐	hand	☐
crib	☐	five	☐
three	☐	mask	☐
flat	☐	clap	☐

Read the Sentences

1. I have one raft.

2. We can see three drops.

3. Two fast cats are with me.

4. Five masks are a lot.

5. Look at the four plants.

Note to Teacher: Children read each word. Children read two sentences.

Scoring for Read the Words: Score 1 point for each correct word.

Consonant Blends (*spot, crib, flat, trap, hand, mask, clap*) _______ / 7

High-Frequency Words (*one, two, three, four, five*) _______ / 5

MONITOR PROGRESS

- Consonant blends
- High-frequency words

DAY 5 Wrap Up your Week

10–15 mins.

Objectives

- Recognize a set of directions.
- Identify steps in directions.

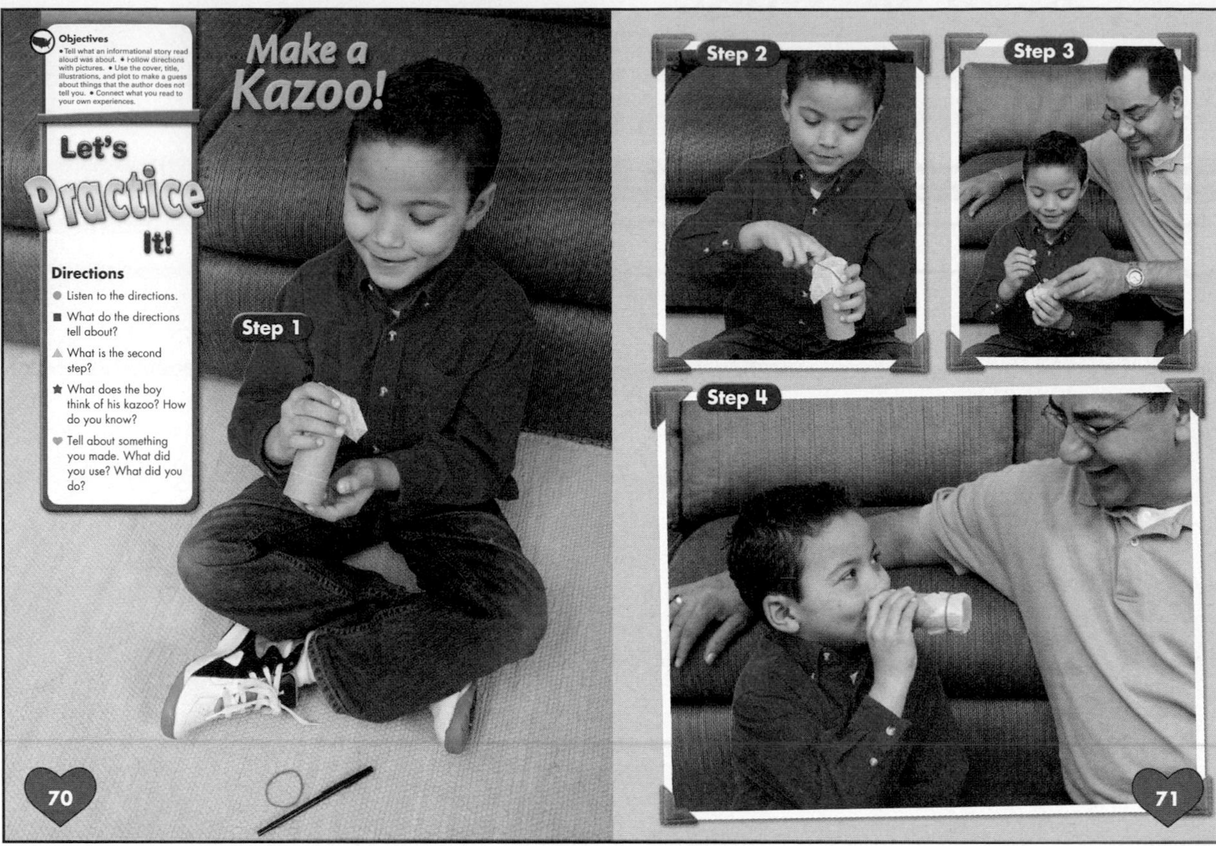

My Skills Buddy, pp. 70–71

Let's Practice It!
Directions

Teach

Today I will read you directions for making an instrument called a kazoo. Directions are steps that tell us how to do or make something. Explain the following features of directions with children:

- Directions tell us how to do or make something.
- Directions have numbered steps.
- Directions must be done in order.

Have children turn to p. 70 of *My Skills Buddy*. I am going to read a selection called "Make a Kazoo!" Look at the pictures as I read. Read the text of "Make a Kazoo!" As you read, direct children to look at the appropriate picture. Point out the numbered steps.

Guide practice Discuss the features of directions with children and the bulleted text on *My Skills Buddy*, p. 70.

- Directions tell us how to do or make something. What do these directions tell us how to do or make? (They tell us how to make a kazoo.)
- Directions have numbered steps. What is Step 4 in these directions? (Hum into the tube.)
- Directions must be done in order. What should you do first when making a kazoo? (Wrap waxed paper over one end of a cardboard tube.)
- We can use directions to tell how to do many things. Pretend you are giving directions on brushing your teeth. What should you do first when brushing your teeth? (Put toothpaste on the toothbrush.)

Differentiated Instruction

Advanced

Support Directions Have children give directions for how to do or make something, such as how to make their bed or tie their shoes.

Make a Kazoo

Here's how you can make a musical instrument called a kazoo.

Here's what you'll need:

- cardboard tube from a bathroom tissue roll
- 4-inch square of waxed paper
- rubber band
- ballpoint pen

Here's what to do:

1. Wrap the waxed paper square over one end of the cardboard tube.

2. Put the rubber band around the tube and over the waxed paper to hold the paper in place.

3. Use the pen to make a hole in the tube just past the waxed paper.

4. Hold the open end of the cardboard tube to your mouth. Hum a tune into the tube.

If you and several friends make kazoos, you can have a kazoo band!

Objectives
◎ Review sequence.

Assess
◎ Identify sequence.

Comprehension Assessment
Monitor Progress

Review

Sequence You have learned that stories are told in a certain order. Something happens first, next, and last. This is called the sequence. What do we call the order in which things happen?

Good readers pay attention to the sequence to help them understand a story.

Read "The Tale of Peter Rabbit"

Tell children that you are going to read a story about a young rabbit that gets in trouble one day. Tell them to listen to the order in which things happen. Listen carefully. I am going to read you a story and then have you tell me what happened in the correct order. Read "The Tale of Peter Rabbit" on p. 48 of the *Read Aloud Anthology*.

Read Aloud Anthology

Check sequence

After you read the story, have children identify the sequence of events.

- What does Peter do first? (Peter goes to Mr. McGregor's garden.)
- What does he do next? (Peter eats vegetables from the garden.)
- Then what does Peter do? (Peter runs through Mr. McGregor's garden trying to get away from him.)
- What does Peter do last? (Peter finally gets out of the garden to go home, where his mother gives him medicine because he is sick.)

Corrective feedback

If... children cannot identify events that happen first, next, then, and last,
then... reteach sequence in *First Stop*.

Assess sequence

Use the blackline master found on p. 299. Make one copy for each child. Have children cut out the three scenes and glue them to another sheet of paper in the correct order. Have children label the scenes 1, 2, or 3.

Name ______________________________

Sequence

Put events from "The Tale of Peter Rabbit" in order.

Note to Teacher: Have children cut out the scenes from the story and glue them onto another paper in sequential order. Have them label the sequence 1–3.

MONITOR PROGRESS

- Sequence

DAY 5 Wrap Up your Week

10–15 mins.

Objectives

- Review complete sentences.
- Write or dictate sentences.

Conventions
Complete Sentences

Review Remind children of what they learned about complete sentences. A complete sentence must start with an uppercase letter and end with a punctuation mark. A complete sentence has a naming part and an action part.

Model Display the *tent* Picture Card. This is a picture of a *tent*. I can say a complete sentence about a tent. *The campers sleep in a tent*. *The campers* is the naming part and *sleep in a tent* is the action part.

Guide practice Have children recall the animals they have read or heard about this week. We have read about a mouse looking for a house and Flap the Cat, and heard about Peter Rabbit. Let's make some sentences about the animals we have read about. Have a volunteer name an animal for the naming part of the sentence and have another child complete the sentence by giving the action part. Write both parts on the board. Have children tell you where to write an uppercase letter and where to add a punctuation mark.

On their own Have children use a complete sentence to tell about an animal they have seen. Have them tell the naming part and the action part in their sentences.

Daily Fix-It Use the Daily Fix-It exercise for more conventions practice.

Writing
This Week We...

Review Display *One Little Mouse,* Sing with Me Chart 21B, Phonics Songs and Rhymes Chart 21, Decodable Reader 21 from *My Skills Buddy,* Kindergarten Student Reader K.4.3, and Get Set, Roll! Reader 21. We read new books and we sang new songs about animal adventures this week. Which book or song was your favorite? My favorite was *One Little Mouse*. Let's share our ideas with each other.

Team Talk Pair children and have them take turns telling which book or song was their favorite and why.

Model writing complete sentences Today we will write about our favorite animals and what they did in the stories or songs.

> **The mouse looks for a house.**
>
> **The frog hops.**
>
> **The rabbit goes to bed.**

Guide practice Continue making sentences with children. Make sure children dictate complete sentences. Read sentences with children, having them echo read after you.

On their own Have children copy the sentence they dictated and illustrate it. Remind children to start their sentences with an uppercase letter and end it with an ending punctuation mark. Collect the sentences for a class book about animal adventures.

Daily Handwriting

Write 5 and *five* on the board. Review correct formation of the numeral 5 and the lowercase letters *f, i, v,* and *e*.

Have children write 5 and *five* on their Write-On Boards. Remind them to use proper left-to-right and top-to-bottom progression and proper spacing between letters when writing 5 and *five*.

Differentiated Instruction

Advanced

Making Connections Have children tell something that was the same about two of this week's selections.

Daily Fix-It

the mouse fell in the hole

The mouse fell in the hole.

This week's practice sentences appear on Teacher Resources DVD-ROM.

English Language Learners

Poster Preview Prepare children for next week by using Week 4 ELL Poster number 22. Read the Poster Talk-Through to introduce the concept and vocabulary. Ask children to identify and describe objects and actions they see.

Objectives
- Review weekly concept.
- Review sequence.

Wrap Up Your Week!

Question of the Week
What adventures can animals have?

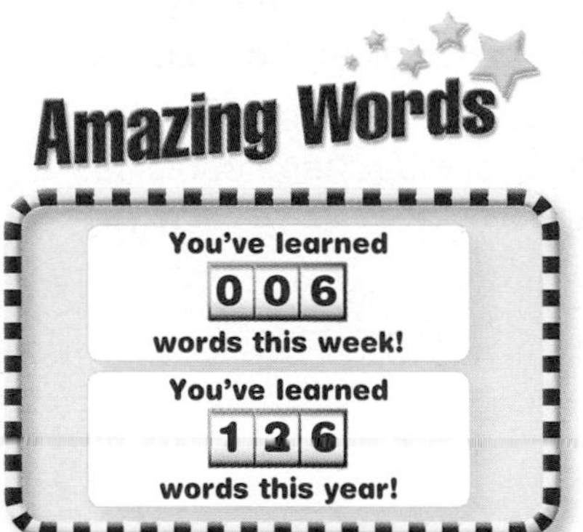

Illustrate sequence

This week we talked, read, and sang about animals having adventures.

- Use a graphic organizer to record what happens in the beginning, middle, and end of *One Little Mouse*.
- When the entire chart has been completed, have children echo read it with you.

Beginning
Middle
End

Next Week's Question
How can an adventure cause trouble?

Discuss next week's question. Guide children in making connections between adventures animals can have and adventures people can have.

Science
Animal Movement

Materials: books showing pictures of animals, chart paper, markers

Study Animals Show pictures of a variety of animals. Explain that each animal moves in its own unique way. Tell children to look at the pictures of these animals and to think of other animals.

- Which animals swim?
- Which animals crawl?
- Which animals fly?
- Which animals climb?
- Which animals hop?

Make a Chart Record children's answers to each question in a chart. Which animals move in more than one way? Have children imitate the movement of each animal in the chart.

swim	crawl	fly	climb	hop
fish	bug	bird	cat	rabbit
shark				
whale				

Math
Animal Addition

Materials: copies of small pictures of animals, paper, pencil

Add Animals Give children a set of animal pictures. Tell them to select two pictures and place them in front of them. Then tell children to select three more pictures and place them below the other two. Have children tell how many animal pictures they have. You may wish to write the problem on the board to show children the addition fact: $2 + 3 = 5$. Continue giving other addition problems.

Comprehension
Where Is Mouse?

Materials: Big Book *One Little Mouse,* chart paper, drawing or writing utensils

Trace Mouse's Travels Draw a long path on a sheet of mural paper. Sketch a mouse head at the beginning of the path on the left side of the paper. Discuss Mouse's travels in *One Little Mouse*. Have children mark off spaces along the path to show all the places the little mouse travels. Then have children draw animals and locations on the map in the order in which the mouse goes to each house.

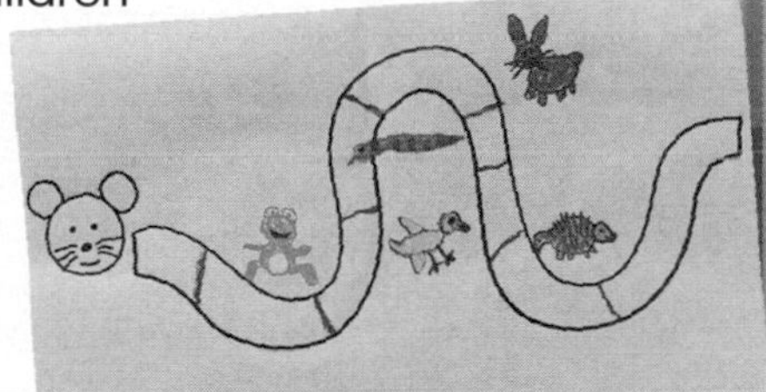

Assessment Checkpoints for the Week

Weekly Assessment

Use the whole-class assessment on pages 294–295 and 298–299 in this Teacher's Edition to check:

- ✔ **Consonant Blends**
- ✔ **Comprehension Skill** *Sequence*
- ✔ **High-Frequency Words**

one	*two*	*three*
four	*five*	

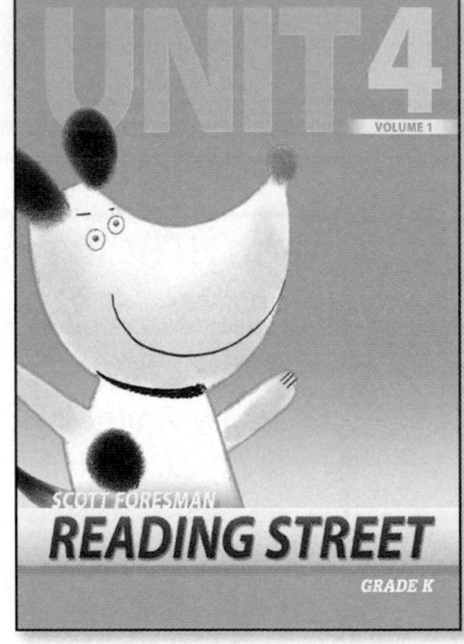

Teacher's Edition, Day 5

Managing Assessment

Use the Assessment Handbook for:

- ✔ **Observation Checklists**
- ✔ **Record-Keeping Forms**
- ✔ **Portfolio Assessment**

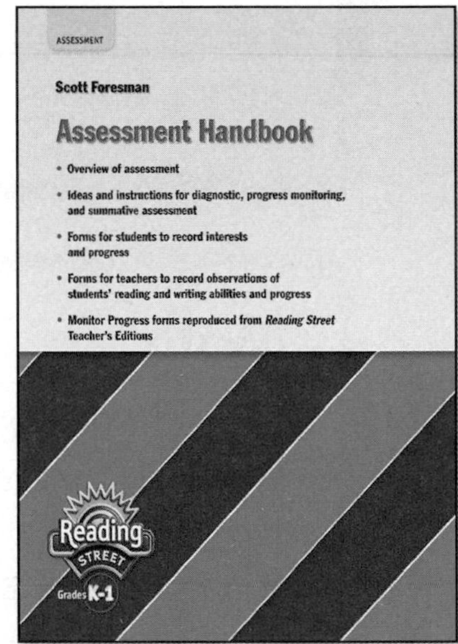

Assessment Handbook

Teacher Notes

Pacing Small Group Instruction

5 Day Plan

DAY 1	• Phonemic Awareness/ Phonics • Decodable Story 21
DAY 2	• Phonemic Awareness/ Phonics • Decodable Reader 21
DAY 3	• Phonemic Awareness/ Phonics • Concept Literacy Reader K.4.3 or Kindergarten Student Reader K.4.3
DAY 4	• Phonemic Awareness/ Phonics • Get Set, Roll! Reader 21
DAY 5	• Phonics Review • Listen to Me Reader K.4.3

3 or 4 Day Plan

DAY 1	• Phonemic Awareness/ Phonics • Decodable Story 21
DAY 2	• Phonemic Awareness/ Phonics • Decodable Reader 21
DAY 3	• Phonemic Awareness/ Phonics • Concept Literacy Reader K.4.3 or Kindergarten Student Reader K.4.3
DAY 4	• Phonemic Awareness/ Phonics • Get Set, Roll! Reader 21

3 Day Plan: Eliminate the shaded box.

DAY 1

Phonemic Awareness • Phonics

- **Isolate Initial Blends** Display the *playground* Picture Card. This is a playground. *Playground* begins with a blend. A blend is two letters whose sounds are blended together to make a sound. What is the beginning sound in *playground?* *Playground* begins with /pl/. Say it with me: /p/ /l/ /pl/, *playground.* What two letters blend together to make /pl/? (*p* and *l*) Repeat with *block, flag, glove, cloud,* and *sled*.
- **Discriminate Blends** I am going to say two words. I want you to tell me which word begins with a two-letter blend. Listen carefully: *plan, pan.* Which word begins with a blend? *Plan* begins with the blend /pl/. Pan does not begin with a blend. Continue discriminating initial blends with the following sets of words: *lip, flip; clap, cap; play, pay; sip, slip; love, glove; block, lock.*

Decodable Story 21

- **Review** Review the high-frequency words *one, two, three, I, have, see, like, is, you,* and *do.* Write each word on the board and have children read the word with you.

  If... children have difficulty reading the words,
  then... say a word and have children point to the word. Repeat several times, giving assistance as needed.

- **Read** Have children read the story orally. Then have them reread the story several times individually.

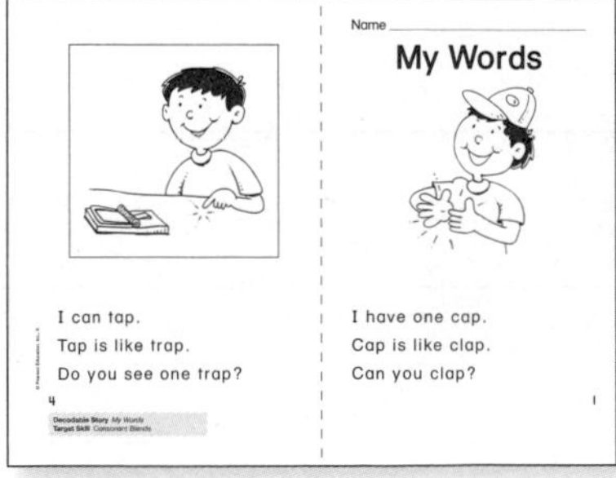

I can tap.
Tap is like trap.
Do you see one trap?
4

Name

My Words

I have one cap.
Cap is like clap.
Can you clap?
1

Reader's and Writer's Notebook, pp. 267–268

Objectives

- Isolate the initial sound in spoken one-syllable words.
- Read at least 25 high-frequency words from a commonly used list.

DAY 2

Phonemic Awareness • Phonics

- **Discriminate Blends** Display Phonics Songs and Rhymes Chart 21. Sing "Sliding Down the Slippery Slope" to the tune of "Jack and Jill Went Up the Hill" with children. When we go down a slide, sometimes we make a sound—like *Weeeee*—to show we are having fun. When you hear a blend, say *Weeeee.*
- **Recognize Blends** List the words *bran, crop, drip, free, grin, slid,* plop, and *glad* on the board. Circle the initial blend in each word. What are the names of these letters? What is the sound of these letters together? The word is *bran*. What two letters does *bran* begin with? What is the sound for that blend? Continue with the other words.

Decodable Reader 21

- **Review** Review the high-frequency words by writing *one* on the board. This is the word *one.* What word is this? Continue with the following words: *two, three, four, five, a.*

  If... children have difficulty reading the words,
  then... say a word and have children point to the word. Repeat several times, giving assistance as needed.

- **Read** Display the cover of *One to Five* on p. 58 of *My Skills Buddy.* Ask a volunteer to read the first page of the story. Have children tell how many animals are on the page. Continue through the story in this manner.

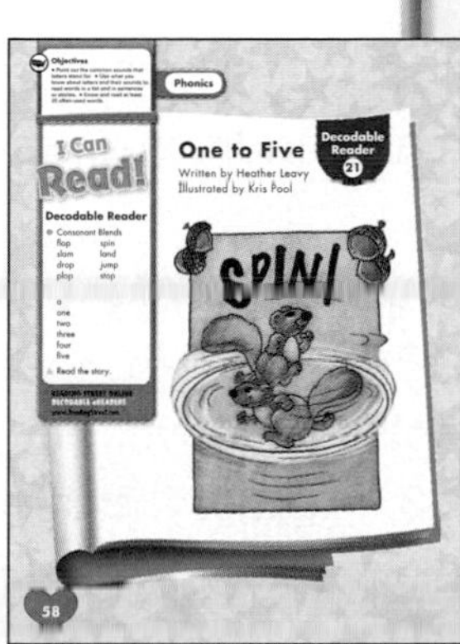

My Skills Buddy

Objectives

- Identify the common sounds that letters represent.
- Read at least 25 high-frequency words from a commonly used list.

More Reading

Use Leveled Readers or other text at children's instructional level.

Phonemic Awareness • Phonics

- **Isolate Final Blends** Display the *desk* Picture Card. This is a *desk. Desk* ends with the blend /sk/. Say it with me: /d/ /e/ /sk/, *desk.* The blend /sk/ is made up of /s/ and /k/. Repeat with these words: *lamp, tent, quilt, vest, mask.*
- **Discriminate Blends** Display the *mask* Picture Card. This is a *mask*. *Mask* has a blend at the end of the word. It is a blend of /s/ and /k/. Say it with me: /s/ /k/, /sk/. Say the word with me: /m/ /a/ /sk/, *mask*. Demonstrate for children how to make a finger mask by making two "okay" signs with your hands and putting them in front of your eyes. When you hear a word that ends with /sk/, I want you to make a finger mask. Use the following words: *west, ask, say, sand, left, right, task, milk, juice, desk, find, one, first.*
- **Blend Sounds** Write *skip* on the board. Have children blend the sound of each letter to read the word. Repeat the routine with the words *milk* and *flip.*
- **Review High-Frequency Words** Write *two* on the board. Have volunteers say the word and use it in a sentence. Continue with the words *three, four, five,* and *one.*
- To practice phonics and high-frequency words, have children read Kindergarten Student Reader K.4.3. Use the Instruction on pp. 254–255.

For a complete lesson plan and additional practice, see the **Leveled Reader Teaching Guide**.

Concept Literacy Reader K.4.3

- **Preview and Predict** Display the cover of the Concept Literacy Reader K.4.3. Point to the title of the book. The title of the book is *Animal Adventures.* What do you think the book is about? Can animals have the same adventures as us? Have children tell about the picture and what they think the book might be about.
- **Set a Purpose** We talked about the title and the cover of the book. Let's read the book to find out what real animals can do. Have children read the Concept Literacy Reader.
- **Read** Provide corrective feedback as children read the book orally. During reading, ask them if they were able to confirm any of the predictions they made prior to reading.

If... children have difficulty reading the book individually,
then... read a sentence aloud as children point to each word. Then have the group reread the sentences as they continue pointing to the words.

- **Retell** Have children retell the content as you page through the book. Help them identify what the book is about. Ask children to discuss whether they can do the same things as the animals in the book.

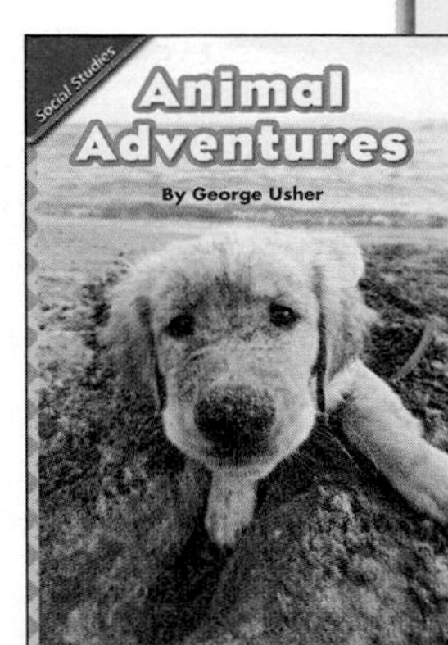

Concept Literacy Reader K.4.3

Objectives

- Identify the common sounds that letters represent.
- Predict what might happen next based on the cover.
- Predict what might happen next based on the title.

DAY 4

Phonemic Awareness • Phonics

- **Say a Rhyme** Say the following rhyme for children several times. Then have them clap when they hear an initial blend.

  Clip and clop, clip and clop,
  Feet are marching, never stop.

- Write the following rhyme on the board. Read it aloud. Have children identify the initial and final blends. What is the blend in *skip?* What letters blend to make that sound? Continue with *left, best,* and *rest.*

  Skip left, skip best,
  Skip better than the rest.

- **Segmenting** Say *hand.* I hear four sounds in *hand,* /h/ /a/ /n/ /d/. /n/ and /d/ make a final blend, /nd/. Let's blend the word, /h/ /a/ /nd/, *hand.* How many sounds do you hear in *flap?* What are they? What is the blend in *flap?* (four; /f/ /l/ /a/ /p/; /fl/) Repeat the procedure with *slim, drip, span, pump,* and *mask.*

Get Set, Roll! Reader 21

- **Review** Review the following high-frequency words with children prior to reading the story: *look, one, two, three, four, five.*
- **Review Names** Write the names *Jack, Dan, Melvin,* and *Gabriella* on the board. Read each word aloud. Show a picture of each truck. Look for these words in the story today. A picture above the word will help you read it.
- **Read** Display Get Set, Roll! Reader 21, *Jack Is It!* Point to the title of the story. What is the title of the story? *Jack Is It!* is the title of the story. Look at the picture and think about the title. What do you think this story will be about?

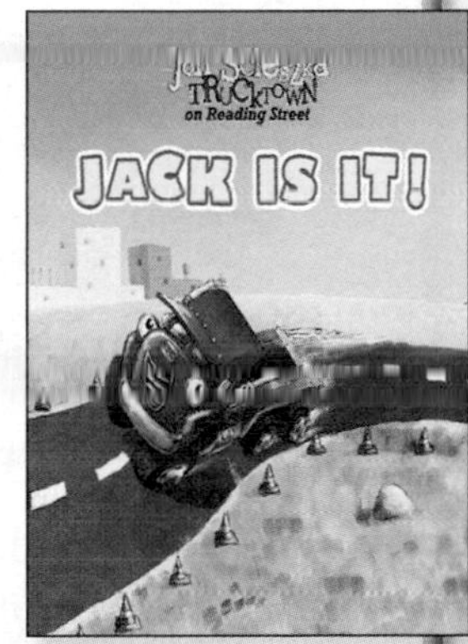

Get Set, Roll! Reader 21

  If... children have difficulty reading the story individually,
  then... read a sentence aloud as children point to each word. Then have the group reread the sentences as they continue pointing to the words.

- **Reread** Use echo reading of Get Set, Roll! Reader 21 to model fluent reading. Use your oral reading to model for children where to pause, when to change pitch, and which words to stress. Then have children reread orally three to four times, or until they can read with few or no mistakes.

Objectives

- Read at least 25 high-frequency words from a commonly used list.
- Predict what might happen next based on the cover.
- Predict what might happen next based on the title.

More Reading

Use Leveled Readers or other text at children's instructional level.

More Reading

Use Leveled Readers or other text at children's instructional level.

Phonics Review

- **Recognize Blends** Write the words *slip* and *sip* on the board. Name the letters in each word. Then ask the class why the words are different. Remind children that for *slip* we blend the sounds of the first two letters, *s* and *l*, to make /sl/.
- **Connect Sounds to Letters** Write *Cc* and *Ll* on the board. What are the names of these letters? What sound do these letters make when they are blended together? Name some words that begin with /kl/. Repeat the routine with /sl/, /gl/, /pl/, /st/, /tr/, and /sp/.

Listen to Me Reader K.4.3

- **Preview and Predict** Display the cover of the book. The title of this story is *Five of Us!* It is written by Susan Yuen. How many children are on the cover? Point to each child as you count him or her. What do you think these five children will do in this story?
- **Set a Purpose** Review children's ideas. Point out that after they read, they will know if they predicted correctly. Tell children that you will read the story with them. Follow along with your finger as I read. Then we will take turns reading this page. Repeat this routine through all of the pages. Guide children to decode words.

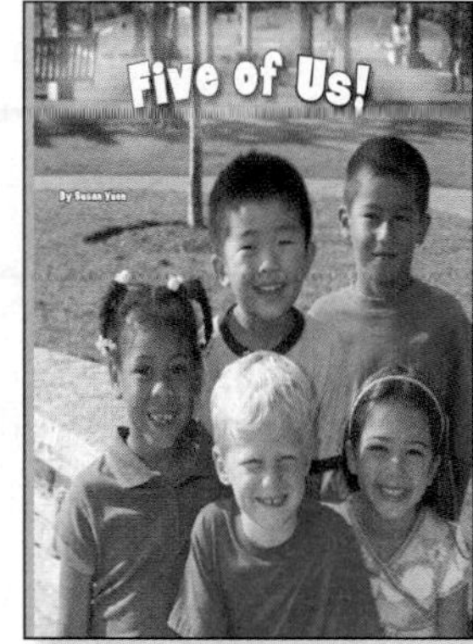

Listen to Me Reader K.4.3

- **Reread for Fluency** Use echo reading of Listen to Me Reader K.4.3 to model reading fluently. Use your oral reading to model for children when to pause, when to change pitch, and which words to stress. Then have children reread orally three to four times, or until they can read with few or no mistakes.

Objectives

- Identify the common sounds that letters represent.
- Predict what might happen next based on the cover.

OL On-Level DAY 1

Phonemic Awareness • Phonics

- **Recognize Blends** Display the *black* Picture Card. This is the color black. The word *black* begins with the blend /bl/. What letters make the blend /bl/? Show children these Picture Cards and have them say each word: *crab, frog, cloud, dress,* and *star.* List the words on chart paper as they say them. Have children echo read the list of words. Then ask children to take turns circling the initial blends in the words on the chart.

Objectives

- Identify the common sounds that letters represent.

OL On-Level DAY 2

Phonemic Awareness • Phonics

- **Listen for Blends** Tell children you will tell them a story and they should listen for initial blends. When you say a word with two-letter blends, children should clap and repeat the word. Tell a simple story, emphasizing the initial blend words and pausing to give children a chance to clap, repeat the word, and name the letters that make the blend. *Grace plans* to take a *trip*. She puts on her *pretty blue dress*. On her *trip*, *Grace* gets to *climb* at a *playground*. She *plays* on the *slide* with her *friends*. When it is time to *fly* back to *Cleveland*, *Grace cleans* up *slowly*. It has been a fun *trip!*

- **High-Frequency Words** Display the following word cards: *one, two, three, four, five, do, that, are.* Say the word *two* and select a child to point to the word. Have children say the word and use it in a sentence. Continue with the other words.

Objectives

- Isolate the initial sound in spoken one-syllable words.
- Read at least 25 high-frequency words from a commonly used list.

Pacing Small Group Instruction

20–30 mins.

5 Day Plan

DAY 1	• Phonemic Awareness/ Phonics • Decodable Story 21
DAY 2	• Phonemic Awareness/ Phonics • High-Frequency Words • Decodable Reader 21
DAY 3	• Phonemic Awareness/ Phonics • Kindergarten Student Reader K.4.3
DAY 4	• Get Set, Roll! Reader 21
DAY 5	• Phonics Review • **Reread** Leveled Books

3 or 4 Day Plan

DAY 1	• Phonemic Awareness/ Phonics • Decodable Story 21
DAY 2	• Phonemic Awareness/ Phonics • High-Frequency Words • Decodable Reader 21
DAY 3	• Phonemic Awareness/ Phonics • Kindergarten Student Reader K.4.3
DAY 4	• Get Set, Roll! Reader 21

3 Day Plan: Eliminate the shaded box.

More Practice

For additional practice with this week's phonics skills, have children reread the Decodable Story (Day 1) and the Decodable Reader (Day 2).

Phonemic Awareness • Phonics

- **Act It Out** Write the following action words on index cards: *skip, spin, drop, stop, clap, stand, hop, sit, tap.* Mix the cards and show one card at a time. Have children read the word and do the action only if the word has a two-letter initial blend. Continue until children are able to read and do the action fluently.

Kindergarten Student Reader K.4.3

- **Preview and Predict** Display the cover of the book. The title of this story is *A Home for Flap.* Look at the cover. Who is Flap? What kind of home do you think Flap needs? Tell me your ideas.

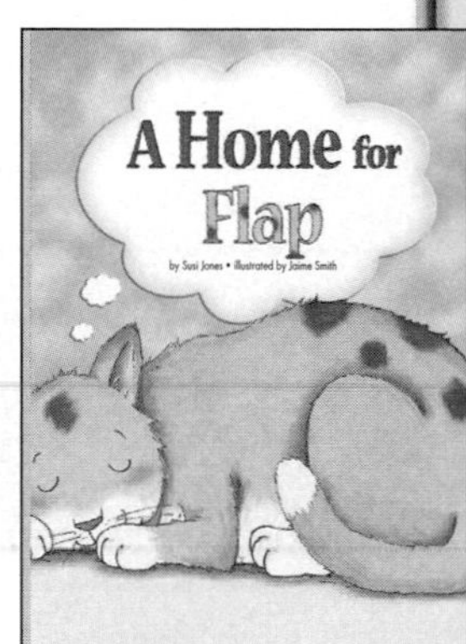

Kindergarten Student Reader K.4.3

- **Set a Purpose** Review the list of things children think might happen in the story. Remind children that setting a purpose for reading can help them better understand the story. Guide children to pay attention to what Flap does.
- **Read** Have children follow along as they read the story with you. After reading p. 3, ask children to tell why they think Nan and Nat stop for Flap. Continue with each page. Ask the following questions:
  - How many times do Nan and Nat clap for Flap?
  - How many times does Flap sip the drops?
  - How many spots does Flap have?
- **Summarize** Have children retell the story to a partner and tell what Flap does in the story.
- **Text to Self** Help children make personal connections to the story as they tell what kind of pet they have or would like to have.

Objectives

- Predict what might happen next based on the cover.
- Predict what might happen next based on the title.
- Make connections to own experiences.

eReaders

DAY 4

Get Set, Roll! Reader 21

- **Review** Review the words *look, is, one, two, three, four,* and *five* by writing each word on the board and saying the word with children. Then give clues to a word and have children tell which word it is.
- **Review Rebus Words** Write *Melvin* on the board and read the word with children. This name is *Melvin.* What kind of truck is Melvin? He is a cement mixer. Continue with the names *Jack, Gabriella,* and *Dan.* Remember, there will be a picture above the words to help us read them.
- **Read** Display Get Set, Roll! Reader 21, *Jack Is It!* Point to the title of the story. What is the title of the story? *Jack Is It!* is the title of the story. Let's read the story together.

Objectives

- Read at least 25 high-frequency words from a commonly used list.

More Reading

Use Leveled Readers or other text at children's instructional level to develop fluency.

Phonics Review

- **Blend and Bend** Give children chenille sticks. Gather the following Picture Cards: *blue, crab, dress, fan, flag, grapes, mug, nut, playground, six, spoon, starfish, train.* If the words have two-letter initial blends, have children bend the chenille sticks into the letters for that blend. If the words do not have initial blends, have them make the chenille sticks straight.

Objectives

- Identify the common sounds that letters represent.

Small Group Time

Pacing Small Group Instruction

20–30 mins.

5 Day Plan

DAY 1	• Phonemic Awareness/ Phonics • Decodable Story 21
DAY 2	• Phonics • Spelling • Decodable Reader 21
DAY 3	• Independent Reader K.4.3 or Kindergarten Student Reader K.4.3
DAY 4	• Get Set, Roll! Reader 21 or Kindergarten Student Reader K.4.3
DAY 5	• Fluency/ Comprehension • Independent Reader K.4.3

3 or 4 Day Plan

DAY 1	• Phonemic Awareness/ Phonics • Decodable Story 21
DAY 2	• Phonics • Spelling • Decodable Reader 21
DAY 3	• Independent Reader K.4.3 or Kindergarten Student Reader K.4.3
DAY 4	• Get Set, Roll! Reader 21 or Kindergarten Student Reader K.4.3

3 Day Plan: Eliminate the shaded box.

More Practice

For additional practice with this week's phonics skills and to develop fluency, have children reread the Decodable Story (Day 1) and the Decodable Reader (Day 2).

A Advanced — DAY 1

Phonemic Awareness • Phonics

■ **Discriminate Blends** Write the following equation on the board six times. ___ + ___ = ___. Explain the equation to children who do not yet understand addition. Tell children that one letter's sound plus another letter's sound can be blended to form a new sound. Have volunteers fill in the spaces to make new blends. Give the following choices for letters: *f, l, s, p, d, r, t, c, k, n.* When a blend is made, help children think of a word that begins with that blend.

Objectives

• Isolate the initial sound in spoken one-syllable words.

A Advanced — DAY

Phonics • Spelling

■ **Connect Sounds to Letters** Display the *dress* Picture Card. What is the initial blend in the word dress? What letters make that blend? Continue with the *blue, brown, cloud, crab, flag, frog, green, playground, sled, spoon,* and *train* Picture Cards.

■ **Spell Sounds** Give each child the following letter tiles: *d, i, l, n, o, p, r, s.* Listen to the sounds in the word *spin:* /s/ /p/ /i/ /n/, *spin*. What are the letters for /sp/? They are *sp.* Place your *s* and *p* tiles in front of you. Continue with the remaining sounds.

Let's blend the sounds to read the word: /sp/ /i/ /n/, *spin*. Continue the routine with *drop* and *slip*.

Objectives

• Identify the common sounds that letters represent.
• Use letter-sound correspondences to spell consonant-vowel-consonant (CVC) words.

DAY 3

For a complete lesson plan and additional practice, see the **Leveled Reader Teaching Guide**.

Independent Reader K.4.3

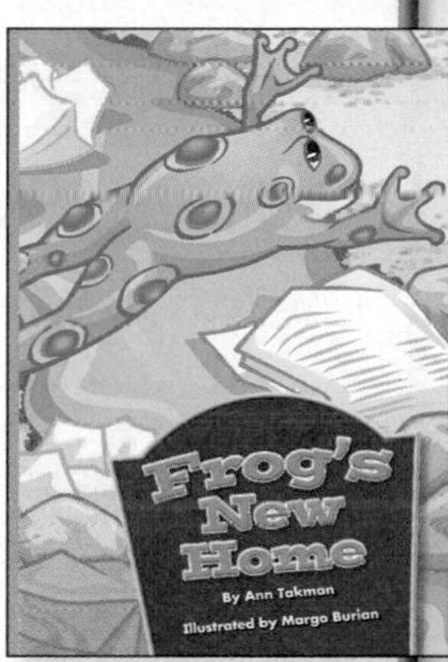
Independent Reader K.4.3

- **Practice High-Frequency Words** Write *are* on the board. Have volunteers say the word and use it in a sentence. Continue with the words *that* and *do*.
- **Activate Prior Knowledge** Have children read the title and look at the picture. What animal is this? Remind children that a frog needs to live in a quiet, moist place that has sun and shade. Do a picture walk through *Frog's New Home* and discuss what Frog encounters along the path. Why is the lake a bad home for Frog? Why might bits of trash be bad for Frog?
- **Sequence** After reading the book, have children draw a picture of what happens first and what happens last.
- **Reread for Fluency** After rereading with children, model reading fluently for them. I am going to read this book aloud. I will read just the way I speak. I will read the words with no mistakes. I want you to read it aloud with me. Try to read the words just as I do.
    - Use echo reading of Independent Reader K.4.3 to model reading fluently. Use your oral reading to model for children where to pause, when to change pitch, and which words to stress. Then have children reread orally three to four times, or until they can read with few or no mistakes.
- For more practice with phonics and high-frequency words and to develop fluency, have children read Kindergarten Student Reader K.4.3. Use the instruction on pp. 254–255.

Objectives

- Read at least 25 high-frequency words from a commonly used list.
- Predict what might happen next based on the illustrations.

More Reading

Use Leveled Readers or other text at children's instructional level.

More Reading

Use Leveled Readers or other text at children's instructional level.

Kindergarten Student Reader K.4.3

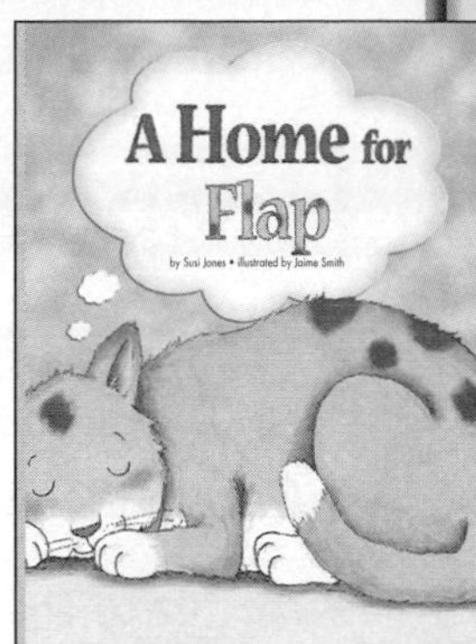

Kindergarten Student Reader K.4.3

- **Revisit Prior Knowledge** Have children discuss what they know about cats. What do cats need at their homes? What kinds of things do cats do?
- **Reread** Kindergarten Student Reader K.4.3 to practice reading fluently.
- **Text to World** Ask children to describe Flap. Then have children tell how other cats look.
- **Read** Have children read Get Set, Roll! Reader 21, *Jack Is It!* Use the instruction on p. 283.

Objectives
- Read at least 25 high-frequency words from a commonly used list.
- Make connections to the larger community.

Fluency•Comprehension

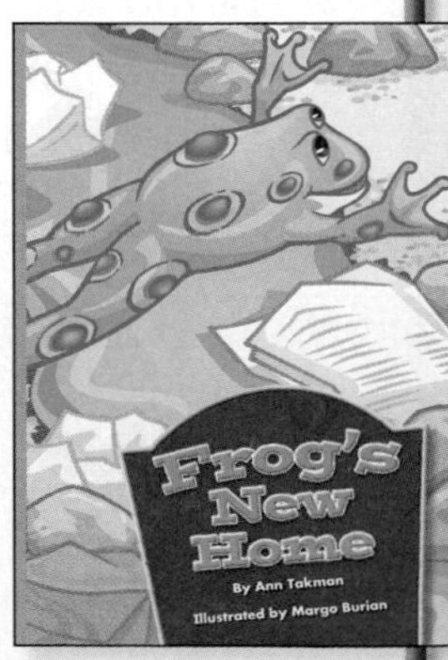

Independent Reader K.4.3

- **Reread for Fluency** Use the Independent Reader K.4.3 to model reading fluently for children. I am going to read this selection aloud. I will read the words with no mistakes. I want you to read it aloud with me. Try to read the words just as I do.
- **Comprehension** After children have finished reading, have them retell what happens in the selection. Then have children write or draw a picture that shows what happens last.

Objectives
- Read at least 25 high-frequency words from a commonly used list.
- Retell a main event from a story read aloud.

DAY 1

Concept Development

- **Read the Concept Literacy Reader** To build background and vocabulary, read *Animal Adventures* with children. Begin by having children look at the pictures in the book. What animals do you see? Which of these animals have you seen before? Read the book aloud, pausing to discuss each page. This is a bunny. A bunny is a small, furry animal. It is eating a leaf. What other things would a bunny eat? (lettuce, carrots, etc.) On a second reading, invite children to talk about the pictures on each page.
- **Develop Oral Language** Revisit *Animal Adventures,* pointing out that different animals can do different things. Then have children sing the following song with you to the tune of "Frère Jacques":

> I'm a rabbit, I'm a rabbit,
> What are you? What are you?
> Eating leaves and lettuce, eating leaves and lettuce,
> Do you too? Do you too?

Repeat the song with other animals from the selection.

Phonemic Awareness/Phonics

- **Frontload Consonant Blends with /l/** Have children look at the picture on pp. 52–53 of *My Skills Buddy*. It is winter in the picture. In the winter it is cold outside. Point to the sled. Have you ever gone sledding? Listen to the word *sled*. What sound does *sled* begin with? *Sled* begins with /s/. What is the next sound in *sled?* The next sound is /l/. Let's put the two sounds together; /s/, /l/; /sl/, *sled*. When a word has two consonants together, the sound can be blended, or put together. /sl/ is a blend. Then use chants to introduce blends with /l/. For example: In this picture the animals sled. Down the hill they ride the sled. Have children point to the animals sledding in the picture. Make up a chant for other words in the picture that begin with consonant blends with *l,* including *slip, flag, plow, fly, cloud, play, clap,* and *blow*.
- **Connect Consonant Blends to Their Spellings** Display the word *plan.* This word is *plan:* /p/ /l/ /a/ /n/, *plan*. Say the blend with me; /pl/. Now say the word with me. Have children write the word *plan* and circle the blend that makes /pl/. Write and read aloud the following sentence: *I am glad I did not flip the sled*. Point to *gl* in *glad.* What blend is this? Repeat with *fl* in *flip* and *sl* in *sled*.

Objectives

• Distinguish sounds of English with increasing ease. • Distinguish intonation patterns of English with increasing ease. • Recognize elements of the English sound system in newly acquired vocabulary. • Learn relationships between sounds and letters of the English language.

Content Objective

- Develop content knowledge related to animal adventures.

Language Objectives

- Understand and use grade-level content area vocabulary.
- Recognize the sounds of English.

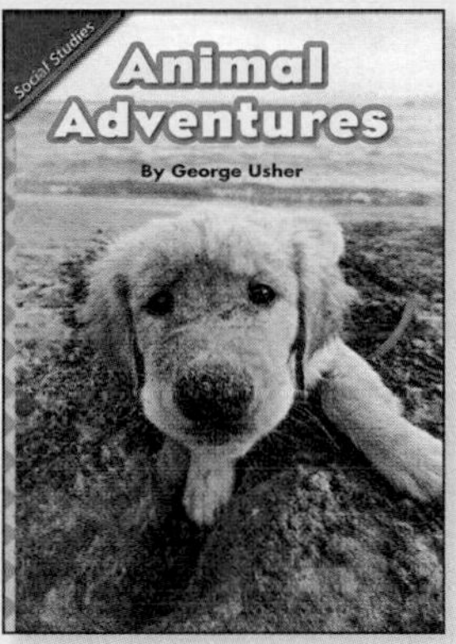

Concept Literacy Reader K.4.3

Daily Planner

DAY 1	• Concept Development • Phonemic Awareness/ Phonics • Listening Comprehension
DAY 2	• Comprehension • Vocabulary
DAY 3	• Phonemic Awareness/ Phonics • Conventions
DAY 4	• Phonemic Awareness/ Phonics • Concepts and Oral Language
DAY 5	• Language Workshop • Writing

Content Objective

- Understand sequence.

Language Objective

- Learn and use academic vocabulary.

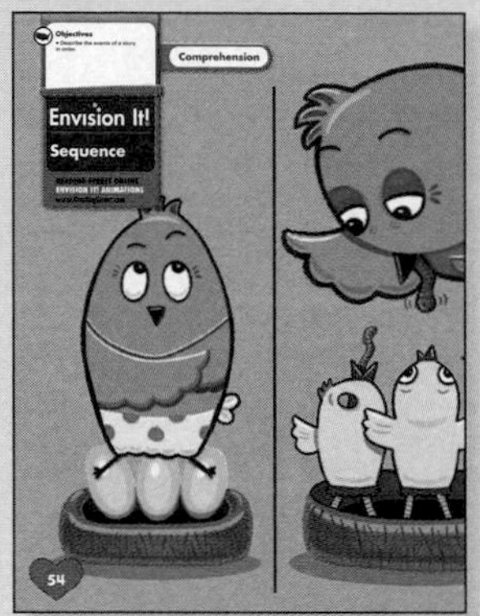

My Skills Buddy, pp. 54–55

DAY 1

Comprehension: Sequence

- **Frontload Vocabulary** Point to each illustration in turn and ask children what is happening and why. For example, point to the first picture. What do you see? (a momma bird sitting on eggs) Why do you think the momma bird is sitting on the eggs? (to keep them warm) Repeat the routine with the other pictures.
- **Provide Scaffolding** Discuss the illustrations on pp. 54–55 in *My Skills Buddy* to frontload vocabulary. Explain what is happening in each illustration. Help children understand that these drawings show events in sequence, or the order they happen. Point to the first picture. The baby birds are in the eggs. They have not been born. The momma bird is keeping them warm. Point to the middle picture. This happens next. The baby birds have hatched. They are being fed by their mother. Point to the third picture. This happens last. Now the babies are old enough to fly away. Tell children that many times sequence is shown from left to right.
- **Prepare for the Read Aloud** The modified Read Aloud below prepares children for listening to the oral reading "Swimming Sally" on p. 225.

Read Aloud

Swimming Sally

Sally Salmon was born in a stream. She swam every day. Every day she got bigger. Soon, she wanted to see more.

"Time to go!" she said. Sally swam down the stream. The stream got bigger. It became a river. Sally kept swimming. The river got bigger. It turned into the ocean.

Sally looked at the ocean. "This is big! Too big! I want to go home!"

Sally turned around. She swam out of the ocean. She swam up the river. She swam into her stream.

"It's good to be home!" she said.

- **First Listening** Write the title of the Read Aloud on the board. This is about a fish named Sally. She wants to see more than her stream. Explain that a stream is a small river. Listen to find out what happens on her trip. After reading, ask children to recall the events.
- **Second Listening** Write the words *stream, river,* and *ocean* on the board and point to them as the children answer questions. Where was Sally born? (stream) Where does Sally go first on her trip? (the river) Where does Sally go after the river? (the ocean) Make sure children understand the sequence of the story.

Objectives

- Expand and internalize initial English vocabulary by retelling simple stories and basic information represented or supported by pictures. • Use visual and contextual support to enhance and confirm understanding needed to comprehend increasingly challenging language.

DAY 2

Comprehension

- **Provide Scaffolding** Display *One Little Mouse*. Lead a detailed picture walk through the story. Focus on the following:
  - **Set the Scene** Use the cover of the Big Book to help children understand that this story takes place in a woodland. Describe what a woodland is like. A woodland is an area covered in trees, bushes, or shrubs. It has many different animals. You can go on a walk in a woodland and see squirrels, mice, frogs, and birds.
  - **Frontload Vocabulary** As you lead the picture walk, use the illustrations to introduce unfamiliar words in the text. Look at the picture on page 21. The birds sleep in a willow. What is a willow? (a kind of tree) Can you name other kinds of trees? (Possible answers: elm, oak, pine) Why do you think the mouse does not want to sleep in the willow? (Possible answer: The mouse might fall and get hurt.) Include some of the following words from the story: *vale* (p. 13); *meadows* (p. 14); *quills* (p. 23); *tidy* (p. 26); *content* (p. 32).

Vocabulary: Words for Shapes

- **Frontload Vocabulary** Have children turn to p. 68 of *My Skills Buddy*. Talk about the shapes, using the words *heart, star, oval,* and *diamond*. Instruct children to take out a sheet of paper. Draw a heart on the board. This is a heart. Draw a heart on your paper. Draw a star on the board. This is a star. Draw a star on your paper. Continue with the oval and the diamond. After children have drawn all four shapes, say each shape name aloud, and have children point to it on their papers.
- **Provide Scaffolding** Write the words *heart, star, oval,* and *diamond* on the board. Draw an example of each shape beside the word. Tell children to point to the answer of each question on the board. Which shape would you see on a Valentine's Day card? (heart) Which shape would you see in a drawing of the night sky? (star) Which shape is a baseball field? (diamond) Which shape looks like an egg? (oval). Encourage children to name things with each shape.

Objectives

• Speak using learning strategies. • Internalize new basic language by using and reusing it in meaningful ways in speaking activities that build concept and language attainment. • Learn new basic and academic vocabulary heard during classroom instruction and interactions.

Content Objective

- Develop background knowledge.

Language Objective

- Learn and use words for shapes.

Use Learning Strategies

Remind children that if they have trouble naming a shape, they can ask the teacher for help.

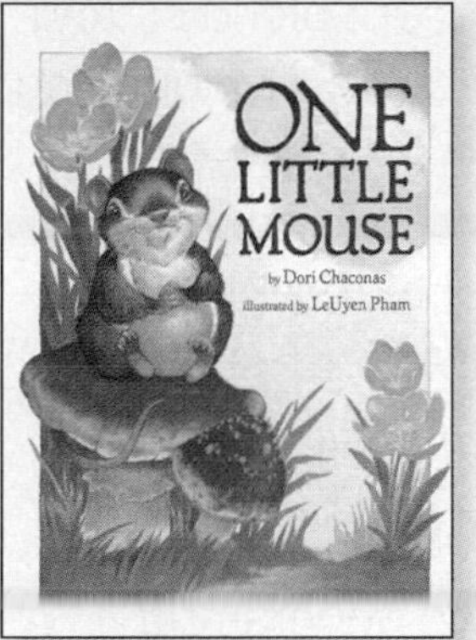

Big Book

Content Objective

- Use learning strategies.

Language Objectives

- Connect consonant blends to their spellings.
- Use complete sentences.

Transfer Skills

Pronouncing Consonant Blends Speakers of Spanish may not be familiar with the initial consonant blend *sl,* and may have trouble pronouncing and spelling it. If they have difficulty, practice connecting the letters *sl* to the initial sound /sl/ in words such as *sleep, slip,* and *slow*.

Use Learning Strategies

Help children understand that in English, a complete sentence starts with a capital letter and ends with a period or other punctuation mark. For example, *The mouse lives in the woodland*. In many foreign languages, capital letters and punctuation are not used.

ELL English Language Learners

DAY 3

Phonemic Awareness/Phonics

- **Isolate Final Blends** Say *left,* and then model segmenting sounds by saying /l/ /e/ /f/ /t/. Emphasize the sound of the final blend /ft/ in the word. Repeat with *milk* and *ask*. Help children identify each separate sound in the blend, and then combine the two sounds. Say *fast,* and then model segmenting the blend by saying /s/ /t/. Then say the blend together, /st/. Finally, have children say the whole word. Repeat with *find* and *past*.
- **Spelling Consonant Blends** Write the words *silk, band,* and *mist* on the board. As you read them aloud, track the sounds and letters with your fingers. Help children recognize that these words end with a consonant blend.

Conventions: Complete Sentences

- **Provide Scaffolding** Point to the image on p. 10 of *One Little Mouse*. Three meadow frogs were leaping from logs. Write the sentence on the board. Remind children that the naming part of a sentence tells what it is about. The naming part of this sentence is *Three meadow frogs*. Remind them that the action part of a sentence tells what happens. The action part of this sentence is *were leaping from logs*. A complete sentence must have a naming part and an action part. Circle the capital letter in *Three* and the period at the end of the sentence. A complete sentence should start with a capital letter and finish with an end mark. What are some end marks? (period, exclamation point, question mark)
- **Practice** Pick out some sentences from the story that clearly display a naming part, an action part, capitalization, and punctuation: *Four bobwhite quail ran up from the vale*. (p. 12); *Nine porcupine waddled by in a line*. (p. 23). Have children identify the naming and action parts of each sentence.

Leveled Support

Beginning/Intermediate Write a group of sentences on the board, some complete, some incomplete. Ask children if the sentence is complete. After they have answered, point out what was missing from the incomplete sentences.

Advanced/Advanced-High Write an incomplete sentence on the board. Have children figure out what is missing. Then have them correct the mistake to make it a complete sentence.

Objectives

- Monitor understanding of spoken language during classroom instruction and interactions.
- Speak using a variety of grammatical structures with increasing accuracy and ease as more English is acquired.
- Learn relationships between sounds and letters of the English language.

ELL English Language Learners DAY 4

Phonemic Awareness/Phonics

- **Review Initial and Final /l/** To review /l/, read a sentence with words that both begin and end with /l/: Nell fell and hurt her leg. Have children repeat the sentence after you. Then have them pronounce the word that begins with /l/; /l/ /e/ /g/. What sound does this word start with? Yes, it starts with /l/. Then have them pronounce the words that end with /l/: /n/ /e/ /l/; /f/ /e/ /l/. What sound do these words end with? Yes, they end with /l/.
- **/l/ Spelled *Ll*** Write the letters *Ll*. What letter is this? Yes, this letter is *Ll*. Use word tiles to form these words: *lid, lap, tell, fill, lob, lip*. Model reading each word, isolating /l/. Show all the sound-letter correspondences (for example, /l/ /i/ /d/ = *lid*).

Concepts and Oral Language

- **Revisit Talk with Me Chart 21A** Display the chart. Have children describe the people, places, and things in the photos. Then say a sentence for each picture. Have children identify the naming part and the action part in each sentence. For example, *The mouse sits in the nest*. *The mouse* is the naming part and *sits in the nest* is the action part.
- **Develop Oral Language** Introduce language patterns that help describe the pictures on Talk with Me Chart 21A. Write this sentence frame on the board: *The picture shows* _____. Let's use this sentence pattern to talk about the pictures. *The picture shows a cozy girl. Another word for cozy is* comfortable. *The picture shows a comfortable girl*. Have children suggest other sentences using the frame. Then ask questions about where you might see the scene in each picture. Have children reply by pointing to the correct picture and answering in a complete sentence.

Beginning Have children point to each picture on the chart and use the Amazing Word to describe the picture.

Intermediate Ask questions to help children notice more details about the people, animals, and objects in the pictures, such as Does the comfortable girl look happy or sad? What is making the shadow?

Advanced/Advanced-High Encourage children to use their prior knowledge and experiences about the actions and objects in the pictures. For example, *The girl is comfortable. I am comfortable when...* or *The woodland is pretty. I saw a woodland...*

Objectives

- Use visual support to enhance and confirm understanding of increasingly complex and elaborated spoken language. • Use support from peers and teachers to read grade-appropriate content area text needed to comprehend increasingly challenging language.

Content Objectives

- Develop oral language.
- Use learning strategies.

Language Objectives

- Connect /l/ with *Ll*.
- Learn English language patterns.

Use Learning Strategies

Draw a one-column chart on the board titled *One Little Mouse* and number it 1 through 5. Beside the chart write these 5 sentences: *The mouse meets three frogs. The mouse goes to sleep. The mouse meets five snakes. The mouse goes to look for a new house. The mouse meets ten opossums*. Ask children to assist you in putting the sentences in sequence in the chart. Have children point to the sentence that should go first. Then have them point to the sentence that should go next, etc. Write the sentences into the chart.

Talk with Me Chart 21A

Content Objectives

- Understand *One Little Mouse*.
- Practice sequence.

Language Objectives

- Express opinions through speaking and writing.
- Write using grade-level vocabulary.

Monitor and Self-Correct

Remind children that if they don't know how to say a word, they can ask other children for help.

Home Language Support

Invite children to share ideas in their home languages before creating their sentences.

ELL English Language Learners

DAY 5

Language Workshop: Share Opinions

- **Introduce and Model** Display p. 17 of *One Little Mouse*. The mouse is sleeping with the cottontails. The mouse does not look very comfortable. But the cottontails look very happy. Where are some places that you have gone to sleep? (bed, sofa, floor, cot, tent, etc.) What is your favorite place to sleep? What is your least favorite place? What you think is called your *opinion*. Everyone has an opinion. Your opinion may be different from mine. That's OK. Opinions are not right or wrong. They are just our thoughts.
- **Practice** What is your favorite place to sleep? List answers in a chart. After every opinion has been given, have the class vote on their favorite place to sleep. Keep track of votes by using tally marks. Then announce the most popular place to sleep.

Writing: Share Opinions

- **Prepare for Writing** We shared our opinions about the best and worst places to sleep. Now let's write about our opinions. Have each child fold a piece of paper in half to create two sections.
- **Create Sentences About Opinions** Have children copy this sentence frame at the bottom of the first section: *The best place to sleep is* _____. Have them copy this sentence frame at the bottom of the second section: *The worst place to sleep is* _____. Have children draw their favorite sleeping spot and their least favorite spot. Have them complete the sentence frames. When children finish their sentences, have them read their sentences to a partner several times.

Leveled Support

Beginning Provide the sentence frame in each section and have children dictate or write words to complete the sentences.

Intermediate Guide children in writing words to complete the sentences.

Advanced/Advanced-High Encourage children to write their sentences on their own. You might also have children help less-proficient partners complete their sentences.

Objectives

• Express opinions ranging from communicating single words and short phrases to participating in extended discussions on a variety of social and grade-appropriate academic topics. • Write using a variety of grade-appropriate sentence lengths in increasingly accurate ways as more English is acquired.

Customize Literacy in Your Classroom

Table of Contents
for Customize Literacy

Customize Literacy is organized into different sections, each one designed to help you organize and carry out an effective literacy program. Each section contains strategies and support for teaching comprehension skills and strategies. *Customize Literacy* also shows how to use weekly text sets of readers in your literacy program.

Weekly Text Sets
to Customize Literacy

The following readers can be used to enhance your literacy instruction.

	Decodable Reader	Concept Literacy Reader	Below-Level Reader	On-Level Reader	Advanced Reader
Unit 4 WEEK 1	*Hob Can Hit*	*What Do I See?*	*Hap*	*A Day to Play*	*The Trip*
Unit 4 WEEK 2	*Can It Fit?*	*My Lucky Day*	*The Rainy Day*	*Our Musical Adventure*	*Pigs*
Unit 4 WEEK 3	*One to Five*	*Animal Adventures*	*Five of Us!*	*A Home for Flap*	*Frog's New Home*

Customize Literacy in Your Classroom

Customize Instruction
to Improve Reading Behaviors

Instruction in comprehension skills and strategies provides readers with avenues to understanding a text. Through teacher modeling and guided, collaborative, and independent practice, children become independent thinkers who employ a variety of skills and strategies to help them make meaning as they read.

Mini-Lessons for Comprehension Skills and Strategies

Unit 1	Character, Setting, Sequence, Classify and Categorize, Predict and Set Purpose, Recall and Retell
Unit 2	Compare and Contrast, Setting, Main Idea, Realism and Fantasy, Sequence, Predict and Set Purpose, Recall and Retell
Unit 3	Compare and Contrast, Plot, Cause and Effect, Draw Conclusions, Main Idea, Predict and Set Purpose, Recall and Retell
Unit 4	Sequence, Cause and Effect, Character, Classify and Categorize, Setting, Predict and Set Purpose, Recall and Retell
Unit 5	Realism and Fantasy, Cause and Effect, Compare and Contrast, Plot, Main Idea, Draw Conclusions, Predict and Set Purpose, Recall and Retell
Unit 6	Compare and Contrast, Character, Main Idea, Plot, Setting, Draw Conclusions, Predict and Set Purpose, Recall and Retell

Envision It! A Comprehension Handbook

Envision It! Visual Skills Handbook
Author's Purpose
Categorize and Classify
Cause and Effect
Compare and Contrast
Draw Conclusions
Fact and Opinion
Generalize
Graphic Sources
Literary Elements
Main Idea and Details
Sequence

Envision It! Visual Strategies Handbook
Background Knowledge
Important Ideas
Inferring
Monitor and Clarify
Predict and Set Purpose
Questioning
Story Structure
Summarize
Text Structure
Visualize

Anchor Chart Anchor charts are provided with each strategy lesson. These charts incorporate the language of strategic thinkers. They help students make their thinking visible and permanent and provide students with a means to clarify their thinking about how and when to use each strategy. As children gain more experience with a strategy, the chart may undergo revision.

See pages 97–113 in the *First Stop on Reading Street* Teacher's Edition for additional support as you customize literacy in your classroom.

Good Readers DRA2 users will find additional resources in the *First Stop on Reading Street* Teacher's Edition on pages 100–102.

Contents

Pacing Guide

This chart shows the instructional sequence from *Scott Foresman Reading Street* for Grade K. You can use this pacing guide as is to ensure you are following a comprehensive scope and sequence. Or, you can adjust the sequence to match your calendar, curriculum map, or testing schedule.

Grade K

LANGUAGE ARTS

UNIT 1	Week 1	Week 2	Week 3	Week 4	Week 5	Week 6
Phonological/ Phonemic Awareness	Rhyming Words	Syllables Sound Discrimination	Discriminate Sounds Segment Syllables	Discriminate Sounds	Isolate /m/ Discriminate Sounds	Isolate /t/ Discriminate Sounds Rhyme
Phonics	Letter Recognition: *Aa, Bb, Cc, Dd, Ee*	Letter Recognition: *Ff, Gg, Hh, Ii, Jj, Kk, Ll, Mm, Nn*	Letter Recognition: *Oo, Pp, Qq, Rr, Ss*	Letter Recognition: *Tt, Uu, Vv, Ww, Xx, Yy, Zz*	/m/ Spelled *Mm*	/t/ Spelled *Tt*
High-Frequency Words	*I, am*	*I, am*	*the, little*	*the, little*	*a, to*	*a, to*
Listening Comprehension	Character	Setting	Sequence	Classify and Categorize	Character	Classify and Categorize
Comprehension Strategies	Preview and Predict, Retell					

UNIT 2	Week 1	Week 2
Phonological/ Phonemic Awareness	Isolate /a/ Oral Blending	Isolate /s/ Oral Blending
Phonics	/a/ Spelled *Aa*	/s/ Spelled *Ss*
High-Frequency Words	*have, is*	*have, is*
Listening Comprehension	Compare and Contrast	Setting
Comprehension Strategies		

UNIT 4	Week 1	Week 2	Week 3	Week 4	Week 5	Week 6
Phonemic Awareness	Isolate /h/ Oral Blending Segment Phonemes	Isolate /l/ Oral Blending Segment Phonemes	Consonant Blends	Isolate /g/ Segment Phonemes	Isolate /e/ Segment Phonemes Discriminate Phonemes	Isolate /e/ Segment Phonemes Discriminate Phonemes
Phonics	/h/ Spelled *Hh*	/l/ Spelled *Ll*	Consonant Blends	/g/ Spelled *Gg*	/e/ Spelled *Ee*	/e/ Spelled *Ee*
High-Frequency Words	*are, that, do*	*are, that, do*	*one, two, three, four, five*	*one, two, three, four, five*	*here, go, from*	*here, go, from*
Listening Comprehension	Sequence	Cause and Effect	Sequence	Character	Classify and Categorize	Setting
Comprehension Strategies	Preview and Predict, Retell					

UNIT 5	Week 1	Week 2
Phonemic Awareness	Isolate /j/, /w/ Oral Blending Segment Phonemes	Isolate /ks/ Oral Blending Segment Phonemes
Phonics	/j/ Spelled *Jj* and /w/ Spelled *Ww*	/ks/ Spelled *Xx*
High-Frequency Words	*yellow, blue, green*	*yellow, blue, green*
Listening Comprehension	Realism and Fantasy	Cause and Effect
Comprehension Strategies		

Are you the adventurous type? Want to use some of your own ideas and materials in your teaching? But you worry you might be leaving out some critical instruction kids need? Customize Literacy can help.”

Week 3	Week 4	Week 5	Week 6
Isolate /p/ Oral Blending	Isolate /k/ Oral Blending	Isolate /i/ Discriminate Sounds Oral Blending	Discriminate Sounds Oral Blending
/p/ Spelled *Pp*	/k/ Spelled *Cc*	/i/ Spelled *Ii*	/i/ Spelled *Ii*
we, my, like	*we, my, like*	*he, for*	*he, for*
Main Idea	Realism and Fantasy	Sequence	Realism and Fantasy
Preview and Predict, Retell			

UNIT 3

Week 1	Week 2	Week 3	Week 4	Week 5	Week 6
Isolate /n/, /b/ Oral Blending Segment Phonemes	Isolate /r/ Oral Blending Segment Phonemes	Isolate /d/, /k/ Oral Blending Segment Phonemes	Isolate /f/ Oral Blending Segment Phonemes	Isolate /o/ Oral Blending Segment Phonemes	Oral Blending Segment Phonemes
/n/ Spelled *Nn* and /b/ Spelled *Bb*	/r/ Spelled *Rr*	/d/ Spelled *Dd* and /k/ Spelled *Kk*	/f/ Spelled *Ff*	/o/ Spelled *Oo*	/o/ Spelled *Oo*
me, with, she	*me, with, she*	*see, look*	*see, look*	*they, you, of*	*they, you, of*
Compare and Contrast	Plot	Cause and Effect	Plot	Draw Conclusions	Main Idea
Preview and Predict, Retell					

Week 3	Week 4	Week 5	Week 6
Isolate /u/ Oral Blending Segment Phonemes	Isolate /u/ Oral Blending Segment Phonemes	Isolate /v/, /z/ Oral Blending Segment Phonemes	Isolate /y/, /kw/ Oral Blending Segment Phonemes
Connect /u/ to *Uu*	Connect /u/ to *Uu*	Connect /v/ to *Vv* and /z/ to *Zz*	Connect /y/ to *Yy* and /kw/ to *qu*
what, said, was	*what, said, was*	*where, come*	*where, come*
Compare and Contrast	Plot	Main Idea	Draw Conclusions
Preview and Predict, Retell			

UNIT 6

Week 1	Week 2	Week 3	Week 4	Week 5	Week 6
Isolate /a/ and /i/ Blend Phonemes Segment Phonemes	Isolate /o/ Blend Phonemes Segment Phonemes	Isolate /e/ Blend Phonemes Segment Phonemes	Isolate /u/ Blend Phonemes Segment Phonemes	Discriminate Sounds Blend Phonemes Segment Phonemes	Discriminate Sounds Blend Phonemes Segment Phonemes
Connect /a/ to *Aa* and /i/ to *Ii*	Connect /o/ to *Oo*	Connect /e/ to *Ee*	Connect /u/ to *Uu*	Consonant and Short Vowels	Consonant and Short Vowels
Review: *here, do, little, with, what*	Review: *where, is, go, that, come*	Review: *the, was, to, like, from*	Review: *for, of, my, we, yellow*	Review: *have, they, four, two, blue*	Review: *you, said, see, look, three*
Compare and Contrast	Character	Main Idea	Plot	Setting	Draw Conclusions
Preview and Predict, Retell					

Pacing Guide

Grade K

LANGUAGE ARTS	UNIT 1 Week 1	Week 2	Week 3	Week 4	Week 5	Week 6	UNIT 2 Week 1	Week 2
Speaking and Listening	Follow Directions	Drama—Respond to Literature	Listen for Rhyme and Rhythm	Talk About Me	Announce-ments and Messages	Drama: Respond to Literature	Listen for Sequence	Listen for Directions
Grammar/ Conventions	Say Our Names	Write Our Names	What We Look Like	What We Can Do	Nouns for People and Animals	Nouns for Places and Things	Nouns for More Than One	Proper Nouns
Writing	Song	Invitation	Poem	Instructions	Caption	Personal Narrative	Label	List

	UNIT 4 Week 1	Week 2	Week 3	Week 4	Week 5	Week 6	UNIT 5 Week 1	Week 2
Speaking and Listening	Give Directions	Compare and Contrast	Listen for Sequence	Discuss Authors and Illustrators	Listen for Story Elements: Character	Listen to Poems	Ask and Answer Questions	Drama: Respond to Literature
Grammar/ Conventions	Subjects (Naming Parts)	Predicates (Action Parts)	Complete Sentences	Telling Sentences	Capital Letters and Periods	Pronouns *I* and *me*	Questions	Question Marks and Capital Letters
Writing	Directions	Poem	Description	List	Informal Letter	List	Caption	Rhyme

Week 3	Week 4	Week 5	Week 6
Discussions	Listen for Setting	Give a Description	Listen for Plot
Adjectives: Colors and Shapes	Adjectives: Sizes and Numbers	Adjectives: Opposites	Adjectives
Notes	Poem	Caption	Story

UNIT 3

Week 1	Week 2	Week 3	Week 4	Week 5	Week 6
Respond to Literature	Sequence	Recite Rhymes	Oral Presentation	Messages and Letters	Ask and Answer Questions
Verbs	Verbs for Now and the Past	Verbs That Add *-s*	Verbs for Now and the Future	Meaningful Word Groups	Sentences
Summary	Invitation	Persuasive Statement	Caption	List	Poem

Week 3	Week 4	Week 5	Week 6
Discuss Literature	Sequence	Oral Presentation: Description	Discuss Literary Elements: Plot
Prepositions	Nouns	Nouns in Sentences	Verbs
Poem	Formal Letter	Invitation	How-to Report

UNIT 6

Week 1	Week 2	Week 3	Week 4	Week 5	Week 6
Recite Language	Discuss Fact and Opinion	Interpret Information	Discuss Literary Elements: Character	Oral Presentation: Book Report	Discuss Literary Elements: Setting
Pronouns *I* and *me*	Prepositional Phrases	Telling Sentences	Questions	Exclamations	Complete Sentences
List	Song	Rhyme	Rhyme	Poem	Report

Teaching Record Chart

This chart shows the critical comprehension skills and strategies you need to cover. Check off each one as you provide instruction.

Reading/Comprehension	DATES OF INSTRUCTION		
Predict what might happen next in text based on the cover, title, and illustrations.			
Ask and respond to questions about texts read aloud.			
Identify elements of a story including setting, character, and key events.			
Discuss the big idea (theme) of a well-known folk tale or fable and connect it to personal experience.			
Recognize sensory details.			
Recognize recurring phrases and characters in traditional fairy tales, lullabies, and folk tales from various cultures.			
Respond to rhythm and rhyme in poetry through identifying a regular beat and similarities in word sounds.			
Retell a main event from a story read aloud.			
Describe characters in a story and the reasons for their actions.			
Identify the topic of an informational text heard.			

Tired of using slips of paper or stickies to make sure you teach everything you need to? Need an easier way to keep track of what you have taught, and what you still need to cover? Customize Literacy can help.

Reading/Comprehension	DATES OF INSTRUCTION		
Identify the topic and details in expository text heard or read, referring to the words and/or illustrations.			
Retell important facts in a text, heard or read.			
Discuss the ways authors group information in text.			
Use titles and illustrations to make predictions about text.			
Follow pictorial directions (e.g., recipes, science experiments).			
Identify the meaning of specific signs (e.g., traffic signs, warning signs).			
Discuss the purposes for reading and listening to various texts (e.g., to become involved in real and imagined events, settings, actions, and to enjoy language).			
Ask and respond to questions about text.			
Monitor and adjust comprehension (e.g., using background knowledge, creating sensory images, re-reading a portion aloud).			
Make inferences based on the cover, title, illustrations, and plot.			
Retell or act out important events in stories.			
Make connections to own experiences, to ideas in other texts, and to the larger community and discuss textual evidence.			

Objectives:

- Children understand that some things happen in a certain order.
- Children identify what happens first, next, and last in a story.
- Children identify sequence in nonfiction selections.

Texts for Teaching

- *Plaidypus Lost*
- *A Bed for the Winter*
- *Rooster's Off to See the World*
- *One Little Mouse*

Leveled Readers

- See pages CL16–CL17 for a list of Leveled Readers.

Sequence

Understand the Skill

My Skills Buddy K.4, pp. 14–15

Sequence means the order in which things happen.
Sequence can also mean the steps we follow to make or do something.
Understanding sequence is the first simple way to comprehend a story.

Teach

Use the Envision It! lesson on *My Skills Buddy* K.4, pages 14–15 to visually teach sequence. Use the pictures to retell the story in order.

Tell children that they know lots of things that happen in order. Use a simple example, such as a chick hatching from an egg. (First, the chick pecks a hole in the egg; next, the chick comes our of the egg; last, the chick stands up.)

Practice

Read aloud the following passage and have children listen for what happens first, next, and last.

Our class planted flowers for Mother's Day. First, we put dirt in a flowerpot. Next, we pushed seeds into the dirt. Last, we watered our seeds. It will take time for our plants to grow.

If... children have difficulty recognizing sequence,
then... retell the story and insert phrases such as *that's the first thing that happens, the next thing that happens is that . . . .*

Apply

Reread the passage and tell children to listen again. Have them ask questions: *What happened first? What happened next? What happened last?* Then have them draw or write to show what happened in the story, in sequence. They can use a graphic organizer like this one.

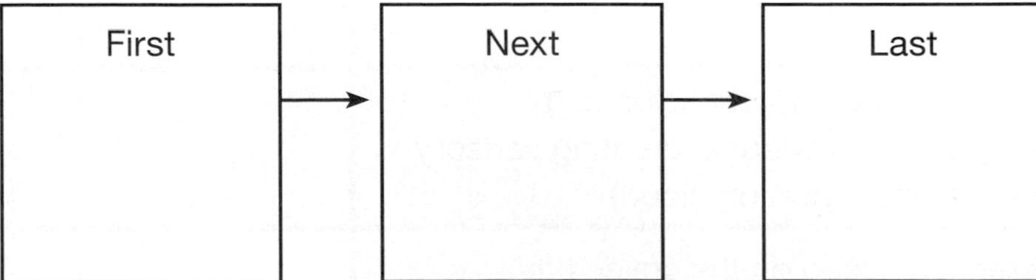

Writing

Children can write sentences about what happens in a favorite story on separate pieces of paper. Then have them put them in order and glue the strips in order. Post them in the classroom.

Objectives:

- Children identify "what happens."
- Children identify "why something happens."

Texts for Teaching

- *George Washington Visits*
- *My Lucky Day*
- *Mayday! Mayday!*

Leveled Readers

- See pages CL16–CL17 for a list of Leveled Readers.

Cause and Effect

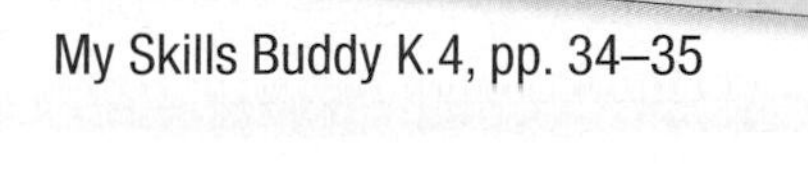
My Skills Buddy K.4, pp. 34–35

Understand the Skill

A **cause** is why something happens. An **effect** is what happens. Children learn that things are sometimes connected to each other. Children think about what happens and why as they listen to stories.

Teach

Use the Envision It! lesson on *My Skills Buddy* K.4, pages 34–35 to visually teach cause and effect.

Tell children that some things happen because of something else. Point to the white dog and ask what happens to it. Use simple physical examples to model cause-and-effect relationships, such as getting cold if you go outside without a coat on a cold day or a snowman melting on a warm day. After each example ask: What happened? Why did that happen?

Practice

Tell children that sometimes something makes another thing happen. Write these sentences on the board or on sentence strips. Read each aloud and ask: What happened? Why did that happen? Have a volunteer draw an arrow from what happened to why it happened.

Rain started to fall.	Maria got wet.
John's dog barked.	Mark was at the door.
The lunch bell rang.	The children got up and formed a line.
Mom turned on the lights.	It was dark inside.

If... children have difficulty explaining why something happened,
then... give them choices and have them choose.

Apply

Tell children to listen carefully as you read to find out what happens and why something happens. After reading, ask: *What is one thing that happened in the story? Why did it happen?*

Writing

Children can write and share something that happened to them. Have them explain why it happened.

Compare and Contrast

Objectives:

- Children tell how things are alike.
- Children tell how things are different.
- Children make groups by identifying likenesses and differences.

Texts for Teaching

- *Flowers*
- *Little Panda*
- *Trucks Roll!*
- *Building with Dad*

Leveled Readers

- See pages CL16–CL17 for a list of Leveled Readers.

Mini-Lesson

My Skills Buddy K.3, pp. 14–15

Understand the Skill

Compare and contrast means to find the likenesses and/or differences between two or more people, places, things, or ideas. Children use the terms *alike* and *different* to talk about stories, characters in stories, their experiences, objects, and so on.

Teach

Use the Envision It! lesson on *My Skills Buddy* K.3, pages 14–15 to visually teach compare and contrast. Have children compare the bikes and the weather.

Remind children that two things can be alike or different. Show children pictures of familiar animals or plants. Think aloud and model comparing and contrasting two of the pictures. One animal is spotted and the other is striped. This animal looks like it lives in the jungle. This animal looks like it lives in a grassland. Continue using other pairs of pictures. Have children add likenesses and differences that they see.

Practice

Use a familiar piece of nonfiction to show children that authors compare things too. Choose a book that compares things, such as seasons, places, or times. Read together and make a chart to show likenesses and differences. For example, the trees in the spring have small green leaves, trees in the fall have red or yellow leaves.

Spring	Fall

As you read with children, point out pictures and words that help compare.
If... children have difficulty finding likenesses,
then... ask leading questions, such as: *Are they the same color? Is one bigger than the other?*

Apply

Tell children to listen carefully as you read a story to find things that are alike and different. Draw a two-column feature chart on the board and use the graphic organizer to list similarities and differences of two things from the illustrations or the sentences.

Writing

Children can write sentences about how school and home are different and alike. Provide sentence frames as needed. Children can illustrate their sentences.

Objectives:

- Children tell what they think will happen in a story and what will happen next in a story.
- Children preview a book and set a purpose for reading.

Texts for Teaching

- *Predicting and setting purposes is a strategy that can be applied to any selection. Encourage children to make predictions and set a purpose before they read.*

Predict and Set Purpose

Mini-Lesson

Understand the Strategy

To predict means to tell what you think might happen next in a story or what the author may tell you next. Predicting goes hand-in-hand with previewing, which involves looking at text features and language to get an overview of a piece of writing. Before reading, previewing and predicting helps readers access what they already know about the topic and so **set a purpose** to guide reading.

Teach

Tell children that readers do things before they listen to or read a book. We look at the book inside and out. We think about what it might be about. Then we think about what we would like to find out as we read. Model predicting and setting purpose using the tips below.

Before We Listen or Read
• Look at the cover. What do you see?
• Look inside. What do you see?
• Think. What will this story will be about?
As We Listen or Read
• Listen or read carefully.
• Did you predict what would happen?
• Think. What will happen next?
After We Listen or Read
• Look back. Did you predict what would happen?
• Think. Do you like this story? Why or why not?

Practice and Apply

Use the strategy on a new story. Record some purposes children have. Record some predictions they make. After reading, return to them and talk about whether their purposes were met. How close were their predictions?

If... children have difficulty making predictions,
then... model the process using text clues and personal experience.

Anchor Chart

Anchor charts help children make their thinking visible and permanent. With an anchor chart, the group can clarify their thinking about how to use a strategy. You might make a chart of the strategy Predict and Set Purpose to hang in the classroom.

Glossary of Literacy Terms

This glossary lists academic language terms that are related to literacy. They are provided for your information and professional use.

A

alliteration the repetition of a consonant sound in a group of words, especially in poetry

animal fantasy a story about animals that talk and act like people

antonym a word that means the opposite of another word

author's purpose the reason the author wrote the text

autobiography the story of a real person's life written by that person

B

background knowledge the information and experience that a reader brings to a text

biography the story of a real person's life written by another person

C

cause why something happens

character a person, an animal, or a personified object in a story

classify and categorize put things, such as pictures or words, into groups

compare and contrast tell how things are the same and different

comprehension understanding of text being read—the ultimate goal of reading

comprehension strategy a conscious plan used by a reader to gain understanding of text. Comprehension strategies may be used before, during, or after reading.

context clue the words, phrases, or sentences near an unknown word that give the reader clues to the word's meaning

D

details small pieces of information

dialogue written conversation

draw conclusions arrive at decisions or opinions after thinking about facts and details and using prior knowledge

E

effect what happens as the result of a cause

expository text text that contains facts and information. Also called *informational text.*

F

fable a story, usually with animal characters, that is written to teach a moral, or lesson

fact piece of information that can be proved to be true

fairy tale a folk story with magical characters and events

fantasy a story that could not really happen

fiction writing that tells about imaginary people, things, and events

folk tale a story that has been passed down by word of mouth

foreshadowing the use of hints or clues about what will happen later in a story

G

generalize make a broad statement or rule after examining particular facts

graphic organizer a drawing, chart, or web that illustrates concepts or shows how ideas relate to each other. Readers use graphic organizers to help them keep track of and understand important information and ideas as they read. Story maps, word webs, Venn diagrams, and KWL charts are graphic organizers.

graphic source a chart, diagram, or map within a text that adds to readers' understanding of the text

H

historical fiction realistic fiction that takes place in the past. It is an imaginary story based on historical events and characters.

humor writing or speech that has a funny or amusing quality

I

idiom a phrase whose meaning differs from the ordinary meaning of the words. *A stone's throw* is an idiom meaning "a short distance."

imagery the use of language to create beautiful or forceful pictures in the reader's mind

inference conclusion reached on the basis of evidence and reasoning

inform give knowledge, facts, or news to someone

informational text writing that contains facts and information. Also called *expository text.*

interview a face-to-face conversation in which someone responds to questions

L

legend a story coming down from the past about the great deeds of a hero. Although a legend may be based on historical people and events, it is not regarded as historically true.

literary elements the characters, setting, plot, and theme of a narrative text

M

main idea the big idea that tells what a paragraph or a selection is mainly about; the most important idea of a text

metacognition an awareness of one's own thinking processes and the ability to monitor and direct them to a desired goal. Good readers use metacognition to monitor their reading and adjust their reading strategies.

monitor and clarify a comprehension strategy by which readers actively think about understanding their reading and know when they understand and when they do not. Readers use appropriate strategies to make sense of difficult words, ideas, or passages.

M

moral the lesson or teaching of a fable or story

mystery a story about mysterious events that are not explained until the end, so as to keep the reader in suspense

myth a story that attempts to explain something in nature

N

narrative a story, made up or true, that someone tells or narrates

narrator the character in a selection who tells the story

nonfiction writing that tells about real things, real people, and real events

O

onomatopoeia the use of words that sound like their meanings, such as *buzz* and *hum*

opinion someone's judgment, belief, or way of thinking

oral vocabulary the words needed for speaking and listening

P

personification a figure of speech in which human traits or actions are given to animals or inanimate objects, as in *The sunbeam danced on the waves.*

persuade convince someone to do or to believe something

play a story that is written to be acted out for an audience

plot a series of related events at the beginning, middle, and end of a story; the action of a story

poem an expressive, imaginative piece of writing often arranged in lines having rhythm and rhyme. In a poem, the patterns made by the sounds of the words have special importance.

pourquoi tale a type of folk story that explains why things in nature came to be. *Pourquoi* is a French word meaning "why."

predict tell what a selection might be about or what might happen in a text. Readers use text features and information to predict. They confirm or revise their predictions as they read.

preview look over a text before reading it

Q

questioning a reading strategy in which readers ask and answer questions to help make sense of what they read

R

reading vocabulary the words we recognize or use in print

realistic fiction a story about imaginary people and events that could happen in real life

R

repetition the repeated use of some aspect of language

rhyme to end in the same sound(s)

rhythm a pattern of strong beats in speech or writing, especially poetry

S

science fiction a story based on science that often tells what life in the future might be like

semantic map a graphic organizer, often a web, used to display words or concepts that are meaningfully related

sequence the order of events in a selection or the order of the steps in which something is completed

sequence words clue words such as *first*, *next*, *then*, and *finally* that signal the order of events in a selection

setting where and when a story takes place

stanza a group of lines in a poem

steps in a process the order of the steps in which something is completed

story map a graphic organizer used to record the literary elements and the sequence of events in a narrative text

story structure how the characters, setting, and events of a story are organized into a plot

summarize give the most important ideas of what was read. Readers summarize important information in the selection to keep track of what they are reading.

supporting detail piece of information that tells about the main idea

T

tall tale a humorous story that uses exaggeration to describe impossible happenings

text structure the organization of a piece of nonfiction writing. Text structures of informational text include cause/effect, chronological, compare/contrast, description, problem/solution, proposition/support, and ask/answer questions.

theme the big idea or author's message in a story

think aloud an instructional strategy in which a teacher verbalizes his or her thinking to model the process of comprehension or the application of a skill

topic the subject of a discussion, conversation, or piece of text

V

visualize picture in one's mind what is happening in the text. Visualizing helps readers imagine the things they read about.

Leveled Readers Skills Chart

Scott Foresman Reading Street provides more than six hundred leveled readers. Each one is designed to:

- Practice critical skills and strategies
- Build vocabulary and concepts
- Build fluency
- Develop a lifelong love of reading

Grade K

Title	Level*	DRA Level	Genre	
Max the Duck	A	1	Fantasy	
Fun for Us	B	2	Informational Text	
Nick the Fix-It Man	B	2	Informational Text	
Red and Blue	B	2	Realistic Fiction	
We Have Fun Together	B	2	Fantasy	
Two or Three?	B	2	Realistic Fiction	
Buds for Mom	B	2	Realistic Fiction	
A Walk in the Forest	B	2	Realistic Fiction	
Looking for Animals	B	2	Realistic Fiction	
Skip and Run	C	3	Fantasy	
A Winter Home	C	3	Informational Text	
A Yard for All	C	3	Fantasy	
The Fawn	C	3	Realistic Fiction	
We Can Do It!	C	3	Realistic Fiction	
Fun With Gram	C	3	Realistic Fiction	
They Will Grow	C	3	Realistic Fiction	
What Can You Do?	C	3	Informational Text	
Sad and Glad	C	3	Realistic Fiction	
The Trip	C	3	Informational Text	
Pigs	C	3	Informational Text	
Frog's New Home	C	3	Informational Text	
Five Bears	C	3	Fantasy	
My Walk in Antarctica	C	3	Realistic Fiction	
A Trip to Washington, D.C.	C	3	Informational Text	
The Bus Ride	C	3	Realistic Fiction	
The Boat Ride	C	3	Realistic Fiction	
Ming on the Job	C	3	Realistic Fiction	
The Big Train	D	4	Realistic Fiction	
Get On the Bus!	D	4	Realistic Fiction	
Catch the Ball!	D	4	Realistic Fiction	
Homes	D	4	Informational Text	
The Best Club Hut	D	4	Realistic Fiction	
A Small Trip	D	4	Informational Text	
The Box	D	4	Informational Text	
Our Camping Trip	D	4	Realistic Fiction	
Safe Places for Animals	D	4	Informational Text	

* Suggested Guided Reading Level. Use your knowledge of children's abilities to adjust levels as needed.

This chart lists titles of leveled readers appropriate for students in Kindergarten. Use the chart to find titles that meet your students' interest and instructional needs. The books in this list were leveled using the criteria suggested in *Matching Books to Readers: Using Leveled Books in Guided Reading, Grades K–3* by Irene C. Fountas and Gay Su Pinnell. For more on leveling, see the *Reading Street Leveled Readers Leveling Guide.*

Comprehension Strategy	Target Comprehension Skill	Additional Comprehension Instruction	Vocabulary
Recall/Retell	Character	N/A	N/A
Recall/Retell	Setting	N/A	N/A
Recall/Retell	Sequence	N/A	N/A
Recall/Retell	Classify and Categorize	N/A	N/A
Recall/Retell	Character	N/A	N/A
Recall/Retell	Classify and Categorize	N/A	N/A
Recall/Retell	Compare and Contrast	N/A	N/A
Recall/Retell	Setting	N/A	N/A
Recall/Retell	Main Idea	N/A	N/A
Recall/Retell	Realism and Fantasy	N/A	N/A
Recall/Retell	Sequence	N/A	N/A
Recall/Retell	Realism and Fantasy	N/A	N/A
Recall/Retell	Compare and Contrast	N/A	N/A
Recall/Retell	Plot	N/A	N/A
Recall/Retell	Cause and Effect	N/A	N/A
Recall/Retell	Plot	N/A	N/A
Recall/Retell	Draw Conclusions	N/A	N/A
Recall/Retell	Main Idea	N/A	N/A
Recall/Retell	Sequence	N/A	N/A
Recall/Retell	Cause and Effect	N/A	N/A
Recall/Retell	Sequence	N/A	N/A
Recall/Retell	Character	N/A	N/A
Recall/Retell	Classify and Categorize	N/A	N/A
Recall/Retell	Setting	N/A	N/A
Recall/Retell	Realism and Fantasy	N/A	N/A
Recall/Retell	Cause and Effect	N/A	N/A
Recall/Retell	Compare and Contrast	N/A	N/A
Recall/Retell	Plot	N/A	N/A
Recall/Retell	Main Idea	N/A	N/A
Recall/Retell	Draw Conclusions	N/A	N/A
Recall/Retell	Compare and Contrast	N/A	N/A
Recall/Retell	Character	N/A	N/A
Recall/Retell	Main Idea	N/A	N/A
Recall/Retell	Plot	N/A	N/A
Recall/Retell	Setting	N/A	N/A
Recall/Retell	Draw Conclusions	N/A	N/A

Section 3 Matching Books and Readers

What Good Readers Do

You can use the characteristics and behaviors of good readers to help all your students read better. But what are these characteristics and behaviors? And how can you use them to foster good reading behaviors for all your students? Here are some helpful tips.

Good Readers enjoy reading! They have favorite books, authors, and genres. Good readers often have a preference about where and when they read. They talk about books and recommend their favorites.

Develop this behavior by giving students opportunities to respond in different ways to what they read. Get them talking about what they read, and why they like or dislike it.

This behavior is important because book sharing alerts you to students who are somewhat passive about reading or have limited literacy experiences. Book sharing also helps you when you select books for the class.

Good Readers select books they can read.

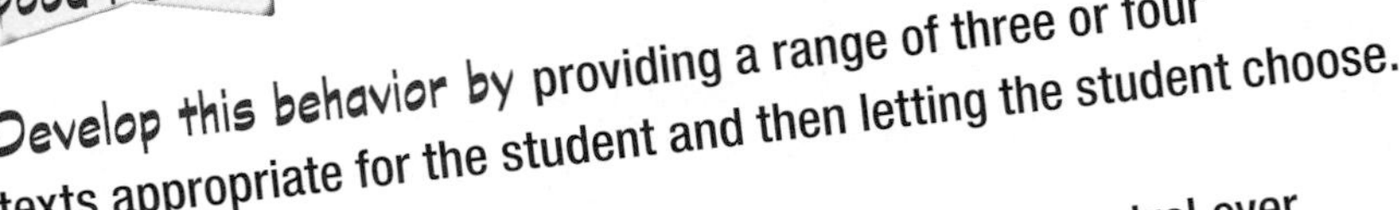

Develop this behavior by providing a range of three or four texts appropriate for the student and then letting the student choose.

This behavior is important because students gain control over reading when they can choose from books they can read. This helps them become more independent in the classroom.

Good Readers use text features to help them preview and set purposes.

Develop this behavior by having students use the title and illustrations in fiction texts or the title, contents, headings, and other graphic features in nonfiction texts to make predictions about what they will be reading.

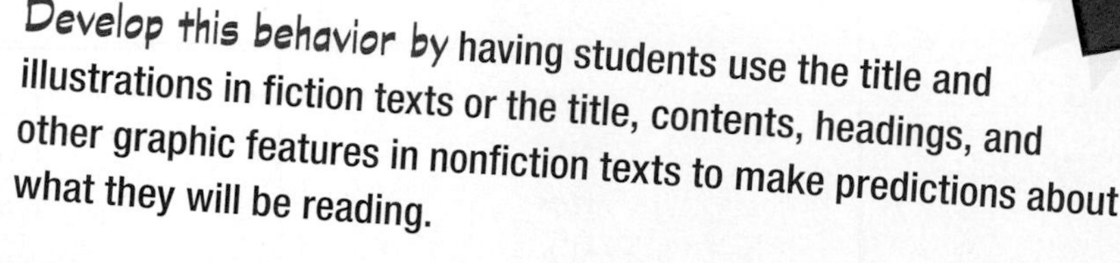

This behavior is important because previewing actually makes reading easier! Looking at features and sampling the text enables readers to predict and set expectations for reading.

Want to improve your students' performance by fostering good reading behaviors? Customize Literacy can help.

Good Readers predict and ask questions before and while they read.

Develop this behavior by asking questions. After reading a passage, ask students what they think will happen next in a fiction text. Have them ask a question they think will be answered in a nonfiction text and read on to see if it is.

This behavior is important because when students predict and ask questions as they read, they are engaged. They have a purpose for reading and a basis for monitoring their comprehension.

Good Readers use effective strategies and sources of information to figure out unknown words.

CH-
QU-
ST-

Develop this behavior by teaching specific strategies for figuring out unknown words, such as sounding out clusters of letters, using context, reading on, and using references.

This behavior is important because when readers have a variety of strategies to use, they are more able to decode and self-correct quickly. Readers who do these things view themselves as good readers.

Good Readers construct meaning as they read and then share or demonstrate their understanding.

Develop this behavior by having students retell what they read or write a summary of what they read in their own words.

This behavior is important because the ability to retell or write a summary is essential for success in reading. It shows how well a student has constructed meaning.

Good Readers make connections.

Develop this behavior by asking questions to help students make connections: *What does this remind you of? Have you ever read or experienced anything like this?*

This behavior is important because making connections helps readers understand and appreciate a text. Making connections to self, the world, and other texts supports high-level thinking.

Conversation Starters

Asking Good Questions Children want to read and listen to interesting and thought-provoking books! You can help them talk about these books. Use questions such as the following to assess listening comprehension and help children think about books. As you read longer books, pause often to ask questions about past and future events.

Cause and Effect

- What happens in this story?
- Why does it happen?

Classify and Categorize

- How are these things alike?
- Do these things belong in the same group?
- Is this thing like the others? Does it belong in the group?
- How do you know that it is like/not like the others?
- How would you group these things?

Draw Conclusions

- What happens in the story?
- What did the characters do to show you that they are kind/mean/strong?
- Which character do you like best? Why?
- Do you like this story? What makes you like it or dislike it?

Character

- Who is in this story?
- What does this character like to do?
- How did the character feel in this part of the book?
- What does this character think about what happens in the book?
- Does this character seem real or made-up? What makes you think so?
- What character would you like to be? Why?

Compare and Contrast

- How are these things/characters/stories alike?
- How are these things/characters/stories different?

Main Idea

- What is this story all about?
- What is the big idea of this story?
- What clues help you know what the story is about?

Plot

- In the story, what happens at the beginning? in the middle? at the end?
- What are other important things that happen in the story?
- What do you think is the most exciting/important thing that happens?
- What is the problem that the character must solve/fix?
- How is that problem solved or fixed?

Realism and Fantasy

- Could this story happen in real life? Why do you think as you do?
- What things in the story could happen in real life?
- Do the people in this story act like people you know?
- How do you know if a story is make-believe or could really happen?

Sequence

- In this story, what happened first? next? last?

Setting

- What do the pictures tell you about when and where this story happened?
- What is this place like? What do you think it would be like?
- Does the place seem real or made-up? How can you tell?
- Do you want to visit this place? Why?

Connecting Science and Social Studies

Scott Foresman Reading Street Leveled Readers are perfect for covering, supporting, or enriching science and social studies content. Using these books ensures that all students can access important concepts.

Grade K Leveled Readers

Science

Earth and Space Science	Life Science	Physical Science
Fiction Books • *We Can Do It!*	**Nonfiction Books** • *A Winter Home* • *What Can You Do?* • *The Trip* • *Pigs* • *Frog's New Home* • *A Small Trip* • *Safe Places for Animals* **Fiction Books** • *A Walk in the Forest* • *Looking for Animals* • *Skip and Run* • *A Yard for All* • *The Fawn* • *Fun with Gram* • *They Will Grow* • *Sad and Glad*	**Fiction Books** • *Catch the Ball!* • *The Best Club Hut*

Grade K Leveled Readers

Social Studies

Citizenship	Culture	History
Nonfiction Books • *Fun for Us* • *Nick the Fix-It Man* • *The Box* **Fiction Books** • *Red and Blue* • *We Have Fun Together* • *Two or Three?* • *Buds for Mom* • *Ming on the Job*	**Nonfiction Books** • *Homes* **Fiction Books** • *Max the Duck* • *Five Bears* • *My Walk in Antarctica* • *The Bus Ride* • *The Boat Ride* • *Get On the Bus!* • *Our Camping Trip*	**Fiction Books** • *The Big Train* **Geography** **Nonfiction Books** • *A Trip to Washington, D.C.*

Connecting Science and Social Studies

Grade 1 Leveled Readers

Science

Earth and Space Science

Nonfiction Books

- *All About the Weather*
- *The Communication Story*
- *Over the Years*
- *Ready for Winter?*
- *Using the Telephone*

Fiction Books

- *Cody's Adventure*
- *Marla's Good Idea*
- *What a Detective Does*

Life Science

Nonfiction Books

- *All About Food Chains*
- *Animals Change and Grow*
- *Around the Forest*
- *Around the World*
- *Baby Animals in the Rain Forest*
- *Bees and Beekeepers*
- *The Dinosaur Detectives*
- *The Dinosaur Herds*
- *Fun in the Sun*
- *Honey*
- *In My Room*
- *Learn About Butterflies*
- *Learn About Worker Bees*
- *Let's Go to the Zoo*
- *Let's Visit a Butterfly Greenhouse*
- *Look at Dinosaurs*
- *A Mighty Oak Tree*
- *Monarchs Migrate South*
- *People Help the Forest*
- *The Seasons Change*
- *Seasons Come and Go*
- *What Animals Can You See?*

Life Science

Fiction Books

- *Bix the Dog*
- *Britton Finds a Kitten*
- *Carlos Picks a Pet*
- *Cary and the Wildlife Shelter*
- *Mac Can Do It!*
- *Mack and Zack*
- *Plans Change*
- *Sam*
- *The Sick Pets*
- *Time for Dinner*
- *What Brown Saw*
- *Which Animals Will We See?*
- *Which Fox?*

Physical Science

Nonfiction Books

- *The Inclined Plane*
- *Simple Machines at Work*
- *Simple Machines in Compound Machines*

Grade 1 Leveled Readers

Social Studies

Citizenship

Nonfiction Books

- *A Class*
- *A Garden for All*
- *Great Scientists: Detectives at Work*
- *Here in My Neighborhood*
- *A New Library*
- *Puppy Raiser*
- *The Story of the Kids Care Club*
- *Ways to Be a Good Citizen*

Fiction Books

- *The Art Show*
- *At Your Vet*
- *Big Wishes and Her Baby*
- *Double Trouble Twins*
- *Fly Away Owl!*
- *Grasshopper and Ant*
- *Hank's Song*
- *Let's Build a Park!*
- *Look at My Neighborhood*
- *My Little Brother Drew*
- *On the Farm*
- *Paul's Bed*
- *A Play*
- *Rules at School*
- *Space Star*
- *Squirrel and Bear*
- *That Cat Needs Help!*

Culture

Nonfiction Books

- *Cascarones Are for Fun*
- *My Babysitter*
- *Special Days, Special Food*
- *We Are a Family*
- *What Makes Buildings Special?*

Fiction Books

- *Go West!*
- *Grandma's Farm*
- *Gus the Pup*
- *Jamie's Jumble of Junk*
- *A New Baby Brother*
- *A Party for Pedro*
- *A Visit to the Ranch*
- *Where They Live*

History

Nonfiction Books

- *School: Then and Now*
- *Treasures of Our Country*

Fiction Books

- *Loni's Town*

Government

Nonfiction Books

- *America's Home*
- *Our Leaders*

Fiction Books

- *Mom the Mayor*

Planning Teacher Study Groups

Adventurous teachers often have good ideas for lessons. A teacher study group is a great way to share ideas and get feedback on the best way to connect content and students. Working with other teachers can provide you with the support and motivation you need to implement new teaching strategies. A teacher study group offers many opportunities to collaborate, support each other's work, share insights, and get feedback.

Think About It

A weekly or monthly teacher study group can help support you in developing your expertise in the classroom. You and a group of like-minded teachers can form your own study group. What can this group accomplish?

- Read and discuss professional articles by researchers in the field of education.
- Meet to share teaching tips, collaborate on multi-grade lessons, and share resources.
- Develop lessons to try out new teaching strategies. Meet to share experiences and discuss how to further improve your teaching approach.

Let's Meet!

Forming a study group is easy. Just follow these four steps:

1. **Decide on the size of the group.** A small group has the advantage of making each member feel accountable, but make sure that all people can make the same commitment!
2. **Choose teachers to invite to join your group.** Think about whom you want to invite. Should they all teach the same grade? Can you invite teachers from other schools? Remember that the more diverse the group, the more it benefits from new perspectives.
3. **Set goals for the group.** In order to succeed, know what you want the group to do. Meet to set goals. Rank goals in order of importance and refer often to the goals to keep the group on track.
4. **Make logistical decisions.** This is often the most difficult. Decide where and when you will meet. Consider an online meeting place where group members can post discussion questions and replies if people are not able to meet.

What Will We Study?

Use the goals you set to help determine what your group will study. Consider what materials are needed to reach your goals, and how long you think you will need to prepare for each meeting.

How Will It Work?

Think about how you structure groups in your classroom. Use some of the same strategies.

- **Assign a group facilitator.** This person is responsible for guiding the meeting. This person comes prepared with discussion questions and leads the meeting. This could be a rotating responsibility dependent on experience with various topics. This person might be responsible for providing the materials.
- **Assign a recorder.** Have someone take notes during the meeting and record group decisions.
- **Use the jigsaw method.** Not everyone has time to be a facilitator. In this case, divide the text and assign each portion to a different person. Each person is responsible for leading the discussion on that particular part.

Meet Again

Make a commitment to meet for a minimum number of times. After that, the group can reevaluate and decide whether or not to continue.

"Have some great teaching tips to share? Want to exchange ideas with your colleagues? Build your own professional community of teachers. Customize Literacy gets you started."

Trial Lessons

Use your colleagues' experiences to help as you think about new ways to connect content and students. Use the following plan to create a mini-lesson. It should last twenty minutes. Get the support of your colleagues as you try something new and then reflect on what happened.

Be Creative!

As you develop a plan for a mini-lesson, use these four words to guide planning: *purpose*, *text*, *resources*, and *routine*.

- **Purpose:** Decide on a skill or strategy to cover. Define your purpose for teaching the lesson.
- **Text:** Develop a list of the materials you could use. Ask your colleagues for suggestions.
- **Resources:** Make a list of the available resources, and consider how to use those resources most effectively. Consider using the leveled readers listed on pages CL16–CL17 and CL22–CL25 of Customize Literacy.
- **Routine:** Choose an instructional routine to structure your mini-lesson. See the mini-lessons in Customize Literacy for suggestions.

Try It!

Try out your lesson! Consider audio- or videotaping the lesson for later review. You may wish to invite a colleague to sit in as you teach. Make notes on how the lesson went.

How Did It Go?

Use the self-evaluation checklist on page CL29 as you reflect on your trial lesson. This provides a framework for later discussion.

Discuss, Reflect, Repeat

Solicit feedback from your teacher study group. Explain the lesson and share your reflections. Ask for suggestions on ways to improve the lesson. Take some time to reflect on the feedback. Modify your lesson to reflect what you have learned. Then try teaching the lesson again.

Checklist for Teacher Self-Evaluation

How Well Did I ...	Very Well	Satisfactory	Not Very Well
Plan the lesson?			
Select the appropriate level of text?			
Introduce the lesson and explain its objectives?			
Review previously taught skills?			
Directly explain the new skills being taught?			
Model the new skills?			
Break the material down into small steps?			
Integrate guided practice into the lesson?			
Monitor guided practice for student understanding?			
Provide feedback on independent practice?			
Maintain an appropriate pace?			
Assess student understanding of the material?			
Stress the importance of applying the skill as they read?			
Maintain students' interest?			
Ask questions?			
Handle student questions and responses?			
Respond to the range of abilities?			

Books for Teachers

Children aren't the only ones who need to read to grow. Here is a brief list of books that you may find useful to fill your reading teacher basket and learn new things.

A Professional Bibliography

Adams, M. J. "Alphabetic Anxiety and Explicit, Systematic Phonics Instruction: A Cognitive Science Perspective." *Handbook of Early Literacy Research.* The Guilford Press, 2001.

Adams, M. J. *Beginning to Read: Thinking and Learning About Print.* The MIT Press, 1990.

Afflerbach, P. "The Influence of Prior Knowledge and Text Genre on Readers' Prediction Strategies." *Journal of Reading Behavior,* vol. XXII, no. 2 (1990).

Armbruster, B. B., F. Lehr, and J. Osborn. *Put Reading First: The Research Building Blocks for Teaching Children to Read.* Partnership for Reading, Washington, D.C., 2001.

Bear, D. R., M. Invernizzi, S. Templeton, and F. Johnston. *Words Their Way.* Merrill Prentice Hall, 2004.

Beck, I., M. G. McKeown, and L. Kucan. *Bringing Words to Life: Robust Vocabulary Instruction.* The Guilford Press, 2002.

Biemiller, A. "Teaching Vocabulary in the Primary Grades: Vocabulary Instruction Needed." *Vocabulary Instruction Research to Practice.* The Guilford Press, 2004.

Blachowicz, C. and P. Fisher. "Vocabulary Instruction." *Handbook of Reading Research,* vol. III. Lawrence Erlbaum Associates, 2000.

Cunningham, P. M. and J. W. Cunningham. "What We Know About How to Teach Phonics." *What Research Says About Reading Instruction,* 3rd ed. International Reading Association, 2002.

Daniels, H. *Literature Circles.* 2nd ed. Stenhouse Publishers, 2002.

Dickson, S. V., D. C. Simmons, and E. J. Kame'enui. "Text Organization: Instructional and Curricular Basics and Implications." *What Reading Research Tells Us About Children with Diverse Learning Needs: Bases and Basics.* Lawrence Erlbaum Associates, 1998.

Diller, D. *Making the Most of Small Groups: Differentiation for All.* Stenhouse Publishers, 2007.

Duke, N. K., V. S. Bennett-Armistead, and E. M. Roberts. "Bridging the Gap Between Learning to Read and Reading to Learn." *Literacy and Young Children: Research-Based Practices.* The Guilford Press, 2003.

Duke, N. K. and C. Tower. "Nonfiction Texts for Young Readers." *The Texts in Elementary Classrooms.* Lawrence Erlbaum Associates, 2004.

Ehri, L. C. and S. R. Nunes. "The Role of Phonemic Awareness in Learning to Read." *What Research Has to Say About Reading Instruction.* 3rd ed. International Reading Association, 2002.

Fountas, I. C. and G. S. Pinnell. *Guided Reading: Good First Teaching for All Children.* Heinemann, 1996.

Fountas, I. C. and G. S. Pinnell. *Matching Books to Readers: Using Leveled Books in Guided Reading,* K-3. Heinemann, 1999.

Harvey, S. and A. Goudvis. *Strategies That Work: Teaching Comprehension to Enhance Understanding.* 2nd ed. Stenhouse Publishers, 2007.

Hiebert, E. H. and L. A. Martin. "The Texts of Beginning Reading Instruction." *Handbook of Early Literacy Research.* The Guilford Press, 2001.

Indrisano, R. and J. R. Paratore. *Learning to Write, Writing to Learn. Theory and Research in Practice.* International Reading Association, 2005.

Juel, C., G. Biancarosa, D. Coker, and R. Deffes. "Walking with Rosie: A Cautionary Tale of Early Reading Instruction." *Educational Leadership* (April 2003).

National Reading Panel. *Teaching Children to Read.* National Institute of Child Health and Human Development, 1999.

Pressley, M. *Reading Instruction That Works: The Case for Balanced Teaching,* 3rd ed. The Guilford Press, 2005.

Smith, S., D. C. Simmons, and E. J. Kame'enui. "Word Recognition: Research Bases." *What Reading Research Tells Us About Children with Diverse Learning Needs: Bases and Basics.* Lawrence Erlbaum Associates, 1998.

Snow, C., S. Burns, and P. Griffin, eds. *Preventing Reading Difficulties in Young Children.* National Academy Press, 1998.

Vaughn, S., P. G. Mathes, S. Linan-Thompson, and D. J. Francis. "Teaching English Language Learners at Risk for Reading Disabilities to Read: Putting Research into Practice." *Learning Disabilities Research & Practice,* vol. 20, issue 1 (February 2006).

Acknowledgments

Acknowledgments

Illustrations

Cover: Rob Hefferan

12 Manja Stojic

19–25 Cale Atkinson

28, 49, 69, 88, 129 George Ulrich

30 Jan Bryan Hunt

32 Aaron Zenz

39–45 Natalia Vasquez

50–51 Steve Mack

52 Marilyn Janovitz

59–65 Dani Jones

72 Steve Simpson

90–91 Jason Wolff

92 Ron Lieser

99–105 Robbie Short

110–111 Vanessa Newton

112 Karol Kaminski

119–125 Wednesday Kirwan.

Photographs

Every effort has been made to secure permission and provide appropriate credit for photographic material. The publisher deeply regrets any omission and pledges to correct errors called to its attention in subsequent editions.

Unless otherwise acknowledged, all photographs are the property of Pearson Education, Inc.

Photo locators denoted as follows: Top (T), Center (C), Bottom (B), Left (L), Right (R), Background (Bkgd)

10 (B) ©Mario Lopes/Alamy

48 ©Andy Sands/Nature Picture Library, ©Envision/Corbis, ©Fusion Pix/Corbis, Dave King/©DK Images

130 (B) ©Thinkstock/Corbis

131 (C) ©Jochen Tack/Peter Arnold, Inc., (T, B) ©Peter Bennett/Ambient Images, Inc., (TL) PhotoLibrary Group, Ltd.

144

Teacher Editions

KWL Strategy: The KWL Interactive Reading Strategy was developed and is used by permission of Donna Ogle, National-Louis University, Skokie, Illinois, co-author of *Reading Today and Tomorrow*, Holt, Rinehart & Winston Publishers, 1988. (See also the *Reading Teacher*, February 1986, pp. 564–570.)

Understanding by Design quotes: Wiggins, G. & McTighe, J. (2005). *Understanding by Design.* Alexandria, VA: Association for Supervision and Curriculum Development.

Illustrations

Cover Rob Hefferan

Running Header Steven Mach

Photos

Every effort has been made to secure permission and provide appropriate credit for photographic material. The publisher deeply regrets any omission and pledges to correct errors called to its attention in subsequent editions.

Unless otherwise acknowledged, all photographs are the property of Pearson Education, Inc.

Teacher Resources

Looking for Teacher Resources and other important information?

- Dear Kindergarten Teacher
- Research into Practice on Reading Street
- Guide to Reading Street
- Assessment on Reading Street
- Writing on Reading Street
- Differentiate Instruction on Reading Street
- ELL on Reading Street
- Customize Literacy on Reading Street
- Digital Products on Reading Street
- Teacher Resources for Kindergarten
- Index

Teacher Resources

Looking for Teacher Resources and other important information?

- Dear Kindergarten Teacher
- Research into Practice on Reading Street
- Guide to Reading Street
- Assessment on Reading Street
- Writing on Reading Street
- Differentiate Instruction on Reading Street
- ELL on Reading Street
- Customize Literacy on Reading Street
- Digital Products on Reading Street
- Teacher Resources for Kindergarten
- Index